THE LAWS OF ESHNUNNA

THE LAWS OF ESHNUNNA

by

REUVEN YARON

Second Revised Edition

THE MAGNES PRESS, THE HEBREW UNIVERSITY
E. J. BRILL
JERUSALEM-LEIDEN

First Edition, 1969
Second Revised Edition, 1988

Printed in Israel
Phototypesetting: Barry Segal International, Jerusalem

Library of Congress Cataloging-in-Publication Data

Yaron, Reuven, 1924-
The laws of Eshnunna.

Includes text of laws in romanized Akkadian and English translation.
Bibliography: p. 305
Includes index.
1. Law—Eshnunna. I. Eshnunna. Laws. English & Akkadian. 1988. II. Title.
LAW 348.35'023 88-1541
ISBN 90-04-08534-3 (Brill) 343.50823

TO DAVID DAUBE
FOR HIS EIGHTIETH BIRTHDAY
8 FEBRUARY 1989

^{D}TIŠPAK *u* ÈŠ.NUN.NA^{ki} *šalim*

(AbB ix 143:6)

PREFACE TO THE SECOND EDITION

Quadragesimo anno, in the fortieth year after the publication of the first edition of the Laws of Eshnunna, and roughly twenty years after this book was first published, I present here — not without apprehension — a revised version.

In reshaping the book I changed my views on some topics, or restated them. I paid more attention than before to the style of the Laws, and to the role mnemotechnic considerations may have played in their formulation. Haddad 116, a small but significant fragment, had to be incorporated into the text of the Laws, relevant new outside sources had to be adduced. One Ebla tablet provided parallels preceding the Laws of Eshnunna by many centuries. Due notice had to be taken of the work of others, Assyriologists and historians of law. The discussion of old problems and controversies had to be followed. As examples one might note the continuing efforts concerning the meaning of *muškenum*, or else about *ṣimdat šarrim*. I wrestled again with my translation, fretting over minutiae, to make my version follow the original even more closely than before.

The lexical tools at our disposal have grown considerably. AHw was completed in 1981. The stately CAD progressed steadily, albeit unavoidably more slowly: currently, in early 1988, it covers — in 18 volumes — the letters A to N, Q, S, Ṣ and Z. They are indispensable, even though one will occasionally be exasperated with this translation or that. The law has — quite appropriately — a jargon of its own, the proper use of which requires expert circumspection. There is also the question of new departures: when a text is translated several times, over a period of years, new departures may reflect new insights, and are not objectionable in principle. But one would wish to have the feeling that recent editors are aware of the work of their predecessors, that they depart intentionally and for some palpable reason.

There have been numerous new translations, into a variety of languages: Czech, French, German, Italian and Portuguese versions have come to my attention. They are referred to on points of controversy — but not routinely, when they unavoidably adhere to the uniformly established. Here I should like to single out for mention the final contribution of Albrecht Goetze who has laid firm foundations for the study of the Laws of Eshnunna. His work on the Laws culminated in his standard edition, published in 1956, and he never returned to deal with them. But in 1969 he used the 3rd edition of ANET, to accept one improved reading, and — no less significantly — to ignore another suggestion. A sole collation of parts of the LE was carried out in 1966, by Mrs. Maria de J. Ellis, after participating in a seminar on the LE, conducted by J.J. Finkelstein. We shall have occasion to refer to it.

During a prolonged stay at Oxford, in 1985/6, I benefited from the helpful wisdom of Professor O.R. Gurney. A meeting, all too brief, with Professor F.R. Kraus, in June 1985, was useful and instructive. Dr. Raymond Westbrook kindly made typescripts of two forthcoming books available to me.

Professor Eckart Otto very generously put at my disposal the proofs of his forthcoming *Rechtsgeschichte der Redaktion im Kodex Eschnunna und im "Bundesbuch"*. Reading them with alacrity, I found that we agreed on many points, and disagreed on others. To my considerable regret, by that time my work had reached a stage at which changes were no longer possible.

To all these gentlemen I wish to express sincere thanks.

This edition is again dedicated to Professor David Daube, on this, his seventy-ninth birthday, in anticipation of his completing fourscore years, *ka'eth ḥayyah*. To his many pupils, colleagues and friends he continues to be an unfailing source of inspiration.

Reuven Yaron

Jerusalem, 8 February 1988

PREFACE TO THE FIRST EDITION

The Laws of the Old Babylonian kingdom of Eshnunna (LE) were discovered in 1945 and 1947, on two parallel tablets, during excavations at Tell Ḥarmal, an outskirt of Baghdad. An *editio princeps*, with English translation, was published already in 1948 by Professor Albrecht Goetze, of Yale University. Since then the LE have been translated into many languages, major and minor, and a considerable literature has grown up around them. Needless to say, these translations differ greatly in their value. Some of them give only the text, others add more or less detailed comment. Goetze himself has repeatedly returned to the Laws of Eshnunna. In 1950 he offered a new translation, in J.B. Pritchard's *Ancient Near Eastern Texts Relating to the Old Testament*, a revised second edition of which appeared in 1955. Goetze's standard edition of the Laws of Eshnunna, now in general use, was published in 1956 (*The Annual of the American Schools of Oriental Research*, Vol. XXXI).

Despite all the effort devoted to the interpretation of the Laws, in commentaries, reviews and in papers dealing with specific topics, much remains obscure and in need of elucidation, with regard to both language and law. The text itself is in numerous instances open to query, a fact due in part to the state of preservation of the tablets. Anyone coming from papyrology — as I do — is also bewildered by the fact that the autograph prepared by the *editor princeps* serves as the near-exclusive basis for research. True, there are the photographs, but I am told on good authority that there is a very significant difference between the best of photographs and studying the original. By contrast, in papyrology the photocopy is almost equivalent to the original; in some cases — thanks to modern techniques of photography — it will even reveal what is not visible to the eye of the scholar examining the papyrus itself. This immediate access to the text is a characteristic feature of papyrological work which seems to be missing in the sphere of cuneiform. Nevertheless, one should beware of exaggerated expectations: independent re-examination of the tablets may lead to improved readings, hence to the better understanding of some provisions, but there is no reason to assume that the results will be revolutionary. The same is true of some interesting corrections which have been made since the *editio princeps*. In sum: The state of the text does not call for a delay in the investigation of the Laws; the more so since a new edition does not appear to be imminent.

The present volume grew out of a course of lectures delivered at the Hebrew University in 1963-1965. It is written by a jurist, and in the first instance addressed to students of legal history. It has no pretensions in the field of philology — beyond the modest, negative aim of avoiding mistakes. Wishing to keep transliteration as simple as possible, I decided to dispense with all marking of vowel length (even when quoting authors who employ such marks). There is as yet no uniform, generally accepted mode of marking, and for the jurist vowel length is largely irrelevant. In the exceptional case, when the identity of a word may depend upon length, the various possibilities were pointed out. Similarly, vowel length was omitted in the transliteration of Hebrew, as was also initial *alef*. On the other hand, I found it occasionally useful and necessary to include elementary remarks, which to the expert Assyriologist may appear superfluous, altogether dispensable.

I thought it desirable to offer a new translation, since knowledge of the Akkadian language is the exception rather than the rule among legal historians. It is important that a translation be meticulous and refrain from "improving" on the original; the difficulties inherent in it, whatever their cause, must not be glossed over. A few of the earlier translations may have been directed to a different type of reader, one able to check each phrase on his own. In due course we shall consider in detail some of the problems one encounters in translating from Akkadian.

Juristic and Assyriological modes of writing differ in some other ways. Having to choose I have preferred to adhere to the traditions of my own field of research. The jurist does not examine the credentials of the authors he quotes, and rejects as unavoidably erratic any "system" of selective reference. Everything that is printed and relevant is to be noted; it will either be accepted, or rejected — with reason given for doing so. If something is passed over, this is due to human failure, not to lofty disdain.

The book is not offered as an authoritative and comprehensive treatment of the Laws; this must remain a remote desideratum. As it is, a frank admission of failure to understand this provision or that is preferable to fanciful conjecture, concealing (or perhaps revealing?) uncertainty behind terms like "no doubt", "obviously", and the like. The noble habit of saying *non liquet* deserves to be practised on a larger scale than is customary.

Numerous private legal texts and letters from the region of Eshnunna have been discovered, the greater part of which are as yet unpublished. In due course the interpretation of the LE may be furthered by these, especially by allowing better insight into regional idiosyncrasies of language. On the strictly legal plane one should not expect too much — if the parallel of the CH is of relevance.

The Laws of Eshnunna attract attention for two main reasons. They are a compilation of legal rules; relative to the mass of private legal material, texts of a general nature will always be rare and of exceptional interest. The Laws of Eshnunna have a further claim to the attention of legal historians, because of the place they occupy in the sequence of cuneiform collections of laws. They are earlier than the Code of Hammurabi, even though it cannot be definitely established by how much. Together with the Laws of Lipit-Ištar, the LE enable us to see, at least in a few instances, how the law developed and changed.

With one possible exception, there is no evidence that the compilers of the Code of Hammurabi borrowed directly from either the Laws of Eshnunna or from those of Lipit-Ištar. Formally, one must bear in mind, all these are legal rules of political entities not dependent on each other. But while it is quite true that each of these states has to be credited with its own, peculiar, local positive law, it is no less true that to a considerable extent we have here customary laws and practices common to the ancient Near East. There was close and continuous contact between the various neighbouring cities and states, and it is not unlikely that there was also considerable traffic in legal notions and practices. We have no reason to assume that the compilers of the Code of Hammurabi would have recoiled in horror from the suggestion that they take into account, in addition to their own materials, also the laws, practices and precedents of their neighbours. Lawgivers are accustomed to cast inquisitive glances, in stealth or openly, on the doing of others. It is a fascinating process which can be observed throughout the ages, for example in the Bible and the Talmud, in early and post-classical Roman law. Nowadays borrowings are, as a rule, openly acknowledged; in ancient times the foreign source would usually remain unmentioned. This tendency of suppressing the source may be due to a variety of reasons. The one is a desire to appear independent and original (such a desire would be especially accentuated when laws were attributed to a divine lawgiver); the other is that antiquity, quite generally, had not developed the notion of copyright and little compunction was felt in appropriating the creation of others. True, the Babylonian Talmud propounds that "he who says something in the name of him who said it, brings salvation to the world" (*Megillah* 15a). But this was a sentiment rarely applied in the present context.

The collection of legal rules contained in the Laws of Eshnunna does not constitute a systematic entity, a code dealing in a comprehensive way with all, or with some, aspects of the law in force. Rather — it will be seen — they are a loose compilation of precedents and ordinances; in this they resemble comparable ancient collections of laws. It was not my intention to supplement the LE from other Old Babylonian sources, so as to give them a semblance of a legal system. I have endeavoured to confine myself to the cases actually mentioned, but have for these adduced comparative material from other sources of ancient laws, down to the Talmud and Rome. It is hoped that the various rules may thereby gain in significance and interest.

The arrangement of the material, the division of the book into chapters, cannot be free of an element of arbitrariness. The present-day lawyer cannot dispense with the categories of thought, the classifications which are his customary tools. One may safely assume that no comparable divisions existed at the early date when the Laws of Eshnunna were compiled and promulgated. Distinctions such as those between public law and private law, property and obligation, crime and tort, are of a much later age. One may use these notions, sparingly and with caution; but they must not be made to serve as a basis for conclusions which have no roots in the text itself.

I should now like to express thanks to some friends and colleagues. Some years ago, when my attention turned to the legal sources in Akkadian, it was Professor H. Tadmor, of the Hebrew University Department of Assyriology, who helped me acquire the minimum knowledge of the language which is indispensable for independent research. I have also greatly benefited from the generous assistance of Dr. A. Shaffer. Professor D. Daube and Professor H.B. Rosén have read the manuscript, and I am grateful for their remarks. I should also wish to record a very stimulating conversation with Professor F.R. Kraus, of the University of Leiden. There is no need to stress that none of these scholars is in any way responsible for the shortcomings of this book. Finally, I ought to mention that this book was already set when the *Symbolae Martino David Dedicatae* appeared, containing two important papers, by Landsberger and Petschow. I have tried to utilize these, but under the circumstances treatment could not be as full as it would otherwise have been. My thanks are due to the publishers and the printers who showed much patience in making the many changes which became necessary.

Reuven Yaron

Jerusalem, August 1968

CONTENTS

CHAPTER ONE

INTRODUCTION

Eshnunna gained a position of political significance after the downfall of the third dynasty of Ur. "Eshnunna was not the least among the powers contending for mastery or at least independence in these centuries of division. Like many other cities it had broken away in the last days of the Ur dynasty ..."[1]

The city of Eshnunna itself (the present Tell Asmar) was situated to the east of the Tigris, on the banks of its tributary, the Diyala. The kingdom occupied an important strategic position between Assyria (in the north), Babylon (in the west), Isin and Larsa (in the south), finally Elam (in the east). Much of the history of Eshnunna is as yet uncertain, and I do not intend (nor am I competent) to trace the fluctuating fortunes of the Kingdom, the victories and defeats of its rulers. "Eshnunna was to have its years of glory under three kings, Naram-Sin, Dadusha and Ibalpiel II, whose reigns occupied the century ending with Hammurabi. The first of these even made himself king of Assyria, and all three were prominent in the affairs of Upper Mesopotamia ..."[2] However, these achievements were not to last: eventually Eshnunna fell victim to the expansionist policies pursued with success by Hammurabi of Babylon, during the fourth decade of his reign. Here it will suffice to refer to some relevant publications.[3]

TABLETS A AND B

It has already been mentioned in the Preface that the LE have reached us on two tablets. These were found in 1945 and 1947, during

1 Gadd *1971:* 635f.

2 *Ibid.*

3 See the Introduction to Goetze *1956*, and references given there. Further, e.g., Edzard *1957* (Index, s.v. Ešnunna); see also Greengus *1979:* 14-22; Indices of *The Cambridge Ancient History*, 3rd ed., I/2, 1971 and II/1, 1973.

excavations at ancient Šaduppum (now Tell Ḥarmal, within the city of Baghdad); they are kept in the Iraq Museum and bear the numbers IM 51059 (Tablet A) and IM 52614 (Tablet B).[4] A fragment of an excerpt from the LE was found during rescue excavations at Tell Haddad. It is Haddad 116, published in 1982.[5]

Of the two major tablets, A is nearer to being complete, but its surface has suffered damage. B is the lower part of a tablet in a much better state of preservation. Also, from a comparison of the two tablets it will emerge that the scribe who wrote B did his work with rather more attention and carefulness.

Date of writing and promulgation

There is a measure of scholarly consensus concerning the age of the two tablets. Archaeological evidence shows fairly conclusively that they are not later than the reign of Dadusha.[6] The time of Dadusha or of an immediate predecessor of his is accordingly suggested by Szlechter *1954:* 10, as the date of the writing of both the tablets. Not very different is the view of Goetze *1956:* 16. After comparing carefully the orthography of A and B,[7] he assigns B to the reign of Dadusha: "A is somewhat older, how much older is difficult to say."

4 For a description of their features and for details concerning their place of discovery, see Goetze *1956:* 3.

5 Al-Rawi *1982:* 117-120.

6 See Goetze *1956:* 5; Lewy *1959:* 438ff., puts the last year of Dadusha in the 29th year of Šamši-Adad of Assyria, which is the 7th year of Hammurabi.

7 The following characteristic differences are pointed out; (i) B shows a predilection for simple two-sound signs; three-sound signs are more frequent in A than in B; (ii) B employs repeated vowels more freely than A (see also Szlechter *1954:* 11); (iii) B doubles normally the middle consonant of verbs whenever grammar requires it, while A in many cases fails to do so (cf. Szlechter, *ibid.*); (iv) B employs phonetic complements more frequently than A (cf. Szlechter, *ibid.*); (v) in a number of cases B spells out words syllabically, while A uses the corresponding Sumerogram; (vi) there are characteristic differences in the way etymological *s (samekh)* is spelled at the end of the syllable, and A reflects an older orthographic system of the region; (vii) on the other hand, mimation — usually regarded as indicating an earlier mode of spelling — is more frequent in B than in A (Goetze *1956:* 12, note 49; Szlechter, *ibid.*) Note, moreover, that in most of these items there are occasional exceptions, going contrary to the predominant tendency.

On the other hand, the date of promulgation of the Laws has not yet been established with any certainty, since the archaeological data supply only a *terminus ad quem*. At one stage it was believed that Tablet A furnished a definite reply concerning the time of promulgation. The *editio princeps* brought, in line 2 of the preamble, the name Bilalama. Consequently the Laws were attributed to that ruler of Eshnunna, who preceded Hammurabi by some 200 years. Both the reading and the dating were accepted without further query by the majority of scholars who discussed the LE soon after their publication. But, within a short time doubts arose concerning the reading of the crucial word, the name Bilalama. These were voiced from various quarters.[8] Finally, in the *1956* edition, Goetze himself abandoned his previous stand;[9] there remained then no link between the LE and that particular ruler of Eshnunna, and the question had to be considered anew.

A comparison of some provisions in the LE with corresponding ones in the CH shows merely that the latter reflects a more developed state of the law.[10] We need not at present go into details, since in our immediate enquiry they cannot carry us beyond the results deriving from the archaeological data. It is not possible to translate the differences between LE and CH into terms of time, and that for two reasons: One must remember that these are laws of two separate political entities, and the assumption that they were both — at a given moment — at an identical stage of legal development is arbitrary. Secondly, it is likely that Hammurabi and his jurists will have introduced numerous amendments and reforms, that is to say that the law of Babylon itself may have undergone significant change within a short time.

MISTAKES

In these circumstances, it remains only to ask whether some clue may not be obtained from the tablets themselves. One must examine the mistakes made by the two scribes (whom, for short, we shall call "scribe A" and "scribe B"); also one must go into the divergences between the two tablets. One should note that mistakes and

8 For details see Landsberger *1968:* 65f.; note also Szlechter *1954:* 6ff.
9 See p. 20, note 18.
10 Cf. Korošec *1954:* 372; differently, Szlechter *1954:* 9, note 33.

divergences may overlap; even so they ought to be considered separately. A mistake in a text is due to some shortcoming of the scribe, his haste, negligence, ignorance perhaps: had he been more attentive or better qualified, he would not have written the way he wrote. A divergence may itself be the result of a mistake (as will shortly be demonstrated). However, it may also be intentional, displaying dissatisfaction with an earlier formulation, a wish to change (the authority for doing so is a different question). Unfortunately a clear distinction between these types of divergences will not always be achievable.

This examination of mistakes and divergences is complicated. It may be said at once that in the end it will not yield much information concerning the textual history of the tablets, yet this somewhat disappointing outcome should not dissuade us from pursuing the topic. It remains essential, and its by-products may be of interest.

Let us commence with the easier part, that concerning scribal mistakes. We can start with Goetze *1956:* 12ff. in distinguishing their varieties: (i) wrong spelling;[11] (ii) omitted (and redundant) signs;[12], [13] (iii) wrong phonetic complements;[14] absent-minded repeti-

11 Tablet A: sec. 4 (i 24) *ka-mi* instead of *ka-la*. Tablet B: sec. 38 (iii 9): Goetze notes *qá-ab-*NE*-it*, but von Soden *1949:* 372 suggests that the correct *qá-ab-li-it* is actually to be read there. In sec. 44/ (iii 23) *ìs-ki-in-ma* is probably wrong for *ìs-ki-im-ma* (cf. Goetze *1956:* 120). On *ú-še-te-eq-ma* (sec. 50, B iv 10) see notes on the text, p. 74, below.

12 Tablet A: sec. 27/ (ii 32) *ri-ik-tim* for *ri-ik-sa-tim*; sec. 30 (ii 45) *a-al*^{ki} (so Goetze *1948* and Szlechter) for *a-al*^{ki}*-šu*; sec. 50 (iv 4) *ḫa-al-qa*, preceded and followed by *ḫa-al-qa-am*, must be regarded as mistaken, and is not satisfactorily explained as a mere routine omission of mimation (so Goetze *1956:* 12, note 49); sec. 54/ (iv 16) *ú-ši-ir-ma* is probably corrupt, see notes on the text, p. 77, below; sec. 58 (iv 26) *ú-nin-ma* instead of *ú-dan-nin-ma*. There are no such omissions in B. Regarding *it-ta-di*, in sec. 33 (B ii 16), we shall argue (pp. 165ff., below) that it may represent a reading which is preferable to *it-ta-di-in* of A iii 7. For a redundance in B see sec 41 (iii 16) *i-na-ad-*[[*ta*]]*-di-šum*.

13 We have disregarded the omission of dispensable particles, such as *-ma*: sec. 29 *šanum(ma)* (omitted in A ii 42); sec./37 *izakkaršum(ma)* (omitted in A iii 20); sec. 50 *irdi'am(ma)* (omitted in B iv 9); or *-šum*: sec. 36/ *iriab(šum)* (omitted in A iii 17).

14 Tablet B: sec. 34/ (ii 21) *marum*^{rum} instead of *maram, martum*^{tum} instead of *martam*.

tion.[15] Of particular interest is (ii), the omission of signs in Tablet A, in four instances. These omissions are all those of scribe A himself.[16] They testify to his haste, and some at least of the divergent omissions, which we shall discuss, may be due to the same cause.[17]

So we tend to conclude that scribe B did a better job than scribe A. But this is of little relevance to the dating and the history of the text. Considerably more important is the question whether there are mistakes common to both A and B. If there are, and if one assumes that the original was free of mistakes, one would have to conclude that A and B were both descended from another tablet (X), which was already faulty. Goetze *1956:* 13 holds that there is at least one such omission: "Sec. 37 shows in the sentence *šumma bit awilim lu imqut* an unmotivated *lu*. The context suggests that house breaking must have been mentioned." Goetze therefore conjectures *lu* <*ip-pališ lu*> *imqut* — "either was broken into or collapsed."[18] There can be no certainty that this is correct. With the *editio princeps*, followed by others, one might prefer to regard *lu* as a particle of emphasis or asseveration.[19] Finally, there is the reading *lu-uq-qú-ut* — "ausgeplündert" (i.e. "plundered, ransacked") which has been suggested by Landsberger *1968:* 99; this we have adopted in our text.

15 Tablet A: sec./ 57 (iv 24): by mistaken association back (to lines 17, 18), the scribe wrote *ikkimma* ("it gored"), instead of *iššukma* ("it bit"), as in line 22. Tablet B: sec. 30 (ii 8) *it-ta-aḫ-bi-it* (instead of *it-ta-bi-it* of A ii 46) may be a phonetic spelling. But see CAD A/i 45b, where this reading of B is noted as a variant.

16 There is little reason to assume that he copied mechanically obvious mistakes from his *Vorlage*.

17 Note that our list of mistakes differs from that given by Goetze *1956:* 12f. We have rather more mistakes in A, fewer in B. A comparison of the two tablets would have to take into account the different length of the texts. Also, our list is not necessarily complete. Landsberger *1968:* 76, note 1, describes A as "mit Fehlern gespickt".

18 Goetze's conjecture and conclusion are accepted by Bottéro *1965/1966:* 89, 94.

19 Von Soden *1956:* 34 would emend by inserting *lu* after *imqut*. This does not necessitate the assumption of a common mistake, since there is a break in B iii 1. But see pp. 249f., below, where we reject this suggestion.

Divergences

We turn now to divergences between the two tablets, to which some scholars were inclined to attach much weight.[20] Our own conclusions will be rather less sanguine.[21]

The most striking divergence, that in sec. 17/18, is but a homoioteleuton, a well known mechanical mistake of scribes. It was recognised as such already by Goetze *1948:* 66. Scribe A, after writing (ii 4) the phrase *ana šimtim ittalak* — "went to the fate" (= died), omitted the apodosis of the first subsection and the protasis of the second one, which ended in the same phrase; he continued with the apodosis of the second subsection. Szlechter and von Soden have attempted to come to the rescue of the truncated version of A, but Goetze *1956:*13 is quite right in holding that through the omission the text of A became meaningless.[22] Even if a sense could, with considerable effort, be

20 See Miles-Gurney *1949:* 176: "The divergences between A and B are such that they cannot be regarded as duplicate copies of a single text ..." Similarly Szlechter *1952:* 245: "Nous sommes, en réalité, en présence d'un texte original, et d'un texte glosé." More cautiously, in *1954:* 10f., he adds "on peut émettre aussi l'opinion qu'il s'agit de deux copies d'un texte unique dont les différences ne seraient dues qu'à l'arbitraire du scribe. Il ne nous paraît possible en l'état d'éclaircir ces points". Kraus *1973:* 107, rejects as "unhaltbar" the view that the tablets constitute different versions of the LE, and I agree with him.

21 We shall submit that even differences which might have legal import (in secs. /28 and 50) do not reflect an evolution of the law, its intentional change.

22 Szlechter *1954:* 48 is well aware of the difficulties involved: in his view the shorter, condensed version is the original one and it was meant to apply "aussi bien aux fiancés qu'aux époux (sans enfants). Cependant en réunissant dans ce même article les deux hypothèses, le législateur n'a pas suffisamment dégagé les différences qui existent entre les deux cas. En effet, en ce qui concerne les fiancés, la question de compensation ne saurait se poser. La dot *(šeriktum)* n'est donnée à la fille qu'au moment du mariage". The unsatisfactory formulation of the original, Szlechter holds, was later corrected by the draftsmen, the result of whose efforts we find in version B. For von Soden *1958:* 519, the point of departure is to read, in A ii 3, *ina kilallin kal!* [*-la-tum*] — "of the two the bride": this is forced and problematic, not only in view of B, which has *ina kilallin išten* — "one of the two", but also because the proposed restoration yields a cumbersome wording: why say "of the two the bride", when "the bride" would be quite sufficient? See Petschow *1961:* 270, note 22, and Landsberger *1968:* 74: "Diskreditierung des klaren Textes B zugunsten

assigned to the version of A, the homoioteleuton remains the simplest, and therefore the best explanation of this divergence between the tablets.

In sec. 18A, the second provision reads "1 kor 1 (pan and) 4 seah barley *(se'am)* interest will bear". The word *še'am* = "barley" occurs only in Tablet B.

Sec. /28 brings the only divergence in which Tablet A offers a fuller version. The final sentence reads as follows: *um ina sun awilim iṣṣabbatu imat ul iballuṭ* — "the day in the lap of a man she will be seized, (one)[23] shall die, shall not live". This all-important statement is missing in B. Szlechter tends to see in this omission in B the disappearance of the death penalty, an evolution of the law.[24] One may question this proposition. What is omitted is not only the (death) penalty, but the crime of adultery altogether. One is left with a mere definition of the term *aššatum* — "wife", devoid of any operative context and consequence. The conscious abandonment of the death penalty for adultery would be in marked (and inexplicable) contrast with all that one finds in this respect in other Near Eastern collections of laws.[25] Rather, one may assume that scribe B (or his *Vorlage*) omitted one line. The occurrence of such a mistake was facilitated by the fact that the part actually written constituted a complete sentence; consequently the scribe need not have been immediately aware of having skipped one line at the end of the section.

Some minor divergences occurring in sections /37 and 38 are not without interest. One constitutes the only case where, if Goetze's reading of the tablet is exact, they actually differ. In /37, Tablet A (iii

von A ist unstatthaft. A lässt Ende von Par. 17 und Anfang von Par. 18 aus." Szlechter *1978:* 152ff., still refuses to contemplate a homoioteleuton.

23 = he?/she?. See pp. 284f., below.

24 *1954:* 12, repeated *1978:* 111.

25 Szlechter's own doubts emerge from his rather different suggestion at *1954:* 123. There he no longer holds that the death penalty for adultery was abolished *sub silentio*: it would still be imposed under customary law. B merely intended to prohibit self-help by the aggrieved party. In our view, Szlechter reads too much into the silence of version B. If such a change had been contemplated, the legislator would have made it explicit, by adding words like *din napištim ana šarrim* — "litigation of life (belongs) to the king" (cf. sec. 48). See also Miles-Gurney *1949:* 176: they regard the final sentence as "a deliberate gloss by the scribe of A", but one fails to see the reason for this.

20), Goetze reads *ina bit* ᴰ*Tišpak* ("in the house of Tišpak"), but in the corresponding B iii 3 *ina bab* ᴰ*Tišpak* ("in the door of Tišpak"); note that Szlechter *1954:* 26 reads *ina bab* in both the tablets. Discussing the divergence, Goetze *1956:*13, note 50, suggests that "the original text probably had *ina bab bit* ᴰ*Tišpak* ('in the gate of the house of Tišpak'); the signs for *bit(um)* and *bab(um)* are so similar to each other that omitting either one amounts to haplography".[26] Actually, Goetze's submission would involve a cumulation of mistakes. First, the omission of one of the two signs, probably in a faulty common source (X), from which in Goetze's opinion (see *1956:* 16) both A and B are descended. This would have been followed by the confusion of the Sumerogram for *babum* (KÁ) or *bitum* (É), in A or B. The second possibility, which is even more unlikely, is the independent omission in both A and B (or in their respective predecessors), in the one case of KÁ, in the other of É. All this is too complicated. It seems then rather that the original contained only one sign: either may be quite possible.[27] Then it will suffice to assume that only one mistake occurred, through misreading.[28]

In other divergences B offers a slightly fuller version, A a slightly briefer one. There is no difference in meaning. All these may be regarded as omissions in A rather than additions in B, since it is not likely that anyone would have bothered to interpolate a legal text for no evident purpose.

In / 37, A iii 18 has *itti maṣṣartim* ("with the deposit") for the fuller *itti buše awil maṣṣartim* ("with the goods of the depositor")[29] of B iii 1.

Still in sec. / 37, the depositee swears (B iii 4) *bušuia lu̯ ḫalqu* — "my goods were verily lost" (with yours), but the version of A (iii 21) omits the particle of emphasis, *lu*.

In sec. 38, B iii 7 has *ana kaspim inaddin* — "will give for silver" (= "will sell"), A iii 24 has only *inaddin* — "will give" (there is no difference

26 Some scholars import Goetze's *Urtext* into their translations: so Haase I, II, Bottéro, Klíma, Borger. One wonders how this came about.
27 See Gelb *1955*, no. 7; Schorr *1913*, no. 169.
28 Compare CH 182, where É is by mistake substituted for KÁ, in the Sumerogram KÁ.DINGIR (RA)ᴷᴵ (= Babylon); see Driver-Miles *1955:* 73. Conversely, note A 21979 (=Ishchali 199, in Greengus *1979*), from which CAD M/ii 273a quotes lines 2 and 3: *ša* KÁ.GAL *ša* MAŠ.KAK.EN. Here KÁ may be wrong for É. If so, it would be the earliest occurrence of the pair *ekallum — muškenum*.
29 Note the strong objection of Landsberger *1968:* 99 to *awil maṣṣartim*.

in the actual import). In the same section, the conjunction *u* — "and", of B iii 8, has no counterpart in A, but is altogether dispensable.

One would indeed wish to know whether all these are merely hasty omissions, the result of hurry, if not boredom. The other possibility is that they may reflect a desire, conscious or not, to cut out what may have appeared as superfluous, not adding to the import of the text. If there was such an inclination, it certainly did not go very far. Also it could hardly be attributed to scribe A, whose handiwork has come down to us. So the choice is between his negligence and some predecessor's brain.

Divergences which have attracted comment occur in sec. 50, dealing with officials remiss in carrying out their duties: they had seized fugitive slaves or stray animals, but had failed to deliver them to Eshnunna. Tablet A gives no details concerning the owner, but B specifies that the objects are *ša ekallim u muškenim* — "of the palace or of a *muškenum*". In the view of Miles-Gurney *1949:* 176 this addition "entirely alters the ambit of the law as it appears in A". More detailed are the remarks of Szlechter *1954:* 114. He sees here an intention to restrict the scope of the provision. The *droit de poursuite*, which under A had been general, is henceforth to be granted only in case the property is that of the palace itself or of a specially protected class, the *muškenum*. There are several objections to this. First, the section does not concern any "right of pursuit", but the duty to deliver up lost property, which is moreover likely to have come into the hands of the officials concerned in the course of their duties. What reason could there have been for the exclusion of another class, the *awilum*? Why should the law condone concealment of property of theirs?[30] Rather, we prefer to hold that *ekallum* plus *muškenum* covers all the possibilities.[31, 32] This disposes also of Szlechter's argument, who points — in distinction from sec. 50 — to the general, unspecific formulation of the two following sections,

30 Underlying Szlechter's view is a conception concerning the *muškenum* with which we disagree. See the detailed discussion, pp. 132ff., below.

31 Perhaps slaves and other property of strangers would be excluded. See Deuteronomy 23: 16-17; also, more generally, *Babylonian Talmud, Baba Qamma* 113b.

32 See also Goetze *1956:* 127, note 6, mentioning the reappearance of *ekallum* in the final passage of the section. In his view this shows that *ša ekallim u muškenim* must have formed part of the original text. But see p. 112, below.

51 and 52. This argument is anyhow quite inconclusive, since it is probable that these sections are derived from a different source.[33]

There is a further divergence in the same section, 50. Tablet B, but not A, specifies that the provisions will become operative (only if) *umi eli warḫim išten ušetiq* — "he let pass days over one month". Goetze regards this phrase as not essential to the sense; from the point of view of grammar or syntax this may be true, but for legal purposes the definition of a suitable period of time is, if not essential, at least useful. It is difficult to decide whether we have before us an accidental omission in A, or an intentional addition to B. We have seen that A is prone to omission, but even if preference is given to the other possibility, this is still not a fargoing "development" of the law, on the basis of which one would have to postulate the passage of a considerable length of time from the version of Tablet A to that of B.

Goetze *1956:* 13f. draws attention to the possibility that B may have contained material not covered by A. "Some important difference between A and B is hidden from us by the fragmentary condition of B." B i and ii contain more than A i and ii, respectively. The end of B i corresponds to A ii 9, that of B ii to A iii 17. "One would therefore expect B iv to begin around the middle of A iv." Instead, it begins already at A iii 42. In other words, the whole of B iii corresponds to only 24 lines of A iii, which is little more than half the column. Goetze suggests two possible explanations: "Either B iii was written out in a much more space consuming fashion, or B must have contained material which did not appear in A at all. A decision is difficult to make, but it seems that the second alternative is more likely. If this proves true, we would have to admit extensive omissions in A." Agreeing with the analysis of Goetze, also with his opting for the second possibility, I added that the cut in A might have occurred before sec. 48, which looked incomplete. All these submissions have been confirmed by Haddad 116, which — after sec. 47 — ends in a new section (incorporated below as LE 47A). In Haddad 116, the new section occupies 3 lines, 9 to 11, in Tablet A it would take up only 2 lines.[34] More than that seems to be missing.[35]

33 See p. 111, below.

34 Compare / 45, 2 lines (3-4) in Haddad 116, 1 line only (38) in Tablet A iii; 46, 47, 2 lines each (5-6, 7-8) in Haddad, but 3 lines (39-41) in Tablet A.

35 Haddad 116 ends with sec. 47A, so we still lack the beginning of sec. 48, and probably some more material preceding it.

An attempt to explain the omission in Tablet A would be no more than a guess. If the tablet is merely a school product, a writing exercise, a pupil may on purpose or else unintentionally have skipped a passage. A further possibility would be to assume extensive additions in B iii, but the rest of the text gives little support to such a suggestion.

We have also to note Goetze *1956:* 88 doubting, for reasons of space, that sec. 31 (B ii 11-12) was ever contained in A. Here I should hesitate to follow suit: it would be rather peculiar that a small section of two lines should have been left out just where, between the end of A ii and the beginning of A iii, some lines are missing or illegible. Some miscalculation seems to have occurred already with regard to the preceding section, 30. To it Goetze allots the lines A ii 45 to iii 2, but — with Szlechter — we prefer to assume that the section ended already in column ii (the lower edge of which seems to have been inscribed — so Goetze, *1956:* 190). Even if one were to assume that sec. 30 ended at the top of column iii, it cannot have taken up there more than one line, and this shows that Goetze's calculation cannot stand. Note that something very similar occurs at the top of A iv, where at first sight it seems that no room is left for sec. 49 (B iv 4-5). Here it seems that Goetze is mistaken in assigning two of the broken lines at the head of the column to the beginning of sec. 50, where one would be perfectly sufficient. This correction, and the addition of one more line at the top of column iv, give us the necessary space for sec. 49.[36]

From all that has been said it emerges that the case for a faulty antecedent, from which both A and B are derived, has not been made out. While one may readily admit that Tablet A is somewhat older than B, there is no proof for Goetze's further contention, *1956:* 16, that the laws are likely to have been issued under a king who ruled Eshnunna prior to the reign, in Babylon, of Sumu-abum, the founder of the First Dynasty.[37] The general trend of scholarly opinion would favour a much later date, holding that the LE are only slightly older than the CH, by some years, or at the utmost by some decades.[38] The truth is that it is impossible to arrive at definite conclusions. Also, one might bear in

36 Differently Szlechter *1954:* 29, who would insert sec. 49 at the bottom of A iii, as lines 45-46.

37 Sumu-abum died 89 years before Hammurabi became king of Babylon.

38 See Szlechter *1954:* 10; Edzard *1957:* 166; Korošec *1964:* 86; von Soden *1964:* 139; Kraus *1984:* 94f.

mind that collections like the LE were not promulgated *ex nihilo*. Some reflections on a pre-promulgation stage of the Laws will be offered later.[39]

Character of the Tablets

When asking about the character or nature of the LE, one ought to distinguish between the Laws as such, and the tablets on which they have been preserved. Concerning the Laws, we follow those who regard them as officially promulgated[40] against those who would deny them that status.[41] As for the two tablets, A and B, Goetze *1956:* 14 is probably right in holding that neither of them was an official copy. Such a copy "would not be faulty to the extent that A, at least, apparently is. The copies, then, were private copies. They still may have been used by officials who had to deal with legal questions in their daily routine. However, they may just have been products of a scribal school in which the Laws were copied and recopied for the instruction and the education of scribal apprentices".

Division into Sections

The tedious question of the division of the text into sections has now to be discussed. This is not merely a matter of convenience: the correct division of a legal text into its component parts may occasionally be of importance for the interpretation of its contents. One should regard as a "section" only a passage which can stand entirely by itself — both with regard to its substance and, especially, with regard to its formulation, the way it is drafted.[42] Where reference to another passage (usually to one preceding) is essential, this shows that one is not dealing with a

39 See pp. 87f., below.

40 E.g., Goetze *1956:* 16; Korošec *1964:* 87; Finkelstein *1981:* 15, note 5: "... the full year-name of the date of its promulgation, which precedes the text, may be taken as an indication of some formal and public status."

41 See Miles-Gurney *1949:* 178: "The tablets are copies, probably made independently, of an extract or selection of laws drawn from the official promulgation of the laws of Eshnunna and from other documents."

42 See already Poebel *1915:* 257ff.

"section", in the proper, legal-technical sense of that term. Size and complexity are only very unreliable guides, since we are entirely dependent on the way in which the ancient draftsman chose to formulate his provisions. It is only natural that there is considerable variety: his sections may be very brief and simple, or else they may be longwinded and intricate; we can but follow in his footsteps.

Quite generally, it may be said that every scholar writing about a text, or about a problem, will desire to go beyond those who preceded him, and will not shrink from contradicting accepted opinion. Indeed, this is, in essence, the purpose of taking part in scholarly discussion. Such a process may be very slow and prolonged, eventually leading to drastic changes in the understanding of a text. If the scholar editing it was mistaken in reading or interpretation, it is likely that in due course the error will be found out and put right.

Matters are entirely different with regard to the particular point under discussion, the division of a legal text into sections. Here, as a rule, the work of the *editor princeps* is endowed with an unparalleled degree of permanence and immutability. Even if the division is criticized and shown to be faulty, one will usually refrain from introducing any changes. The greater the interest evoked by a text, the sooner the modes of referring to it — as fixed in the *editio princeps* — come to be regarded as parts of a canon, deviation from which is very difficult. Reviews are not a suitable occasion for changing the division, nor are the hurried translations into a host of languages which follow the *editio princeps* in a short time, or papers devoted to particular topics. By the time a new edition is published, the old division into sections will be firmly entrenched, and one will instinctively shrink from the confusion which would, at least temporarily, result from a fresh departure. The Code of Hammurabi is the classical example for such a process. V. Scheil, the first editor of the Code, split the text of the stele — on which the sections were not marked in any way — into units which in many instances were but fragments. He appears to have been guided by the desire to make quotation easy and convenient: *šumma* — "if", introducing a conditional sentence, was usually regarded as starting a new section. Some years later, copies of parts of the code, written on tablets, were published. These bore divisions by the scribe, and Scheil was shown to have been wrong in many instances. The matter was discussed in detail by A. Poebel (see note 42), who proposed principles of division which ought to have gained general adherence.[43] In spite of all this, as the centenary of the discovery and publication of the CH slowly approaches, and after it has been through many editions, Scheil's faulty division is still with us. It is a safe guess that it will never be deviated from: any innovation would involve too much inconvenience.[44]

The task facing the editor of the LE resembled that of Scheil, in that on the tablets sections were not marked off in any way. Nor was it possible to deduce much from the lines. In Tablet A, the scribe has not attempted to employ the line as a structural unit: sections start often in the middle of a line,[45] though not — as a rule — quite near its end.[46] In Tablet B, by contrast, sections invariably start at the beginning of a line. But scribe B goes much farther: he has taken pains to utilize the line for purposes which one achieves nowadays by means of punctuation (which, needless to say, does not exist in cuneiform and is altogether a modern invention). In this fashion, the lines may divide the section into its various logical components, not just into protasis and apodosis. As example one may mention sec. 33: there the protasis splits logically into two parts different in time, and is followed by a short apodosis. Each of these components has one line for itself. Since they are of different length, the writing is rather unequal: 18 signs are crammed into B ii 16, there are 15 signs in line 17, only 11 in line 18. Better still is the example of sec. 38: there the main part of the protasis, consisting of 23 signs, is pressed into one line (iii 7), while the two following lines, containing the second part of the protasis and the apodosis, have between them only 22 signs (10 and 12, respectively). There are only a few instances in which this desire for neat subdivision is not evident. Where then a scribe is so

43 Driver-Miles *1952:* 42 give a list of sections in the CH, which are to be combined. For a critical discussion of Scheil's division see also Finkelstein *1981:* 16.

44 So the new numeration proposed by Friedrich *1959* for tablet II of the HL has found little adherence.

45 See secs. 4, 7, 10, 12, 21, 22, 27/, 30, 34/, 38, 39, 44/, 47, 51, 53, 54/, — altogether sixteen sections!

46 However, in some regulatory sections Tablet A is neatly organized. So especially in secs. 1 and 2 (for which the counterpart in Tablet B is not preserved). In 1 the data are arranged in 4 columns over 10 lines; in 2, in 3 columns over 3 lines. Note also the full correspondence of A and B in the arrangement of sec. 18A.

keen on dividing his material, each section — but also each subsection — will naturally start a new line. For our present purpose, then, Tablet B will not help, though for reasons opposite to those noted for Tablet A.

In the absence of any formal, exterior, mechanical indicator, there remained the legal and linguistic criteria. Goetze has not dwelt upon the principles which guided him in fixing the sections of the LE. His division has drawn the criticism of several of the reviewers of the *editio princeps*; especially to be noted are the remarks of von Soden *1949:* 368, who pointed out — in a general fashion — that the editor had carried the division much too far; von Soden referred to Poebel's paper (mentioned above), and called for a new division of the text, to be truly in accord with its import.[47]

It is cause for regret that the criticisms voiced by von Soden have had very little practical effect. Szlechter missed the opportunity of putting the division on a sounder basis; instead, he preferred to follow Goetze and limited himself to a few suggestions (*1954:* 13, note 1). Goetze himself could easily have put the matter right, already in *1950* (ANET) and especially in *1956*, his standard edition. But, with one exception, all the remarks — general as well as particular — of his reviewers concerning the division of the LE into sections went unheeded.

Bowing to von Soden and San Nicolò, Goetze conceded that his original section 18 was made up of two unrelated laws, and gave to the final part the number 18A, "so as not to disturb the numbering adopted in the *editio princeps*". This division into two sections is followed by most authors, over the attempt of Landsberger *1968:* 73f. to re-establish the unity of 18 and 18A: "Par. 18A kann kein selbständiger Gesetzesartikel sein; wäre er es, so müsste er anders lauten; *uṣṣab* hat kein Subjekt, dies kann nur dem Par. 18 entnommen werden, obgleich Härte des Subjektwechsels zugegeben werden muss. Somit: Der Brautvater, bzw. seine Erben, erstattet zwar das Eingebrachte nicht zurück, wohl aber den durch seine Investierung erzielten Gewinn, der in der Form von Zinsen zum normalen Satze abgefunden wird."

Difficulties inherent in Landsberger's proposal have been pointed out by Finkelstein (*1970:* 249f.) Better translations, proposed by Bottéro and Finkelstein, and incorporated below, should dispose of the matter altogether. As for the absence of a subject in sec. 18A, one may mention the generally elliptic, slogan-like formulation of the regulatory

47 See also San Nicolò *1949:* 261.

provisions. This would distract considerably from the force of Landsberger's argument.

Scholarly work on the LE has by now reached a stage at which it appears no longer practicable to introduce a new division. There is little likelihood that a new numeration would gain wide, not to say general, acceptance; even if it did, the resulting confusion would be too great.[48] However, some compromise may be feasible: this will indeed retain the current numeration, but will also give expression to some of the suggestions made by various scholars, as well as to my own examination of the matter. Compound sections are to be quoted by joining their component numbers: e.g., Goetze's sections 34 and 35 become sec. 34/35. Often, when referring to a specific part, one may use the existing numeration, writing 34/, or /35: the stroke gives expression to the view that the passage referred to is the beginning, respectively the end, of a compound section. Let us now consider the details.

It will be seen in due course that a significant part of the LE is devoted to the regulation of economic life. When dividing these passages into sections, one is up against an immediate difficulty: contrary to what one finds in the legal parts proper, the regulations on prices and hire contain few indications of language and structure which could be relied upon in delimiting sections. It may even be asked whether the term "section", in its usual technical sense, is here at all applicable. Rather, we have here lists, on the one hand stating prices (or exchange values) of certain commodities (secs. 1, 2), on the other hand the hire of chattels and persons (secs. 3, 4, 7, 8, 9A, 10, 11, and 14). In a class apart is sec. 18A, fixing the rate of interest for loans of silver, respectively barley. In these lists division is necessarily somewhat arbitrary. There would be little difficulty in combining sections 1 and 2; 3 and 4; 7 and 8. More radically, one might even contemplate joining sections 1 to 4, regarding the distinction between sale and hire as not of the essence of the matter.[49] Nevertheless, after all has been said, it appears impossible to make out a compelling case for a different division, on the lines suggested. Change must not become an aim in itself. Therefore, we have deviated from Goetze's numeration of the regulatory sections only in

48 Similar considerations bid us refrain from another change: in view of the superiority of Tablet B, it might have served as the basic text, the starting point. We have been content with one minor change, which will cause no trouble: the line division in our English version is based on B.

49 On the structure of these lists see also pp. 97f., below.

one instance, by splitting his section 9, into 9 and 9A.[50] Our numeration might have been different if the matter had been *res integra*.

In the legal parts proper of the Laws, we suggest combining sections in eight instances:

Sec. 17/18 provides for the restitution of the bride payment *(terḫatum)*, in case either the bridegroom or the bride dies (17/), and for the set-off of dowry and bride payment in case death follows shortly upon the consummation of the marriage (/18).[51]

Sec. 23/24 deals with death caused in the course of unlawful distress, for a debt which does not exist. The first part (23/) fixes the penalty in case the victim is a slave woman taken in distress; the second part (/24) imposes the death penalty in case the victim is the wife or child of the alleged debtor.

The complex structure of sec. 27/28, concerning adultery, will be discussed in detail.[52] It is the final part of the section which provides for the punishment of the offence.[53]

Sec. 34/35 concerns only one case, and /35 is but the second part of the apodosis. If the child of a slave woman belonging to the palace has been handed over to another person, the palace may take it away (34/). The exact import of /35 is in dispute: some hold that the person who received the child may give another one as a substitute, some are of the view that the additional child is to be given in any case, as a penalty. For the present purpose the result is the same.[54]

Sec. 36/37 deals with the loss of goods which had been deposited. The first part (36/) makes the depositee liable to compensate the loss, in case his house has not been burgled. The second part (/37) deals with a different situation: the house was plundered and the owner also incurred loss. The combined section is the largest in the LE, and rather cumbersome. This does not change the fact that the second part (/37) is

50 For doubts on the unity of Goetze's section 9, see already Szlechter *1954:* 16, note 37. Secs. 9 and 9A are separated also by Bottéro *1965/1966:* 91, and this has become commonplace in recent translations of the LE. Landsberger *1968:* 72 still regards 9 and 9A as one section, but is not followed by Finkelstein *1970:* 249.

51 See also pp. 101, 179ff., below.

52 See pp. 102f., below.

53 On the unity of sec. 27/28 see already von Soden *1956:*34.

54 The unity of sec. 34/35 has been stressed by many scholars: San Nicolò *1949:* 261; Korošec *1953:* 90; Szlechter *1954:* 25, note 93; von Soden *1956:* 34; Petschow *1961:* 271; Bottéro *1965/1966:* 93.

— in its formulation — dependent on the preceding one. If one adheres to the criteria proposed above, 36/37 constitutes only one section.[55]

The three instances of combined sections which remain to be considered are simple and present no problem. Sec. 44/45 deals with two similar cases of bodily injury, the breaking of an arm (44/), and the breaking of a leg (/45).[56] Sec. 54/55 deals with the death of a human being, caused by a goring ox, with variations according to the status of the victim: in the first part (54/) he is a free man *(awilum)*, in the second (/55) a slave *(wardum)*. Sec. 56/57 is essentially similar, only the place of the goring ox is taken by a vicious dog.[57]

So far the discussion has turned on the criticism of Goetze's division of the LE, but matters are rather more complicated. Some of Goetze's critics have been too hasty in suggesting mergers; they tend to prefer substance over form. While usually commendable, it is the wrong approach to the question in hand. Von Soden (*1956*: 33) would combine sections 4 and 5, but there appears to be no warrant for this. Sections 5 and 6 have indeed been attracted by the subject matter of sec. 4 (hire of a boat), but they constitute an interruption in the regulatory list concerning hire, of which sec. 4 is part. The formulation of sec. 5 is not dependent on the preceding section.[58] Szlechter *1954:* 19, note 58, wishes to combine secs. 15 and 16. True, these resemble each other in their mode of formulation, and are probably taken from the same source. One may even find a common heading for both of them,[59] but they are nevertheless independent, in both syntax and content. The former applies only to slaves, the latter also — indeed primarily — to a free *mar awilim la zizu*. Grammatically the subject is different: in sec. 15 it is the merchant (or alewife), in 16 the *mar awilim* or the slave.[60] Von Soden (*1958*: 520) regards secs. 18A and 19 as forming one section; here too the justification for his view eludes me. The former contains a

55 See already Miles-Gurney *1949:* 185.

56 See already Szlechter *1954:* 28, note 110; also Bottéro *1965/1966:* 94.

57 The combinations 54/55, 56/57 are accepted by Bottéro *1965/1966:* 95.

58 Note that CH separates the two topics: hire of a boat (corresponding to LE 4) is regulated in secs. 275, 276, 277, while negligent sinking (corresponding to LE 5) has already been disposed of, in secs. 236, 237.

59 Goetze *1956:* 56: "Incapacity to contract".

60 Klíma *1956:* 439: "Nel testo del par. 16 non si ripete più il soggetto." In 1982, secs. 15 and 16 are still lumped together in CAD Q 97b. See also pp. 158f., 162, below.

general statement on rates of interest. The latter does indeed deal with a case of loan, and is thereby in logical contact with the preceding section (and with the one that follows). But both in formulation and in its actual contents it stands by itself.[61] Bottéro *1965/1966:* 92 combines secs. 20 and 21, but these two provisions on loan are independent in their formulation. A combination of sections 22 and 23/ has also been suggested;[62] the two are indeed closely related, but they have been drawn up as true and proper separate sections.

Bottéro (*1965/1966:* 94, 99) splits sec. 42 into two parts, the one (42) concerning the case of biting a nose and severing it, the other (42A) constituting a tariff of penalties for (the destruction of) an eye, a tooth, an ear, and for a slap in the face, His reason for so holding is that the verbs "to bite" and "to sever" are not suited to the other injuries (with the possible exception of the ear). This is so, but on the whole the objection seems too pedantic: it is the injured organ that matters, not the selection of verbs to suit each specific case. In addition, the unity of section 42 is suggested by its neat tripartite structure. Only the first and the last of the five injuries listed are set out in full. The three in between (referring to eye, tooth and ear) are formulated elliptically, in slogan-like fashion: the compensation is fixed, but the noun determining it, *kaspam* ("silver") and the verb *išaqqal* ("he shall weigh out") are omitted.

Finally, we have to mention secs. 47 and 48, the unity of which has been confidently asserted by von Soden already in 1949.[63] Our understanding of sec. 48 is hampered by its poor state of preservation, but as far as one can see the section is formulated in a strange fashion: it is introduced by the conjunction *u*, an unlikely beginning for a new section. However, its contents are quite general, distinguishing — for the purpose of assigning jurisdiction — between cases from 1/3 of a mina (= 20 shekels) to 1 mina, and capital cases. Even then it was not probable that these provisions were to be regarded as continuing the very specific sec. 47, which laid down the payment of 10 shekels (a sum smaller than that mentioned in 48!) for some bodily injury.[64] Now, sec.

61 Von Soden is followed by Bottéro *1965/1966:* 92; cf. Petschow *1968a:* 137. *Contra*, Landsberger *1968:* 73. See also pp. 105, 235f., below.

62 See Haase *1965:* 144, note 51; Klíma *1966:* 253.

63 See von Soden *1949:* 368: "eindeutig nur ein einziges Gesetz". At one time I adhered to that opinion: *1962b:* 138f.

64 See p. 288, below.

47A separates 48 from 47, and this — by itself — is sufficient to dispose of von Soden's suggestion. On the other hand it still remains likely that sec. 48 is not an independent section, i.e. that its beginning is still missing (from Tablet A).[65]

Problems of translation

We ought now to discuss briefly some of the difficulties hindering the proper translation, and consequently the proper understanding, of a legal text in Akkadian. These may reflect various causes. Ambiguities may be due to the fact that some particles, which occur very frequently, have more than one translational equivalent. The same form of the Akkadian verb may give expression to very different notions. Finally, there are phenomena of Akkadian grammar and syntax which have not yet been sufficiently explored. All this accounts for a great many uncertainties and differences of rendering.

First and foremost among the ambiguous particles is the conjunction *u*: it may denote cumulation ("and") or alternation ("or"). On the basis of comparison with other Semitic languages, it is customary to distinguish between *u* — "and", and *û* — "or".[66] However, both are often spelled exactly the same way — *ù*: so in LE, CH and MAL. It follows that one cannot derive any assistance from this distinction, correct as it is.[67] The choice of the one or the other of the two renderings may in a given case make a great deal of difference. In many instances that choice will indeed be obvious, and there will be no room for doubt: e.g., *še'am u ṣibassu* (sec. 20) means "the barley and its interest", *ina bitim u mala ibaššu* (sec. 59) — "from the house and whatever there is"; on the other hand one has, e.g., *ša ekallim u muškenim* (sec. 50) — "of the palace or of a *muškenum*", *wardum u amtum* (sec. 51) — "slave or slave woman". In other cases careful examination of the substantive legal import may be necessary. In our translation we render *u* either "and/", or "/or". The choice of the one or the other expresses our preference in a given case; the stroke recalls the fact that an alternative

65 See p. 28, above.

66 See, e.g., GAG, sec. 117b, c; Driver-Miles *1955:* 362 (Glossary).

67 AHw (1979) 1398: "... nur nach dem Zusammenhang zu unterscheiden."

rendering is also feasible, at least *in abstracto*.[68] Where necessary, the matter is examined in detail in the commentary.[69]

Next one ought to mention the enclitic particle *-ma*, which may give expression to several different nuances.[70] E.g., between two verbs it may serve as a simple conjunction, "and", "and then", etc. denoting a logical connection between two actions; it may also express contrast, "but", "yet", etc. These two nuances will occasionally occur in one sequence: e.g., *la išuma ... iklama uštamit* — "had nothing (upon a man), yet ... detained ... and caused (the distress) to die" (sec. 23/24); *issima ... ikšišuma ... ittadin* — "he claimed, but ... wronged him, and gave ..." (sec. 25). It may be attached to a noun or pronoun for the sake of emphasis: *ana belišuma* — "to its owner indeed ..." (sec. 17/; cf. sec. 31); *din napištimma* — "a case of life indeed" (sec. 26); *ina bitišuma* — "in his house indeed" (sec. 50). Sometimes emphasis may carry with it an element of exclusiveness, of restriction: *wataršuma* — "its excess only" (sec. /18); *šuma šaraq* — "he himself is the thief" (sec. 40); *ana šarrimma* — "to the king himself", "to the king only" (sec. 48).[71]

To be especially noted is the creation of conditional sentences without *šumma* — "if", by means of the precative and *-ma* in the protasis: *libilma* — "should he bring" (secs. 14, 17/); *lišimma* — "should she dwell" (sec. 27/).[72] Another instance of a conditional sentence without *šumma* is that of sec. 50 (Tablet B): *ušetiqma ... itawwi* — "(if) he let pass ... (the palace) will charge ..."[73]

68 This is different from lawyerese "and/or", which is meant to include both the possibilities. By contrast, Akkadian *u*, in full "and?/or?", is an *ambigua sermo*, in the sense of *Digesta Iustiniani* 34.5.3: "... non utrumque diximus, sed id dumtaxat quod volumus."

69 In some instances the text leaves cumulation or alternation without expression: *ipram piššatam lubuštam* — "rations of food, oil (and) clothing" (sec. 32), but *kaspam še'am šipatam ellam* — "silver, barley, wool, (or) sesame oil" (sec. 15). Cf. GAG, sec. 140a. As a rule we have followed the Akkadian in omitting the conjunction altogether.

70 Cf. GAG, sec. 123a; Driver-Miles *1955:* 387f. (Glossary); Bottéro *1965/1966:* 92; AHw 569f.

71 See GAG, sec. 126 (and especially 126e) on the use of *-ma* in nominal sentences.

72 See GAG, sec. 160c; Goetze *1956:* 55; and see ARM VIII 33:13 (CAD A/ii 116a)

73 This construction, following *ušetiq*, is frequent in Old-Babylonian texts, some of which come from the region of Eshnunna: e.g. *ušetiqma ṣibtam uṣṣab* — "if he let (the term) pass, he shall pay interest"; for references

Akkadian prepositions are notorious for the wide range of their import. The prepositon *ina* may — *inter alia* — have to be rendered "in" and "from": compare *ina bitišu* — "in his house" (sec. 23/34) and *ina bitim* — "from the house" (sec. 59).[74] Again, *ana* may denote motion in a certain direction ("to"), but also purpose ("for"): see *ana bitišu irub* — "she entered to his house" (sec. /18), but *ana tarbitim* — "for upbringing" (secs. 32, 34/).[75] Other renderings may also be necessary. It would not have been practicable to include consistently a cumulation of various renderings within the translation, so the choice had to be made already at this early stage. In some cases of ambiguity care was taken that this should not go unnoted (see, e.g., secs. 9, 19, 36/).

Some peculiarities of the Akkadian verb call for attention. These are (a) the connotations of the present tense; (b) gender; (c) the import of the *t*-form.

The tense employed ordinarily in the apodosis[76] is the present; it may cause uncertainties of translation, since it has several connotations.[77] So it may denote the simple future, as in *ekallum itabbal* — "the palace will take away" (sec. 34/), *šurqam ittišu itawwi* — "(with) theft will charge him" (sec. 50). Occasionally its import will be one of permission, e.g. *ipaṭṭar* — "he may redeem" (sec. 39). Usually, however, it will refer to a duty, as in *išaqqal* — "he shall weigh out" *(passim), iriab* — "he shall replace" (sec. 23/, 36/). In a particular case the nuance chosen may make a great deal of difference. For example, there are secs. 3, 4, and 10, dealing with the hire of a wagon, a boat, a donkey, and their respective drivers. All three terminate in the sentence *kala umim ireddeši(-šu).* In *1948 (editio princeps)* Goetze rendered this by "he may drive it the whole day", making the provision refer to the hirer, permitting a certain behaviour of his; in *1950* (ANET) he changed his rendering slightly, to

see CAD E 392a b. Von Soden *1958:* 521, remarks that "in § 50 gehört *ušetiqma* nach Ausweis des *-ma* bereits zum Nachsatz". This is strange, in view of what he had written in GAG (sec. 160) about "Bedingungssätze ohne einleitende Partikel" (conditional sentences without introductory particle), and the function of *-ma* in them.

74 See GAG, sec. 114c.

75 GAG, sec. 114d.

76 The use of the present in the protasis is more complex: see the detailed discussion by Hirsch *1969:* 120ff.

77 See GAG, sec. 78d.

"he shall drive it the whole day"; in other words, the passage refers to the duties of the driver (or boatsman). It is to this last rendering that we shall give preference.[78] Throughout our translation we have had to opt for the one or the other of these possible renderings, introducing once more an interpretative element at an early stage. It may therefore be well to emphasize that from the formal point of view of language the renderings will/may/shall are equally valid; the actual rendering depends in each case on the substance of the provision.

The second point concerns gender. Semitic languages have usually different verb forms for the masculine and the feminine of the third person singular. This is true also for Akkadian: for the masculine there is the prefix *i*-, or *u*-, for the feminine *ta*-, or *tu*-.[79] This difference in forms may sometimes be of help; one finds it, e.g., in MAL, not however in LE and CH: these employ only the masculine form. Already in 1933, von Soden could state, quite categorically, that "im Altbabylonischen ist der Präfix *i* (bzw. *u*) in der Amtssprache ausnahmslos *generis communis*".[80] The LE conform to this rule: in six instances, in which the subject is unavoidably feminine, ostensibly masculine forms are employed. So in (a) sec. /18 *(iḫusima) ana bitišu irub* — "(he took her and) she entered his house"; (b) /28 *um ina sun awilim iṣabbat* — "the day in the lap of a man she will be seized"; (c) 29 *maram ittalad* — "she bore a son"; (d) 33 *amtum usarirma marša ana mạrat awilim ittadin* — "a slave woman cheated and gave her son to the daughter of a man"; (e) *marša ... ittadin* — "gave ... her son"; (f) 41 *sabitum ... inaddinšum* — "the *sabitum* ... shall sell to?/for? him". Whenever the context, for one reason or another, is not conclusive, i.e., the subject is undefined, this uncertainty ought to be reflected in the translation. In three sections, /18, /28, 59, I have used "(one)": this is not a final translation, not even a *Verlegenheitslösung*. It merely

78 See the notes on sec. 3, pp. 46f., below.

79 See GAG, sec. 75d.

80 *1933:* 149. A similar situation exists in Sumerian: in an unclear context, no assistance can be derived from the verb, due to the absence of gender. So in LUY 4 (on servile marriages), where the editor F. Yildiz (*1981:* 96) rendered "... he may not leave the house (of his master)"; she was at once followed by Haase (in a *Nachtrag* to Haase *1979*) and by Römer (*1982:* 20). Relying on the parallel in Exodus 21: 2ff., I preferred "... she may not leave the house (of her master)" (*1985a:* 138f.).

indicates that the text, as it is, does not offer the modern reader a definite answer. Further discussion will (or will not) supply it.[81]

Finally, difficulties are caused by the *t*-form of the verb. This has been the subject of detailed discussion by Driver: "One of the most vexed questions in Akkadian grammar is the force of the *t* infixed in certain stems or themes of the verb. Until this has been decided, scarcely a single text can be accurately translated."[82] This means that we face here an ever-present factor of inaccuracy. I do not feel competent to make any suggestions of my own on the matter; rather I should confine myself to some few observations based on the LE themselves, which were not yet taken into account by the authors quoted above. The *t*-form is usual at the end of the protasis,[83] but there are some exceptions.[84] In the LE it does not occur after the negation *la*.[85] The *t*-form and *-ma* are mutually exclusive — even if the verb with infix occurs in the middle of the protasis.[86] Especially striking is LE 29, with its string of *t*-verbs, but without a single *-ma*.[87] A painstaking analysis of the *t*-forms in the LE, offered by Hirsch, has also not reached definite conclusions.[88] In our translation we do not take account of a specific import of the infixed form.

Some few remarks now, a kind of *apologia pro domo mea*, before I pass to the translation. In this second edition I have continued to grapple with it, making some changes in substance, but many more in form.

Translations may vary according to the nature of the text being translated: the rendering of a poem will differ from that of a section of law. With regard to a legal text, close adherence to the original must be

81 See further, remarks on style, pp. 94f., below, and the detailed discussion of each of the sections, below pp. 180ff. (/18), 284f. (/28), and 213ff. (59).
82 Driver-Miles *1955:* 350-361.
83 As observed by Oppenheim *1933:* 182, the form occurs frequently "am Ende von Sinnesabschnitten".
84 See secs. 9, 21, 32, 40, 47.
85 Secs. 9, 27/, 32, 40. But accident cannot be ruled out, in view of the occurrence of the form after *la* in CH: see, e.g., secs. 1, 2, 3, 10 11, 16, etc.
86 See sec. 23/24; this too does not hold true for the CH: see, e.g., secs. 16, 27, 30, 135.
87 See also sec. 30.
88 *1969:* 119-131.

a paramount consideration, and the demands of the receptor language — however legitimate in themselves — will take second place only. Yet "second place" does not mean that the needs of the receptor language can be disregarded altogether. There must be a limit even to a translator's endeavour to bring the reader as close as possible to the position in which the reader of the original finds himself. Especially in matters of syntax excessive adherence to the original would have yielded a version which a modern reader would digest only with difficulty. The Akkadian of the LE (and of similar texts) very consistently puts the verb at the end of the clause ("Jack Jill loves"), where English has the verb follow the subject and precede the object ("Jack loves Jill"). A rendering into Latin, true to the Akkadian structure, would have been easy to achieve; it would also have been satisfactory to accommodate some of the problems mentioned above.

For just a fleeting moment, I toyed with the idea of a Latin translation. But I realized at once how strange this would seem, how completely out of tune with the spirit and the needs of the present. It might have been suitable for some serious students of Roman law; for others it would have constituted an unnecessary, puzzling and hardly surmountable barrier.

So I offer an English translation, which cannot claim to be elegant. Not only a better translator could have offered a smoother translation, I myself could have done so. But my aim was different: the starting point is the original, even while I recognize that excessive violence must not be done to English usage. What constitutes "excessive violence" will necessarily remain a matter of individual taste. For example, I thought it feasible to adhere to the Akkadian sequence in the apodosis (which is relatively simple), but not in the protasis. The end result is a compromise, and I harbour no illusions about compromises: it is often their fate that they please a few, but displease many more.[89]

89 For some further remarks about translation from the Akkadian, see Yaron *1985b:* 23-33.

CHAPTER TWO

THE TEXT*

The Heading: A i 1-7

1 [.........................]X U$_4$.21.KAM
2 [.........................]X ^{D}EN.LÍL.LÁ DINGIR. X X
3 [.........................] NAM.LUGAL Èš-nun-na^{ki}
4 [.........................]X.A É.AD.DA.A.NI.ŠÈ
5 [.........................]X.RA.ÀM Ṣúpu-ur-^{D}Šamaš^{ki}
6 [.........................]X BAL.RI.A ^{ÍD}IDIGLAT
7 [........] MU.1.KAM ^{GIŠ}TUKUL.KALAG.GA BA.AN.DÁB

Section 1: A I 8-17

8	1 kùr še'um (ŠE)	a-na	1 šiqil (GÍN)	kaspim (KÙ.BABBAR)
9	3 qa šaman ruštim (Ì.SAG)	[a]-na	1 šiqil	kaspim
10	1 sut 2 qa ellum (Ì.GIŠ)	[a]-na	1 šiqil	kaspim
11	1 sut 5 qa naḫum (Ì.ŠAḪ)	a-na	1 šiqil	kaspim
12	4 sat Ì.ÍD	a-na	1 šiqil	kaspim
13	6 ma-na šipatum (SÍG)	a-na	1 šiqil	kaspim
14	2 kùr ṭabtum (MUN)	a-na	1 šiqil	kaspim
15	1 kùr uḫulum (NAGA)	a-na	1 šiqil	kaspim
16	3 ma-na erum (URUDU)	a-na	1 šiqil	kaspim
17	2 ma-na erum ep-šum	a-na	1 šiqil	kaspim

* Italics in the text or the translation indicate uncertainty. References by name of author only, relate to translations (for details see Bibliography, pp. 305ff., below).

The Heading: Restorations of the missing left side of the tablet are disputed; here they are omitted altogether. In addition to the proposals of Goetze *1956*, see those of Landsberger *1968:* 66f. There are few divergences between the two in the reading of the actually extant text. At the end of line 2, Landsberger reads ^{D}NIN-A-ZU (~~—Tishpak~~). Their opinions differ on the import of the heading. Goetze speaks of a "preamble", Landsberger sees no more than a date formula: so also Finkelstein *1970:* 247.

The Heading
[........................] on the 21st day
[........................] of Ellil, the ... god
[........................] the kingship of Eshnunna
[........................] so that into his father-house
[........................] (and when) Ṣupur-Šamaš
[........................] across the Tigris
[....] (same) one year were seized with mighty (force of) weapon.

Section 1

1 kor barley	for	1 shekel	silver
3 qa *ruštum* oil	for	1 shekel	silver
1 seah (and) 2 qa sesame oil	for	1 shekel	silver
1 seah (and) 5 qa lard	for	1 shekel	silver
4 seah "river oil"	for	1 shekel	silver
6 minas wool	for	1 shekel	silver
2 kor salt	for	1 shekel	silver
1 kor potash	for	1 shekel	silver
3 minas copper	for	1 shekel	silver
2 minas wrought copper	for	1 shekel	silver

Goetze *1948* gave a very different reading (since abandoned) for the decisive line 2; this led to the assumption that the LE had been promulgated by Bilalama, King of Eshnunna, who had preceded Hammurabi of Babylon by some 200 years.

Sec. 1: **9**: Ì.SAG: *šaman ruštim*: so with Szlechter and Landsberger *1968:* 68f. The meaning of *ruštum* is not certain. Goetze renders Ì.SAG by *ul šamnim* — "very light oil". **10**: *ellum* (Goetze *ullum*): see Landsberger *cit.* 69f.; CAD E 106b, AHw 205a. **12** Ì.ÍD ("river oil"): Goetze gives no Akkadian equivalent. Szlechter reads Ì.ESIR = *šaman ittim* ("naphte"). Cf. further Miles-Gurney *1949:* 180; Goetze *1956:* 27; Landsberger *cit.* 70. **15**: NAGA (=*uḫulum* — "alkali,

Section 2: A i 18-20

18	1 qa ellum (Ì.GIŠ)	ša ni-ís-ḫa-tim	3 sat še-šu (ŠE.BI)
19	1 qa naḫum (Ì.ŠAḪ)	ša ni-ís-ḫa-tim	2 sat 5 qa še-šu
20	1 qa Ì.ÍD	ša ni-ís-ḫa-tim	8 qa še-šu

Section 3: A i 21-23

21 ^{is}ereqqum (GIŠ.MAR.GÍD.DA) qá-du-um alpi-ša (GUD.ḪI.A-ša) ù re-di-ša
22 1 pan 4 sat še'um idi-ša (Á.BI) šum-ma kaspum 1/3 šiqlim idi-ša
23 ka-la u$_4$-mi-im i-re-de-e-ši

Section 4: A i 23-24

idi(Á) ^{is}eleppim (GIŠ.MÁ) 1 kurrum^{um} 2 qa
24 ù [....] qa idi malaḫim (MA.LAḪ) ka-la$^{!!}$ u$_4$-mi i-re-de-ši

Section 5: A i 25-26

25 šum-ma malaḫum i-gi-ma ^{is}eleppam uṭ-ṭe$_4$-eb-bé
26 ma-la ú-ṭe$_4$-eb-bu-ú ú-ma-al-la

Section 6: A i 27-28

27 šum-ma awilum (LÚ) i-na nu-la-a-ni ^{is}eleppam la ša-at-tam
28 iṣ-ṣa-ba-at 10 šiqil kaspam išaqqal (Ì.LÁ.E)

potash"); so following von Soden *1956:* 33, *1958:* 519, who is supported by Landsberger *cit*. 70. Goetze gave for NAGA the Akkadian equivalent *qaqullum* ("cardamon"). Szlechter suggested IN.NU(?) = *tibnum* ("paille" — "straw"). **17**: *ep-šum*: so CAD E 323a; confirmed by Landsberger *cit*. 70. Goetze *1948*, Szlechter *1954*, von Soden *1956:* 33: *ma-šum* — "refined". See Goetze *1956:* 28 for *ma-sum*$_6$, and the objections of von Soden *1958:* 519.

Sec. 2: **18**ff.: *ša nisḫatim*: meaning uncertain. See Goetze *1956:* 31f. The commodities described as *ša nisḫatim* are more expensive than the ordinary ones, listed in sec. 1 (lines 10-12); the differences amount to 20, 25 and 6 2/3 percent, respectively. One school sees in *ša nisḫatim* a reference to better quality; so von Soden, since *1949:* 363; Diakonoff, Lipin *1963*; Bottéro. Others, relying on comparison with Old Assyrian texts, see here a reference to a tax, included in the price: so San Nicolò *1949:* 258; Böhl *1949/1950:* 98, note 6; Korošec *1953:* 93; Szlechter *1954:* 14, 66. Von Soden *1956:* 33 denies a connection with the Old Assyrian "Abgabebezeichnung *nisḫatum*, da diese in babylonischen Urkunden nicht vorkommt". Finally, Landsberger *1968:* 71: "Kleinverkaufpreis"; so also AHw 794b.

Sec. 3: **23**: *kala umim ireddeši*: time not defined; it might mean "from dawn to dusk". Goetze *1948* regarded the hirer as subject: "he may drive it the whole

Section 2

1 qa sesame oil	*ša nisḫatim*	3 seah (is) its barley
1 qa lard	*ša nisḫatim*	2 seah (and) 5 qa (is) its barley
1 qa "river oil"	*ša nisḫatim*	8 qa (is) its barley

Section 3

A wagon together with its oxen and/ its driver:
1 pan (and) 4 seah barley (is) its hire. If silver — 1/3 shekel (is) its hire.
All the day he shall?/may? drive it.

Section 4

The hire of a boat (per) 1 kor (of capacity, is) 2 qa, and/ [....] qa (is) the hire of the boatman. All the day he shall?/may? drive it.

Section 5

If a boatman was negligent and caused the boat to sink — whatever he caused to sink, he shall pay in full.

Section 6

If a man *ina nullani* seized a boat (which was) not his — 10 shekels silver he shall weigh out.

day" (followed by Diakonoff). Miles-Gurney *1949:* 180: "he shall return it in the evening" (followed by Böhl, Lipin *1954*, but rightly rejected by Goetze *1956:* 34, note 3). Much the better rendering is that of Goetze *1950* and *1956*, Szlechter, Lipin *1963*, Bottéro, Landsberger *1968:* 71: "he (the driver) shall drive" — is obliged to drive.

Sec. 4: **24**: Due to a break at the beginning of the line, the hire of a boatman is uncertain. Goetze *1956* reads [1 *su*]*t 1qa*, but this would amount to little more than the pay of a winnower (sec. 8) or a donkey-driver (sec. 10), and would be considerably less than the pay of a harvester (sec. 7). For this reason von Soden *1949:* 368f. restored [2 *su*]*t*; but see also San Nicolò *1949:* 258. According to Landsberger *1968:* 72, the hire of the boatman, just as that of the boat itself, is related to the size of the vessel: he reads (or restores) [1/3] *qa* (per kor), that is 1/9 % (300 *qa* = 1 kor). *ka-la*[!!] : tablet has *ka-mi*, by mistake of the scribe.

Sec. 6: **27**: *ina nullani*; meaning uncertain. Goetze *1948:* "at (its) berth" (?); followed by Diakonoff, Lipin *1954*. Miles-Gurney *1949:* 181; San Nicolò *1949:* 258 suggest *furtum usus*. Böhl, Korošec *1953*; AHw 803a; CAD N/ii 333, think of "dishonest behaviour". Goetze *1950* and *1956* would prefer "in a peril", "in an emergency". See further pp. 274f., below.

Section 7: A i 28-29

2 sat še'um idi eṣidim (ŠE.KUD.KIN)

29 šum-ma kaspum 12 uṭṭeti (ŠE) idi-šu (Á.BI)

Section 8: A i 29

1 sut še'um idi za-ri-i

Section 9: A i 30-33

30 awilum 1 šiqil kaspam a-na e-ṣe-di a-na $^{aw.}$agrim (LÚ.ḪUN.GÁ)
31 [li]-di-in-ma šum-ma re-su la ú-ki-il-ma
32 [e]-ṣe-dam e-ṣe-dam la e-ṣí-su 10 šiqil kaspam
33 išaqqal

Section 9A: A i 33-34

1 sut 5 qa idi *niggallim* (URUDU.KIN.A) ù *ku-ṣi-rum*

34 [*a-na b*]*e-lí-šu-ma* i-ta-a-ar

Section 10: A i 34-35

1 sut še'um idi imerim (ANŠE)

35 ù 1 sut še'um idi re-di-šu ka-la u$_4$-mi-im i-re-de-šu

Section 11: A i 36-37

36 idi $^{aw.}$agrim (LÚ.ḪUN.GÁ) 1 šiqil kaspum 1 pan še'um ukulle-šu (ŠÀ.GAL.BI)
37 warḫam išten (ITU 1.KAM) i-la-ak

Sec. 7: **28**: Á.E for *idi* is unusual, with no ready explanation for the addition of the second sign. Cf. Moran *1957:* 219. Moran objects also to ŠE.KUD.KIN (instead of the usual ŠE.KIN.KUD), but this has parallels in Susa: see CAD E 349a, AHw 253a.

Sec. 9: **30**: *e-ṣe-di*, not *e-ṣé-di* (Goetze *1956). ana*: "for" or "to"? See p. 226, below. **31**: [*li*]-*di-in-ma*: Goetze *1948*, *1956*, also Szlechter, and Hirsch *1969*: 121, note 28, restore [*i-na-*]*di-in-ma*, with little apparent justification. Considerations of space do not help, since *li* takes much the same as *i-na*. The present occurs in the LE in the protasis only in secs. 38 and 41, referring to a desire (or duty); sec. 9 is different. The construction of sec. 9 (on which see p. 101, below) is similar to that of sec. 17/ *(mar awilim ... libilma)*, and this is the basis for our restoration. The hypothetical [*i-na-*]*di-in-ma* led Artzi and Lipin *1954* to render the introductory passage of sec. 9 as laying down a duty of the employer; this in turn creates difficulties of syntax, and leaves no import for the final *-ma.* **32**: [*e*]-*ṣe-dam e-ṣe-dam*, not *e-ṣé-dam e-ṣé-dam* (Goetze *1956*, AHw 250b). There are differences of opinion on the import of the

Section 7
2 seah barley (is) the hire of a harvester. If silver — 12 grains (is) his hire.

Section 8
1 seah barley (is) the hire of a winnower.

Section 9
Should a man give 1 shekel silver for harvesting to?/for? a hired man; if he (the worker) was not ready for him, and did not *at all* harvest for him the harvesting — 10 shekels silver he shall weigh out.

Section 9A
1 seah (and) 5 qa (is) the hire of a *sickle* and/ a *band* ... *to its owner* shall return.

Section 10
1 seah barley (is) the hire of a donkey, and/ 1 seah barley (is) the hire of its driver. All the day he shall?/may? drive it.

Section 11
The hire of a hired man (is) 1 shekel silver; 1 pan barley (is) his provender. One month he shall serve.

repetition: CAD E 339a, K 517a treat the case as a mere dittography. Goetze *1948* and *1950* (also Lipin *1954* and Szlechter) see here a reference to non-completion of the task. Cf. Goetze *1956:* 48, speaking of a failure to perform "wherever he is sent". Our tentative rendering "not at all" is a mere conjecture: it takes the repetition as indicating "total failure to perform".

Sec. 9A: On the separation of the passage from the preceding section, see pp. 34f., above. The import is obscure. **33**: *idi nigallim* (URUDU.KIN.A) *ù kuṣirum*: this reading is suggested by CAD Ḫ 145b, and accepted by Goetze *1957b:* 82a, also by von Soden *1958:* 519. The reading *kuṣirum* is rejected by Finkelstein *1970:* 247f. **34**: *ana b*]*elišuma* suggested by von Soden, *ibid.*, in comparison with sec. 17/; followed by Bottéro; Landsberger *1968:* 72. Goetze *1948* and *1956*, also Szlechter read [*ù* ŠE.]Ì.TÚG.BA — "and the rations of barley, oil, (and) cloth ..." CAD, *ibid.*, continued *ša iḫ*]-*ḫi-šu-ú* ("with which it is bound") but von Soden and Goetze reject this as irreconcilable with the traces still visible on the tablet. The reading of CAD Ḫ, suggested by Landsberger *1964*/*1966:* 61, note 51, was abandoned by him in *1968:* 72.

Section 12: A i 37-40

awilum ša i-na eqel (A.ŠÀ) muškenim (MAŠ.KAK.EN)
38 i-na ku-ru-lim i-na mu-uṣ-la-lim iṣ-ṣa-ba-tu
39 10 šiqil kaspam išaqqal [ša i-na mu-š]i-im i-na ku-ru-lim
40 iṣ-ṣa-ba-tu i-ma-a-[at] ú-ul i-ba-lu-uṭ

B i 1-3

1 [...] x
2 [...] i-ṣa-ab-ba-tu
3 [.......................] ú-ul i-ba-al-lu-uṭ

Section 13: A i 41-42

41 awilum ša i-[na bitim ša muš]kenim i-na bitim (É) i-na mu-uṣ-la-lim
42 [...š]a i-na mu-ši-im
43 [..]

B i 4-7

4 [awilum š]a i-na bitim (É) ša muškenim i-na bitim i-na mu-uṣ-la-lim
5 iṣ-ṣa-ab-ba-tu 10 šiqil kaspam išaqqal
6 ša i-na mu-ši-im i-na bitim iṣ-ṣa-ab-ba-tu
7 i-ma-a-at ú-ul i-ba-al-lu-uṭ

Section 14: B i 8-9

8 idi $^{\text{aw.}}$x x x (LÚ. x x x) 5 šiqil kaspam li-bíl-ma 1 šiqlum idi-šu (Á.BI)
9 10 šiqil kaspam li-bi-il-ma 2 šiqlan idi-šu

Sec. 12: **38**: *ina kurullim*: meaning uncertain. The rendering "in the crop" is that of Goetze *1948* and *1950* (followed, e.g., by Böhl, Diakonoff, Lipin, Petschow *1968a:* 134). But see the remarks of Miles-Gurney *1949:* 182 and von Soden *1949:* 369. Variants, still treating *ina kurullim* as referring to a location, were offered by Szlechter *1954* and *1978*, and by Goetze *1956*, "inside the fence (?)" Others, notably Bottéro ("avec une gerbe-liée"), Landsberger *1968* ("mit einer Getreidegarbe"), Borger, see *ina kurullim* as referring to an object seized in the hands of the intruder. CAD vacillates: K 572b, M/ii 243b, render "among the shocks"; Ṣ 40a, M/ii 274a have "with (stolen) sheafs". See further p. 273, note 68, below. *ina muṣlalim*: "in broad daylight": so with Böhl, "op klaarlichte dag"; Landsberger *1968:* 72: "bei hellem Tageslicht". In suitable contexts *ina muṣlalim* may refer to a specific part of the day, "high noon", "Siesta-Zeit": San Nicolò *1950a:* 441; Goetze *1956:* 52; AHw 679a. But in the present context too strict a delimitation does not appear indicated.

Section 12
A man, who will be seized in the field of a subject, in the *crop*, in broad daylight, 10 shekels silver shall weigh out.
(He) who will be seized at night in the *crop* —
he shall die, shall not live.

Section 13
A man, who will be seized in the house of a subject, in the house, in broad daylight, 10 shekels silver shall weigh out.
(He) who will be seized at night in the house —
he shall die, shall not live.

Section 14
The hire of a ....: Should he?/it? bring 5 shekels silver, 1 shekel (is) his hire;
should he?/it? bring 10 shekels silver, 2 shekels (is) his hire.

Sec. 13: **B 4**: *ina bitim ... ina bitim*: Miles-Gurney *1949:* 182 suggest that the second *ina bitim* may be a misreading in the archetype from which both the tablets are derived; *contra* Lipin *1954:* 48, note 2. Hartmann *1956:* 442 thinks of a dittography, but the text is supported by the parallel wording in the preceding section, *ina eqel muškenim ina kurullim*. Goetze's observation (*1956:* 12, note 48) that "the second *ina bitim* of B i 4 ... has no correspondence in A (i 41)" must be due to inadvertence, in view of his own remarks at p. 52. Bottéro renders the second *ina bitim* by "avec un coffre (?)"; no explanation is offered. Landsberger *1968:* 72 reads *ina* GIŠ = *iṣim* — "mit einem Scheit Holz" (followed by Finkelstein *1970:* 249). This, while epigraphically possible, is not at all plausible. A log is not a typical object of theft from a house. We follow Petschow *1968a:* 134: "in einem Raum".

Sec. 14: On the construction of the section cf. GAG 212 (sec. 160c). **B 8**: *idi* $^{aw\cdot}$*x x x* — "the hire of ..."; the name of the profession is quite uncertain. Von Soden *1949:* 369 suggests a reading LÚ.NIMG[IR?].KI? (Akkadian equivalent

Section 15: B i 10-11

10 i-na qa-ti wardim (SAG.ÌR) ù amtim (GEMÉ) tamkarum (DAM.GÀR) ù sa-bi-tum

11 kaspam še-a-am šipatam (SÍG) ellam (Ì.GIŠ) a-di ma-*di*/*ṭi*-im ú-ul i-ma-ḫa-ar

Section 16: A ii 1

1 mar awilim (DUMU.LÚ) la zi-z[u..]

B i 12

12 mar awilim (DUMU.LÚ) la zi-zu ù wardum (SAG.ÌR) ú-ul iq-qí-a-ap

unknown). Böhl *1949/1950:* 99, note 15, suggests *šamallum* — "agent" (so also Lipin *1954*). Both suggestions are rejected by Goetze *1956:* 55, note 1, where he disapproves also of the reading subsequently put forward in CAD I/J 17b, *idi* LÚ.TÚG 1 TÚG 5 *siqil kaspam libilma* 1 *šiqlum idišu* — "as to the wages of the fuller, if the garment is worth 5 shekels of silver, his wage is 1 shekel"; cf. Bottéro "tailleur"; Landsberger *1968:* 73: "apprêteur"; Petschow *1968a:* 133: "Schneider". Szlechter *1954:* 18 suggests LÚ.ÍL = *kinattum* ("proposé, commis"), but see on this von Soden *1956:* 33. Goetze's suggestion *babbilum* — "porter" is opposed by von Soden *1958:* 519 and Kraus *1958:* 124.

Sec. 15: **B 11**: *adi ma-di?/ṭi?-im*: reading and rendering uncertain. Goetze (since *1948*) reads *madim* (from *madum* — "much, numerous"; AHw 573) and arrives at the meaning "as an investment"; this is termed "unacceptable" by Miles-Gurney *1949:* 183, who offer no suggestion of their own; von Soden *1949:* 363 regards Goetze's rendering as too specific and suggests "bis zum Vielwerden", that is "in grösserer Menge", followed by Bottéro, "en notable quantité". Goetze *1956* has "(accept money [or its equivalent]) at the multiple (of its value)", i.e. "for speculation". On the basis of the same reading, but from a different interpretation of the preposition *adi*, Diakonoff arrives at

Section 15
From the hands of a slave /or of a slave woman a *tamkarum* /or a *sabitum*
silver, barley, wool, sesame oil *adi mad/ṭim* shall not receive.

Section 16
A coparcener son of a man, /or a slave, shall not be given credit.

the rendering "(vmeste) c mnogim" (= "together with many things", i.e. "*et cetera*"); similarly CAD A/i 122b — "(silver, barley, wool, oil) and other things" (lit. "inclusive many others"); Landsberger *1968:* 73: *et cetera*. So also Borger, Saporetti. Without going into the complicated lexical aspects of CAD's *adi* B (joined with *qadum* etc. and translated "together with, inclusive of, pertaining to") it will suffice to note that it does not suit the given context: in LE 15 there is no joining of one thing with another (as in sec. 3: *ereqqum qadum alpiša u redišа* — "a wagon together with its oxen and its driver"), hence nothing more than a conjunction (*u* or *lu*) is called for and justified (cf. sec. 40 ... *alpam u šimam mala ibaššu* — "... an ox, / or [any other] purchase, however much it be"). Other scholars read *maṭim* (from *maṭum* — "little"); so Böhl: "zelfs niet de geringste hoevelheid" — "not even the smallest quantity"; followed by Korošec *1953:* 92 — "aucun"; Szlechter *1954:* 18 — "même de peu de valeur" (lit. "jusqu'à peu"); AHw 635b — "bis zum Geringsten". Lipin interprets *maṭim* as an adverbial phrase, of time — "daje na vremia" (= "even temporarily"). See on *adi mad/ṭim* also San Nicolò *1949:* 259; Klíma, e.g., *1953c:* 144f.; Leemans *1950:* 36. Petschow *1961:* 269 "noch immer dunkel" retains its validity.

Sec. 16: **B 12**: *mar awilim la zizu*: see duscussion, pp. 159f., below. *ul iqqiap*: see discussion pp. 158f., below.

Section 17/18: A ii 2-5

2 mar awilim a-na bit e[-mi-im.....................]
3 šum-ma i-na ki-la-al-li-in i[š-te-en]
4 a-na ši-im-tim it-ta-la-ak ma-la ub-[lu]
5 ú-ul ú-še-eṣ-ṣé wa-tar-šu-ma i-le-qé

B i 13-18

13 mar awilim a-na bit e-mi-im ter-ḫa-tam li-bi-il-ma
14 šum-ma i-na ki-la-al-li-in iš-te-en a-na ši-im-tim
15 it-ta-la-ak kaspum a-na be-lí-šu-ma i-ta-a-ar
16 šum-ma i-ḫu-ús-si-ma a-na biti-šu i-ru-ub
17 lu-ú a-ḫi-za-nu lu-ú kal-la-tum a-na ši-im-tim it-ta-la-ak
18 ma-la ub-lu ú-ul ú-še-ṣe wa-tar-šu-ma i-le-eq-qé

Section 18A: A ii 6-7

6 1 šiqlum šadištam (IGI.6.GÁL) ù 6 uṭṭeti (ŠE) ṣibtam (MÁŠ) ú-ṣa-ab
7 1 kurrum 1 (pan) 4 sat ṣibtam ú-ṣa-ab

B i 19-20

19 1 šiqlum^{um} šadištam ù 6 uṭṭeti ṣibtam ú-ṣa-ab
20 [1] kurrum^{um} 1 (pan) 4 sat še'am ṣibtam ú-ṣa-ab

Section 19: A ii 8-9

8 awilum ša a-na me[-eḫ-ri-šu] i-na-ad-di-nu
9 i-na maš-kán-n[im ú]-ša-ad-da-an

B i 21-22

21 [awilum ša] a-na me-eḫ-ri-šu i-na-ad-di-nu
22 [i-na maš-]kán-nim ú-ša-ad-da-an

Sec. 17/18: On the construction of the section see pp. 101f., below. Part of the section in Tablet A is lost, due to a homoioteleuton: see discussion pp. 24f., above. **3/ B 14**: *inna kilallin ištēn*: CAD K 355b renders "one of the two (brothers)": a new suggestion, or inadvertent mistake? **B 17**: *lu-ú*: this reading is generally accepted, but Goetze *1956* substitutes *ù*: see p. 180, note 28, below. *a-ḫi-za-nu*: reading much disputed. Goetze *1948: a-aḫ-ḫa-ru-ú*; Goetze *1956: a-aḫ-ḫa-ru-um*(?). Goetze renders *aḫḫarum* as adverb — "afterward, thereafter", etc. (followed by Diakonoff, Lipin; see also Lewy *1959:* 436); von Soden *1949:* 370 sees *aḫḫarum* as adjective — "delayed, being in delay"; followed, with nuances, by Böhl and Szlechter *1954*. Von Soden *1958:* 519: *a-aḫ-ḫa-ru-ma*; see also AHw 20a: "im Rückstand befindlich". A radical departure was the reading proposed in 1964, in CAD A/i 192b (= Landsberger *1968:* 73): *lu a-ḫi!-za!-n*[*u-u*]*m lu kallatum* — "either the bridegroom or the

Section 17/18
Should a son of a man bring bride payment to the house of his father-in-law:
(i) if of the two one went to the fate, the silver to its owner indeed shall return;
(ii) if he took her and she entered to his house,
(and) *either the groom or* the bride went to the fate,
whatever (one) has brought, (one) will not cause to go forth; its *excess* only (one) will take.

Section 18A
1 shekel — one sixth and/ 6 grains interest will bear;
1 kor — 1 (pan and) 4 seah of barley interest will bear.

Section 19
A man,who will give for its equivalent,
at?/from? the threshing floor will collect.

bride". The reading *aḫizanum* has since found near-total acceptance; and note Finkelstein *1970:* 249, note 34, who reports that the reading is confirmed by collation. I have finally adopted this reading into the above text. My misgivings are detailed at pp. 188ff., below. *kallatum*: see Kraus *1973:* 50ff.

Sec. 18A: Goetze *1948* and *1950* treats this passage as part of sec. /18; it is supposed to provide for the payment of interest, in case *terḫatum* or dowry has to be refunded. A late adherent to this view was Landsberger (see p. 33, above); he is followed by Klíma *1979* and Borger *1982*. But in the main the separation of the two sections is widely accepted. Our translation follows Bottéro *1965/1966*: 92 and Finkelstein *1970*: 250. **6/B 19**: *šadištam*: von Soden *1956:* 33 suggests *šuššum* as the correct reading of IGI.6.GÁL.

Sec. 19: **8**: *awilum ša*: Kraus *1984:* 197 would translate "Ein Mann lässt sich das, was ...", but does not reject "ein Mann, der ...": this is the common usage of *awilum ša*, hence preferable. **B 21**: *ana meḫrišu*: see discussion, pp. 236f., below.

Section 20: A ii 10-13

10 šum-ma awilum *še-a-am* a-na x x x x x
11 id-di-in-ma še-a-am a-na kaspim i-te-pu!-u[š]
12 i-na e-bu-ri še-a-am ú ṣibassu (MÁŠ.BI) 1 kurrum 1 (pan) 4 s[at]
13 i-le-eq-qé

Section 21: A ii 13-15

šum-ma awilum kaspam a-na pa-ni-šu
14 id-di-in kaspam ú ṣibassu 1 šiqlum šadištam ú [6 uṭṭeti]
15 i-le-eq-qé

Section 22: A ii 15-18

šum-ma awilum e-li awilim mi-im-ma
16 la i-šu-ú-ma amat (GEMÉ) awilim it-te-pé be-el amtim ni-iš ilim i-[za-ka]r
17 mi-im-ma e-li-ia la ti-šu-ú kaspam
18 ma-la *Š[ÁM]* amtim^{tim} išaqqal

Section 23/24: A ii 19-25

19 šum-ma awilum e-li awilim mi-im-ma la i-šu-ma
20 amat awilim (GEMÉ LÚ) it-te-pé ni-pu-tam i-na biti-šu ik-la-ma
21 uš-ta-mi-it 2 amatim a-na be-el amtim i-ri-ab
22 šum-ma mi-im-ma e-li-šu la i-šu-ma
23 aššat muškenim (DAM MAŠ.KAK.EN) mar muškenim (DUMU MAŠ.KAK.EN) it-te-pé
24 ni-pu-tam i-na biti-šu ik-la-a-ma uš-ta-mi-it di-in na-pí-iš-tim
25 ne-pu-ú ša ip-pu-ú i-ma-a-at

Sec. 20: **10**: *še-a-am*: reading contested. Goetze *1948* restored *ka*[*spam*]; followed by San Nicolò *1949:* 260; Böhl 100; Leemans *1950:* 14; Loewenstamm *1957:* 197; von Soden *1958:* 520, AHw 267a; Bottéro *1965/1966:* 102; Petschow *1968a:* 137, note 4. Korošec, since *1951:* 88 and Szlechter *1954:* 20, 76 preferred [*šeam*], on substantive grounds; this view was followed in YLE 156ff. Landsberger *1968:* 74 reads *še-a-am* and this is supported by collation (as reported by Finkelstein *1970:* 250). *a-na*: rejected by Finkelstein, *ibid.* At the end of the line, Szlechter *1954* read *ana na?-aš?-p*[*a-ku-ti*]*m-ma* — "pour (payer) l'engagement"; rejected by von Soden *1956:* 33 as "mit der Photographie unvereinbar und auch nicht sinnvoll". Goetze *1956: ana qa?-aq-qa?-di?-ma* — "to the amount recorded"; von Soden *1958:* 519: "Lesung ganz unsicher, so dass man auf eine Erklärung besser verzichtet". Landsberger *1968:* 74 suggests *ana* GIŠ.APIN *u* GIŠ.TÙN — "zum (Anbau mit) Pflug oder Hacke". **11**: *i-te-pu!-u*[*š*: for discussion, see p. 244, below. Goetze *1948: i-te-wi-šum* —

Section 20
If a man has given barley for?/to? ... but has made the barley (in)to silver, at?/from? the harvest the barley and/ its interest, (per) 1 kor 1 (pan and) 4 seah, he will take.

Section 21
If a man has given silver *ana panišu*, the silver and/ its interest, (per) 1 shekel one sixth and/ [6 grains], he will take.

Section 22
If a man had nothing upon a man, yet distrained the man's slave woman: the owner of the slave woman shall swear by (a) god, "Thou hast nothing upon me"; silver as much as the *price* of the slave woman he (the distrainor) shall weigh out.

Section 23/24
If a man had nothing upon a man, yet distrained the man's slave woman, detained the distrainee in his house and caused (her) to die, 2 slave women to the owner of the slave woman he shall replace.
If he had nothing upon him, yet distrained the wife of the subject, the son of the subject, detained the distrainee in his house and caused (her/him) to die — (it is) a case of life; the distrainor who distrained shall die.

"expresses to him" (followed by Böhl, Szlechter); von Soden *1949:* 370: *i-te-pi-i*[*r*? (from *eperum* — "verpflegen"; followed by Korošec *1953*; von Soden *1956:* 33: *i-ṭe₄-pi-š*[*um* — "er ihm (Korn) hinbreitet" (from *ṭepum*). Goetze *1956* read *i-te-wi-š*[*um* — "he has equated for him(self)"; cf. von Soden *1958:* 520, and the discussion, pp. 238f., below. Landsberger *(ibid.)* suggests *uš-te-pi-e*[*l* — "will verwandeln"; rejected by Finkelstein *1970:* 250, who prefers *i-te-wi-š*[*um?*].

Sec. 21: **13**: *ana panišu*: see the discussion, pp. 245f., below.

Sec. 22: **18**: *mala š*[ÁM] *amtim* Goetze, since *1948*, read *mala taḫḫi amtim* — "in full compensation for the slave woman"; followed by Diakonoff, Lipin, Szlechter *1954* and *1978*, Haase *1962*, Bottéro, Saporetti; von Soden (since *1949:* 370) read *mala idi amtim* — "as much as are the wages of the slave woman"; followed by Böhl, Landsberger *1968:* 74, Borger, Haase *1979*. Against von Soden, see Finkelstein *1970:* 250. CAD M/i 148a has *mala* š[ÁM] *amtim* — "(silver) to the amount of the price of the slave girl", which in substance is in agreement with Goetze. See the discussion, pp. 276f., below.

Section 25: A ii 26-28

26 šum-ma awilum a-na bit e-mi is-si-ma e-mu-šu
27 ik-ši-*šu*-ma mara(t)-su (DUMU.SAL-šu) a-na [*ša-ni-im* i]t-ta-di-in
28 a-bi ma-ar-tim ter-ḫa-at im-ḫu-ru ta-aš-na ú-ta-ar

Section 26: A ii 29-31

29 šum-ma awilum a-na marat awilim ter-ḫa-tam ú-bil-ma
30 ša-nu-ú ba-lum šá-al a-bi-ša ù um-mi-ša im-šu-u'-ši-ma
it-ta-qa-ab-ši
31 di-in na[-pí-i]š-[ti]m-ma i-ma-[at]

Section 27/28: A ii 31-37

šum-ma awilum marat awilim ba-lum ša-al
32 a-bi-ša ù um-mi-ša i-ḫu-si-ma ú kir-ra-am ú ri-ik-<sa>-tim
33 a-na a-bi-ša ù um-mi-ša la iš[-ku-u]n u_4-mi šattim ištiat
(MU 1.KAM) i-na biti-šu
34 li-ši-im-ma ú-ul aššat (DAM) šum-ma ⌜ḫi-pí⌝ ri-ik-sa-tim
35 ù kir-ra-am a-na a-bi-ša ù um-mi-ša iš-ku-un-ma
36 i-ḫu-us-si aššat u_4-um i-na su-un awilim iṣ-ṣa-ab-ba-tu i-ma-at
37 ú-ul i-ba-al-lu-uṭ

B ii 1-2

1 [..................................ri-]ik-sa[-tim....................................]
2 [.......................] ù um-mi-ša iš-ku-un-ma i-ḫ[u-us-si..........]

Sec. 25: **26**: *ana bit emim issima*: rendering of this phrase, and with it the interpretation of the section, has been greatly influenced by the publication of the documents U. 16900 F (discussed in Yaron *1965:* 23ff.) and BM 80754 (published by Finkelstein *1967b:* 127ff.; republished by Kraus as AbB vii 188); for further references and discussion, see pp. 191ff., below. **27**: *ikšišuma* — "wronged him"; reading with CAD E 154b (= Landsberger *1968:* 75) and von Soden *1958:* 520, AHw 463b, deriving the verb from *kašum* — "Unrecht tun, ungerecht behandeln". Diakonoff's reading *iklimšuma* is possible *(lim = ši)*, but a verb *kalamum* is not known in Akkadian. Goetze *1956* reads *ikšisuma*, from *kašašum* — "to take into bondage" (cf. his comment at p. 77); followed by Kraus *1958:* 158, note 1; *contra* von Soden *ibid*. See also Finkelstein *ibid.* 135, note 1. In *1969a:* 76 Finkelstein suggests *ik-kir(?)-šu-ma* (from *nakarum* — "to deny"?). [*šanim*]: restoration uncertain; other possibilities are [*ibrim*] — "(to) a fellow", or [*ibrišu*] — "(to) his fellow".

Sec. 26: **29**: *ana*: the rendering "for" seems preferable (but note CAD A/i 12a "to"). **30**: *im-šu-u'-ši-ma*: see von Soden *1956:* 34 and AHw 625a: he

Section 25
If a man claimed (his bride) at the house of his father-in-law, but his father-in-law wronged him and gave his daughter to [another] — the father of the daughter the bride payment he received shall twofold return.

Section 26
If a man brought bride payment for?/to? a man's daughter, but another without asking her father and?/or? her mother, forcibly seized her and deflowered her — (it is) a case of life indeed; he shall die.

Section 27/28.
If a man took a man's daughter without asking her father and?/or? her mother: —
(i) and also (subsequently) did not fix marriage feast and?/or? contract for her father and?/or? her mother, — should she (even) dwell in his house the days of one year, (she is) not "a wife".
(ii) If he (subsequently) fixed contract and?/or? marriage feast for her father and?/or? her mother and took her, (she is) "a wife". The day in the lap of a man she will be seized, (one) shall die, shall not live.

stresses that the verb is *maša'um* ("gewaltsam fortführen"), not *mašaḫum*; so also CAD M/i 361a. And see already Goetze *1956:* 79.

Sec. 27/28: **32**: *abiša u ummiša* — "her father and?/or? her mother"; see discussion, pp. 156ff., below. *(iḫussi)-ma u*: cf. CH 45, 156: "the precise force of *-ma u* ... is uncertain" (Driver-Miles *1955:* 173). *kirram* (also line 35): "marriage feast", or "drinking party", following Landsberger *1968:* 76ff. in his critical examination of the texts, against the submission of Greengus *1966:* 55-72, who rendered "libation". Landsberger renders *kirrum* freely by "Hochzeitsgelage". Earlier Landsberger had read *qer-ra-am*, rendering this by "Hochzeitsmahl"; see Koschaker *1950*: 241f. He was followed by Korošec *1953:* 30, note 48 and von Soden *1956:* 34; but note Landsberger's self-criticism (*1968:* 77, note 2). Other interpretations proceed from a different reading, *girram*: the phrase *girram u rik<sa>tim* (line 34f. *riksatim u girram*) is taken as a hendiadys; so Goetze (since *1948*): "formal marriage contract"; also Böhl (but see p. 101, note 27); Diakonoff; Lipin; Driver (as quoted by Miles-Gurney *1949:* 184). Szlechter renders *girrum* by "communauté (d'acqêts)"; CAD G 93a: "travel provisions". **34**: *ḫi-pí*: long disputed. Landsberger, *ibid.*, 76, note 1, critical of readings proposed by Goetze *1956:* 80 and von Soden *1949:* 370. See, finally, Finkelstein *1981:* 20, note 1: "*ḫi-pí*, 'broken' the conventional scribal notation signalling that at that point the original tablet which was being copied was damaged ... it would appear from

Section 29: A ii 38-45

38 šum-ma awilum i-na ḫarran^{an} (KASKAL) še-e[ḫ-ṭi]m
39 ù sa-ak-pí-im it-t[a-*aš-la-al*]
40 ù lu na-aḫ-bu-tum it-ta-aḫ-ba-at
41 [u$_4$-m]i ar[-ku-tim i-na ma-]tim ša-ni-tim-ma
42 [.......................] ša-nu-um
43 [.......................] it-ta-la-ad
44 [.......................a]m ašša(t)-su (DAM-šu)
45 [.......................]

B ii 3-7

3 šum-ma awilum i-na ḫarran (KASKAL) še-eḫ-ṭim ù sa-ak-p[í-im *it-ta-aš-la-al*]
4 ù lu-ú na-aḫ-bu-tum it-ta-aḫ-ba-at u$_4$-m[i ar-ku-tim]
5 i-na ma-a-tim ša-ni-tim-ma it-ta[-*ša-ab*]
6 aš-ša-su ša-nu-ú-um-ma i-ta-ḫa-az ù maram it[-ta-la-ad]
7 i-nu-ú-ma it-tu-ra-am aš-ša-su i-ta-[*ab-ba-al*]

Section 30: A ii 45-48 ? (iii 1 ?)

[šum-ma] awilum a-al^{ki}
46 [...]it-ta-bi-it
47 [...]
48? iii 1(?) [.......................]

B ii 8-10

8 šum-ma awilum al^{ki}-šu (URU.KI-šu) ù be-el-šu i-ze-er-ma it-ta-aḫ-bi-it
9 aš-ša-su ša-nu-ú-um-ma i-ta-ḫa-az i-nu-ú-ma it-tu-ra-am
10 a-na aš-ša-ti-šu ú-ul i-ra-ag-ga-am

the context that very little, if anything, was actually missing in the original ..." (reading *ḫi-pí* based on collation by Mrs. Ellis). **36**: *aššat*: written DAM, not *aš-ša-at* (Goetze *1956*); *i-ma-at*: not *i-ma-a-at (ibid.)*. Line 36f., the operative part of sec. /28, is omitted in Tablet B (see p. 25, above). .

Sec. 29: **39/B 3**: *sakpum* (Goetze *1956*), *sagbum* (Landsberger *1968:* 98): meaning not quite certain. *itt*[*ašlal*]: verb missing in both the tablets, but restoration (by Goetze, Landsberger) is supported by CH 134, 135. Szlechter *it*-[*ta-aṣ-ba-at*] — "was seized". **40**: *naḫbutum*: AHw 304a reads *na-aḫ-bu-tum*-[*ma!*: a break in the tablet leaves ample space for this addition, not paralleled in B 3. **41/B 4**: *ar*[*-ku-tim*] — "long" Goetze; von Soden *1949:* 370 and Szlechter *1954* suggest [*ma-du-tim*]. **B 5**: *it-ta*[*-ša-ab*] — "dwelt": perhaps

Section 29
If a man has been [*made prisoner*] during a raid/ or an invasion, or has been carried off forcibly, (and) [*dwelt*] in another land for a l[ong] time,
another indeed took his wife and/ she bore a son:
whenever he returns, his wife he may [*take back*].

Section 30
If a man hated his city and his master and fled,
another indeed took his wife: — whenever he returns,
to his wife he shall have no claim.

it-ta[*-aṣ-ba-at*] — "was held" would convey more clearly his being prevented from returning home; cf. MAL 36 (lines 106, 108). **B** 7: *i-ta*[*-ab-ba-al*]: so Goetze and others; alternatively, *i-ta*[*-a-ar-šum*] — "sie kehrt zu ihm zurück": von Soden *1949:* 370, and others.

Sec. 30: On the placing of the section in Tablet A see p. 29, above. **45:** Goetze *1956* reads *a-al-šu!*, but the copy supports *a-al*^{ki} of Goetze *1948*. **B 8**: *alšu u belšu* — "his city and his master"; Bottéro: "sa ville ou son maître"; CAD A/i 384: "his city and its ruler". On Old Assyrian parallels of the phrase, see pp. 116f. below. **46**: *it-ta-bi-it* as against **B 8** *it-ta-aḫ-bi-it*: see p. 23, note, 15, above. Opinions differ on the derivation of *ittabit*: GAG, sec. 97L (p. 128), Goetze *1956:* 85, note 1, speak of a verb *nabatum* — "to flee", occurring only in the N-form. Driver-Miles *1955:* 363 (Glossary), and especially CAD A/i 45 have *abatum* (some Old Assyrian texts in which the G-form is used are not listed in AHw). AHw 700b includes the subject of *nabatu* in LE 30 under "Sklave, Dienstverpflichteter", not under "politischer Flüchtling"; why?

Section 31: B ii 11-12

11 šum-ma awilum amat awilim it-ta-qa-ab

12 1/3 ma-na kaspam išaqqal ù amtum ša be-lí-ša-ma

Section 32: A iii 3-5

3 [.......................................]x

4 id-[di-]i[n-ma..................]............-na

5 tar-b[i]-it mari-šu i[šaqqal-ma mar-šu] i-ta-ar-ru

B ii 13-15

13 šum-ma awilum mar-šu a-na šu-nu-qí-im a-na tar-bi-tim id-di-in-ma

14 ipram piššatam lubuštam (ŠE.BA Ì.BA SÍG.BA) šalaš šanatim (MU 3.KAM) la id-di-in 10 *ma-na*

15 tar-bi-it mari-šu išaqqal-ma mar-šu i-ta-a-ar-ru

Section 33: A iii 6-9

6 šum-ma amtum ú-sa-ri-ir-ma [mar-ša] a-na mar[at] awilim

7 [i]t-ta-di-in i-nu-ú-ma ir-ta-bu-ú

8 [be-]el-šu i-mar-šu i-ṣa-ba-su-ma

9 i-ta-ar-ru-ú-šu

B ii 16-18

16 šum-ma amtum ú-sa-ar-ri-ir-ma mar-ša a-na marat awilim it-ta-di

17 i-nu-ú-ma ir-ta-bu-ú be-el-šu i-ma-ar-šu

18 i-ṣa-ab-ba-su-ma i-ta-ar-ru-šu

Sec. 31: On the section being contained in Tablet A, see p. 29, above. **B 12**: 1/3 *ma-na*: so with von Soden *1949:* 370; Böhl; Korošec; Goetze (since *1955* [ANET]); Bottéro. 2/3 *ma-na*: Goetze *1948* and *1950*; Diakonoff; Landsberger *1968:* 50.

Section 31
If a man deflowered a man's slave woman,
1/3 a mina silver he shall weigh out, and/ the slave woman (remains) her owner's indeed.

Section 32
If a man gave his son for suckling, for upbringing,
but did not give food-rations, oil-rations, clothing rations (of) three years, 10 *minas* the (cost of) upbringing his son he shall weigh out, and his son he will take back.

Section 33
If a slave woman cheated and gave (B: *cast*) her son to the daughter of a man,
(and) when he has grown up, his master recognizes him: —
he may seize him and take him back.

Sec. 32: **B 13**: *ana šunuqim*: one would expect *ana mušeniqtim* (as in CH 194); for the construction "to a person for a purpose", see LE 34/, 36/. **B 14**: SÍG.BA: *lubušu* (CAD L 237a) or *lubuštu* (AHw 561a)? *ma-na*: see discussion pp. 253ff., below. **5/B 15**: *itarru* — "will take back", with von Soden *1949*: 371, Goetze *1956*, and others; alternative rendering "they shall return (his son)"; see YLE *ad locum*.

Sec. 33: **B 16**: *it-ta-di* against 7 *it-ta-di-in*: discussed, pp. 165ff., below.

Section 34/35: A iii 9-13

šum-ma amat ekallim^{lim} (É.GAL) mar-ša
10 lu mara(t)-sa a-na muškenim a-na tar-bi-tim
11 it-ta-di-in maram lu-martam ša id-di-nu ekallum^{lum}
12 it-ta-ba-al ù le-qú-ú ša mar amat ekallim^{lim}
13 il-qú-ú me-ḫe-er-šu a-na ekallim^{lim} i-ri-a-ab

B ii 19-23
19 šum-ma amat ekallim^{lim} mar-ša lu-ú mara(t)-sa
20 a-na muškenim a-na tar-bi-tim it-ta-di-in
21 marum^{rum} lu-ú martum^{tum} ša id-di-nu ekallum^{lum} i-ta-ab-ba-al
22 ù le-qú-ú ša mar amat ekallim^{lim} il-qú-ú
23 me-ḫe-er-šu a-na ekallim^{lim} i-ri-a-ab

Section 36/37: A iii 14-23
14 šum-ma awilum bu-še-šu a-na na-ap-ṭà-ri a-na ma-ṣa-ar-tim
15 id-di-in-ma bitum la pa-li-iš si-ip-pu la ḫa-li-iš
16 a-ap-tum la na-às-ḫa-at bu-še-e ma-ṣa-ar-tim
17 ša id-di-nu-šum uḫ-ta-li-iq bu-še-e-šu i-ri-a-ab
18 šum-ma bit awilim lu-uq-qú-ut it-ti ma-ṣa-ar-tim
19 ša id-di-nu-šum ḫu-lu-uq be-el bitim ḫa-li-iq
20 be-el bitim i-na bit ^{D}Tišpak ni-iš ilim (DINGIR) i-za-kar-šum
21 it-ti bu-še-e-ka bu-šu-ia ḫal-qú i-wi-tam
22 ù sà-ar-tam la e-pu-šu i-za-kar-šum-ma mi-im-ma
23 e-li-šu ú-ul i-šu

B ii 24-iii 6
24 šum-ma awilum bu-še-e-šu a-na na-ap-ṭà-ri-im
25 a-na ma-ṣa-ar-tim id-di-in-ma bitum^{tum} la pa-li-iš
26 si-ip-pu la ḫa-li-iš a-ap-tum la na-ás-ḫa-at
27 bu-še-e ma-ṣa-ar-tim ša id-di-nu-šum uḫ-ta-al-li-iq
28 bu-še-e-šu i-ri-a-ab-šum
1 šum-ma bit awilim lu-uq-qú[-ut] it-ti bu-še-e awil [ma-ṣa]-ar-tim
2 ša id-di-nu-šum ḫu-lu-uq be-el bitim ḫa-li-iq
3 be-el bitim^{tim} i-na bab (KÁ) ^{D}Tišpak ni-iš ilim i-za-kar-šum-ma
4 it-ti bu-še-e-ka bu-šu-ia lu-ú ḫa-al-qu
5 i-wi-tam ù sà-ar-tam la e-pu-šu i-za-kar-šum-ma
6 mi-im-ma e-li-šu ú-ul i-šu

Section 34/35

If a slave woman of the palace her son or her daughter gave to a subject for upbringing,
the son or the daughter whom she gave the palace will take away;
and?/or? the taker, who took the son of the slave woman of the palace,
his equivalent to the palace shall?/may? replace.

Section 36/37

If a man gave his goods to?/for? a *napṭarum* for a deposit, and — the house not having been broken into, the threshold not having been scraped off, the window not having been torn out —
he caused the goods of the deposit, which he had given to him, to be lost,
his goods he shall replace (B: to him).
If the house of the man was plundered, (and) with the goods of the deposit(or?), which he had given to him, loss of the owner of the house was incurred —
the owner of the house shall in the house (B: in the gate) of Tišpak swear to him by god:
"Together with thy goods my goods were (B: verily) lost, I have not done evil and/ fraud." He shall swear to him,
and nothing upon him he shall have.

Sec. 34/: **12**: *it-ta-ba-al*, not *i-ta-ba-al* (Goetze *1956*). Sec. /35: **12/B 22**: *u* — "and?/or?". The interpretation of the section depends on the import of the particle: "and ... shall" imposes a duty on the person who took the child, "or ... may" endows that person with a power. Following San Nicolò *1949:* 261, we give preference to "imposition of a duty". See further pp. 168ff., below.

Sec. 36/37: Compare the translation given by CAD B 353b (but botched in M/i 339a). **14/B 24**: *napṭarum*: Landsberger *1968:* 98f.: Standesbezeichnung — "ein Immuner"; Kraus *1973:* 63 and *1976:* 165ff. **18/B 1**: *luqqut* — "was plundered", following Landsberger, *cit.* 99. Landsberger's suggestion is based on BM 87398 (= AbB i, no 47). Goetze *1948: lu imqut* — "indeed collapses",

Section 38: A iii 23-25

šum-ma i-na at-ḫi-i iš-te-en zi-it-ta-šu
24 i-na-ad-di-in a-ḫu-šu ša-ma-am ḫa-še-eḫ qá-ab-li-it
25 ša-ni-i ú-ma-la

B iii 7-9

7 šum-ma i-na at-ḫi-i iš-te-en zi-it-ta-šu a-na kaspim i-na-ad-di-in
8 ù a-ḫu-šu ša-ma-am ḫa-še-eḫ
9 qá-ab-li-it ša-ni-i-im ú-ma-al-la

Section 39: A iii 25-27

šum-ma awilum i-ni-iš-ma
26 bi(t)-su ana kaspim it-ta-di-in u_4-um ša-ia-ma-nu
27 i-na-di-nu be-el bitim i-pa-ṭà-ar

B iii 10-11

10 šum-ma awilum i-ni-iš-ma bi(t)-su a-na kaspim it-ta-di-in
11 u_4-um ša-a-ia-ma-nu i-na-ad-di-nu be-el bitim^{tim} i-pa-ṭà-ar

Section 40: A iii 28-29

28 šum-ma awilum wardam amtam alpam ù ši-ma-am ma-la i-ba-šu-ú
29 i-ša-am-ma na-di-na-nam la ú-ki-in šu-ma šar-ra-aq

B iii 12-13

12 šum-ma awilum wardam amtam alpam ù ši-ma-am ma-la i-ba-aš-šu-ú
13 i-ša-am-ma na-di-na-nam la ú-ki-in š[u-m]a šar-ra-aq

taking *lu* as particle of emphasis; so also Böhl, Korošec, Diakonoff, Szlechter. For emendations proposed by Goetze and von Soden see p. 23, above, and 249f., below. *itti (B: buše awil) maṣṣartim*: note criticism of *awil maṣṣartim* by Landsberger *cit.* 99, note 1: "sowohl in der akkadischen Sprache unmöglich wie für einen Depositor unpassend"; but CAD M/i 339a retains LÚ(= awil). **19/B 2**: *bel bitim*: see Kraus *1973:* 84. **20**: *bit ^{D}Tišpak* against **B 3** *bab ^{D}Tišpak*: see pp. 25f., above. **21/B 5**: *iwitam*:— "evil": Goetze *1948, 1950f.* [ANET]:

Section 38
If one of brothers will sell his share,
and his brother wishes to buy,
the *average (price)* of another he shall pay in full.

Section 39
If a man became impoverished and sold his house —
the day the buyer will sell, the owner of the house may redeem.

Section 40
If a man bought a slave, a slave woman, an ox, / or (any other) purchase, however much it be, and has not established the seller — he himself is the thief.

"improper", *1956:* 101: "conspiracy" (connecting *iwitum* with *awum* — "to speak"). Böhl *1949/1950:* 103, note 36, connects *iwitum* with Hebrew *'awah* and *'awon* — "sin, misdeed"; AHw 408a (cf. 267a): "böswillig falsche Behauptung" (abandoning von Soden *1956:* 34: "grobe Nachlässigkeit"). Kraus *1958:* 72 follows Goetze *1956*. **22/B** 5: *sartam*: cf. Hebrew *sarah*: Deuteronomy 13:6, 19:16; Isaiah 1:5.

Sec. 38: **B 9**: *qá-ab-li-it*: Goetze reads *qá-ab-*NE*-it*: see p. 22, note 11, above. On the import of the phrase *qablit šanim umalla*, see in detail pp. 228ff., below.

Section 41: A iii 30-31

30 šum-ma ubarum (U.BAR) na-ap-ṭà-rum ù mu-du-ú šikar-šu (KAŠ-šu) i-na-di-in
31 sa-bi-tum ma-ḫi-ra-at i-la-ku šikaram i-na-di-in-šum

B iii 14-16

14 šum-ma ubarum na-ap-ṭà-rum ù mu-du-ú šikar-šu i-na-ad-di-in
15 sa-bi-tum ma-ḫi-ra-at i-il-la-ku
16 ši-ka-ra-am i-na-ad-[[ta]]-di-šum

Section 42: A iii 32-34

32 šum-ma awilum ap-pé awilim iš-šu-uk-ma it-ta-ki-ís
33 1 ma-na kaspam išaqqal inum (IGI) 1 ma-na šinnum (ZÚ) 1/2 ma-na
34 uz-nu 1/2 ma-na me-ḫe-eṣ le-tim 10 šiqil kaspam išaqqal

B iii 17-20

17 šum-ma awilum ap-pé awilim iš-šu-uk-ma it-ta-ki-ìs
18 1 ma-na kaspam išaqqal
19 inum 1 ma-na šinnum 1/2 ma-na uz-nu 1/2 ma-na
20 me-ḫe-eṣ le-tim 10 šiqil kaspam išaqqal

Section 43: A iii 35-36

35 šum-ma awilum ú-ba-an awilim it-ta-ki-ís
36 2/3 ma-na kaspam išaqqal

B iii 21-22

21 šum-ma awilum ú-ba-an a-wi-lim [it-t]a-ki-ìs
22 [... m]a-na kaspam išaqqal

Sec. 43: **36**: 2/3 *ma-na*: so most, but Lipin, Bottéro read 1/3 *ma-na*.

Section 41
If an *ubarum*, a *napṭarum*, / or a *mudum* will give his beer,
the *sabitum* at the current rate
the beer to?/for? him shall sell.

Section 42
If a man bit and severed the nose of a man, —
1 mina silver he shall weigh out.
An eye — 1 mina; a tooth — 1/2 mina; an ear — 1/2 mina.
A slap in the face — 10 shekels silver he shall weigh out.

Section 43
If a man severed a man's finger, —
2/3 a mina silver he shall weigh out.

Section 44/45: A iii 36-38

šum-ma awilum a-wi-lam i-na ik/g-x-x
37 ís-ki-im-ma *qa(t)*-su (ŠU-su) iš-te-ber$_5$ 1/2 ma-na kaspam išaqqal
38 šum-ma šep-šu (GÌR-šu) iš-te-ber$_5$ 1/2 ma-na kaspam išaqqal

B iii 23-25

23 [.......................] a-wi-lam i[-na ....ì]s-ki-in-ma
24 [...]am išaqqal
25 [...] išaqqal

Haddad 116: 1-4

1 [...]
2 è[š-te-b]er$_5$ 1/2 ma-na kaspam išaqqal
3 šum-ma šep-šu èš-te-ber$_5$
4 1/2 ma-na kaspam išaqqal

Section 46: A iii 39-40

39 šum-ma awilum a-wi-lam im-ḫa-aṣ-ma ḫa-x-x-šu iš-te-ber$_5$
40 2/3 ma-na kaspam išaqqal

Haddad 116: 5-6

5 šum-ma awilum awilam im-ḫa-aṣ-ma
6 ki-ir-ra-šu èš-te-ber$_5$ 1/3 ma-na kaspam išaqqal

Section 47: A iii 40-41

šum-ma awilum i-na x x x -tim
41 awilam i-še-el 10 šiqil kaspam išaqqal

Haddad 116: 7-8

7 šum-ma awilum i-na ši-gi-èš-tim
8 awilam ik/q-te-el 10 šiqil kaspam išaqqal

Sec. 44/: **36**: *ina ik/g-x-x*: Szlechter restores ina [*ṣa-al-tim*] — "au cours d'une lutte" (but see Nörr *1958:* 9, note 35). Possibly *ina ik-ki-im* — "in a (bad) temper" (for *ikkum* see CAD I/J 59b, AHw 369b). *ina ek*[*litim*]: Böhl *1949/1950:* 104, note 39, "in het donker"; Bottéro, "dans l'obscurité"; similarly Landsberger *1968:* 101: *ina ek-lu-tim* — "in der Finsternis" (see already CAD I/J 61a); the reading is disputed by Finkelstein *1970:* 254f. CAD S 70a, also Borger, read *ina suqim* — "in the street". **37/B 23**: *ís-ki-im-ma* — "threw ... to the floor"; loosely rendered "ein Bein gestellt hat": Landsberger *(ibid.)*, followed by Haase *1979*.

Section 44/45
If a man threw a man to the ground in an *altercation* and broke his *arm*, — 1/2 a mina silver he shall weigh out.
If he broke his leg, — 1/2 a mina silver he shall weigh out.

Section 46
If a man hit a man and broke his *collarbone*, — 2/3 a mina silver he shall weigh out.

Section 47
If a man *injured* a man in a *brawl*, — 10 shekels silver he shall weigh out.

Sec. 46: **39**: *ḫa-x-x-šu*: various restorations have been proposed, none of them really satisfying. They may all have been superseded by Haddad, line 6: *ki-ir-ra-šu* — "his collarbone" (cf. CAD K 410b). If the first sign in Tablet A is definitely *ḫa-*, one would have to postulate variant readings. **40**: 2/3 *ma-na*: reading disputed. 2/3: Goetze (since *1948*); Diakonoff; Szlechter; Borger (and others). The reading 1/3 is preferred, e.g., by Miles-Gurney *1949*: 186; Korošec; von Soden *1956:* 34; Bottéro. The reading 1/3 would now seem to have the support of Haddad, line 6 (but Al-Rawi is not quite certain about it).

Sec. 47: **40/Haddad 7**: the reading *i-na ši-gi-èš-tim* might supersede earlier conjectures for the break at the end of line 40, but the meaning remains in doubt. Al-Rawi connects with *šagaštum* (AHw 1127a), but this seems tenuous. The rendering "in a brawl" is *ad sensum* only.

Section 47A: Haddad 116: 9-11

9 šum-ma awilum i-na ri-ès-ba-tim
10 mar awilim uš-ta-mi-it
11 2/3 ma-n[a k]aspa[m] išaqqal

Section 48: A iii 42-44

42 ù a-na x x x iš-tu 1/3 ma-na a-di 1 ma-na
43 [...............] di-nam ú-ša-ḫa-zu[-š]u-[ma]
44 a-wa-at na-pí-iš-[tim.........]

B iv 1-3

1 [.......................] ma-na a-di 1 ma-na
2 [.......................] ú-ša-ḫa-zu-šu-ma
3 [.................. na-]pí-iš-tim a-na šarrim-ma (LUGAL-ma)

Section 49: B iv 4-5

4 šum-ma awilum i-na wardim šar-qí-im amtim ša-ri-iq-tim
5 it-ta-aṣ-ba-at wardum wardam amtum amtam i-re-ed-de

Sec. 47A: **Haddad 9**: *ina ri-ès-ba-tim*: cf. CH 206. AHw 988b: "Schlägerei".

Sec. 48: Section possibly incomplete; see p. 28, above. **42:** *ana x-x-x:* Miles-Gurney *1949:* 187 suggest *ana daiane* — "to the judges"; followed by Szlechter *1954*. Böhl *1949/1950:* 104, note 43: *ana* [*dinim*] — "for litigation"; so also Bottéro. Landsberger *1968:* 101: *ana dinim ša* KÙ.BABBAR; so also Szlechter *1978*. **43**: At the beginning of the line, Goetze restores *awilam*; CAD D 29a (= Landsberger, *ibid.*) suggests *daiane* (DI.KUD.MEŠ), but CAD A/i 178a reverts to the suggestion LÚ *(awilam).*

Section 47A
If a man in an affray
caused the death of a son of a man,
2/3 of a mina silver he shall weigh out.

Section 48
And/ for ...? from 1/3 of a mina to 1 mina
they shall cause him to seize litigation,
but a charge (concerning) life (belongs) to the king himself.

Section 49
If a man was seized in (possession of) a stolen slave, a stolen slave woman, — slave a slave (shall bring along) slave woman a slave woman shall bring (along).

Sec. 49: **B 5**: *wardum wardam amtum amtam* (SAG.ÌR SAG.ÌR GEMÉ GEMÉ) *iredde* — "slave a slave (shall bring along) slave woman a slave woman shall bring (along)"; with von Soden *1949:* 372, *1958:* 521 (followed by Böhl; Korošec; Szlechter; Bottéro), — *pace* Goetze *1956:* 126, note 1. Goetze *1948: wardam wardam amtam amtam* (accusative throughout); *1956: warad warad amat amat iredde* — "he shall surrender slave for slave (and) slave girl for slave girl". Decisive proof for von Soden's reading and interpretation is provided by BM 80195 (= AbB ii 107), line 19: [KUBA]BBAR^{um} KUBABBAR^{am} *lirdi* — "dann möge das Silber dem Silber folgen" (and see AHw 965 [bottom]: "zusätzlich bringen"). One may compare Mishnaic idiom: *miṣwah gorereth miṣwah wa'averah gorereth 'averah* — "a pious deed carries with it (lit. draws, drags) a pious deed, and transgression carries with it transgression" (*Mishnah Avoth* 4.2); and see similar constructions in *Babylonian Talmud, Shabbath* 71a, *Baba Meṣi'a* 4a.

Section 50: A iv 2-7

2 [.. te-]er-tim
3 [..] wardam ḫa-al-qá-am
4 [.....................................] alpam ḫa-al-qá imeram ḫa-al-qá-am
5 i[ṣ-ba-a]t-ma [a-n]a Èš-nun-na^{ki} la ir-di-a-am-ma
6 i-na biti-šu-ma ik-t[a-la] ekallum^{lum} šu-ur-qá-am
7 it-ti-šu i-ta-wi

B iv 6-10

6 šum-ma šakkanakkum (GÍR.NITÁ) ša-pir$_6$ narim (ÍD) be-el te-er-tim ma-la i-ba-aš-šu-ú
7 wardam ḫal-qa-am amtam ḫa-li-iq-tam alpam ḫal-qa-am imeram ḫal-qa-am
8 ša ekallim^{lim} ù muškenim iṣ-ba-at-ma a-na Èš-nun-na^{ki}
9 la ir-di-a-am i-na biti-šu-ma ik-ta-la u$_4$-mi e-li warḫim išten (ITU 1.KAM)
10 ú-še-te-eq-ma ekallum^{lum} šu-ur-qa-am it-ti-šu i-ta-wi

Section 51: A iv 7-9

wardum ù amtum ša Èš-nun-na^{ki}

8 ša ka-an-nam maš-ka-nam ù ab-bu-tam ša-ak-nu
9 abul (KÁ.GAL) Èš-nun-na^{ki} ba-lum be-lí-šu ú-ul uṣ-ṣí

B iv 11-13

11 wardum ù amtum ša Èš-nun-na^{ki} ša ka-an-nam ma-aš-ka-nam
12 ù ab-bu-ut-ta-am ša-ak-nu
13 abul (KÁ.GAL) Èš-nun-na^{ki} ba-lum be-lí-šu ú-ul uṣ-ṣí

Sec. 50: We commence column iv of Tablet A with line 2, in order to conform to Goetze's numbering; see p. 29, above. **B 9:** *umi eli warḫim išten* — "days over one month", so with CAD E 392a (see also AHw 262b). Goetze (since *1948*) reads *umi se-bé warḫim išten* — "seven days in a month", which does not make much sense. See also von Soden *1958:* 521. **B 10**: *ú-še-te-eq-ma*: Goetze *1948* read *ú-še-li-ik-ma*; but we follow (with Szlechter *1954* and Goetze *1956*) the suggestion of von Soden *1949:* 372, that *te* is the correct reading of the third sign; differently CAD E 392a: *ú-še-te* (text *-li*)*-eq-ma*.

Section 50
If a *šakkanakkum*, a canal commissioner (or) whatever official there may be, seized a fugitive slave, a fugitive slave woman, a stray ox, a stray donkey (B only: of the palace / or of a subject), but did not bring (it) to Eshnunna, in his house indeed detained (it) (B only: [if] he let pass days over one month), the palace (with) theft will charge him.

Section 51
A slave / or a slave woman of Eshnunna, who is marked with a *kannum*, a *maškanum* and?/ or? an *abbuttum*,
(from) the gate of Eshnunna without his owner shall not go forth.

Sec. 51: On the meaning of the technical terms *kannum*, *maškanum* and *abbuttum* see pp. 162f., below. **8/B 12**: *u*: the rendering "or" seems to be preferable; differently von Soden *1949:* 372f.; and cf. p. 163, below. **8**: *ab-bu-tam*: not *ab-bu-ut-tam* (Goetze).

Section 52: A iv 10-13

10 wardum ù amtum ša it-ti mar ši-ip-ri-im
11 na-aṣ-ru-ma abul Èš-nun-na^{ki} i-te-er-ba-am
12 ka-an-nam maš-ka-nam ù ab-bu-tam iš-ša-ka-an-ma
13 a-na be-lí-šu na-ṣer

B iv 14-16

14 wardum ù amtum ša it-ti mar ši-ip-ri-im na-aṣ-ru-ma
15 abul Èš-nun-na^{ki} i-te-er-ba-am ka-an-nam ma-aš-ka-nam
16 ù ab-bu-tam iš-ša-ak-ka-an-ma a-na be-lí-šu na-ṣe-er

Section 53: A iv 13-15

šum-ma alpum (GUD) alpam (GUD) ik-ki-im-ma
14 uš-ta-mi-it ši-im alpim ba-al-ṭì ù šir (UZU) alpim mi-tim
15 be-el alpim ki-la-la-an i-zu-uz-zu

B iv 17-19

17 šum-ma alpum alpam ik-ki-im-ma uš-ta-mi-it
18 ši-im alpim ba-al-ṭim ù šir alpim mi-tim
19 [.......................] ki-la-al-la-an i-zu-uz-zu

Section 54/55: A iv 15-19

šum-ma alpum nakkapi^{pí}-ma ($\frac{\text{UL}}{\text{UL}}$pí-ma)
16 ba-ab-tum a-na be-lí-šu [ú]-še-di-ma alap-šu la ú-ši-ir-ma
17 awilam ik-ki-im-ma uš-ta-mi-it be-el alpim
18 2/3 ma-na kaspam išaqqal šum-ma wardam ik-ki-im-ma
19 uš-ta-mi-it 15 šiqil kaspam išaqqal

B iv 20

20 [..] be-lí-šu

Sec. 52: **13/B 16**: *ana belišu naṣer*: CAD N/ii 34b — "remains under guard for his master"; similarly Borger.

Sec. 53: **14/B 18**: *šir* (UZU) — "meat, carcass": so, with CAD Z 79a (= Landsberger *1968:* 102) and Goetze *1969* [ANET 3rd ed.]. Earlier reading was *taḫḫi alpim mitim* — "the value of the dead ox".

Section 52
A slave / or a slave woman who is in the custody of an envoy, and has entered the gate of Eshnunna, shall be marked with a *kannum*, a *maškanum*, and?/ or? an *abbuttum*, and in the custody of his owner shall remain.

Section 53
If an ox gored and killed an ox,
the price of the live ox and/ the carcass of the dead ox
both ox owners shall divide.

Section 54/55
If an ox (was) a gorer and the ward (authorities) have had (it) made known to its owner, but *he did not guard his ox* and it gored and killed a man, — the owner of the ox 2/3 a mina silver shall weigh out.
If a slave it gored and killed, — 15 shekels silver he shall weigh out.

Sec. 54/ **15**: ***nakkapi^{pi}-ma***: Landsberger *1968:* 102 reads *na-ka-pi-ma*. **16**: *ú-ši-ir-ma*: so von Soden *1949:* 373 (followed by Böhl *1949/1950:* 105, note 49; Szlechter). This reading is endorsed also by Landsberger, *ibid.*; but note Goetze *1956:* 136, note 8: "... *ú-ši-ir* ... was considered by me when I copied the tablet and was rejected with the original at hand". Goetze (since *1948*) reads *pa-ši-ir-ma*, but this too is not free of difficulty. Secs. 56/ and 58 lead one to expect a definite verb form not a stative. The meaning is also doubtful. Von Soden *1956:* 34 proposes the emendation *ú-<še->ši-ir-ma* — "(nicht) in Ordnung bringt"; also *1958:* 522. Followed by Finkelstein *1966:* 364, note 30 (also on later occasions), rendering "he did (not) keep ... in the direct march".

Section 56/57: A iv 20-24

20 šum-ma kalbum (UR.ZÍR) še-gi-ma ba-ab-tum a-na be-lí-šu
21 ú-še-di-ma kalab-šu la iṣ-ṣu-ur-ma
22 awilam iš-šu-uk-ma uš-ta-mi-it
23 be-el kalbim 2/3 ma-na kaspam išaqqal šum-ma wardam
24 ik-ki-im-ma uš-ta-mit-it 15 šiqil kaspam išaqqal

Section 58: A iv 25-28

25 šum-ma i-ga-rum i-qa-am-ma ba-ab-tum a-na be-el i-ga-ri
26 ú-še-di-ma i-ga-ar-šu la ú-<dan>-nin-ma
27 i-ga-rum im-qú-ut-ma mar awilim uš-ta-mi-it
28 na-pí-iš-tum ṣí-im-da-at šar-ri-im

Section 59: A iv 29-32

29 šum-ma awilum mari (DUMU.MEŠ) wu-ul-lu-ud-ma ašša(t)-su
30 i-zi-im-ma [ša]-ni-tam i-ta-ḫa-az
31 i-na bitim ù ma-l[a i-b]a-šu-ú in-na-sa-aḫ-ma
32 wa-ar-ki ša i-*ra-a*⌜*m-m*⌝*u-ma* it-ta-la-ak
33 [.................................?]

Sec. 56/57: **21**: *iṣ-ṣú-ur-ma* — "he did (not) guard": this is the accepted reading, following von Soden *1949:* 373. Goetze *1948* read *is-ki-ip-ma* — "he did (not) subdue". **24**: *ikkimma* — "it gored":mistake of the scribe for *iššukma* — "it bit"; noted already in Goetze *1948*.

Sec. 58: **25**: *iqamma*: see Hirsch *1969*: 120; CAD Q 98a.

Sec. 59: **31**: [*i-b*]*a-šu*: Finkelstein *1970:* 255: "There is almost certainly no *i* before *ba-šu-ú.*" **32**: *ša i-ra-a*⌜*m-m*⌝*u-ma* — "whom (one) will *love*": one of many restorations which have been suggested; for a detailed discussion see Goetze *1956*: 143ff., and below, pp. 214ff. Landsberger *1968:* 102 continues sec. 59 into line 33, where he reads [DA]M-*sú (= aššassu)* É *(= bitam) te-re-de* — "seine (erste) Gattin erbt das Haus". Landsberger is widely followed; see, e.g., Kraus *1969:* 53, note 137; Finkelstein *1970:* 255; von Soden (AHw 966b). Slightly different, Szlechter *1978* reads [*ù*] *bitam terede*. And see the discussion, pp. 221f., below.

Section 56/57
If a dog (was) vicious and the ward (authorities) have had (it) made known to its owner, but he did not guard his dog and it bit a man and caused (him) to die — the owner of the dog 2/3 a mina silver shall weigh out.
If a slave it gored and caused (him) to die, — 15 shekels of silver he shall weigh out.

Section 58
If a wall was threatening to fall and the ward (authorities) have had (it) made known to the owner of the wall, but he did not strengthen his wall and the wall collapsed and killed a son of a man:
(it is a case concerning) life: decree of the king.

Section 59
If a man begot sons and divorced his wife and took another, — (one) shall be torn out from the house and/ whatever there is and after whom (one) will love? (one) shall?/may? go.
[.....................................?]

Sec. 60: In spite of all the efforts devoted to it, the reading, hence also the import, of this poorly preserved text remains quite uncertain. It is for this reason that I restrict my comment to this note only.
A reading was first attempted by von Soden *1949:* 373 (followed by Szlechter). Further contributions were made by Goetze *1956*. For all these see YLE, p. 50. A new departure was proposed in CAD E 48b (= Landsberger). The beginning of line 33 was left aside (and reappeared later in Landsberger's extension of sec. 59, which has just been noted). The following text was offered:

> *š[umm]a* ... LÚ.EN(!).NUN(!) [*bi-tam a-na n*]*a-ṣa-ri-im i*[*gu*]*-ma* [*pa*]*-al-li-šu* [... *irub*] LÚ.EN.NUN [*šu-ú i-ma-a-at*] — "if a watchman has been careless in watching the house and a housebreaker has entered (the house), this watchman will be put to death".

Landsberger *1968:* 102 improved it somewhat, and his final text was then this:
33. *š*[*um-m*]*a* LÚ.EN.NUN
34. [É *i-na n*]*a-ṣa-ri-im i-gu-ma pa-al-li-šu*
35. [É *ip-lu-uš*] LÚ.EN.NUN.É *ša ip-pa-al-šu*
36. [x x x *i-du*]*-uk-ku ba-lum* [*qa*]*-ab-ri-šu*
37. [*i-na pa-ní pí*]*-il-ši-im iq-qa-bi-ir*

"Wenn ein Wächter beim Bewachen eines Hauses nachlässig ist und ein Einbrecher in das Haus einbricht, so wird man den Wächter des Hauses, in das eingebrochen wurde, [ohne Prozessverfahren] hinrichten; man wird ihn, ohne ein Grab für ihn zu graben, gegenüber der Einbruchstelle begraben."

I am worried by this extreme *Straffreudigkeit*, without parallel in the LE. Negligence of a watchman is treated as a capital case, further aggravated by the denial of proper burial. And all this "ohne Prozessverfahren" (in square brackets, indeed). One can but wonder. Finkelstein *1970:* 255 calls Landsberger's restoration of sec. 60 a "tour de force". Does this express admiration, or reserve, or perhaps a mixture of both?

Major, heroic restorations — especially of a new text, for which there are no parallels to rely upon — are unavoidably risky and questionable. They are largely a matter of hit and miss, with the latter greatly in excess of the former. One should instinctively beware of them. This reserve applies equally to any written text, irrespective of script and writing-material; in that respect cuneiform is not different from papyrus, nor even from a damaged modern text. For another example, see Yaron *1985a:* 139f., on LUY 5 (= F 2).

For LE 60, the problem is vividly demonstrated by another "tour de force" — the restoration (plus translation and commentary) by Sauren *1986:* 76ff. Where Landsberger had added 3 words (the beginning of line 33) to LE 59, Sauren incorporated into it 24 words, all the lines 33 to 37, to the very end of Tablet A. The result: LE 59 is doubled, sec. 60 has disappeared.

CHAPTER THREE

PRELIMINARIES

This chapter, continuing the Introduction, deals with a variety of preliminaries. After a brief analysis of the contents of the Laws, we shall consider the question whether a system can be discovered which underlies the sequence in which the material is presented. Some remarks on style will be followed by an examination of the forms in which the sections are couched. This will in turn lead to a discussion of the types of sources which were at the disposal of the compiler (or the compilers) who gave the LE their present form.

CLASSIFICATION OF THE LAWS

A classification of contents will often involve an element of arbitrariness: sometimes inadvertently, but almost unavoidably, one will make use of distinctions which were not known to the ancient lawgiver or draftsman. Yet, one should heed well-founded *caveats*, such as the following: "Unsere Bemühungen um Kenntnis und Verständnis des altmesopotamischen Rechtes müssen darauf gerichtet sein, die Quellen zu erschliessen und auszuschöpfen. Es gilt nicht, unsere eigenen Anschauungen und Systeme im Rechte jener Zeit wiederzufinden, sondern im Gegenteil, jede einzelne Erscheinung des altmesopotamischen Rechtes in ihrer Eigenart und ihren Zusammenhängen zu erfassen" (Kraus *1960:* 296).

There is another, lesser, point to be taken into account: a section of law purports to solve a problem arising out of a given set of facts. These may touch upon different spheres, so that a section may have to be included under more than one heading. In the order of the subsequent chapters, the material may then be divided as follows:[1]

1 For a more systematic analysis of specific parts of the LE, respective to particular chapters, see pp. 223f., 256f., below.

One section, LE 48, deals with jurisdiction.

The law of persons is represented by secs. 15, 16 (restrictions on capacity), 17/18, 25 to 30 (marriage and matrimonial offences), 33, 34/35 (concerning slave children),[2] 51, 52 (regulations concerning the movement of slaves), finally 59 (on divorce).

A major part of the LE deals with aspects of the law of property and contract: secs. 1, 2 (prices), 3, 4 (hire), 5 (negligent sinking of a boat by the boatman), 7, 8 (hire), 9 (breach of contract for harvesting), 9A, 10, 11, 14 (hire), 15, 16 (already listed under the law of persons), 18A to 21 (loans), 32 (breach of contract), 36/37 (deposit: loss of property deposited), 38, 39 (on special cases of sale), and 41 (a regulatory provision on sale). Elements of both contract and delict may be involved in the badly damaged section 60.

Cases of delict are the concern of secs. 6 (unauthorized use of a boat?), 12, 13 (trespass or burglary), 22, 23/24 (unlawful distress), 26, 27/28 (sexual offences; both sections have already been mentioned in connection with marriage), 31 (defloration of a slave girl), 34/35 (receiving a slave child; see already under persons), 40 (theft by purchase from unidentified seller), 42 to 47 (bodily injuries), 47A (culpable homicide), 49, 50 (theft of slaves and animals), 53 to 58 (dangerous animals and a ruinous wall). Section 60 has already been mentioned.

Arrangement of the Laws

Under the various headings we have adhered to the sequence of the sections in the Laws, and no attempt has been made to rearrange the material. The question has now to be considered whether there is any order in all this, or whether we are rather faced with a haphazard collection of unconnected rules. We would suggest that the correct answer is somewhere between these two possibilities.[3] Obviously, in

2 Questions of property and delict are also involved in these two sections.

3 See the cautious remarks of Klíma *1950:* 355f.: it is not justified to speak of a system, at the utmost one might assume a "Zusammenfassung auf Grund gewisser Anhaltspunkte"; but in *1952:* 566, note 93 he remarks: "Unsystematik nur im Sinne der modernen Auffassung"; see further *1966:* 253. A more positive assessment is offered by Petschow *1968a:* 131ff., also by Cardascia *1969:* 476ff. Petschow is noted with approval by Finkelstein *1981:* 22, note 2.

examining this question it would be misleading to start from Roman or modern concepts, but a convenient means of comparison is available — in the Code of Hammurabi. The fact that particular care was not taken to arrange the LE in an orderly, coherent fashion, emerges clearly from the rules concerning marriage (including the provisions on matrimonial offences) and divorce. In the CH all these form one coherent block, from sec. 127 to sec. 164. The LE are much less comprehensive, yet the provisions are split into three: there is a main part, comprising sections 25 to 30, and separate from it the single sections 17/18 and 59. Section 17/18 provides for the disposition of the *terḫatum* (respectively for the set-off of *terḫatum* and *šeriktum*), in case death causes the failure of the marriage.[4] By its contents it is closely connected with sec. 25, where the marriage fails as a consequence of an action by the father of the bride, who gives her in marriage to another person. So in the CH these types of failure are indeed considered together, in secs. 159 to 164. In the sequence of CH, LE 59 (on divorce) might have followed upon sec. 30.[5] LE 17/18 and 59 are in no way related to the rules immediately preceding or following them, and in neither case is it possible to find any reason, formal or substantive, for the dislocation; rather, one has to conclude that the sections dealing with various problems relating to marriage never did form a unit.[6]

Sec. 14, dealing with the hire of a service (the nature of which is not yet clear) is separated from the introductory part of the LE — devoted to prices and hire — by the unexplained intrusion of secs. 12 and 13, on trespass and burglary. Petschow *1968:* 134, thinks of attraction to the topic "harvest", but this is not quite convincing.

4 See the detailed discussion, pp. 179ff., below.

5 Petschow *1968a:* 142, on LE 59: "sachlich wäre dieser Paragraph im Anschluss an Par. 30 zu erwarten, während er jetzt wie ein nachträglich systemlos angefügter Nachtrag erscheint".

6 But note the suggestion of Bottéro *1965/1966:* 101 and Petschow *1968a:* 136, that LE 17/ may have been attracted by the term *mar awilim*, following the preceding sec. 16. This does not explain why the other provisions relating to marriage do not follow at once. Korošec *1964:* 86 speaks of the impression "dass man wohl anlässlich einer zweiten Redaktion die ursprünglich zusammenhängenden eherechtlichen Bestimmungen (Par. 17/18, 25-31) durch das Einschalten von Rechtssätzen über das Darlehen und die Pfändung (Par. 18A-24) auseinandergerissen habe". But why should a compiler or an editor have made such a change, reducing order to disorder?

The sections on slaves (49 to 52) are rather oddly placed, between bodily injuries (42 to 47A, followed by sec. 48, on jurisdiction) and damage caused by dangerous animals, etc. (53 to 58).

Even so, a measure of integration can be discerned. Some coherent blocks may indeed have been taken over *in corpore* from earlier collections of sources: one might refer to the groups of sections, just mentioned, dealing with bodily injuries, respectively with damages caused by dangerous objects.[7] Of greater interest are other groupings, where diversity of formulation gives rise to an assumption of differences of origin, but the substance of the provisions (or some factor common to them) has caused them to be attracted to each other.

It has already been noted that LE 5 and 6 break into the lists of prices and hire, and that they have been attracted by sec. 4:[8] the three sections have been put together because of their common concern with boats.[9] This measure of integration caused the breaking up of another group of provisions. Secs. 3, 4, and 10 deal with the hire of means of transport (wagon, boat, donkey), and their personnel (driver or boatsman). They all end in the same phrase: *kala umim ireddeši (-šu)* — "all the day he shall/ drive it". It is a plausible assumption that originally the three provisions formed a unit, — in the sequence 3, 4, 10, or else 3, 10, 4. The text of the LE, as it is before us, suffers from two inelegancies, namely the interposition of 5 and 6, and the deferment of sec. 10 to its present place. If all this was due to the draftsmen who gave the LE their shape, one might observe that no, or only very little effort was required to retain intact both groups of sections, the earlier one dealing with means of transport, and the concentration of boats. If the original sequence was 3-10-4, no change was needed; if the original sequence was 3-4-10, all one had to do was to change the place of the last two (have 10 follow upon 3). In this way there would have been two coherent, overlapping sets of altogether 5 sections: 3-10-4 and 4-5-6. It might then seem that the draftsmen did not care.

There is indeed another possibility: we may recall that the first part of the LE, up to sec. 12, is preserved on tablet A only. Hence, the disarray may be due to scribe A. The recurring phrase *kala umim ireddeši (-šu)*

7 But note that the last of these, sec. 58, may probably be an addition: see p. 302ff., below.
8 See Goetze *1956:* 37.
9 Note that in their substance secs. 5 and 6 are not related.

may have furnished an occasion for a homoioteleuton, — the skipping of the provision concerning the donkey. He may have soon become aware of his omission, and would have corrected his mistake, putting the provision at its present place (i.e. after sec. 9A).[10]

Attraction may also have placed sec. 9 (breach of a contract for harvesting) next to the provision fixing the wages of a harvester (sec. 7).[11] The sections on loan, 18A to 21, we shall submit, may be derived from two, possibly three separate sources: the common subject matter has brought them together.

Unless it is entirely due to chance, the placing of sec. 31 (concerning the defloration of a slave girl) may also be noteworthy. By its contents it could properly have been connected with sec. 26, on the rape of a betrothed girl. But there it would have constituted an intrusion into the set of rules devoted to marriage. So the compiler seems to have preferred postponing this item until he had finished with those provisions, in sec. 30.[12]

Secs. 32 to 34/35 have a common factor, the upbringing of children, but deal in fact with quite different topics: breach of a contract for nursing, ownership in a slave child, a penalty payable for the wrongful reception of a slave child. Here, too, they may have been collected from

10 Differently, Petschow *1968a:* 133: "Die zunächst ordnungswidrig erscheinende Einschaltung des Tarifs für Esel und Treiber (Par. 10) zwischen Ernte- und sonstige Arbeiter statt nach dem Thema 'Transportmittel' (Par. 3, 4 bis 6) wird damit begründet sein, dass man die Esel- (plus Treiber-) Miete vorwiegend unter dem Gesichtspunkt der Miete für Erntearbeiten betrachtete." And see his references, note 3, there.

11 We have suggested (p. 34, above) that secs. 7 and 8 ought possibly to be regarded as one section only.

12 Differently, Finkelstein *1966:* 356, and especially p. 369: "... LE 31, by its context, is not related to the standard question of sexual offences, but is considered under another rubric. It is an illustration of the deprivation of economic rights, especially in wives and children, a topic which, in the general way, extends from LE 29 through LE 35. That can be the only explanation for the concluding stipulation of LE 31 — 'the slave girl remains the property of her master' — which otherwise appears to be self-evident and redundant."
We beg to differ. "Deprivation of economic rights, especially in wives and children" is much too general and vague; yet even so it is difficult to bring LE 32 under it. For the final passage of LE 31 we have submitted a different explanation: see p. 282, below.

different sources, as suggested also by differences in style.[13] Secs. 38 to 41 deal with a number of unrelated cases; but they have a common factor, in that — one way or another — they touch on sale. This may have caused their concentration. Finally, the passage on slaves (secs. 49 to 52) seems to have been put together from two sources, each of which accounts for two sections.

One may sum up by saying that to some degree like and like were put together, but that systematization did not go very far. This was then a desire to which the compiler did indeed devote some thought, but not too much.[14] That he could have done considerably better is demonstrated by the CH.

Lack of Comprehensiveness

Another matter of interest, which emerges at once on perusal of the LE, is the lack of any desire for comprehensiveness. Important spheres of the law, e.g., lease, partnership, adoption, succession,[15] are not at all considered. More significant is another fact: even where a particular topic is considered in some detail, in a number of sections, attention is often devoted primarily to isolated, marginal questions. The emphasis is on the exceptional, and no attempt is made to provide comprehensive solutions for the variety of problems which might be envisaged as arising in a particular context. A knowledge of basic rulings is presupposed, hence no need is felt to set them out explicitly.

So there are no rules concerning proper, lawful distress: secs. 22, 23/24 deal only with unwarranted, wrongful distress. The law of marriage is another example. E.g., no details are given about the way "inchoate marriage" is contracted; secs. 17/18 and 25 deal only with frustration (through supervening death), respectively breach of the undertaking. In due course, we shall see that in the sphere of marriage the LE are much less systematic than the CH, not to mention the MAL, where the whole of Tablet A deals in effect with one topic only, the law of women.

13 See p. 112, below.
14 As here, already Korošec *1964:* 86: "Die Systematik ist ziemlich primitiv. Immerhin bemerkt man das Streben des Urhebers, inhaltlich Verwandtes zusammenhängend zu behandeln."
15 Sec. 34/35 may remotely touch on adoption. Secs. 16 and 38 may have cases of succession as their background. See Klíma *1953a:* 192ff.

Even more striking is another peculiarity of the LE. In some sections the actual decision (the apodosis) takes account only of part of the situation. That is to say, questions which arise directly from the statement of facts, as set out in the protasis, may be passed over in silence. LE 26 deals with the rape of a betrothed girl, and lays down the death penalty for the perpetrator. Nothing is said about the girl, in significant contrast to what one finds in other sources: CH 130, MAL 12 provide that the girl (or wife) raped goes free; HL 197 and Deuteronomy 22:23-27 introduce further distinctions.

In LE / 28 the death penalty is laid down for adultery, — but only for one of the offenders (in the singular!) and that in a fashion which leaves room for doubt which of the two is meant; what makes this case particularly noteworthy is that elsewhere (in CH 129, MAL 12-15, HL 198) the fate of the two culprits is made interdependent: pardon of the wife by her husband leads to pardon of her paramour by the king.[16] LE 29 deals with the wife of a prisoner of war, who was taken in marriage by another man, and bore a child to him. The returned prisoner, we are told, is entitled to take back his wife; nothing is said about the child. CH 135, more explicit, provides that *maru warki abišunu illaku* — "the sons after their father will go".[17]

In each of these cases one will be inclined to postulate for Eshnunna rules similar to those obtaining elsewhere, especially in CH;[18] however, in view of the silence of the Laws, there will remain room for more than a modicum of doubt. The assumption of the identity of laws is a good starting point, but is not altogether reliable.

STYLE AND MODES OF EXPRESSION

The style of a considerable number of sections in the LE seems to reflect mnemotechnic needs, the desire to facilitate memorizing. They flow smoothly, can be chanted, and committed to memory without much difficulty. I have not attempted a metric analysis of the texts. What matters to me — and may have mattered to those who fashioned them almost 4000 years ago — is the ease of remembering the text.

16 For a detailed discussion of adultery, see pp. 282ff., below.
17 See also MAL 45; note that in MAL 36 the solution is different.
18 See pp. 198ff., below, concerning LE 25.

Scholarly interest has concentrated on the relationship between the two tablets, and their presumed date of promulgation. But I would believe that parts of the Laws may reflect their pre-promulgation "Entstehungsgeschichte".

Indeed, an investigation of style depends considerably on "Sprachgefühl", — one's feeling for language — not easy to achieve for something as remote as Akkadian. However, one can rely on comparison, both within the LE and with CH.

We shall restrict our examples to two sets of pairs, chosen because of the identity or proximity of their content. First within LE, secs. 33 and 34/35:

LE 33: *šumma amtum usarrirma marša ana marat awilim ittadi<n>*
inuma irtabu belšu imaršu
iṣabbašuma itarrušu

LE 34/35: *šumma amat ekallim marša lu marassa*
ana muškenim ana tarbitim ittadin
maram lu martam ša iddinu ekallum itabbal
u lequ ša mar amat ekallim ilqu
meḫeršu ana ekallim iriab

Both the sections deal with children who had been fraudulently (i.e. without the master's consent or knowledge) passed on by their slave-mothers, presumably in order to have them escape their status as slaves. Both sections uphold the right of the master. One sees at once, that 34/35 is considerably longer, but — to compare equals — it may be better to disregard the two last lines, constituting the second part of the apodosis (misnumbered 35), which has no parallel in sec. 33.

Sec. 33 consists of three parts; each of these is made up of two sentences, and occupies (in Tablet B) one line. Note the decreasing number of words, 8-4-2. The last three words of the section describe three acts, in urgent sequence: (the master) recognizes him, seizes him and takes him back. It is an almost Caesarean frugality of style. Intentional or not, the overall result is very memory-friendly, and may — as it is before us — be the exact transcript of early, pre-promulgation, oral tradition. As for sec. 34/, there are two possibilities: it too may have proceeded from an oral basis, but it has undergone revision, in the course of which some largely superfluous words accrued to it. So *lu marassa* (in the first line) and *lu martam ša iddinu* (in the third). If these are deleted, we are left with a text that is not very dissimilar to sec. 33, — even though without its refinement of structure. Alternatively, 34/ may have been altogether new, based from inception on a written text, not catering to mnemotechnic needs or considerations. Writing overcomes live memory: it was an unequal contest.

Our second couple are LE 30 and CH 136, both dealing with a husband who had fallen out with the authorities and absconded:

LE 30: *šumma awilum alšu u belšu izerma ittabit*
aššassu šanumma itaḫaz inuma ituram
ana aššatišu ul iraggam
CH 136: *šumma awilum alšu iddima ittabit*
warkišu aššassu ana bit šanim iterub
šumma awilum šu ituramma aššassu iṣṣabat
aššum alšu iziruma innabitu
aššat munabtim ana mutiša ul itar

> "If a man his city abandoned and fled, thereafter his wife entered to the house of another: if that man returned and seized his wife — because his city he has hated and fled, the wife of the fugitive to her husband shall not return."

LE 30 is straightforward. A protasis of altogether 12 words states the reasons for the husband's absence ("hated his city and/ master and fled"), tells of his wife's second marriage ("another ... took his wife"), and his eventual return. A brief apodosis (4 words) denies his claim to his wife. Again, the section as a whole is easy to remember.

CH 136 did not fare well at the hands of Hammurabi's draftsmen. Reformulation will almost unavoidably add to the length of a text. This need not be objectionable, if it passes some simple test: it should contribute to the clarity of the text, or else it should deal with some significant point, which was by-passed in the original. (One must bear in mind that brevity, however aesthetically pleasing, may also be excessive.) CH 136 does not meet these demands. The section grows from 16 words to 27. Its form has suffered, but to no visible purpose: the reader is left exactly where he was before.

CH 136 shows signs of extensive revision, but there remains the impression that LE 30, or some version close to it, was the actual starting-point for Hammurabi's compilers. The following divergences may be noted: in the introduction, vis-à-vis LE's *alšu u belšu izerma ittabit*, CH drops *u belšu*, and substitutes for *izerma* the weaker *iddima* (from *nadu* — "to abandon"), to read *alšu iddima ittabit* — a saving of two words! The statement concerning the second marriage commences with *warkišu* — "thereafter" (unnecessary but harmless); marriage itself is approached from the woman's side: instead of *(aššassu) šanumma ittaḫaz* we have *(aššassu) ana bit šanim iterub*; no substantive difference: the two phrases are but two sides of the same coin (and note how they combine in LE / 18). The drafters of CH 136 may simply have continued the phrasing in secs. 133-135.[19] Imbalance begins seriously with the statement about the husband's return: for LE's terse *inuma ituram*, CH has *šumma awilum šu ituramma aššassu iṣṣabat*, where *šumma* is no improvement on *inuma*,[20] *awilum šu* is unneeded but harmless. *aššassu iṣṣabat* has somewhat puzzled translators ever since Scheil, who rendered "veut reprendre sa femme";[21] note that the phrase has no parallel in LE (but one does not miss it) nor in CH 135, where its slot is taken by *alšu iktašad*.[22] What exactly *aššassu iṣṣabat* was meant to convey is not clear.[23]

Now the apodosis. Rather unexpectedly, its substance is preceded by a clause setting out the *ratio decidendi*: the actual decision which follows is based on the circumstances of the husband's absence, — *aššum alšu izirumma innabitu* — "because his city he hated and fled". Indeed, such explanatory preambles occur elsewhere in CH, in secs. 107, 146, 194, and 232:[24] in each case this *ratio* is an exact quote from the protasis, of the decisive element. In the present case, there is a noteworthy discrepancy: the quote is not from the protasis of CH 136 (as we have it), rather from LE 30 (or a text with an identical wording). The return to the original may be inadvertent; it may also reflect

19 But a nuance of calamity may be faintly more detectable in "another took her" than in the more restrained "she entered another's house" (see also AO 9066 [p. 143, below] and Deuteronomy 20:7).
20 In the preceding CH 135, the corresponding phrase has *ina warka*.
21 Followed, e.g., by Winckler *1902* — "seine Ehefrau nehmen will"; Meek *1950* — "wishes to take back his wife"; Finet *1973* — "a voulu reprendre sa femme". *Ad sensum* only is the rendering of Driver-Miles *1955* — "finds his wife".
22 In CH 27 and 135 *alšu iktašad* follows *ituram-ma*, to form a hendiadys. In CH 32 it stands by itself without loss of import.
23 Note the comment of Driver-Miles *1952:* 286: "... a man ... 'attaches' or claims his wife by a formal seizure."
24 See Driver and Miles, *ibid.*

dissatisfaction with the actual wording of the protasis. The phrase *iddima ittabit* — "he abandoned and fled" may have been regarded as too weak, too vague, not quite adequate to justify that the wife shall not return to her husband (who is described, very officially, and maybe somewhat pompously, as *munnabtum* — "fugitive").

When all has been said, the rewriting of CH 136 is a clear case of miscorrection: the reader is burdened with a text that has grown by two-thirds, but he gets nothing in return for this increase.[25]

There are some inherent differences between the protasis and the apodosis. The former, since it consists of a recital of facts, may relate some which are of no specific legal import, rather are mentioned as part of the *res gestae*, the series of events which accumulated on a given occasion. It will not always be easy to distinguish between what is legally material and those parts of the protasis which would be dispensable.

Sec. 25, dealing with the case of the rejected bridegroom, states as one of the facts that the bride was given to another man. Is this material, and are we to deduce that the rights of the disappointed bridegroom depend on this particular occurrence? In other words, would he be left without remedy if the father merely refused to give his daughter, as promised?

Several factual elements are cumulated also in sec. 27/. Here we hear of a man "taking" *(aḫazum)* a man's daughter without the consent of "her father and ?/or? her mother", without "marriage feast" and?/or? contract: in this case — we are told — she is not an *aššatum* ("wife"), even if she dwell in his house for a full year. What is the impact of the cumulation of these negative elements, viz., the absence of parental consent, of feast, of contract? Does the mention — here and already in sec. 26 — of both father and mother imply that the cooperation of both parents is essential, or is the mother brought into the picture only for the case that the father has died (or is for some other reason incapable of acting)? And what is the purpose of the further statement (perched between protasis and apodosis) that the passage of time will not heal the original defect?

25 Compare and contrast also LE 54/ (19 words) and CH 251/ (24 words); there is no meaningful difference. In the Bible, contrast Proverbs 20:10 (an eight-word condemnation of fraudulent weights and measures) with its lawyerese elaboration in Deuteronomy 25:13-16. And see Yaron *1986:* 156.

In sec. 39, mention is made of the fact that the seller of a house was in a difficult financial position *(iniš)*. Is this a material part of the situation, and does it imply that the power of redemption granted in the section was not of general application?

In sec. 59, the facts include not only the divorce of the wife who had given birth to children, but also the taking of another woman. What, if any, is the import of this addition? Does it mean that the section did not provide for the case of arbitrary divorce as such, as long as that arbitrary divorce was not followed by a second marriage?

With regard to all these cases we are for the moment content with merely putting questions, and defer suggesting any answers until we deal with each section in its proper context.

On the other hand, in some instances the protasis is formulated in an elliptic fashion. In sec. 40 we hear of a buyer who is unable to establish the identity of the seller. With Goetze *1956:* 113 we deny that it was intended to proclaim an abstract principle, by which "every purchase has to conform to certain rules, and that he who violates the rules can be prosecuted as a thief". Rather, it is a necessary implication that the buyer is charged with having in his possession stolen goods. What is missing here is an introductory sentence, like that of CH 9: *šumma awilum ša mimmušu ḫalqu mimmašu ḫalqam ina qati awilim iṣṣabat* — "If a man, some of whose property was lost, seized his lost property in the hands of a man ..."

Elliptic is also the formulation of the protasis in sec. 25. There the apodosis imposes a duty of returning double the bride payment *(terḫatum)* which had been received, even though such payment is not mentioned *expressis verbis* in the protasis.[26]

Sec. 50 does not define the duties of the official who seized fugitive slaves or stray animals. Rather it deals at once with the fact that he has not delivered his find to Eshnunna.

Elliptic formulations need not be sloppy: rather they testify to a desire for brevity, to omit what is taken as self-understood or implicit. A good example is the biblical provision on succession (Numbers 27.8ff.): the son's right to inherit — indeed as sole heir, to the exclusion of the deceased's daughter — is indicated only *en passant*, by necessary implication: "... if a man die without having a son, ye shall transfer his

26 Cf. Goetze *1956:* 78 and the detailed discussion, pp. 196f., below.

inheritance to his daughter."[27] In the Bible, the writing of a bill of divorce — so meticulously regulated in later Jewish law — is mentioned only as part of the *res gestae*, leading up to a narrow provision, the prohibition of a reunion with the divorcee, in case she had in the interim been married to another man (Deuteronomy 24:1-4).

We see then that the protasis may veer between an excess of detail and ellipsis. It is the former deviation rather than the latter which is likely to occasion difficulties of interpretation.

Rather different is the picture presented by the apodosis. By contrast to the protasis, it is necessarily restricted to essentials: there is little occasion to introduce anything superfluous, and redundancies are few. In sec. /24, there is the phrase *nepu ša ippu* — "the distrainor who distrained"; here one could do without the relative clause *(ša ippu)*, which merely repeats the facts of the protasis. The same applies also to the relative clause in sec. /35: *(lequ) ša mar amat ekallim ilqu* — "(the taker,) who took the son of the slave woman of the palace". Some slight verbiage, no doubt; but it creates no problems.

In two sections the apodosis contains a definition, or classification, of an act as *din napištim* — "a case of life". So in sec. /24, the case of the wrongful distrainor who caused death, and in sec. 26, that of the rapist of an inchoately married girl.[28] And in both the concrete result is expressed by a single word: *imat* — "he shall die". In sec. 58 we have another formulation, *napištum ṣimdat šarrim* — "(a case concerning) life: decree of the king"; *din napištim* is shortened to *napištum*, but then we have a singular reference to a source of the punishment provided for: "decree of the king". The actual imposition of the death penalty is not mentioned.[29]

We must return to the phenomenon of brevity, this time with emphasis on the apodosis. As an outstanding example of brevity (and resulting elegance) one may mention sec. 39, concerning the sale of a

27 Strikingly similar, in formulation rather than substance, is the corresponding Roman provision, XII Tables 5.4: *Si intestato moritur cui suus heres nec escit* ... Here there is a double ellipsis: the narrative protasis refers to the absence of a testament, as well as to the absence of an offspring-heir *(suus heres)*.

28 One is reminded of the "diagnosis pattern", analysed by Daube *1945:* 39ff. See further Yaron *1961:* 110ff.

29 See pp. 259, 302f., below, on the import of this, ostensibly defective formulation.

house by its impoverished owner. The final part of the protasis, and the apodosis do not repeat the object: "the day the buyer will sell, the owner of the house may redeem". Brevity goes here beyond what one might expect, but in this specific case does not result in uncertainty. Another brief apodosis, in sec. 38, is not yet clear; but the problem is not due to brevity, rather to the obscurity of the key phrase *qablit šanim mullum*.

But in a number of sections our difficulties can be directly attributed to excessive "elegant" brevity. All the necessary verbs are given, but their subjects are not made explicit: one can but try to select suitable subjects from the preceding statements of facts, in the protasis. If the protasis itself is complex, it may be difficult to understand properly the "elegant" apodosis.

In sec. /18 the apodosis is *mala ublu ul ušeṣṣe wataršuma ileqqe*: 6 words, 3 of them verbs; forms of *wabalum* — "to bring, carry", of *šuṣum* (causative of *waṣum* — "to go forth"), hence "cause to go forth",[30] and of *lequm* — "to take". Each of the three verbs is preceded by one word which throws but feeble light on the import; these are *mala* — "whatever", *ul* — a negation ("shall) not", *wataršuma* — "its excess only" (or perhaps "its remainder only"?).[31]

We have already had occasion to fret about the final apodosis of sec. /28, laying down the punishment for one offender only, in the unavoidably joint crime of adultery. Here the apodosis, stern and elegant, consists of 3 words; these form an idiomatic expression in which two antithetic verbs, "to die" and "to live", become synonyms by the insertion of the negation *ul* — ("shall) not".[32] In other words, when it comes to the import of the apodosis as a whole, these three words are telescoped, become as if one only: *imat* — (someone) "shall die", without telling expressly who that person is.

Finally, in sec. 59, once more three verbs without explicit subjects: *ina bitim u mala ibašu innassaḫma warki ša ira*[*mmu*]*ma ittallak*. These tell, somewhat enigmatically, of an expulsion from house and property, and about going after one's choice.

There is, may we note again, a certain attractiveness in these ultra-short formulations. These are literary modes of expression, prose

30 On *šuṣu* — "cause to go forth", see pp. 183f., below.
31 See Petschow *1968:* 137, note 1: dealing with sec. /18, he observes that "... der akkadische Wortlaut wegen seiner lapidaren Kürze nicht eindeutig ist."
32 Concerning *imat ul iballuṭ* see further pp. 259ff., below.

bordering on poetry. In searching — not too successfully — for the correct interpretation of the texts, one should not be unfair to the ancient compilers of the LE, who were culling these passages from earlier sources, or possibly putting into writing what may have been oral tradition. Their phrasing need not have posed a problem for a knowledgeable contemporary reader, familiar as he would have been with context and background. And, after all, it was to that contemporary reader that the Laws were addressed, — to him and not to the historian of law, groping to find his way almost four millennia later.

Nevertheless and even so, there remains a further aspect: there is considerable difference between the "abridged" formulation of the apodosis in secs. /18, /28 and 59, and the "full" wording, up to the verbose one, e.g. in 34/35. No less clear is the difference between the excessively brief apodosis in the sections discussed and their "normal" counterparts in the corresponding CH secs. 163/164, 129, 137.

Faced with these uncertainties, Goetze *1956:* 142f. looked for firm ground in asserting that "in a formally ambiguous sentence it cannot be assumed that the subject changes unless the change is made explicit". Rephrased in simpler language this would mean that one has to assume an identity of subjects "unless the change is made explicit". It is such an assumption that guides Goetze (and some others); however, it can be shown that the assumption of identity of subjects is unreliable, i.e. that within the LE there are instances of non-explicit change of subject.

So in sec. 9: "Should a man give 1 shekel of silver for harvesting to?/for? a hired man — if he (the worker) was not ready for him, and did not ... harvest for him the harvesting — 10 shekels silver he shall weigh out."

Here the employer is the subject of the introductory passage; "Should ... a hired man", but later on — in both the protasis and the apodosis — the subject is the harvester (or the person by whom he is owned or managed). Yet one looks in vain for an explicit indication of the reversal.[33]

Sec. 22, one may recall, concerns a case of wrongful distress: "If a man had nothing upon a man, yet distrained the man's slave woman, the owner of the slave woman shall swear by (a) god: 'Thou hast nothing

33 Goetze solves the problem by rendering "... he (i.e. the hired man) does not hold himself in readiness ..."; I do the same by inserting "(the worker)".

upon me'; silver, as much as the *price* of the slave woman, he shall weigh out."

Here too, there is no formal indication of the change of subjects. Strict adherence to Goetze's approach would lead to the result that both the verbs in the apodosis refer to the owner of the slave woman, who will both swear and pay. Needless to say, Goetze does not go that far, but inserts an explanation: "... he (i.e. the distrainor) shall pay", and so do we.

Finally, the apodosis of sec. / 37 (the longest in the LE): "... the owner of the house shall in the house (or door) of Tišpak swear to him by god: 'Together with thy goods my goods were lost, I have not done evil and / fraud.' He shall swear to him, and nothing upon him he shall have." Again, there is no formal indication of the switch — at the very end — from depositary to depositor. Goetze has no difficulty in making the proper insertions.

One may then conclude that in the style of the LE there is no insistence on the identity of subjects; on the contrary, the subject may change without any indication.[34] Consequently, where there are substantive legal grounds leading to the assumption that the subject has indeed changed, there is no *a priori* difficulty involved. In such cases, a possible change of subject will widen the choice of available interpretations (and with it the scope for scholarly controversy).

FORMS

The forms employed in the LE ought now to be considered. It is a generally accepted hypothesis that the Code of Hammurabi is a compilation, taken from a variety of earlier sources. This *communis opinio* is the result of detailed critical enquiries into the substance of the Code. As far as forms are concerned, the CH is almost completely uniform, with only a few exceptions. Its provisions are formulated as conditional

34 This is stressed also by Bottéro *1965/1966:* 97: "...nul critère grammatical ne permet de décider, dans le texte, quel est le sujet d'un verbe, quand il y en a plusieurs possibles; et le cas n'est pas rare où, sans autre indication, le sujet change d'un verbe à celui qui le suit." For the same phenomenon in CH see e.g. sec. 186, and the comments of Driver-Miles *1955:* 244. Adherence to an unwarranted assumption of identity of subjects may lead to a mistaken interpretation: see, concerning CH 186, Szlechter, *1967:* 83, note 10.

sentences: if a man does so and so the following legal consequences will ensue. A typical section in CH begins with the words *šumma awilum* — "if a man"; variations consist in the main in the substitution of more specific designations for the general *awilum*. However, comparison with the LE shows that the uniformity of drafting in CH is the work of its compilers. Out of several modes of formulation which were in use in ancient Babylonia — as evidenced by LE — the draftsmen of Hammurabi selected *šumma awilum* as the one most common and convenient, and imposed it upon his collection of legal rules. On the whole the results were quite satisfactory, with some exceptions to which we shall refer. From the point of view of the legal historian it may be regrettable that this process of reformulation obliterated the differences of origin; however, such a levelling down to a common form would be one of the aims which the compilers would wish to achieve.

It is of interest and importance that the LE underwent no comparable process of reformulation and levelling down. The marked variety of forms shows for this corpus of rules at one glance what for the CH could be established only by means of a laborious examination of the substance: like the CH, the LE are a compilation of legal rules collected from earlier sources. There is no reason to assume that any one legislator would wish to express his rules in greatly divergent ways. Indeed, the approach to this matter of forms ought not to be too exacting and meticulous; some slight measure of variety is almost inevitable, in any given collection of texts. But in case the divergences of formulation become very pronounced, and concrete reasons for them cannot be found, different origin may be a plausible explanation.[35]

Several sections in the LE are atypical; these are in the main the regulatory sections, fixing prices, hire and rates of interest.[36] After dealing with these we shall try to distinguish four kinds of formulation.

PRICES AND HIRE

Price regulations are different from ordinary legislation; they are not meant to resolve conflicts or establish rights. It follows that when they display formulations of their own, this cannot be taken as indicating

35 Note, however, reservations of Jackson *1982:* 50, 57.

36 Atypical is also sec. 48, on jurisdiction, which may be incomplete.

differences of origin. The eleven regulatory sections deal with a variety of topics. Sec. 1 fixes the price of various commodities; sec. 2 lays down the ratio of certain kinds of oil vis-à-vis barley. Sec. 3 fixes the hire of a wagon, 4 that of a boat. Secs. 7, 8, 10 and 11 fix the hire of agricultural workers, the hire of a donkey and its driver. Obscure and not yet understood are secs. 9A and 14. Finally, sec. 18A fixes the rate of interest on loans of silver and grain.

The formulation of the various sections is quite straightforward. Yet, even where the subject matter is similar or comparable, there is not full uniformity of expression. In the eight sections dealing with hire there are two main formulations. The one starts with the object of the contract: "The hire of X is Y." So in secs. 4, 11, 14; a variant of this form is that of sec. 3: "A wagon together with its oxen and its driver — Y is its hire": here the compound nature of the object may have caused the postponing of *idiša* — "its hire". The other four sections, 7, 8, 9A and 10, have the inverted sequence, stating first the amount to be paid: "Y is the hire of X." The more usual means of payment in hire is grain; secs. 3 and 7 give alternatives in silver, sec. 14 has only payment in silver. Sec. 11 fixes payment in silver, and in addition the supply of a quantity of grain. There is certainly a degree of variety in all this; but when all has been said, that variety does not exceed what may have been done by one person (or by one group of persons) not particularly careful in drafting or not attaching great importance to uniformity.

What is of interest in the formulation of the regulations regarding prices and hire concerns not so much the LE as the CH, and it emerges from a comparison of the two sources. In the Code, the desire of using throughout the conditional form, *šumma awilum*, seems to have been the decisive consideration. As a result of this tendency, one finds ordinary, everyday transactions — e.g., the hire of a farm worker (sec. 257), or that of an ox (sec. 268) — couched in the formal language of the lawcase; in these contexts *šumma awilum* looks artificial, slightly pompous, and altogether out of place.[37]

37 Also Finkelstein *1981:* 35 — "patently unsuited". But one may note possible antecedents in Sumerian: a conditional formulation of hire occurs already in the fragmentary AO 10638 (a fragment of LI), republished and discussed by Nougayrol *1952:* 54. The fragment corresponds to CH 271.

The legal sections of the LE employ the following four forms: (i) the conditional sentence *(šumma awilum)*; (ii) the split protasis; (iii) the apodictic command; and (iv) the relative formulation *(awilum ša)*.

THE CONDITIONAL SENTENCE *(šumma awilum)*

The form which is most frequent, occurring in 33 sections,[38] is the conditional sentence, starting off with *šumma*. The subject follows at once. In 23 sections the beginning is *šumma awilum*.[39] The remaining 10 sections are limited by their subject, and consequently more specific in their wording: here one finds *malaḫum* (sec. 5), *amtum* (33), *amat ekallim* (34/), *ubarum* etc. (41), *šakkanakkum* etc. (50), *alpum* (53, 54/), *kalbum* (56/), and *igarum* (58); in sec. 38 the subject following *šumma* is more complicated, made up of a compound expression: *ina atḫi išten* — "one of brothers".

The conditional sentence introduced by *šumma awilum* (or a specific subject) goes back to very early times. The Ebla tablet TM.75.G.2420 takes us back to the middle of the third millennium. While the actual import is not always clear, the opening *su-ma* LÚ (= *šumma awilum*), used in several instances, is not in doubt.[40] The collections of laws written in Sumerian use the equivalent TUKUMBI LÚ. We have just noted that the conditional formulation is predominant in the LE; it has a virtual monopoly in the CH,[41] and also in the rules of law given in Tablet 7 of *ana ittišu*. It occupies only a minor position in the edict of Ammi-ṣaduqa.[42] Subject to some exceptions,[43] *šumma awilum* is the form employed almost exclusively in the MAL. On the other hand, it is

38 Our count of sections ends with sec. 59. Of sec. 60 one does not even know where it actually begins.

39 6, 20, 21, 22, 23/24, 25, 26, 27/28, 29, 30, 31, 32, 36/37, 39, 40, 42, 43, 44/45, 46, 47, 47A, 49, 59.

40 See Sollberger *1980:* 136ff., lines 112, 117, 128, — probably also in line 183. Different is the construction in lines 133ff.: *su-ma in 10* NU-BÀNDA *ma-nu-ma* — "If (of a group of) 10 'sergeants' someone ...". This may be compared with the compound subject in LE 38. In other constructions, *su-ma* occurs in TM.75.G.2420 in 11 more places: see lines 191, 202, 221, 261, 415, 419, 427, 435, 475, 581, 587. The significance of the early use of *šumma* is noted by Artzi *1984:* 39.

41 For some exceptions, see pp. 104f., below.

42 Edited twice, in Kraus *1958* and Kraus *1984*.

43 See p. 106, below.

altogether absent from the Neo-Babylonian Laws, having been displaced by the relative formulation *awilum ša* — "a man, who ...", to be discussed in due turn, under (iv).

THE SPLIT PROTASIS

A typical section of the LE is made up of two parts, a protasis and an apodosis. We have already noted that of these two the latter — setting out the consequences of the occurrence(s) related in the former — is usually relatively simple. In the majority of cases the apodosis concentrates on one of the parties only, and that more often the party duty bound to do something, e.g., pay compensation or make restitution (e.g., secs. 5, 6, 9, 23/, 25, etc.); in other instances, the subject of the apodosis may be the person entitled, who will "take, fetch" some object (e.g., secs. 20, 21, 33).[44] In sec. 17/ the apodosis is formulated in a neutral fashion, speaking objectively of the "reversion" of the silver to its owner (cf. also the end of sec. 31). Sometimes the apodosis will contain provisions concerning both the parties to the transaction or occurrence. So in sec. 34/35 (with express indication of the change of subjects): "the palace will take away, and?/or? the taker ... shall replace", etc.; sec. 22 (without indication of the change of subjects); [45] similarly at the end of sec. /37: "He shall swear to him, and nothing upon him he shall have." In one case, sec. 53, the parties are joint subjects of the apodosis: "both ox owners shall divide ..."

While then the apodosis is relatively simple, the protasis will often be more complicated, relating to a whole chain of events. For example, in sec. 23/: "If a man had nothing upon a man, yet distrained the man's slave woman, detained the distrainee in his house and caused her to die ..."; or in sec. 26: "If a man brought bride payment for a man's daughter, but another without asking her father and?/or? her mother forcibly seized her and deflowered her ...". Not all the events listed in each of the protases adduced are of equal, immediate proximity to the

44 For minor variants, see sec. 30, where the right of a claimant is denied (see also /37). A mixed case, stating a duty and a consequent right, is that of sec. 32: "he shall weigh out" (duty), followed by "he will take back" (right).

45 See pp. 96f., above.

ruling laid down in the apodosis. Some state the background, legal and factual, the circumstances which combine to make up the situation occasioning that specific, final occurrence for which the legislator wishes to provide in his ruling. In our two examples, the background is in the one case the distress in absence of a claim (23/), in the other case the fact that bride payment has been made for the girl (26). These circumstances are in each case an essential part of the whole, a part *sine qua* the section cannot stand, or at least would not reflect the intention of the legislator. But the immediate cause of the provision is some further occurrence, viz., in sec. 23/24 the death of the distress, in 26 the rape of the bride.

A formal separation of these two elements in the protasis, obviously making for greater clarity, is achieved in two sections by means of a simple expedient: the sections start with an introductory passage, and *šumma* is postponed until that final occurrence for which a remedy is being sought. Thereby, attention is at once focused on the decisive part of the protasis. The two sections are 9 and 17/18:

Sec. 9: "Should a man give 1 shekel silver for harvesting ... if he (the worker) was not ready for him and did not ... harvest for him the harvesting ..."

Sec. 17/18: "Should a son of a man bring bride payment to the house of the father-in-law:
(i) if one of the two went to the fate ...
(ii) if he took her and she entered to his house ..."

In section 9, the split in the protasis shows at once that the provision does not deal in a general fashion with the hire of harvesters but rather that it is desired to regulate the particular case when the undertaking, that the harvester be at the disposal of the employer, is not honoured. This mode of formulation is even more useful in sec. 17/18: here the separation of the earlier occurrence, that is the bringing of the bride payment, makes it possible to append two different provisions, the one dealing with death prior to the marriage, the other with death after the marriage has already taken place.

This formulation appears more advanced, more delicate and elegant than the ordinary *šumma awilum*. It is possible that these very characteristics caused its disappearance: the form did not meet the desire for the uniformity and standardization of sections, all of which should start in the same way. I have not found the form outside the

LE,[46] and even here it occurs only exceptionally,[47] while other sections which could employ it with profit, employ the ordinary *šumma awilum*; see already secs. 23/24 and 26, also 27/28.

However, there is in the LE yet another formulation which splits the protasis, even though in less clear a fashion. The section starts indeed with *šumma*, but the part immediately material is construed as a temporal sentence, separately introduced by a conjunction, "at the day (when)" — *um* (secs. /28, 39), or "whenever" — *inuma* (secs. 29, 30, 33):

Sec. /28: "If he (subsequently) fixed contract and?/or? marriage feast ... (she is) a 'wife'. The day in the lap of a man she will be seized ..."

Sec. 39: "If a man ... sold his house: ... the day the buyer will sell ..."

Sec. 29: "If a man ... has been carried off forcibly ... another indeed took his wife ...: whenever he returns ..."

Sec. 30: "If a man hated his city ..., another indeed took his wife: whenever he returns ..."

Sec. 33: "If a slave woman ... gave her son to the daughter of a man, (and) when he has grown up ..."

Sec. 27/28 is complex in its construction.[48] First there is an introduction telling that a man took a man's daughter without parental consent. This introduction has to be read twice, with each of the two passages that follow. The first (comprising the remainder of 27/) concerns the case where subsequent to the unapproved "taking" of the girl no remedial steps were taken to obtain — albeit after the event — the approval of the parents. There is a negative decision: in the circumstances described, the woman *ul aššat* — "is not a wife". The second passage (i.e. sec. /28) offers an alternative set of facts: the parents gave their belated blessing to the union, hence their daughter is

46 But see two Roman instances of split protasis, *Digesta Iustiniani* 36.4.5.26 and 27. The former reads: "In possessionem missus legatorum servandorum causa si litem eo nomine contestatus sit ..."

47 Somewhat similar is CH 163/164. It starts with *šumma awilum*, and each of the two subsections is again introduced by *šumma*. The construction is basically similar to that of LE 17/18, but the triple *šumma* within one section does not occur in LE. Sec. 17/18 avoids the first, 27/28 omits the second. The Bible achieves the separation of early and subsequent events, or else of subsections, by the distinct use of two synonymous conjunctions: a provision will often start with (*iš*) *ki* — "if (a man)", then continue with *im* — "in case". See, e.g., Exodus 21:2ff.; 21:7ff.; Leviticus 25: 29f.; 27:2ff.; Numbers 27:8ff.; 30:3ff.; Deuteronomy 22:13ff.; 22:23ff.

48 See already p. 35, above.

a "wife". There is a logical consequence, which constitutes the final part of /28: being a "wife", she is capable of committing adultery. The construction as a whole is the following: *šumma* starts the introduction, which flows directly, without any break, into the rest of the protasis of 27/; 27/ terminates in the brief, two-word, negative apodosis. Sec. /28, also commencing with *šumma*, leads up to the conclusion *aššat* — "she is a wife". This (parallel to *ul aššat* of 27/) is strictly speaking an apodosis. But this is not yet the end: a final passage (not contained in Tablet B), beginning with *um* — "the day (when)", tells of the adulterous relationship, and the "elegant" apodosis decrees the death of one of the culprits.[49]

Sec. 39, by contrast, is quite simple and straightforward. In this instance the original sale, introduced by *šumma*, constitutes the "prehistory" of the case; *um* starts the final part of the protasis, dealing with subsequent alienation by the buyer.[50] In secs. 29 and 30, the introductions detail the (differing) circumstances of a husband's absence; the final part of the protasis, concerning the return of the absentee, starts with *inuma* — "whenever".[51]

These constructions, being less conspicuous than *awilum ... šumma*, survived also in later sources. In CH there are several sections using *inuma* to introduce the final part of the protasis: see, e.g., secs. 165, 166. Cf. also MAL B 13, 19, and the biblical passages just mentioned.

However, I should stress that one should not rely on any of the forms of split protasis when it comes to the question of differences of origin. The split protasis may well be nothing more than an attempt to improve on the ordinary *šumma awilum* formulation.

THE APODICTIC COMMAND

Four sections, 15, 16, 51 and 52,[52] are formulated as terse commands. Secs. 15 and 16 forbid certain business transactions with slaves, respec-

49 For the apodosis of sec. /28, see also pp. 87, 94, above, and pp. 284f., below.

50 In sec. /28 *um* may perhaps carry a minatory undertone, hinting at the swiftness of retribution; such an implication is entirely absent in sec. 39: on this section, see Petschow *1965a:* 26, note 19. In the Bible compare, on the one hand, Genesis 2:16-17, I Kings 2:36-37, 42; on the other hand, Deuteronomy 21:15-17.

51 For *inuma*, see also LE 33, where a purpose of separation is less evident.

52 Secs. 51 and 52 might also be included with those having a relative *(ša)*

tively with "a coparcener son of a man".[53] Secs. 51 and 52 concern slaves. The former lays down that a marked slave must not leave the gate of Eshnunna without (the consent of) his owner. The latter is the only section of this kind in the LE which is couched in positive terms: it requires the proper marking of certain slaves, and states that they will remain in the custody of their owner.[54]

It has been pointed out that no sanction is laid down in any of these four sections; we are therefore in the dark concerning the consequences which might follow in each case. However, it ought not to be taken for granted that these are all true *leges imperfectae*, which can be disregarded with impunity. On the other hand, it would be wrong to assume that the absence of a sanction is a necessary feature of the apodictic formulation: one finds sanctions added to that formulation by means of a conditional sentence *(šumma awilum)*,[55] or by means of a relative sentence (*awilum ša* — "the man, who").[56]

Several instances of apodictic formulation survive in the CH: these are secs. 36/37, 38/39, 40, all dealing with the alienation of feudal

formulation; so Petschow *1965a:* 29. The point is not of much significance for our discussion.

53 See the detailed discussion, pp. 158ff., below.

54 See pp. 164f., below.

55 See CH 36/37. Compare, in Roman sources, Sextus Iulius Frontinus, *De aquis urbis Romae* 2.97: Ne quis aquam oletato dolo malo, ubi publice saliet. Si quis oletarit, sestertiorum decem milium multa esto: "No one shall pollute the water with malice, where it issues publicly. If anyone pollute (it), 10,000 sestertii the fine shall be" (based on the translation of Ch. E. Bennet, in *Loeb Classical Library*); see also *ibid.*, 2.127.
See further Aulus Gellius, *Noctes Atticae* 4.3.3: Paelex aedem Iunonis ne tangito; si tangit, Iunoni crinibus demissis agnum feminam caedito: "A concubine the temple of Juno shall not touch; if she touch (it), to Juno with hair unbound an ewe lamb she shall sacrifice" (based on the translation of J. C. Rolfe, in *Loeb Classical Library*).

56 See AbB iii, no. 1: "A man or a woman, a son of Ida-maraz or Arrapḫum, from the Sutaeans no one shall buy. [The merchant] who a son of Ida-maraz or Arrapḫum, from the Sutaeans for silver buys, his silver he shall forfeit." See also an edict of the king of Nuzi, in AASOR 16 (1936), text 51 (the sanction is introduced by *mannumme* — "whoever"). Finally, see MAL 40.

holdings,[57] and sec. 187, concerning cases of adoption. Actually, these are in CH the only exceptions to *šumma awilum*.[58] In MAL, the main example is the list of prohibitions and commands, set out at the beginning of sec. 40; cf. also the very fragmentary secs. 58 and F 2.

The Relative Formulation

LE 12, 13, and 19 have a relative formulation: a man, who will do such and such a thing, etc. The first two, closely connected in their contents, are of a penal character: they deal with trespass on a field, respectively on a house. Sec. 19, on the other hand, is purely civil; apparently it fixes the date for the collection of debts arising out of a certain type of loan.[59]

The relative formulation too makes its first appearance — at the side of *šumma* LÚ — in the Ebla text TM.75.G.2420; it is introduced by *mannumme* — "whoever".[60] Next, the relative formulation is attested in Old-Akkadian times, in the inscription of Annubanini, king of Lullubi: *ša ṣalmin annin … ušassaku* — "whoever desecrates these two representations …".[61]

The draftsmen of Hammurabi, probably guided by their desire for uniformity, suppressed the relative formulation. But a short time later, in the edict of Ammi-ṣaduqa, we find it in prominent use.[62] In the

57 The sections are not uniform. Sec. 36/ is a prohibition, /37 adds the sanction. Sec. 38/ prohibits the assignment of certain types of property to a wife or a daughter, /39 permits the assignment of other types. Sec. 40 allows certain persons to alienate their holdings.

58 See Driver-Miles *1952:* 125: "The only explanation that suggests itself of this anomaly in the drafting is that the old law is being reproduced verbatim."

59 See pp. 273f. (on LE 12 and 13), pp. 236f. (on LE 19).

60 Lines 106ff: *ma-nu-ma* EN ÁS *u* UB ÁS *u* KALAM-*tim* ÁS UG$_6$. Sollberger *1980:* 136 renders: "Whomever the king curses, or the district curses, or the country curses, shall die." I would prefer to regard king-district-country as objects, and death as punishment of the offender, rendering: "Whoever curses the king … shall die". While the passage as a whole is still disputed, the first word *ma-nu-ma*, which concerns us primarily, is not in doubt. For the relative *ma-nu-ma* see also lines 575ff. (and cf. at once note 63.)

61 Thureau-Dangin *1907:* 172, no. xiii, i: 9 (quoted in CAD A/ii 136b). On Annubanini, see Gadd *1971:* 444.

62 Perhaps because the relative form is eminently suited for proclamations; see pp. 109f., below.

Middle Assyrian Laws *awilum ša* is only of very minor importance: it occurs only in two sections, 40[63] and B 6. Finally, in the Neo-Babylonian laws, *awilum ša* has prevailed, displacing *šumma awilum* completely. The Hebrew equivalent of *awilum ša, iš ašer*, is in frequent use in the priestly legislation (see especially Leviticus 20:9-21).

This completes our description of forms in the LE. It is submitted that the use of several different formulations justifies the assumption that the LE have been compiled from a variety of earlier sources.

THE "SETTING IN LIFE"

Admittedly more speculative is the attempt to trace the origin, the "setting in life", of some of these forms. It is because of this difference in definiteness that it may be convenient to separate the two parts of the discussion: what has already been said is in no way dependent on the validity of what follows.

Lists of prices. Lists of prices, such as that given in LE 1, may have their origin in the actual life of the retail market. It is striking that we are not told the prices of the various commodities listed per basic unit of weight or measure; rather we see that a simple unit of weight of the silver, one shekel, is made the constant by which the quantities of the goods vary.[64] This is not the way one would expect an administrator to draw up a list of prices, and indeed in sec. 2, where the equivalents in barley of certain kinds of oil are given, it is the barley (the medium of exchange) which is the variant while the quantity of oils is constant. But the practice of referring to a simple unit of money, rather than to a simple unit of the commodity being offered for sale, is one that can be observed even today in actual retail market life, with the vendors loudly proclaiming the cheapness of their merchandise: "Only today, X (units of weight) for one (unit of money)." The origin of the formulation as a market slogan is suggested also by its elliptical way of expression. Contrary to what one finds in the sections on hire, the corresponding

63 On the peculiarities of MAL 40, see Yaron *1962b:* 147f; also Petschow *1965a.*
The mixed use of relative and conditional formulation in the same passage — where the main clause commences relatively, and subprovisions are introduced by *šumma* also makes its début in TM.75.G.2420, lines 575-590.

64 Cf. Lewy *1949:* 48.

word "price" is omitted altogether: "1 kor barley for 1 shekel silver", etc.[65] The legislator makes use of everyday market language for his purposes, which may be the restriction of prices, or even their reduction.

Comparable lists of prices occur in a variety of sources.[66] There are differences of formulation, but there is no need to go into minutiae. I consider the sequence of LE 1 (commodity first and then "1 shekel" at the end of each line, altogether 10 times!) much the best:[67] it is excellent advertising.[68] By contrast, the opposite sequence, having the price proclaimed first, seems dull and listless, because of the delay in offering the actual information.

The conditional sentence. The casuistic *šumma awilum* formulation is well known and has been much discussed.[69] Many scholars maintain that it originated in the courts of law, but one ought to beware of being too definitive. It has been pointed out that the conditional form is prominent in the so-called omina literature, and this leads to the description of the CH as being part of the Mesopotamian "scientific literature" (wissenschaftliche Literatur).[70] Indeed, one should not overestimate the significance of the use of the conditional *šumma awilum* (and its Sumerian equivalent TUKUMBI LÚ) in sources of different nature. It is convenient to use, and wanders easily. The

65 Contrast the formulation in the HL: e.g., sec. 178: "Of a plow-ox, 12 shekel silver (is) its price."

66 See Goetze *1956:* 29; Petschow *1968a:* 135.

67 Fully parallel to the formulation in LE is the list in the Old Aramaic inscription of Panammuwa II (2nd half of 8th century), no 215 in Donner-Röllig *1962*. Close in time with this is II Kings 7: 1, 16, 18.

68 In our times, it could have served as a TV-jingle: a single person announcing quantities and commodities, and a chorus chanting the refrain *ana 1 šiqil kaspim*.

69 See, e.g., Meek *1946:* 64ff.; Driver-Miles *1952:* 42 (note 1), 443 (note 2); Alt *1934:* 12ff.

70 See, above all, Kraus *1960:* 288. This description is to be read with the more modest definition of Old Mesopotamian "wissenschaftliches Schrifttum ... als systematische Aufzeichnung von Wissenswertem in nicht poetischer Form". For a detailed discussion see also Westbrook *1985a:* 251ff. The discussion concerning the nature of CH (and no less so that of LE), is still in the stage of speculation. A resolution of these problems is not attempted within this book, but see some further remarks, pp. 121ff., below, in the discussion of *ṣimdatum*.

substantive import of the similarity, even if the result of borrowing, is difficult to assess. But, above all, one should bear in mind that *šumma awilum* is well attested — and that in a specifically legal context — already in Ebla, at a period for which there is no evidence of any "scientific" writings, nor reason to postulate their existence. All that can be asserted with confidence is the existence of well-developed scribal schools, but these would concentrate on the immediate tools of their trade (word-lists etc.) and on copying for purposes of practice.

Within the sphere of law itself, priority may indeed go to courts: they may well have preceded legislation. But, even if *šumma awilum* was first used in the courts, it might later have been adopted by the legislator, for a variety of purposes. We have mentioned its use, by Hammurabi, even for the regulation of prices and hire; but we shall see that for some purposes it was not quite satisfactory.

As for the split protasis, *awilum* ... *šumma*, we have already suggested that it may be closely related to *šumma awilum*. Its rarity in the collections of laws, and more frequent occurrence in contracts, may mean that it actually originated in notarial practice,[71] and was in a few instances transplanted into laws (in the LE), merging with *šumma awilum*. We have tried to elucidate the reasons which may account for its failure to take root.

The apodictic formulation. From the point of view of style, the apodictic formulation is the simplest of all. The "ifs" and "buts" have been discarded, what remains is the naked command: "he shall not do",[72] or, less frequently, a positive order (or permission).[73] The very peremptoriness of the apodictic form, its tone of "no-nonsense", show that it comes from the ruler himself, or from some subordinate authority to whom he has seen fit to delegate his powers.[74]

71 And see already Kraus *1960:* 289, and note 42, there.

72 In biblical legislation the usual form is that of direct address, employing the second person, singular ("thou shalt" or "thou shalt not"), or plural ("you shall" or "you shall not"). This divergence should not be regarded as basic.

73 See LE 52, CH /39 (permission following upon the prohibition in 38/), 40. In the Bible, see, e.g., Genesis 2:16 (general permission), followed by verse 17 (specific prohibition plus sanction); see also the dietary laws, Deuteronomy 14:3ff.

74 A. Alt regarded the apodictic formulation as specifically Israelite, but this view must be abandoned, especially because of LE 15, 16. Other early

The relative formulation. Contrary to *šumma awilum*, the relative formulation *(awilum ša)* has so far received little attention. *šumma awilum* and *awilum ša* are both "natural" modes of expression; it need cause no surprise that their equivalents occur in many different sources, by no means confined to the ancient Near East. The basic considerations and conclusions will apply to all of these, even though the use of identical or closely similar forms of this kind need not be regarded as indicating dependence or contact between the various sources.

Daube *1956:* 6ff. has contrasted the conditional form *(si)*, which was predominant in early Roman legislation, with the relative form *(qui, quicumque)*, which gained prominence at a later stage. He sees here "an evolution from what we might call folk-law to a legal system". The relative form is "more general, abstract, detached". The conditional form is "contemplating a particular emergency, the other of a systematic character". However valid these observations may be in the Roman context, for the early Orient they are open to question, once one finds conditional and relative formulations side by side as early as Ebla. So early a date makes it difficult to postulate still earlier developments.

In any case, there still remains the question of origins. It does not seem probable that the relative form owes its emergence to a draftsman's desire for abstraction and systematization. More likely the legislator, in his quest for these, made use of a form which had developed very early in a particular sphere — that of proclamation. In this particular sphere the conditional formulation is much too leisurely, academic, does not rise to the urgency of the situation. Proclamations may differ widely in the nature of their contents. Possibly the earliest and most important use of the proclamation is the issue of a command, and more particularly the threat of punishment for disobeying it. But there may also be the offer of a reward ("Auslobung") for some service (especially a difficult one). There are also "neutral" proclamations, involving neither threat nor offer. For all these the relative sentence is a suitable form; it is addressed to the public at large, but not in its capacity as an entity, rather to every individual in it. The proclamation was not the exclusive domain of the authorities. Any humble citizen might use it, e.g., offering a reward for the return of lost property, or for

parallels have been adduced: see Gevirtz *1961:* 137ff.; Kilian *1963:* 185ff.; Williams *1964:* 484ff.

some information.[75] However, the public proclamation is very much in the foreground, and that not only because of the nature of our sources.

Some texts, chosen at random, may serve as examples for the various types of proclamation. For threats, one may mention two situations which will have been common: (i) the military call-up, and the need to ensure obedience to it,[76] (ii) improper dealing with booty.[77] In cuneiform sources I am not aware of any proclamation embodying an actual offer of a reward, but this is probably merely an accident of transmission. There is no reason to doubt that they occurred from time to time, and that they were couched in the form which we are discussing. Biblical examples refer to difficult military exploits,[78] and to the interpretation of a royal dream.[79] As examples of "neutral" proclamations one may mention some provisions in the edict of Ammi-ṣaduqa.[80]

In a majority of cases the proclamation looks to the future, is aimed at encouraging (or discouraging, as the case may be) certain behaviour.[81] But this desire to influence future behaviour need not always be present, especially not in those cases where the proclamation is a neutral one.

75 A good example of a proclamation for private purposes is that contained in MAL B 6. The intention to purchase land had to be proclaimed in public, so that whoever *(ša)* objected might have opportunity to come forward.

76 See ARM I, 6 (lines 16ff.): All are to assemble. "The sheikh whose *(suqaqum ša)* men will not assemble ... will have eaten the *asakkum* of the king." ("Eating the *asakkum* of the king" probably implied sacrilege, with obvious consequences.) For threats in case of failure to obey a call-up see also I Samuel 11:7. And compare Ezra 10:8.

77 ARM II, 13 (lines 25ff.); V, 72 (lines 12ff.). Two points may be noted. Where the antecedent is the general term *awilum*, it may be omitted (II, 13). In order to make the threat more impressive the construction of the sentence may be changed, so that the sanction is mentioned first (so in both these texts). For further threatening proclamations in the Bible see Yaron *1962b:* 151.

78 Joshua 15:16 = Judges 1:12; Judges 10:18; I Samuel 17:25.

79 Daniel 5:7.

80 E.g., secs. 5, 8, 9, 16, 17. In the Bible see Deuteronomy 20:5-8, the proclamation — on the eve of battle — releasing certain persons from the army.

81 Note, in particular, proclamations in Deuteronomy 25:9, and in Esther 6:9-11: both deal with past occurrences, but with the eye clearly also on the future; and see Yaron *1962b:* 152.

Sources of the LE

This ends our discussion of forms and their origins, and it remains now to apply the results which we have obtained to the LE. The attempt to attribute various sections of the LE to particular sources is necessarily of a tentative character, and our suggestions are presented with all reserve. Quite generally speaking, one may assume that the rules of behaviour embodied in the Laws will in the main have had their origin either (i) in the activities — in various spheres — of the ruler, or (ii) in litigation (judge-made-law). It will indeed be difficult to separate the two, but one may, for a start, rely on the formal elements set out above. Our hypothesis will be the following: all sections not using *šumma awilum* reflect one form or another of "statute" law; most of the sections using *šumma awilum*, but not all of them, reflect litigation and precedents ("common law").[82] Let us now see how this works out.

The regulations concerning prices, hire etc., will necessarily have their origin in the command of a competent authority. This disposes of 11 sections.[83] To these we should be inclined to add also sec. 41, which is essentially of a regulatory nature, even though the conditional *šumma* formulation is used.

Other sections issuing from an authoritative source are secs. 12, 13 (proclamations concerning trespass), 15, 16 (apodictic restrictions on the contracts of certain persons), 19 (a provision on loans — in proclamation form), 51, 52 (apodictic police [?] regulations). Of these, sec. 19 deserves special attention, in view of its subject matter: Why should a provision concerning a loan be couched in terms of a proclamation? The verb *šuddunum* — "to cause to give" (that is, to exact, to collect), which occurs in the section, may provide the clue. In its actual import, it is the equivalent of the verb *lequm* — "to take", used in the two subsequent sections, 20 and 21; *šuddunum* does not occur in the CH, but is regularly employed in the edict of Ammi-ṣaduqa, in the negative expression *ul ušaddan* — "he shall not collect".[84] It is therefore suggested that LE 19 may have been "lifted" out of an early edict providing, like that of Ammi-ṣaduqa, for the abolition of certain debts. If this is correct, it would follow that the text underwent alteration. The

82 Compare also the remarks of Finkelstein *1960:* 102f.
83 See p. 98, above.
84 See secs. 3, 17. For a discussion of *šuddunum* see Kraus *1958:* 47ff., revised in Kraus *1984:* 196ff.

original proclamation will probably have read *awilum ša ana mehrišu iddinu ul ušaddan* — "a man who has given *ana mehrišu*[85] shall not collect". When incorporated in the LE, the passage was emended (i) by changing the tense of *nadanum* ("to give"), from praeteritum to present, so as to make it accord with the formulation usual in proclamations relating to future events (see secs. 12, 13); (ii) more important — a date of payment was substituted for the negative provision of the original.

So far we have in the main relied on formal indications, but in some cases the substance may also be suggestive. So one may assume that sec. 50, concerning the behaviour of certain officials, and the reaction of the palace which is to be expected, were of an official character. Sec. 34/35 proclaims rights of the palace, and may be assumed to have been issued by it. Our deliberations concerning the *muškenum* (pp. 138f., 153, below) lead us to believe that every occurrence of this term indicates an authoritative source; this would add to our list sec. /24, which is a complement of the precedents laid down in secs. 22 and 23/.[86] Sec. 48 belongs to this group because of its contents, the delimitation of jurisdiction; sec. 58 because of its reference to *ṣimdat šarrim* — "decree of the king". Finally, because of their wide formulation and concern for detail, I should include also secs. 40 and 49.

These considerations yield two groups of sections: (i) those derived from a decree (of one kind or another); in addition to the directly regulatory provisions, we should assign to this group sections 12, 13, 15, 16, 19, /24, 34/35, 40, 41, 48, 49, 50 51, 52, and 58; (ii) those based on precedent, including sections 5, 6, 9, 17/18, 20, 21, 22, 23/, 25, 26, 27/28, 29, 30, 31, 32, 33, 36/37, 38, 39, 42, 43, 44/45, 46, 47, 47A, 53, 54/55, 56/57, and 59.

Comparison of the two groups may be of interest. It suggests that the sections based on precedent are, on the whole, of a rather narrowly defined formulation. A judgement may have to start from a complicated set of facts, it may even include two different results, based on alternative factual data (see secs. 17/18, 27/28, 36/37), but it will only rarely cumulate parallel, equivalent facts.[87] A typical example of

85 See pp. 236f., below.
86 See a similar suggestion by Haase *1965:* 144.
87 We speak of derivation; this does not exclude compilatorial interference. While secs. 27/28, 36/37 are likely to be based on precedent, their top-heavy form suggests reshaping.

precedent is furnished by secs. 22 and 23/, concerning a slave woman seized in distress.[88] This is a very specific formulation, which suggests that these sections may reflect an actual occurrence.[89] The combination of equivalents indicates the "statutory" origin of a provision, or at least reformulation by the compiler. Such a cumulation may occasionally be useful, when it serves to bring within the scope of a provision cases which are not obviously identical; so in sec. 16, referring to a *mar awilim la zizu* ("a coparcener son of a man") and to a slave *(wardum)*.[90] But this is the exception, not the rule. A favourite cumulation is that of the sexes, where identity of the ruling (as has just been noted) would anyhow not have been in doubt. The difference becomes pronounced when one contrasts the precedent-derived sections 22, 23/, /55, /57, with those based on "statute", secs. 15, 50, 51, 52.[91] Equally significant is the contrast between sec. 33, concerning the son of a slave woman, and sec. 34/ which takes care to specify (twice) "son or daughter".

We may sum up as follows: The LE are a collection of provisions derived from a variety of sources; they show a measure of integration, but this has not been carried through in a systematic fashion. There is no way of knowing whether the Laws in their present form represent the efforts of a compiler, or whether the material had already undergone change before it reached his hands.

88 See in detail, pp. 275ff., below.

89 Note that an *amtum* ("slave woman") is mentioned, not a *wardum* ("slave"), in contrast to CH 116. As a rule, and in the absence of any inherent impossibility or specific reason to the contrary, it may be assumed that the masculine (*awilum, marum, wardum* etc.) includes the feminine (*sinništum, martum, amtum,* etc.), but not *vice versa*. Cf. *Digesta Iustiniani* 31.45 pr: "... non est ex contrario accipiendum, ut filiarum nomine etiam masculi contineantur: exemplo enim pessimum est feminino vocabulo etiam masculos contineri." See also the detailed discussion of this problem of interpretation in Yaron *1968:* 60ff.

90 See pp. 158ff., below.

91 We disregard secs. 40 and 49, so as not to become involved in circuitous reasoning.

CHAPTER FOUR

ADMINISTRATION, COURTS, PROCEDURE

Fragmentary information

Concerning the administration of the kingdom of Eshnunna, its system of courts and the procedure followed in them, the LE convey only very limited and fragmentary information. It may be said to consist only of some odds and ends, a word here, a phrase there, to be collected from all over the material. In this respect the LE are in marked contrast with CH, which allots a prominent place, at the very beginning, to such matters as false accusations, evidence, ordeal, misbehaviour of judges, and the like. This difference becomes especially marked where a topic is treated in both sources. LE 40, on the purchase of stolen property, limits itself to the laconic statement that the buyer *la ukin* — "has not established" the identity of the seller; this is to be compared with the enumeration of details and possibilities, step by step, in CH 9-13. One gets the impression that the interest of LE centers on the question of substance rather than on procedure and proof. This state of the material will necessarily determine the character of the chapter, since it cannot be our wish to deal in any detail with matters not reflected in the text itself.

Organization of the realm: King and Palace

One is left almost completely in the dark about what might be called in modern terminology — the constitutional structure of the realm, and the organization of its administration. At the top there are the king (LUGAL = *šarrum*) and the palace (É.GAL = *ekallum*). Though closely related, they are by no means freely interchangeable, and their demarcation might be significant. Certain powers are specifically reserved to the king. So the jurisdiction in capital cases (LE 48; incidentally, such reservation need not preclude delegation). He is mentioned (LE 58) as the source of a particular provision, the promulgator of a *ṣimdatum* ("decree, ordinance, regulation").[1] Beyond the specific, one may assume that residuary powers, i.e. powers not expressly allotted to others, will also have been vested in the king.

By contrast, the palace is rather elusive, impersonal, amorphous. It may denote the "administration",[2] those who run the day-to-day affairs of the realm, ultimately at the king's behest, — but in fact relieving him of a great part of the burden and presumably often acting on their own. The palace too occurs twice in the LE, in secs. 34/35 and 50.[3] In the first it figures in a private capacity, as the owner of a slave child which had been delivered by its mother to an outsider. Its function in sec. 50 is not as obvious: the palace is indeed mentioned (together with the *muškenum*) as owner of lost property which had been misappropriated (Tablet B iv 8), but the final provision, threatening intervention by the palace, need not depend on ownership. It may reflect the fact that the culprit is a public official.

"CITY AND MASTER"

An expression *alšu u belšu* — "his city and his master", occurs in LE 30; this section concerns the marital rights of a man who "hated *(izir)* his city and his master", and absconded.[4] The city figures in Old Babylonian legal texts, *inter alia*, in compound phrases, like *alum u rabianum* — "the city and the mayor",[5] or *alum u šibutum* — "the city and the elders",[6] but there is in them no parallel to *alum u belum* — "city

1 Note also the reference to "kingship", in line 3 of the heading.
2 For *ekallum*, see Driver-Miles *1952:* 107, note 4; a good description is "die Beamten im Regierungsgebäude" (Kraus *1973:* 75); in substance, this is not very different from "Verwaltung" (offered already by Walther *1917:* 149). The rendering "Palast, palace" (for which lastly Kraus *1984:* 329) has the advantage of avoiding too close links with modern terminology. The term "Obrigkeit", occasionally employed by Kraus, is too German in its flavour.
3 The actual situation may have varied from king to king: see Kraus *1974a:* 259, remarking that "die eigentlichen Entscheidungen dem König persönlich vorbehalten waren, von dessen Laune und Charakter es wohl auch abhing, wie intensiv er sich mit der Verwaltung beschäftigte".
4 The same situation is dealt with also in CH 136; for a different case of political entanglement see MAL B 3.
5 See CH 23, 24.
6 Schorr *1913*, no. 259: 19f.; for additional references see CAD A/i 383.

and master" (or "lord"), which seems altogether vague and of uncertain import.[7] If *belum* refers to the king, one wonders why his usual title — *šarrum* — is not employed; also one would expect him to be mentioned first. An explanation may possibly be found, if one is justified in tracing the origin of this expression to a similar one occurring several times in Old Assyrian texts close in time to the LE.[8] It is usual to interpret *alum* in these texts as referring to Assur, the City (just as *urbs*, without further specification, often refers to Rome[9]), and *belum* as the *Stadtfürst*, the Prince of Assur.[10] The fact that the City is given precedence over the Prince is explained by its being endowed with divine attributes, being actually identified with the god Assur. The personification (or rather deification) of the city finds expression also in the oath formulae *niš alim* — "oath of the City",[11] or *niš alim u ruba'im* — "oath of the City and the Prince",[12] in which *alum* takes the place which is ordinarily reserved for the deity.[13]

It is then submitted that *alšu u belšu* of LE 30 may have been derived from an Assyrian provision, dealing with one who hated "the City and his Lord" *(alam u belšu)*, in other words became involved in subversive activities, directed against the ruler, hence by implication also against the patron deity.[14] If this is correct, it may bear also on the dating of the

7 For *alu u belu* in omen texts see CAD A/i 383b (top), 388b (top).

8 See Eisser-Lewy, nos. 253 (and VAT 9261, quoted there), 325a: *ana alim u belia awati bila* — "bring my matter to the City and my master". Eisser-Lewy, no. 298 provides that certain tablets *maḫar alim u belini iššakkunu* — "be deposited before the City and our master". In Eisser-Lewy, nos. 325 and 326, there is a request that *alum u belum dini liddin* — "the City and the master may judge my case". And see already Szlechter *1965:* 290, note 6.

9 See Quintilianus 6.3.103: "urbis appellationem etiamsi nomen proprium non adicieretur, Romam tamen accipi, sit receptum."

10 See Landsberger *1925:* 8; Goetze *1957:* 72; Garelli *1963:* 324f.; Larsen *1974:* 295; CAD A/i 383, 388a.

11 E.g., Eisser-Lewy, nos. 6, 9, 239, 241, etc.

12 E.g., Eisser-Lewy, nos. 253, 306, 325a.

13 The name of the city as part of the oath formula occurs occasionally also in documents from Sippar: e.g., in Schorr *1913:* nos. 2, 32, 86, 87, 169, 182. There is, however, the significant difference that in the Sippar documents the city usually comes last, after god(s) and the king (no. 32 has town before king; in text 169 the king is omitted).

14 Cf. I Kings 21: 10, 13. For a close connection of the spiritual and the temporal, see also *Digesta Iustiniani* 48.4.1 pr: "Proximum sacrilegio est crimen quod maiestatis dicitur."

LE, since the short period when Assyria is believed to have been governed by Naramsin, King of Eshnunna,[15] would be particularly suitable for such a reception. This would bring the Laws very near to the times of Hammurabi.[16]

It should be stressed that our remarks are confined to the phrase as such. The import, context and consequences need not have been the same. As for the import, one ought to note that in LE the suffix *-šu* is added: the City becomes "his city", any city. It is a return to the local, provincial level. Thereby the reference to *belum* becomes awkward and incongruous, giving rise to the questions which have already been noted. If the king is meant by *belum*, what place remains for *alum* at his side, as the object of "hatred"? As for the context, in LE 30 only the highly personal matter of a fugitive's rights vis-à-vis his wife is in issue, but the postulated Assyrian source of "hating the City and his master" may have dealt with the situation on a much wider basis. The consequences are in turn determined by the context: in LE all that happens is that on his return home the husband is denied the power of interfering with a second marriage which his wife may have contracted.[17] A political undertone is indeed present in LE 30, but it is weak and no stress is put on it.

While the Assyrian element in this provision of the LE is admittedly a matter of hypothesis only, one is on considerably firmer ground when comparing LE 30 with the corresponding section 136 of CH.[18]

OFFICIALS

LE 50 mentions the title of some officials, who may possibly have been involved in the misappropriation of fugitive slaves or stray cattle. Those specified are the *šakkanakkum* (GÌR.NITÁ), *šapir narim* and *bel tertim*. The task which they ought to have fulfilled — the seizure of lost property and its delivery to Eshnunna — is of a purely administrative

15 Cf. Landsberger *1954:* 35, note 24; Edzard *1957:* 164.
16 Naramsin was followed on the throne of Eshnunna by his brother Dadusha, who was an early contemporary of Hammurabi; see p. 20, note 6, above.
17 See pp. 208f., below.
18 For a detailed discussion of the relation between the two sections, see pp. 89ff., above.

nature, but it does not enable us to delimit exactly the scope of their functions. The *šakkanakkum* is the king's highest representative in a particular town;[19] as such he takes an active and leading part also in the adjudication of lawsuits.[20] He is usually designated as the *šakkanakkum* of a town, e.g. of Šaduppum,[21] in one text also as *šakkanak šarrim* — "*šakkanakkum* of the king".[22]

The position occupied in the hierarchy by the *šapir narim* is below that of the *šakkanakkum*, and this is indicated also by his place in the list. In Old Babylonian texts there occur various officials who bear the title of *šapirum* — "one who issues commands" *(Gebieter)*; the noun is derived from *šaparum*, basically "to send", hence "to send an order, to command", etc. As for the *šapir narim*, his main task will have been to supervise the system of irrigation, of vital importance to the economy of the country, but one finds him exercising also other functions, including judicial ones.[23] By contrast, it would appear that *bel tertim* is not the designation of a specific official, rather it is a general term denoting "person of authority";[24] there is then no room for any further definition of it.

THE WARD *(babtum)*

Another legal entity occurring in the LE is the *babtum* — "ward, district". In secs. 54/, 56/, and 58, the *babtum* has the function of giving the owner due warning (*ana belišu ušedi* — "had [it] made known to its owner") concerning the dangers arising out of the fact that his ox is a gorer (respectively, that his dog is vicious, or a wall of his house is sagging). We do not know how the ward went about its business, e.g., by what procedure it gained cognizance of the matter; but the occurrence of such functionaries as the *wakil babtim* — "overseer of the

19 For remarks on this official and the variety of his functions, see Schorr *1913:* 341; Landsberger *1915:* 508; Walther *1917:* 127ff.; Förtsch *1917:* 160ff.; Krückmann *1932:* 445a; Goetze *1956:* 127.

20 See, e.g., HG III (1909) no. 743; Schorr *1913*, no. 275.

21 See Goetze *1958:* 14, text 1 (IM 51503).

22 Quoted by Goetze, *ibid.*, p. 11, note 19, from IM 51652 (unpublished).

23 See Walther *1917:* 143ff.; Krückmann, *ibid.*

24 So Goetze *1956:* 127. AHw 120b renders "Beauftragter", "Kommissär". Note also ARM I, 61, lines 29-30: *šumma bel tertim* UD 2 KAM UD 3 KAM *la uwer tertum ul iḫalliq* — "If a *bel tertim* did not issue orders for two days (or) three days, would the administration not disappear?"

ward",[25] and its *redum* — "runner",[26] shows that the *babtum* had developed a definite organizational structure.

In LE, and also in CH 251/ (which corresponds to LE 54/), the task of the *babtum* is one of supervision and prevention: on the one hand it is desired to anticipate trouble and forestall it, on the other hand the notice given serves to lay the foundation for the liability of the owner — in case he does not heed the warning and damage ensues.[27] Although in the LE the occurrence of the *babtum* is confined to this one topic, it adds to our knowledge in one respect: LE 58 goes beyond CH 251/, in that it concerns a source of imminent danger which is inanimate; this widening of the ward's duty and of its competence would not necessarily have been obvious.

CH 126 and 142/143 show us further functions of the *babtum*. The former gives expression to duties of the ward, rather than to its powers: a man claims that property of his has been lost, and accuses his *babtum* in this connection. When his allegation is shown to be unfounded, he has to pay a double penalty to the *babtum*. It is a necessary implication that in certain circumstances, that is to say if the claim had been true, the *babtum* might have been liable to make good the loss.[28] In sec. 142/143 the *babtum* is charged with the finding of facts in a severe conflict between a husband and his wife; it is unlikely that the *babtum* was itself competent to render judgement, since the case may have involved the capital punishment of the wife.

JURISDICTION

LE 48 should now be considered. The section is poorly preserved, and perhaps altogether incomplete;[29] it deals with matters of jurisdiction, assigning cases involving a penalty from 20 to 60 shekels to some tribunal the designation of which has been lost,[30] but reserving *awat*

25 See, e.g., ARM VI, 43, line 18.
26 Schorr *1913*, no. 123, line 6.
27 See pp. 297f., below.
28 It would take us too far to go into all the details and difficulties. But see the comment of Driver-Miles *1952:* 244f., who regard CH 126 as concerning a case of deposit.
29 See p. 28, above.
30 For various restorations which have been proposed, see the notes to the section, p. 72, above.

napištim — "a charge (concerning) life" (i.e., "capital" cases) for the king. Nothing comparable occurs in any other cuneiform collection of laws.[31] It has been noted that the extant text does not provide for the adjudication of cases where the penalty is below 20 shekels, as in the preceding sections 42 (for *meḫeṣ letim* — "a slap in the face") and 47 (for a bodily injury, the nature and circumstances of which are not yet clear to us). The absence of any provision for cases in excess of 60 shekels (= 1 mina) may be due to the fact that the LE (just as later the CH) do not impose fixed penalties higher than that sum.

The term *awat napištim* (and also *din napištim* — "a case of life") has usually been understood as implying that the life of the accused is in jeopardy: his conviction will (or may) result in the imposition of the death penalty. This may indeed be the rule, but a document from Mari shows that a stiff pecuniary penalty may sometimes have been substituted. In ARM VIII, 1 a payment of 200 shekels is provided in case of contravention of an undertaking, and this sum is termed *kasap din napištim* — "silver of a case of life".[32] Indeed, one must not lose sight of the difference of context: the document from Mari is a contract. Nevertheless, it seems reasonable to assume that the substitution of silver for life will have had its origin in the sphere of judgements in matters of delict, with the sovereign exercising his power of mercy.[33] The fact that the death penalty is not expressly mentioned in LE 58 may indicate that composition was possible.

Another point emerges rather clearly from the fragmentary LE 48. There was in legal Akkadian of the Old Babylonian period (or at least in the LE) no abstract term for "jurisdiction". As a somewhat clumsy substitute, LE 48 uses the preposition *ana*, in the clause *awat napištim ana šarrimma* — "a charge (concerning) life (belongs) to the king himself".[34]

31 See Korošec *1964:* 90.

32 See already the remarks of Boyer *1958:* 168; also Petschow *1958:* 562, note 60. Compare further the phrase *napšate mullu* in MAL 50, 52, C 3; ARM XIII 145. For a discussion of this phrase see Driver-Miles *1935:* 110ff.; Cardascia *1969:* 242; Paul *1970:* 72; Finkelstein *1981:* 22, note 1.

33 Cf. Yaron *1962a:* 245ff.

34 Somewhat loose is Landsberger's rendering (*1968:* 101), ". . . obliegt dem König"; *ana* does not carry the notion of a duty incumbent on someone. See GAG, sec. 114d; AHw 47f.

THE ROYAL ORDINANCE *(ṣimdat šarrim)*

The phrase *awat napištim unu šarrim* has to be juxtaposed with the phrase *(napištum) ṣimdat šarrim* of LE 58, which has repeatedly been rendered by "jurisdiction of the king".[35] I found "jurisdiction" questionable, either way: if it were the correct rendering of *ṣimdatum*, why was that term not used in sec. 48 (which clearly concerns jurisdiction)? If "jurisdiction" had been intended in sec. 58, would they not have repeated the wording of sec. 48 ... *ana šarrim*? True, the argument is by no means conclusive, but it justifies a closer look at the matter.

The exact import of *ṣimdatum* and *ṣimdat šarrim* has been the subject of repeated discussion, a detailed survey of which was given by Lautner.[36] If some early, overly literal renderings are disregarded, the predominant view could be formulated, with San Nicolò,[37] as follows: *ṣimdat šarrim* is a royal ordinance ("Satzung"), concerning substantive law or procedure.

Enter Landsberger, with a paper which was to have much impact, "Die babylonischen Termini für Gesetz und Recht".[38] While the discussion of *ṣimdatum* occupies central place, it is in fact ancillary to another question, that of the role of (written) laws in Old Babylonian society. In an isolated, but revealing sentence, Landsberger notes: "Wir müssten Gesetzen oder gesetzesartigen Bestimmungen hervorragende Bedeutung im Denken und sozialen Leben der alten Babylonier einräumen, wenn wir berechtigt wären, *ṣimdatu* mit 'Gesetz' oder 'Satzung' zu übersetzen" (p. 225). This observation is not continued. It is only its formulation, as an unreal supposition, which guides the reader to supply his own (negative!) conclusion: "wir sind nicht berechtigt".

Why this concentration on *ṣimdatum*? The term occurs in a considerable (and growing) number of Old Babylonian texts, and its accepted rendering by "Gesetz" or "Satzung" was a major obstacle in the endeavour to redefine the nature of the CH (and, one may add, also

35 So Goetze, in all his translations; followed by Böhl, Korošec, Haase (both translations), Bottéro. See also CAD Ṣ 195b; Petschow *1968a:* 140, note 5. Similar is the term "Verfahren", Kraus *1979:* 61.

36 Lautner *1936:* 177-190; and see especially p. 177, note 527.

37 *1931:* 68f.

38 *1939:* 219-234.

the other Old Babylonian law texts).[39] But, perhaps, that obstacle was imaginary only, and would disappear once one had achieved a better, more penetrating understanding of *ṣimdatum*?

An examination with ulterior motives in mind has its obvious risks. Too easily one might be led astray by the desire to achieve a particular result. "Der Wunsch ist der Vater des Gedankens": even scholars should heed the warning implicit in this proverb. Peer criticism is an important corrective, but unfortunately it is not always applied impartially. Towering figures may — in fact though never in theory — be exempt from it.

At the very beginning of his paper (p. 220, top), Landsberger observes that *ṣimdatum* "wurde bisher allgemein mit 'Gesetz' oder 'Satzung' übersetzt...;[40] insbesondere in der Verbindung *ṣimdat šarrim* schien diese Übersetzung voll gerechtfertigt; aber im folgenden soll gezeigt werden, dass sie viel zu eng ist, dass *ṣimdatu* zwar die Gesetze mit einschliesst, aber die gesamte geltende Rechtsexekutive, einschliesslich aller ungeschriebenen Regeln und Praktiken, umfasst". In this fashion, the alleged semantic scope of *ṣimdatum* is considerably broadened. In effect, this means also that the concrete import of the term is much diluted: what had been specific, more or less well-defined, has become non-descript, vague.

39 For a description of the switch in attitude, see Kraus *1960:* 283f. "Seit ihrer Entdeckung gilt die Inschrift der in Susa gefundenen Stele des Ḫammurabi, als ein Gesetzbuch ... Der Codex Ḫammurabi, wie die Inschrift seit ihrer Veröffentlichung heisst, wurde als Gesetzbuch behandelt, interpretiert, kommentiert, analysiert. Koschaker half 1917 der Meinung zum Durchbruch, es handle sich um 'einmal Kodifikation und zum anderen Reform' ..."
"Für die vergleichenden Rechtshistoriker war der Codex Ḫammurabi längst zum Mittelpunkte des altbabylonischen Rechtes und zum Fundament aller ihrer Arbeiten über altmesopotamisches Recht geworden, als Eilers *1932:* 8, ein Schüler von Koschaker und Landsberger, unter dem Einflusse Landsbergers 1932 den Verdacht äusserte, dass 'das grosse Gesetzgebungswerk des Königs nur Repräsentation geblieben und niemals Rechtswirklichkeit geworden sei'."

40 There are many near-synonymous renderings into German. AHw 1102 renders throughout "königliche Verordnung". Kraus, *1979:* 58, uses, for part of the texts "(königliche) Massregel". We shall stick with "Satzung", without objecting to any of the others.

It is of significance, that Landsberger does not, cannot exclude the rendering "Satzung"; this finds expression also elsewhere.[41] Incidentally, this points to a major weakness in Landsberger's position. Unable to replace "Satzung" throughout by one different term, he is forced to opt for multiple renderings.[42] As a matter of method, this means that the basic rendering, accepted by all (i.e., also by Landsberger) which sees *ṣimdatum* as a royal *fiat*, must serve as a starting point, for every single text. He who wishes to deny it can do so only for particular occurrences, and has to show why "Satzung" is not suitable. Otherwise too much room is left for arbitrariness, and resulting uncertainty. So, for example, Landsberger's rendering of *ṣimdat šarrim* in CH 51 and M (= 89) has not found response.[43]

In his detailed discussion Landsberger accords excessive significance to the host of prepositions by which *ṣimdatum* is governed. The import of *ṣimdatum* does not depend upon the divergences in import of *kima, ana, ina* (and the like). An interesting point is made concerning *warki* ("after"): this has to be taken in a temporal sense, and refers to legal acts which are later than a given *ṣimdatum* (and therefore not affected by it).

41 See p. 226: "Wir entnehmen diesen Belegen, dass *ṣimdatum* sich auf ein Gesetz oder dessen Inhalt beziehen kann", or, at p. 230, where he renders *ṣimdatam šakanum* by "(allgemein) Recht schaffen", and explains this as "synonym mit *mešaram šakanu* — 'gerechte Ordnung schaffen'".

42 Multiple renderings may be necessary, but require justification. And see the discussion on *muškenum*, pp. 132ff., below (and already YLE, pp. 83ff.).

43 For Landsberger *ṣimdat šarrim* in these two sections means "dass für die in ausserordentlichen Fällen zugelassene Umwandlung von Geld- in Naturaldarlehen gerichtliche Regelung vorgeschrieben war" (p. 230). The reasoning that follows is tortuous, leading even to the assertion that in CH 51 the phrase *ana pi ṣimdat šarrim* may be an addition ("Zusatz"). By contrast, Driver-Miles render "ordinances of the king"; and so Finet, "ordonnances du roi". Meek (*1950:* 168f.) has "ratio fixed by the king", and comparably, CAD Ṣ 195b, "royal tariff". Lastly, see Kraus *1979:* 61f.: "So kann ich nicht glauben, dass in CH 89/M mit den Worten *kima ṣimdat šarrim* 'gerichtliche Regelung' vorgeschrieben wurde, wie Landsberger … denkt." And, "… nach modernem Gefühl scheint mir hier 'nach diesem Paragraphen' beabsichtigt … Der nur einmal belegte Ausdruck *ana pi ṣimdat šarrim* in CH 51 scheint mir die Auffassung 'gemäss diesem Paragraphen' zu bestätigen. Landsbergers Erklärung ist gezwungen."

But even here the essence of *ṣimdatum* as a royal ordinance remains the same. That ordinances may have a wide range of use, may differ considerably, is not denied.

Occasionally correct, literal renderings are modified by "explanatory" paraphrases. At p. 226, note 33, the phrase *kima ṣimdati ša maḫrika ibaššu* is translated "... gemäss der *ṣimdatum*, die vor Dir ist (die Du besitzest) ...". The literal rendering is quite sufficient, but if a paraphrase is desired, then "die Dir vorliegt" would have been preferable. At p. 227, Landsberger's paraphrase is utilized in forming the notion "richterliche Gewalt, die der Besitz der *ṣimdatum* dem Rechtssprecher gab". If possession indeed enters the picture,[44] it would be simpler and better to see it as referring to the physical possession of a tablet on which the *ṣimdatum* is written out,[45] rather than the abstract power with which a judge would be endowed. Arbitrary is the paraphrase (at p. 231), of *ina ṣimdatim ina manaḫtika ušellika* — "ich werde dich 'nach dem Recht' (durch ein Gerichtsurteil) Deiner Investition verlustig erklären lassen". One fails to see why "nach dem Recht" is preferable to "nach der Satzung", nor why the circumscription "durch ein Gerichtsurteil" is necessary.

So far about Landsberger's paper. It has been much acclaimed, with "grundlegend" as its often-repeated attribute. Its influence peaked in publications such as Kraus *1958:* 244ff.; Kraus *1960* (passim), and Finkelstein *1961:* 103f. I am not aware that Landsberger ever returned to the issues which he had raised.[46]

Later one can discern a gradual retreat from the theses of Landsberger. His propositions concerning the character of Old Babylonian laws were scrutinized by Wolfgang Preiser, and greatly modified, in an important paper, hidden away in a little-read *Festschrift*.[47] 15 years later the views of Preiser were endorsed by Kraus:[48] "Zur Frage der Geltung der 'Gesetze' im modernen Sinne, die ich früher geleugnet

44 This is possible; even more so in the phrase *kima ṣi[md]atim ša ina qatikunu ibaššu,* ABIM 33: 12ff. (quoted in CAD Q 189b).

45 And see AbB i 14: 22, *ana pi ṭuppi ṣimdatim* (noted in YLE, p. 79). Regarding this document, see further Kraus *1984:* 9.

46 Not necessary for our discussion is the footnote inserted by Landsberger, *apud* Kraus *1951:* 158, note 5.

47 *1969:* 17-36.

48 *1984:* 114f.

habe,[49] verweise ich jetzt ... vor allem aber auf Preiser ... eine rechtshistorische Stellungnahme, welche in diesem Punkte meine einseitig philologische Ansichten in für mich akzeptabler Weise korrigiert."

We must return briefly to our immediate topic, *ṣimdatum*, to note how matters developed after the 1939 publication of Landsberger's paper. He gained wide adherence, but there were notable exceptions. Driver-Miles *1952:* 19 continued to hold that "*ṣimdatum* is a concrete term denoting certain definite ordinances and does not mean abstract law or justice". And we have already mentioned the uniform rendering "königliche Verordnung" offered by von Soden in 1974 (AHw). The adherence of CAD Ṣ (1962) to the views of Landsberger was hesitant and lukewarm.

Of additional texts in which *ṣimdatum* occurs, one might note especially two. In 1967 Finkelstein published an Old Babylonian fragment of CH.[50] This is what he says about the colophon: "The colophon, although only partially preserved, is of considerable importance. The preserved lines may be restored and read as follows: DUB *ṣi-im-da-*[*at Ḫa-am-mu-ra-pí*] // ŠU *I-na-é-ul-maš-*NUMUN // DUB.SAR.TUR. This reveals the fact that the term *ṣimdatum* could be used to denote the 'laws'."[51] Two years later Finkelstein published a new fragment of the Edict of Ammi-ṣaduqa.[52] Sec. 4 ends in the following statement: *ša ana ṣimdat šarrim la utaru imat* — "Whoever does not make refund in compliance with the king's ordinance, shall die."[53] Kraus renders "wer nach (diesem) Paragraphen (*scil.* des vorliegenden Edikts) nicht restituiert, muss sterben", and I accept this as "inhaltlich korrekt".[54]

49 Kraus refers to *1960:* 288-292, II and III.
50 *1967:* 39-48.
51 *Ibid.*, p. 42; see also note 4, there.
52 *1969c:* 45-64.
53 *Ibid.*, p. 50; see however, the elaboration in the "Commentary by Sections", p. 58, there: "whoever refuses to make such refund as required by the standing orders of the king shall be put to death"; and see, further, note 4, there: "Here I take *ṣimdat šarrim* as referring not to the edict, but to royally endorsed usage in general, as applicable to any specific set of circumstances" (with reference to Landsberger, p. 220).
54 Kraus, *1979:* 62. Note that here Kraus is in disagreement with Finkelstein (as quoted here, note 53).

Particularly interesting are some texts apparently using *ṣimdatum* in interstate treaties,[55] referring jointly to both the parties. An interpretation, even within the wider, more varied framework suggested by Landsberger, is difficult. Quite hypothetically, one might mention some possibilities. In treaties between unequal partners, an overlord might impose his *ukaz* on his subordinate. This reality might be hinted at by the use of *ṣimdatum*, even though it is called "their" *ṣimdatum*. Treaties between equals might contain provisions necessitating separate decrees in the area subject to each. But all this is quite speculative. One might also contemplate a further possibility, namely that we have here a genuinely different use of *ṣimdatum*.

To sum up: just as in other aspects of the paper, there is growing erosion in the support for Landsberger's analysis of *ṣimdatum*. This process is not yet complete, as long as the division between "Satzung" and "Verfahren" (the terms distilled by Kraus from Landsberger's propositions) continues to be in use, even though with greater caution. As for *ṣimdatum* in LE 58, I see no reason for a switch from "decree"[56] to "jurisdiction", and the like.[57]

Procedure

It remains now to consider those few elements of the procedure followed at Eshnunna, which are discernible in the LE. In sec. 25 occurs the phrase *ana bit X šasum* — "to claim at the house of X". This phrase, it appears, reflects the moment when performance is due. At this stage, resort to a court is not yet actively contemplated, but litigation may follow if a positive response is not forthcoming. It should however be noted that ordinarily the claim is one put by a public authority for the performance of feudal services and extra-judicial coercive measures will have been taken to ensure compliance.[58] In LE 25 the context is one

55 Put together and discussed by Kraus, *1984:* 10f. See also von Soden *1985:* 134.
56 "Decree", and equivalents in other languages, are offered in a series of translations; so in Szlechter *1954* and *1978*, Borger, Saporetti, Bouzon, Kunderewicz. On *ṣimdat šarrim* in LE 58, see further pp. 302f., below.
57 On *ṣimdatum* see lastly Gurney *1987:* 197f.
58 See Kraus *1958:* 54ff. Walther (*1917:* 215) and Lautner (*1936:* 22) regard *šasum* as one of the terms for "to bring an action", "start litigation". The detailed examination by Kraus does not support this view.

of private law: a bridegroom *ana bit emim issi* — "claimed consummation of the marriage" (lit. "claimed at the house of the father-in-law"), but was rejected by him.[59]

The verb *ṣabatum* — "to seize" occurs in LE in several contexts, prior to litigation. It can refer to a person being held in connection with some offence, whether seizure is *in flagranti delicto*,[60] or not.[61] Again, if a person sees a chattel of his in the possession of another, he will "seize" it, that is to say, will formally claim it. So in LE 33, where a man recognizes his slave child, who had come into the hands of a free woman.[62] Of no technical legal import is "to seize" in LE 6 and 50.[63] Not evidenced in LE and CH is the use of *ṣabatum* to denote a preliminary stage, in the commencement of proceedings: a claimant "seizes" his adversary and hales him into court. Finally, a person may be "seized" in the demand that he give evidence.[64]

Not every conflict need develop any further. A claimant might obtain satisfaction directly from his opponent. But in case he did not, he would wish to start a suit *(dinum, awatum)*. To express the act of suing, some verbs meaning "to speak, shout", etc. are in prominent use. So *ragamum*, which is employed as a general term, in the sense "to claim, to sue"; in LE it occurs only once (sec. 30), and there in a negative way, *ul iraggam* — "he shall have no claim".[65] This is an elliptic formulation, equivalent in its import to a fuller version *dinum šu rugummam ul išu*

59 See the detailed discussion, pp. 190ff., below.
60 So in LE 12, 13; possibly also in LE 26, /28.
61 So in LE 49, where a man is seized *ina wardim šarqim* — "in possession of a stolen slave"; cf. pp. 267ff., below. And contrast AbB viii 82, where the writer tells of having seized some persons *ina šaraqim* — "while stealing".
62 Cf. CH 19. Note also CH 136, where the returning fugitive would lay claim to his wife. See already p. 90, above.
63 Similar to the usage of LE 50 is that of CH 17 and 20 (*ṣabitanum* — "seizer").
64 On *ṣabatum* see further Walther *1917:* 213; Lautner *1936:* 12f. See also the full treatment of the verb in CAD.
65 So also in CH 162, 171, 175; slightly different is the use in CH 163/: there the husband, who is the subject of *ul iraggam*, is in actual possession of the object of possible contention, the dowry brought by his late wife; "he shall not claim" means there "he is not entitled (to retain)". In CH 126 the verb occurs without negation; so also in many documents.

— (lit.) "that case has no claim", i.e., an action brought on these facts is bound to fail.[66] The brief *ul iraggam* may reflect the language of the private legal documents, in which the undertaking not to sue is often one of the main clauses.[67, 68]

Rather undefined is *awum* — "to speak". There is no evidence for attributing to it the technical import "to sue", even though its derivative, the noun *awatum* (lit. "word, matter") is a term denoting "case, charge, litigation" (LE 48). The use of *awum* in LE 50 may be due to the identity of the offenders, and the notion behind *ekallum šurqam ittišu itawwi* — "the palace (with) theft will charge him" may be one of extra-judicial, disciplinary retribution. This interpretation may find support in a document from the region of Eshnunna, IM 51234.[69] An official is warned: in case there is a deficiency in the harvest of some sesame, *ekallum ittika itawwu* — "the palace will have words with you".[70] *Prima facie*, an actual, definite offence need not at all have been present in this case.

Not used in the sense "to sue" (we have just seen) is *šasum* — "to call"; nor is *qabum*, another verb meaning "to speak". This occurs in the documents at the final stage of the proceedings, in the sense "to pronounce" a decision.[71] A more specific term for "to sue" is *baqarum*: the proper use of this is in the sphere of claims of ownership, in vindication. It does not occur in the LE, but is frequent in CH,[72] and also in the documents.[73]

After suit has been brought, there follows a stage expressed by the phrase *(daiani) dinam ušaḫazušu/nuti* — "(the judges) caused

66 See CH 115, 123, 250.
67 See the detailed discussion by San Nicolò *1922:* 39ff.
68 The verb *dababum* — "to speak" does not occur in LE and CH, but is used in contemporary documents in the sense "to sue"; see, e.g., Schorr *1913*, nos. 269: 4; 308: 18; 313: 21; see also Lautner *1936:* 23.
69 Goetze *1958:* 35f., text 14: 19ff.
70 Literally, "the palace will talk with you". Less pregnant is Goetze's rendering: "When the sesame in question falls due, the palace will negotiate with you."
71 See Schorr *1913*, nos. 269: 26; 271: 11; 293: 10. Cf. the remarks of Walther *1917:* 244; Lautner *1936:* 36.
72 Secs. / 118, 150, 179; also in the context of adoption, secs. 185, 187, 188.
73 On *baqarum*, see Walther *1917:* 217; Lautner *1936:* 6ff.; San Nicolò *1922:* 154ff.

him/them to 'hold' the proceedings" (or " ... the decision").[74] This literal rendering is far from providing a satisfactory interpretation, and consequently widely divergent opinions have been voiced as to the exact import of the phrase. Vague in itself is the favourite German rendering "Prozessverfahren gewähren";[75] very broad and consequently diffuse is the rendering "to conduct a trial, try".[76] Lautner *1936:* 27 sees *dinam šuḫuzum* as expressing the court's readiness to entertain the case; Walther *1917:* 218 relates the phrase to the opening of the proceedings ("Aufnahme des Verfahrens"), but would extend it to cover also later stages ("die Rechtssprechung überhaupt"). Landsberger suggests that by *dinam šuḫuzum* the parties express their submission to the powers of the court.[77] Driver-Miles *1952:* 71 render literally, "let (the parties to the case) have the law", and explain this to mean "to deliver the judgement".[78] Altogether, then, one is faced with a bewildering variety of suggestions.

Of all these, that of Landsberger seems closest to the phrase as it is before us. *šuḫuzum* is a causative form: while the judges are indeed the express or implied formal subjects, it is the litigants (or one of them) who are caused to do something, namely to proclaim their readiness to abide by the decision which will be rendered in due course.[79] This interpretation is also well in accord with the central position occupied in Babylonian proceedings by the *ṭuppi la ragamim* — "document of not suing", by which the parties bind themselves not to renew the litigation.[80]

It is a moot question whether the formal *dinam šuḫuzum* of LE 48 still reflected the realities of its time, or rather was a fossilized remain of earlier periods, when in each case the submission of the litigants had to

74 The object is as a rule in the plural, occasionally in the singular, i.e. referring to one party only, the defendant: so in LE 48, and in NBC 8237 (see p. 271, below).

75 See AHw 19b.

76 Goetze *1956:* 119; CAD A/i 178a.

77 *1939:* 228: "... die Streitenden ... sich unter die Bindung der richterlichen Gewalt begeben *(dinam aḫazu).*" And cf. Roman *iudicium accipere, Oxford Latin Dictionary*, p. 210 (no. 16); *Vocabularium Iurisprudentiae Romanae* I, col. 84.

78 Similarly Bottéro *1965/1966:* 95: "rendre jugement à l'(accusé)".

79 See AbB vi 96: subsequent to *dinam šuḫuzum*, a litigant refuses to obey. He is summoned before the judge to Babylon.

80 See, instead of all others, Lautner *1936:* 35ff.

be exacted beforehand. It is notorious that terminology tends to remain as it was, even if no longer corresponding to the actual state of matters.

EVIDENCE AND OATHS

The LE tell us very little concerning the steps which a litigant (whether claimant or defendant) would take in order to establish *(kunnum)* his case.[81] It may be noted that in comparison with CH documents occupy only a minor place in the LE: the only reference to a written instrument may be in sec. 27/28, in the context of marriage.[82] Again, it must be borne in mind that quite possibly the Laws in this respect lag behind reality, and one should hesitate to draw conclusions from their silence. We are once more up against the very fragmentary character of the information supplied.

There is no reference at all to witnesses, nor is there mention of an ordeal.[83] On the other hand, oaths occur in secs. 22 and /37. In both the instances the oaths are assertory ones, a party's solemn declaration concerning a past occurrence (/37), or concerning an existing state of affairs (22); promissory oaths do not occur in either LE or CH. In sec. /37 the oath is taken by the defendant, who thereby clears himself (exculpatory oath), and is absolved of liability: *mimma elišu ul išu* — "he shall have nothing upon (= against) him".[84] While this may appear as essentially similar to *dinum šu rugummam ul išu*, considered above, there is the difference that in LE /37 this result is reached only after litigation, when each party has had his say, and — more particularly — subsequent to the oath. The situation is more complicated in sec. 22: there the oath is taken by the complainant, who has to swear that there was no justification for the distress of his slave woman. On having

81 Cf. Goetze *1956:* 108f.; Walther *1917:* 223ff.; Lautner *1936:* 32ff.

82 On CH 128, see pp. 201, 203f., below. Documents are mentioned in connection with sale (CH 7), loan (47, 52), deposit (7, 122, 123) and the hire of a shepherd (264).

83 In CH see secs. 2, 132; and cf. Driver-Miles *1952:* 63ff.

84 For the same phrase in a different context, see LE 22 and 23/24. It may have originated in the sphere of loan, with *išu eli* taken quite literally: "to have something upon" = "to have something owing from". In sec. /37 the import is more abstract.

sworn he becomes entitled to compensation.[85] It is a necessary assumption that neither party was able to produce written proof or witnesses.

In both sections the oath is taken by the deity: *niš ilim izakkar* — "he shall swear by a (or: the) god". In sec. / 37 it is further specified that the ceremony of swearing takes place at the temple of the patron deity of Eshnunna, the God Tišpak.[86]

Ostensibly, the right to take the oath improves the position, of the claimant in sec. 22, of the defendant in sec. / 37. There is another side to the coin: he who refuses to exercise his right has lost his case.[87] Judgement will be given against him.

Nothing in the LE tells about the termination of proceedings and the execution of the judgement rendered.

85 See pp. 276ff., below. Cf. CH 120: there also it is the claimant who swears and obtains satisfaction.

86 On oaths, see Driver-Miles *1952:* 466ff.; Walther *1917: 191ff.*

87 Cf. *Digesta Iustiniani* 12.2.38: "Manifestae turpitudinis et confessionis est nolle nec iurare nec iusiurandum referre."

CHAPTER FIVE

CLASSES AND PERSONS

muškenum AND *awilum*

"The ever-vexing problem of the *muškenum*", as it has rightly been called,[1] is a suitable starting point for an enquiry concerning classes in the LE. This problem has occupied the attention of many scholars, yet a consensus has not been reached and opinions are as widely divergent as ever. It is not intended to go here into all the literature which has grown up in the course of the years;[2] rather we shall concentrate on those proposals which have been made subsequent to the publication of the LE, roughly since 1950.[3]

Arguments based on etymology have been put forward by some scholars,[4] in our view to little purpose. Etymological enquiries are part of a search for origins; in case these origins are very remote in time, the results obtained cannot assist in establishing the late meaning of a term, its exact scope. So, research into classical Roman law is in no way helped by the fact that *pecunia* ("money") is derived from *pecus* ("cattle"); or that the verb *spondeo* ("to promise solemnly") is to be connected with the Greek *σπένδω* ("to make a drink-offering"). Pertinent as these observations may be when one tries to understand

1 Finkelstein *1961:* 96.
2 For a survey of earlier opinion, see Klíma *1976:* 267-274.
3 Driver-Miles *1952:* 90ff., 409ff.; Szlechter *1954:* 37ff.; Goetze *1956:* 51; Diakonoff *1956:* 37f.; Cardascia *1958:* 107ff.; Speiser *1958:* 19-28; Finet *1959:* 64; Kraus *1958:* 144ff.; Finkelstein *1961:* 96ff.; Evans *1963:* 23f., note 22; von Soden *1964:* 133-141; Landsberger *1968:* 72, note 3 (who gives more references); Petschow *1968a:* 134; Haase *1965:* 143ff. Finally, note Finkelstein *1970:* 249, and in particular Kraus *1973:* 92-125 and *1984:* 329-331.
4 Especially Speiser, *ibid.*, pp. 25f.

early Roman economic reality and legal practice, they are mere learned curiosities when the interest focuses on later centuries.[5]

As for the term *muškenum*, it has been observed that it is one of the oldest Akkadian words known to us. Already in the Fara period, that is not much less than a thousand years before the LE, it was taken over into Sumerian, in the form MAŠKA'EN.[6] It is widely held that *muškenum* is to be connected with the rare verb *šukenum* — "to bow, to kow-tow"; even if this is correct, which is by no means certain,[7] it does not yield any concrete result. One cannot rely on this verb for delimiting the import of *muškenum* in Old Babylonian society and law, since there would have been ample time for far-reaching changes.[8] There is then no point in stressing that it is hardly "denkbar, dass der normale Bürger in altbabylonischer Zeit als derjenige charakterisiert wird, der sich dauernd niederwerfen muss".[9] To arrive at valid conclusions, one must concentrate on the sources specifically relevant, in our case on those of the Old Babylonian period.[10]

The occurrences of *muškenum* in LE and CH can be divided into three groups:

(a) In the LE only, there are four sections in which *muškenum* stands by itself: secs. 12, 13, /24[11] and 34/.

(b) In a number of instances, in LE and CH, the term *muškenum* occurs in association with *ekallum* ("palace"). This is so mainly in situations deriving from the ownership of slaves. The pair *ekallum u muškenum* occurs first in LE 50 (Tablet B only), which provides equal protection for both of them, in respect of fugitive slaves and stray

5 And see the apt remark of Landsberger *1967:* 189: "Die berufsmässigen Lexicographen haben längst eingesehen, dass man bei der Ermittelung von Bedeutungen nichts auf Etymologie aufbauen kann."

6 See von Soden *1964:* 134; Landsberger, *1968:* 72, note 3, and the critical remarks of Kraus *1973:* 110f.

7 See the view of Kraus, as quoted by Edzard *1960:* 246, note 35.

8 Kraus *1958:* 154 already remarks that the basic meaning of the word "bietet keinen Anhaltspunkt für eine Begriffsbestimmung, denn das Wort stammt aus grauer Vorzeit, deren soziale Verhältnisse uns unbekannt sind."

9 So von Soden, *ibid.*

10 For the non-legal occurrences we rely in the main on Kraus *1958*. Only the legal texts will be discussed in detail.

11 But note the connection between *muškenum* of /24 and *awilum* of 23/; see p. 141, below.

animals. In CH, secs. 15, 16 impose equal punishment (death) on those who aid fugitive slaves of the palace or of a *muškenum*. In secs. 175, 176, marriages of a slave of the palace or of a *muškenum* have identical legal consequences. CH 8 widens the scope of objects, referring to theft of a variety of domestic animals or of a boat. More important in the present context: CH 8 shows that "palace" and *muškenum* are not always a pair, marching *pari passu*; the penalty for theft from palace (and temple) is 30-fold, from a *muškenum*, only 10-fold.

(c) In three groups of sections, in CH only, the *muškenum* is cast as member of an inferior class, in contrast with the *awilum* (or *mar awilim*). So in sec. /139/140, regarding the "divorce payment" *(uzubbum)*; in the block of sections 196/ to /214, on various bodily injuries; finally, in secs. 215/ to /223, dealing with medical treatment (fees, and penalties for malpractice).[12]

These data may be tabulated as follows:

(a) *muškenum* by itself (without) specific point of reference	LE 12, 13, /24, 34/	
(b) *muškenum* in association with *ekallum*	LE 50 (Tabl. B) [Ishchali 199 (?)][13]	CH 8, 15, 16 175, 176
(c) *muškenum* in contrast with *awilum (mar/marat awilim)*		CH /139/140, 196-214, 215-223

The question then arises: Is the division into classes, reflected by those sections of CH which have been listed under (c), to be followed up and applied uniformly throughout the CH (and also the LE, which are often added, almost as an afterthought)? Three main answers, with minor nuances, emerge from the writings which have been mentioned: (i) *awilum* and *muškenum* are to be strictly separated; (ii) *awilum* includes *muškenum*, except when the two are contrasted; (iii) as a rule, the two are not to be differentiated: hence, not only does *awilum*

12 Concerning bodily injuries and medical provisions a further class, that of the slave *(wardum)* is distinguished.

13 See p. 26, note 28, above.

include *muškenum*, but *muškenum* also includes *awilum* — only those cases excepted where they are contrasted.

(1) Some scholars insist on full and consistent separation of *awilum* and *muškenum*. Szlechter states categorically that *awilum* is to be understood solely as "citizen", to the exclusion, on the one hand of *muškenum* and *wardum*, on the other hand of the foreigner.[14] Basically similar is the opinion of Finkelstein: "If it be suggested that LÚ (= *awilum*) in the *šumma awilum* sections of the laws is to be construed in a more general sense in contrast to those rules where there is explicit contrast with other social classes, this would amount to a kind of arbitrary distinction in usage in the same text, which, in view of the relatively precise language of the Old Babylonian laws would be an unwarranted supposition."[15]

Views like these commend themselves readily to the historian of law: by professional inclination, as a lawyer, he will be all in favour of a clear-cut terminology, to be followed strictly, without deviation. However, on closer examination it will emerge that in the present case this "segregationist" approach leads to results which are extremely implausible. One has to choose the lesser of two evils: (a) the admission of human frailty, i.e. of a degree of laxity and inconsistency in the use of terminology (possibly mitigated by the fact that for a contemporary reader, familiar with the circumstances, this laxity need not have caused

14 Szlechter *1954:* 37: "... il faut entendre sous ce vocable [*awilum*] uniquement 'citoyen', à l'exclusion du *muškenum* et du *wardum* d'une part, et de tout étranger, d'autre part."
Unexpectedly, chapter 1, "Les classes sociales", is omitted from Szlechter's *1978* edition.

15 *1961:* 97. I have not always found it easy to follow Finkelstein. He continues that "it is bad enough to have to contemplate the possibility that the *muškenum* in CH 8, 15-16, 175-176 — in contrast to the meaning of the term elsewhere in CH — might denote the general civilian population as contrasted with 'palace' and 'temple' ..." Yet, in a concluding passage (*ibid.*, p. 99) he concedes that "it may well be that in specific contexts the term [*muškenum*] may denote the entire civilian citizenry, which is of course subservient to the king, and — more importantly — for whose well-being the king is morally responsible." In his article, in Hebrew, on "Law in the Ancient Near East" (*1968:* 595) he remarks (in the context of LE 12 and 13) that *muškenum* "apparently refers to all the citizens of Eshnunna". But in *1969b:* 524, note 21, Finkelstein renders *muškenum* by "crown dependent". See also pp. 282f., note 102, below.

serious ambiguity); or else (b) the excessive and inexplicable fragmentation of the sources, which will follow if the distinction between *awilum* and *muškenum* is carried through in a consistent fashion, without admitting any exception.

We have had occasion to stress that the modern desire for comprehensiveness was alien to ancient corpora of legal rules, such as LE and CH, but the present case would carry us much farther. This difficulty has been present to the mind of several of the authors quoted, and they have offered at least partial answers to it. The solution was sought in the assumption that the position of the *awilum* (or his slave) in cases corresponding to LE 12, 13, CH 8, 15, 16, 175, 176, was regulated by customary law. Concerning burglary committed in daytime (LE 12, 13), it has been suggested that the sanction may well have been more rigorous, in case the person against whom the offence was committed was an *awilum*.[16] On these lines it would follow that it was the *muškenum* whose remedies and rights had to be laid down explicitly. Yet we have noted that in these sections of the CH mention is made also of the palace *(ekallum)*: would its rights also have been in need of redefinition? Further, it seems somewhat inconsistent to suggest that LE 50 (Tablet B) detracted materially from earlier recognized rights of the *awilum*, with respect to stray cattle and fugitive slaves.[17] We have already remarked that there appears to be no good reason for such an intentional discrimination against the *awilum*.[18] But even if one is willing to accept, for the sake of argument, this *deus ex machina* — customary law — there remains a further question: What about those sections, the overwhelming majority in both LE and CH, which mention only the *awilum*? E.g., would the rights of a depositor (LE 36/37, CH 124, 125) not be in equal need of protection, and equally deserving it, if he happened to be a *muškenum*? What about the cases concerning the goring ox (LE 54/55, CH 251/252) and the vicious dog (LE 56/57); in both LE and CH the draftsman distinguishes neatly between *awilum* and *wardum*; is there to be no remedy in case the victim was a *muškenum*, or would here too the matter have been regulated by customary law?

16 See Szlechter *1954:* 41f. Cf. Cardascia *1958:* 108. Differently Haase *1965:* 145.

17 Szlechter does so, *ibid.* p. 42.

18 See p. 27, above.

(ii) A step in the right direction is the view holding that the usual introductory phrase *šumma awilum* refers to any free person, including the *muškenum*.[19] This would to a considerable extent answer the objection raised above concerning excessive fragmentation.

With regard to the sections which mention specifically the *muškenum*, two views can be distinguished. Some scholars would supply corresponding (but not necessarily identical) rules for the *awilum* from customary law; we have just discussed this and found it unsatisfactory. The majority would tackle the matter in a different, more pregnant fashion: "All in all, the *muškenum* is singled out for protection by the state ... the palace has an interest in the *muškenum* above and beyond its normal interest in the *awilum* ... the state had special obligations to the *muškenum* in view of the latter's services to the state."[20] We dissent on both counts. First of all, there is no evidence to show that the *muškenum* was rendering special services to the state, in excess of and different from those rendered by others.[21] These services are a mere hypothesis, developed in order to account for the alleged preferential treatment accorded to the *muškenum*.[22]

19 See, e.g., Driver-Miles *1952:* 409; Cardascia *1958:* 107.

20 Speiser *1958:* 21; supported by Finkelstein *1961:* 97: "Speiser is certainly right in emphasizing that the essential legal status of the *muškenum* is that he is singled out for protection, as a ward of the state or crown." See also Driver-Miles *1952:* 92; Diakonoff *1956:* 38; von Soden *1964:* 141; Haase *1965:* 145. An early opponent was Kraus *1958:* 144, note 2 *(Korrekturzusatz).*

21 For the interpretation of an earlier Sumerian text, UM 5 no. 74, see Kraus *1958:* 146.

22 Speiser himself has some misgivings: "The logical assumption would be that the *muškenum* was some sort of fief-holder, who was bound to specified tasks in return for being a free tenant of the Crown. Yet the Code [of Hammurabi], in addressing itself directly to such tenants, fails to mention the *muškenum*" (p. 21). But subsequently (p. 22), Speiser would yet ingeniously introduce the *muškenum* into these sections of CH. Secs. 36ff. have the sequence *redum ba'irum u naši biltim* (Speiser: "soldier, fisherman, and taskbearer"). "Now the same type of sequence recurs in a letter from Samsuiluna, where we find, however, *ša redi ba'iri u muškeni* [TCL 17 76:13f.]. Taken together, these two passages yield the equation *naši biltim* = *muškenum*." We beg to differ: the results obtained by "equations" of this kind are unreliable and potentially misleading.

Prior to discussing in detail all the relevant sections of LE and CH, suffice it to point to CH 175 and 176, concerning the marriage of the slave of the palace, respectively of the slave of a *muškenum*, with a free woman. These sections, in brief, ensure the freedom of children issuing out of such a marriage, and their right to half the property acquired by the slave subsequent to the marriage (the other half goes to the master). It has been maintained that "the slave of the palace or of a *muškenum* who married a free woman enjoyed certain privileges that other slaves lacked".[23] This is open to doubt: one could understand a privileged position for the slave of the palace, a kind of *servus publicus*, but hardly for the slave of the lowly *muškenum*. Also, it makes little sense to hold that the legal position of a slave would change, and very considerably so, merely by his being owned by a *muškenum* or an *awilum*. What explanation is there for special protection at the extremes, with neglect and disregard at the centre? However, more important is another point emerging from CH 175 and 176: the privileges granted to the slave, or rather to his issue, amount at the same time to restrictions, to disabilities on the part of his owner, the palace or the *muškenum*. True, it is a necessary assumption that the owner's assent was an essential prerequisite of the proposed marriage, but once that had been given, the family of the slave was protected by the law. It follows that in this case the roles would be reversed: palace and *muškenum* emerge as the true underdogs, but the *awilum* owning slaves is in a better position, simply because he is not mentioned in these sections. I would submit that CH 175 and 176 are sufficient to explode the "special protection theory" of the *muškenum* and dispose of it.

(iii) The parallel use of *muškenum* and *awilum*, subject to the necessary exceptions, has been proposed — in detailed argument — by Kraus.[24] He takes as his starting point the statement of Goetze (*1956:* 51) that *muškenum* "has a relative meaning, which for its clarification needs a specific point of reference". Accordingly, Kraus suggests the meaning "Untertan", i.e. "subject", for *muškenum*, when that term occurs in conjunction with *šarrum* — "king", or — as in LE and CH —

23 So Speiser, p. 21.

24 *1958:* 144f. Kraus is supported by Matouš *1959:* 95. Also, rather more cautiously, by Petschow *1961:* 268; cf. Petschow *1960:* 413. CAD renders *warad muškenim* consistently by "private slave" (lastly K 96b, 572b). Kraus has encountered the vigorous opposition of many, prominently that of Finkelstein and von Soden.

in conjunction with *ekallum*.[25] In these contexts the import of *muškenum* is "(normaler) Bürger" — "ordinary citizen" (*1958:* 151). In the sense of Kraus one might say that vis-à-vis the palace everyone is a *muškenum*. The definition of *muškenum* when contrasted with *awilum* is rendered difficult by the fact that the latter term has within CH several related meanings.[26] At any rate it is certain that the distinction is here between an upper class *(awilum)* and a lower one *(muškenum)*.[27] The approach advocated by Kraus seems to be altogether the correct one, although one may disagree with him on some specific points.

To sum up: in all the sections in groups (a) and (b) one may replace *muškenum* by *awilum*, and this would not change the import of the various provisions.[28] Only in the sections of CH listed in group (c), i.e. CH /139/140, 196-214, 215-223, has the term *muškenum* a more narrow, limited import.

This is the thesis. We have now to examine it in the light of the sections of LE and CH. We shall also endeavour to explain, at least tentatively, how it happened that the terminology became confused.

The *muškenum* occurs in five sections of LE and in five of CH, group (b). The majority of these ten sections deal with the invasion of property rights, in other words they are not concerned with matters of status. LE 12 and 13 make unlawful entry a delict even prior to the commission of theft. There seems to be no reason why a provision of this kind would be promulgated in such a fashion that only part of the population would be protected by it. Surely the repression and punishment of unlawful entry is a matter of general interest, not one of special class privilege.[29] In LE 34/35 the right of the palace to recover the slave child would have

25 LE 50 (Tablet B), CH 8, 15, 16, 175, 176. Note also the interaction of *ekallum* and *muškenum* in LE 34/35.

26 Kraus *1958:* 147: "*awilum* ist ...... insofern ein sehr ungünstiger 'specific point of reference', als das Wort bekanntlich im CH in mindestens drei verschiedenen, wenn auch verwandten Bedeutungen vorkommt, (1) 'Mann', 'jemand', 'einer'; (2) 'freier Mann', d.h. jeder der kein Sklave ist; (3) im Sinne von *mar awilim*, 'Angehöriger einer bestimmten gehobenen Schicht', und die Nuance der dritten noch gefunden werden muss."

27 For a juxtaposition of *muškenum* and *ṣuḫarum* ("servant, subordinate") see ARM XIII, 141. On *ṣuḫarum* see CAD Ṣ 232ff.

28 For further discussion of *muškenum* in groups (a) and (b), see p. 153, below.

29 See Kraus *1958:* 151.

been equally valid, whatever the status of the person who had taken it. In any case, the section does not reveal any privilege of the *muškenum*. LE 50 (Tablet B) has been interpreted as abolishing deliberately an earlier right of the *awilum* to have fugitive slaves or stray animals returned to him, when they happen to be seized by an official;[30] such a change of the law would have been little short of the preposterous. But even scholars who do not accept that radical interpretation of LE 50, rather regard the version of Tablet B as the original one, would still have to account for a differentiation according to classes in a matter of this kind.

CH 8 concerns the theft of animals or of a boat: if the stolen object is the property of the palace, a thirtyfold penalty is imposed, if it is that of a *muškenum*, a tenfold one; the death penalty is envisaged in both instances, in case the thief cannot pay up. Important is the fact that in secs. 7 and 9ff., where the owner is described as *awilum*, death is the only punishment provided for certain cases of ordinary, non-aggravated theft. This inconsistency is probably best explained by the assumption that CH combines here laws of different times.[31] In any case, it is clear that the sections on theft do not show the *muškenum*-owner of stolen property as in any way privileged. CH 15 deals with aiding the escape of a slave belonging to the palace or to a *muškenum*, CH 16 with the harbouring of such a slave. In both instances the death penalty is imposed; there seems again to be no room for class distinctions.[32] CH 175 and 176 have already been considered.

30 So Szlechter, as quoted pp. 27, 136, above.

31 See Müller *1903:* 84; quoted with approval by Koschaker *1917:* 75. See there also for other interpretations.

32 With reference to CH 17-20, Speiser suggested that "... the penalty is less severe if the slave belongs to an *awilum*" (*1958:* 21) This is not quite exact. There is in these sections nothing that would identify the owner as an *awilum*, nor do they reveal any leniency; rather it is the contents that are different. CH 17 fixes the reward of a man who detained a slave; CH 18 deals with problems of identification, in case the slave does not cooperate; CH 20 provides for the case where the slave escaped from the custody of the person who had detained him. CH 19, comparable to CH 16, concerns a man who (acting properly) caught a fugitive slave, but later on concealed the matter; this is then a case akin to theft by a finder. As in CH 16 the penalty is death. And see Kraus *1973:* 99f. Compare CH 227, punishing with death the wrongful shaving of a slave's *abbuttum* (see p. 163, below).

There remains LE 23/24, a section concerning cases of death caused in the course of wrongful distress.[33] Kraus holds that here it is possible to establish the identity of *awilum* and *muškenum: eli awilim* (A ii 19) is later referred to by *elišu* — "upon him" (line 22), and then once more, but this time he is described as *muškenum* (line 23).[34] This suggestion of Kraus has met with the opposition of Finkelstein:[35] "Sec. 22 concerns the case of distraint of the slave woman of an *awilum* in the absence of a valid claim, sec. 23, the same case aggravated by the distrainor's having then caused the death of the slave, while sec. 24 deals with the same situation except that the distrainee was the wife or son of a *muškenum* ... From this progression through the three rules Kraus concludes that *awilum* in the first two of these rules and *muškenum* in the last, must be identical ..." It is then pointed out that "these law collections were not logically organized, and the cases chosen for inclusion are often random".[36] One need not quarrel with the last, general statement;[37] but on the whole Finkelstein's objections fail to do justice to the argument of Kraus. This is not based on the logic of the sequence of cases, but on considerations concerning grammar and syntax: *awilum* and *muškenum* are linked by *elišu*, which refers back to the former, and is taken up again by the latter.

Summing up, one may say that in cases concerning the protection of property rights there appears to be no reason which would account for a distinction between *awilum* and *muškenum*. In one section, LE 23/24, the two terms appear to be synonymous. CH 175 and 176 cannot be

33 See pp. 144, 275ff., below.

34 Kraus *1958:* 151: "Hier sind LÚ oder, genauer gesagt, das zweite LÚ von § 23 und MAŠ.KAK.EN (= *muškenum*) nicht etwa Gegensätze, sondern identisch. Denn in § 24 wird das zweite LÚ von § 23, worauf sich das Pronomen von *elišu* bezieht, durch MAŠ.KAK.EN wiederaufgenommen; beide bedeuten ganz allgemein 'jemand', 'ein Einwohner', 'ein Bürger'."

35 *1961:* 97. Finkelstein's views are followed and elaborated by Haase *1965:* 144f.

36 Finkelstein tries to explain the sequence by assuming that it is unlikely that a *muškenum* would have owned slaves. But at p. 98, note 7, he observes that this assumption is contradicted by CH 15, 16 (we may add also LE 50, Tablet B), yet thinks that this is "by no means fatal" to his argument.

37 Similarly Haase, p. 145: "Angesichts des Reformcharakters der altorientalischen Rechtssammlungen ist es nicht verwunderlich, wenn nur ganz bestimmte Probleme des Rechtslebens geregelt werden und manches andere fehlt."

reconciled with the theory that the law gave special protection to the *muškenum*.

We turn now to those provisions in which *awilum* and *muškenum* are contrasted. Let us recall that there are no such cases in LE. The relevant sections of CH are devoted to three topics: divorce payment, bodily injuries, and medical treatment. The most significant of these are the sections on bodily injuries, with their provision of talion in case the victim was an *awilum* (or *mar awilim*).[38] As we see it, here it is the *awilum* (or *mar awilim*) who is singled out for special consideration and protection, whereas the *muškenum* (or *mar muškenim*) is in a position very similar, one might say identical, to that of the *awilum* in LE 42-47. A comparable situation obtains with regard to the sections on medical treatment; this can be seen especially from CH 218, which provides that an unsuccessful surgeon will have his fore-hand cut off, in case he caused the death of an *awilum*, or the loss of his eye.[39,40] Quite singular is the provision of CH / 140, reducing the amount of divorce payment by a *muškenum* (in case there had been no *terḫatum*).[41] Altogether then, the picture of the *muškenum* which emerges from these sections is fairly clear and generally accepted: his is a lower class, financially weaker. His injuries are cheaper to settle, he pays smaller medical fees, and incurs less expense in divorcing his wife.

So far we have analysed the material. It remains now to propose a hypothesis which would account for the state of the sources. More specifically there are two questions to be considered: first, what explains the apparently indiscriminate use of *awilum* and *muškenum* in LE and in parts of CH; second, what explains the very different usage in parts of the same source, that is in CH.

38 On this point I find myself in essential agreement with Finkelstein *1961:* 98, against Kraus *1958:* 149. Talion is not "eine altertümliche, rein 'moralische' Satisfaktion", but more probably an innovation introduced into Babylonian law by Hammurabi. On talion see further pp. 262ff., below.

39 A case of "mirroring punishment"; see Driver-Miles *1935:* 347.

40 I accept the suggestions of Driver-Miles *1952:* 418ff., on omissions in CH 219/220; and see already Kraus *1958:* 146.

41 See Driver-Miles *1952:* 296. Compare, however, a provision in the Laws of Ur-Nammu, LUY 9 and 10 (= F 6 and 7): there the amount of the divorce payment depends on the status of the divorcee: "If it is a (former) widow (NU.MA.SU) whom he divorces, he shall pay 1/2 a mina silver." And see Petschow *1968b:* 7.

We would find the answer to the first question in the assumption that all the provisions mentioning the *muškenum* originate in the legislative or judicial activities of the ruler, the king, not in ordinary court practice. This does not mean that the ruler might not use *awilum* or *mar awilim*, but whenever the *ekallum* occurs, and in association with it the population is mentioned (collectively or individually), the term *muškenum* is employed: it is never *ša ekallim u awilim*, always *ša ekallim u muškenim*. So in the six sections of LE and CH listed in group (b). And this combination, *ekallum u muškenum* is an expression of comprehensiveness, not meant to confine or to exclude anyone.

In texts of a more personal nature, *šarrum* may replace *ekallum*. In omina, signs may be interpreted separately, divergently, for the king and for private persons. Some examples: in a hepatoscopic omen text AO 9066[42] we have ... *šarrum ṣalma ipušma šanum ušerib* [*a*]*na muškenim imatma bisu isappaḫ* — "le roi fera une statue mais c'est un autre qui l'introduira (dans le Temple);[43] pour un homme du commun: il mourra et sa maison sera détruite". CT 20 3:22: *ana šarri bartu ana* MAŠ.EN.KAK *la mitgurtu* — "for the king: rebellion; for the people: discord".[44] King and private persons are joined in a *kispu* (funerary offering) text from Mari, no. 12803: 24, in the phrase *niq šarrim u muškenim* — "le sacrifice du roi et des *muškenum*.[45]

Whenever the legal position of the palace is defined, that definition — one may assume — will have its source in the palace itself, and the same will necessarily apply to the *muškenum*, whenever it occurs in association with *ekallum*.

We have already noted that in four sections in the LE, the term *muškenum* occurs without specific "point of reference". In two of them, LE 12 and 13, the authoritative source is revealed by the use of the proclamation form *(awilum ša)*.[46] In LE 34/35 the palace itself is party to the conflict situation. It is only the remaining section /24 which does not readily reveal, either by substance or by form, some connection with the activity of the palace. One might indeed attempt to justify its attribution to an authoritative source by merely pointing out that the

42 Published by Nougayrol *1950:* 30.
43 Compare Deuteronomy 20: 5, 6, 7.
44 Quoted CAD M/ii 274b.
45 Published by Birot *1980:* 142.
46 See pp. 67f., above.

origin of the term in three other instances can serve as indication also for the remaining one, but this is an argument which does not give satisfaction. Examining again the substance of the related sections 22 and 23/24, one might suggest that "common law" rulings on the distress of a slave woman (sec. 22) and on distress followed by her death (23/), were completed by legislation concerning the death of a free person taken in distress.[47] Sec. 23/ (like 22) deals with a very specific case, the distress of a slave woman (not a male slave). Sec. /24 is broader in its formulation, in that it refers both to the wife and the son of the alleged debtor. The sequence is unusual: one would expect the distress of free persons to be considered first, as in CH 116.[48] It is indeed not impossible to explain the sequence given in LE 22, 23/24: it might be held to signify that the distress of a slave (woman?) will have been the more frequent occurrence.[49] Or else one might regard it as due to the influence of the preceding section 22; but this brings us again to assume that that very specific case was the starting point. A certain verbosity and unnecessary repetition can also be detected.[50] LE 23/24, as presently before us, is indeed one section, but it is far from integrated, and its formulation is not concise. All this gives one the impression that the second part (/24) is a later addition, loosely connected with what precedes.[51]

47 On possible differences in the origin of LE 23/ and /24 see already Haase *1965:* 144.

48 Cf. also LE 54/55, 56/57; CH 117/118, 229/230/231/, 251/252.

49 See Petschow *1968a:* 142, note 4.

50 Note the repetitive *nepu ša ippu* — "the distrainor who distrained", separating *din napištim* — "(it is) a case of life" from *imat* — "shall die"; this has a parallel *in lequ ša ... ilqu* ("the taker who ... took") of LE /35. In both instances the impression is one of "officialese" verbosity (contrast LE 26: *din napištimma imat*). But I realize that one might disagree on grounds of "Sprachgefühl", and would not press the point.

51 A unified section (for which CH 116, *in pari materia*, may serve as an example) could have been formulated more concisely, on the following lines: *šumma awilum eli awilim mimma la išuma niputam iteppe ina bitišu iklama uštamit šumma aššat awilim mar awilim din napištim imat šumma amtum 2 amatim ana bel amtim iriab* — "If a man had nothing upon a man, yet distrained a distress, detained (it) in his house and caused (it) to die — if (it was) a man's wife, a man's son, (it is) a case of life, he shall die. If (it was) a slave woman, he shall replace 2 slave women to the owner of the slave woman."

In searching for an answer to our second question, concerning the difference of usage within CH, one might take as point of departure the suggestion that in the central part of the sections based upon a contrast of *awilum* and *muškenum*, the part dealing with bodily injuries (CH 196 to 214), the provisions concerning talion are an innovation of Hammurabi. It may then not be impossible that the other provisions which display this contrast, the provisions on divorce payment and on medical treatment, are also due to him. It may be well to avoid any possible misunderstanding: it is not intended to attribute to Hammurabi the creation of social classes *ex nihilo*. A distinction between *awilum* and *muškenum* is evidenced also by other, non-legal sources. So in a private letter, Leiden 1892;[52] the writer is dissatisfied with the degree of generosity shown to him by the addressee. He imputes to him the following thoughts: "To your heart you have spoken as follows: 'How will you return my (act of) favour? I am a *mar awilim* (Frankena: Patrizier), he is a *mar muškenim* (Frankena: gewöhnlicher Bürger). How will he return my (act of) favour?'" Kraus (*1958:* 148) deduces that the population itself saw in *awilum* and *muškenum* "zwei sich gegenüberstehende Gruppen verschiedenen sozialen und wirtschaftlichen Standards". Perhaps more important is a letter from Mari, B. 63:[53] it deals with the preferential treatment proposed for some persons described as *awilum* (here further described as connected with the palace), and the resulting indignation of the *muškenum*.[54] However, it seems likely that under the rule of Hammurabi for the first time the class distinctions existing in Old Babylonian society found their way into the law; thereby *de facto* inequality became *de iure* inequality. Needless to say, a suggestion of this kind can reflect only the evidence available at present. One will not hesitate to abandon it once it is superseded by new material.

As for terminology, it would probably not have been practicable to

52 = AbB iii, no. 33.

53 Published by Jean *1948:* 72ff.; discussed by Kraus *1958:* 152. See the later edition by Finet *1959:* 57ff.

54 We have already mentioned (note 27, above) another letter from Mari, ARM XIII, 141: there the contrast is between *ṣuḫarum* and *muškenum*. But there is no way for determining whether *muškenum* in this text denotes "(free) subject" generally, or a specific class.

introduce one entirely new. The easier way for avoiding inconsistency would have been to dispense with the term *muškenum* in the sections of CH included above under (b), which represent the earlier usage.[55] However, it seems that no such attempt was made. Can such looseness of terminology be attributed to the draftsmen of the CH? An examination of the use of the terms *awilum/mar awilim* should settle any doubts and reservations one might have felt in answering this question positively. Driver-Miles (*1952:* 88) assert that in CH "*awilum*, when used alone, never indicates a person's status. Accordingly, an *awilum* has to be described as *mar awilim* if his status is in question". This is at best only a desideratum; it is not carried through in the provisions on bodily injuries, nor in those on medical treatment.[56] More than that, *awilum* may have different connotations within the same section. See secs. 215/216/217 and 221/222/223: at the beginning of each, *awilum* denotes status, at the end it is used in the general sense; *warad awilim* means merely "a person's slave".

mar/marat awilim

Are at least *mar awilim* ("the son of a man") and the feminine *marat awilim* used in a consistent fashion? They are not. The masculine occurs in eight sections of CH, the feminine in three. In these eleven sections three imports of the term can be discerned: it may denote (i) a state of dependence or minority, in CH 7, 14,[57] 116; (ii) a designation of social status, in contrast with *muškenum*: so in secs. 196, 203, 205, /207; in this sense there is *marat awilim* in CH 209/;[58] finally (iii) it is used as a general term, meaning merely "free man", in no way distinguishable from *awilum*. The *mar awilim* of CH 251/ has his exact counterpart in the awilum of LE 54/: in other words, the addition of *mar(um)* does not

55 The earlier date for the combination *ekallum u muškenum* is assured by LE 50 (Tablet B). And recall — with the necessary reserve — Ishchali 199, p. 26, note 28, above. For occurrence at Mari, roughly contemporary with CH, see Kraus, *1958:* 145.

56 And see Driver-Miles themselves (*1952:* 410).

57 This section adds the qualification *ṣiḫrum* — "young".

58 *mar muškenim* occurs in CH /208, /216/, /222/ as a designation of social status; so does *marat muškenim* in sec. /211/.

affect the import.[59] *marat awilim*, in the indefinite, general sense of "free woman", occurs in CH 175 and 176.[60]

One may at once consider the import of *mar awilim* and *marat awilim* in the LE. The masculine occurs in secs. 16, 17/, 47A and 58, the feminine in 26, 27/ and 33. They can all be placed with two of the three groups discernible in CH. In sections 16, 26 and 27/, the *mar/marat awilim* conforms to the sense of group (i), that is, he/she is in a state of minority or dependence.[61] In secs. 17/, 33, 47A and 58 *mar/marat awilim* correspond to CH, group (iii) — "(free) man, woman": there is no difference between the *mar awilim* of sec. 17/ and the *awilum* of sec. 25, between the *mar awilim* of sec. 47A and the *awilum* of secs. 42 to 47, nor between the *mar awilim* of sec. 58 and the *awilum* in two preceding sections, 54/ and 56/. In LE 33, *marat awilim* is equivalent to *sinništum* (SAL) — "woman" (the term, frequent in CH, does not occur in LE); her status, her belonging to a particular class is irrelevant.[62]

These data can be tabulated as follows:

(i) *mar/marat awilim* in a state of dependence or minority	CH 7, 14, 116	LE 16, 26, 27/
(ii) *mar/marat awilim* as a designation of status	CH 196, 203, 205, /207, 209/	
(iii) *mar/marat awilim* — "(free) man/woman"	CH 175, 176, 251/	LE 17/, 33, 47A, 58 [Ishchali 326]

59 In other instances *awilum* may be redundant: the *warad awilim* of CH /252 is identical with *wardum* of LE /55 (cf. also *warad awilim* in CH 7, 116, 199, 205, /217, /223; *amat awilim*, CH 213/). Similarly, I am not inclined to see in *aššat awilim* — "an *awilum*'s wife" (CH 127, 129, 130, 131, 132, 141, 153) a reference to the husband's class; differently Malamat *1966:* 220, note 1, in his discussion of ARM XIII, 114; and cf. also p. 282, note 75, below.

60 Driver-Miles *1952:* 88f., include *marat awilim* of CH 175 and 176 under "social status". For this too I can see no justification. The marriage of upper class women with slaves would have been quite extraordinary.

61 To these one should add the comparable *mar muškenim* of sec./24.

62 One should not lose sight of *mar awilim* (and *warad awilim*) in Ishchali 326 (which is close in time to the LE). See further p. 289, below.

The fusion of these data once more shows up the one difference between the two collections: In LE *mar/marat awilim* (and *mar muškenim*) have no status connotation. For the rest, the situation is similar in both. The exact import — hence our assignment to groups (i) or (iii) — has in each instance to be deduced from the context.

These variations in the import of *mar/marat awilim* within CH (and to a lesser extent within LE) allow us to say, without being unfair, that consistent terminology does not seem to have been a major concern of their draftsmen. In their defence it may be pointed out that their looseness of usage need not have caused real difficulties; at any rate they can hardly be blamed for some excesses of modern scholarship. And, if that be any consolation, the same has happened elsewhere too: it will suffice to mention that *ius civile*, a technical term *par excellence*, may in classical Roman sources have at least two different meanings, depending on "a specific point of reference", that is, on being in juxtaposition either with *ius honorarium* or with *ius gentium*.[63] Within the LE there are no clear class distinctions of legal import. The attempt to postulate already for them a developed "Dreiklassengesellschaft" is not sustained by any substantial evidence.[64] Within the CH, class distinctions are confined to very specific spheres. The numerical ratio of *awilum* and *muškenum* in the society of Hammurabi cannot be established, but one ought to bear in mind the extraordinary nature of the provisions concerning talion, applying to the *awilum*. Also, on the whole, upper classes tend to be more limited in number. With Kraus *1958:* 153 we should then tentatively regard the *awilum/mar awilim* as the exception rather than the norm.

So far this chapter has restated what was presented in YLE, pp. 82-95. It was retouched here and there, with little change in substance. During the years which have passed since, there has been but little movement. There is then still a "dominant" or "majority" view, in a variety of nuances, centered around the theses put forward by Speiser, seconded by Finkelstein, also by von Soden's rendering of *muškenum* by "Palasthöriger" (AHw, in 1967). The central idea is the uniform

63 See the remarks of Kaser *1971:* 201.

64 For suggestions along this line, see, e.g., Klíma *1953b:* 227; Korošec *1951:* 83; Szlechter *1954:* 37; Cardascia *1958:* 107; von Soden *1964:* 133. Different (and correct) Bottèro *1965/1966:* 103; Landsberger *1968:* 72, note 3.

interpretation of *awilum* and — slightly less rigidly — also of *muškenum*. Opposed to it is the "relativist" minority view, pronounced by Kraus *1958*,[65] and adopted in YLE. Kraus endowed the *muškenum* with a much broader role, the exact meaning of which was in each case to be derived from the context, and varying according to points of reference *(ekallum* or *awilum).*

Finkelstein continued to wrestle with his "ever-vexing problem". Some of his occasional remarks gave the impression that he might have modified his views, towards a wider sense for *muškenum.*[66] However, his subsequent reference to the *muškenum*, in *1970:* 249, shows him again as a firm defender of orthodoxy. He reproves Landsberger (*1968:* 72) for rendering *muškenum* by "Untertan", in effect concurring with the view of Kraus, "to which, however, the present reviewer and von Soden raised substantial objections which have not yet been disposed of."

Finkelstein's remark, that his objections of 1961 had not yet been disposed of, was technically correct. Some rejoinders were offered in YLE, but by the time it could have reached him his 1970 remarks may already have been submitted for publication. And the detailed reply in Kraus *1973* was still to come. Even so, Finkelstein could easily have recognised that some basic arguments of Speiser, whose views he had so emphatically endorsed, were palpably mistaken.

Finally, Finkelstein's posthumous *1981* again brought conflicting definitions. At p. 34, the *muškenum* are "personally 'free', but were economically dependent on the crown, either wholly or in a large part". This repeats Speiser's view. But at p. 41, note 5, dealing with CH 8, he says, that "in the context of this rule that term must be understood as 'commoner, ordinary citizen'." This is heterodox relativism.

KRAUS *1973*

The most significant contribution to the twin-topic *awilum* and *muškenum* was the publication of Kraus *1973*. Over 34 pages (92-125) Kraus adduced some new sources, and reformulated, restated his views,

65 Kraus takes as his starting point the distinctions suggested by Meek *1950:* 166, note 39 and 44.

66 See already p. 135, note 15, above.

in constant confrontation with Speiser, Diakonoff, Finkelstein, von Soden, and others.

Kraus had hoped that his detailed presentation would spark a new discussion, but in this he was disappointed.[67] His respondents might primarily have been those scholars whose statements he had subjected to his acute criticism. But Speiser, who more than others had shaped the prevailing opinion on the *muškenum*, had died already in 1965. Finkelstein, his follower in all that concerned our topic, died young and suddenly, the year after the publication of Kraus *1973*. He might have been the one scholar who would not refuse to join battle, to re-examine texts and theories, to modify his views, or abandon them, if necessary. Indeed, I assess undeclared intentions, so my assumptions may be doubtful. But who if not the dead deserve the benefit of doubt?

One who refrained from returning the fire he had drawn in Kraus *1973:* 96f. was von Soden. Reviewing another book of Kraus, *Altbabylonische Briefe* vii, 1977, he speaks of *muškenum* as "a notion still disputed between us", and stands by his early rendering "Palasthöriger".[68] Kraus *1984:* 330 reacts sharply: "Seine ... leicht überraschende Bezeichnung von *muškenum* als 'der zwischen uns noch immer strittige Begriff' muss ich zurückweisen. Wer wirklich streiten will, widerlege meine Ansätze mit Gegenargumenten. Auf der Stelle Treten und ältere Meinungen Wiederholen, deren Unhaltbarkeit ich nachgewiesen habe, fördert die Erkenntnis nicht." A reply was eventually offered by von Soden *1985:* 135 (reviewing Kraus *1984*): the rendering of *muškenum* by "Untertan" is "ganz ungeeignet"— because "vom König aus gesehen, die anderen Gruppen auch aus Untertanen bestehen". This conclusion can indeed be drawn from the analysis offered by Kraus, but does not detract from its validity. Concurring with Kraus, I have used language similar to that of von Soden.[69] In effect, "Untertan" does not differ from "(normaler) Bürger".

Now to some remarks of my own concerning the views of Kraus, as

67 Some ten years later he remarks: "Bedauerlicherweise hat niemand ... es für nötig befunden die Diskussion fortzusetzen, oder gar neue, eigene Hypothesen aufzustellen" (*1984:* 329). Unsatisfactory were half a dozen reviews, the last as late as 1980 (OLZ, vol. 75). Faint praise was usually followed by unsubstantiated reserve.

68 *1978:* 207.

69 See p. 139, above, and already YLE, p. 88.

set out in *1973*. Again, I find myself in agreement with his general approach, and especially with its central feature, the emphasis put on the relativist interpretation of *awilum* and *muškenum*, its dependence on "specific points of reference", if one may return once more to that often repeated phrase.

Two brief, summarizing passages may be quoted. At p. 108 he writes: "Zusammenfassend lässt sich folgendes sagen. Wo *muškenum* als Kollektiv *ekallum* gegenübersteht, bezeichnet es die gesamte freie Bevölkerung des Staates, von der Staatsspitze her gesehen. Nicht kollektivisch bezeichnet es ein Mitglied dieser Gesellschaft." And at pp. 116-117: "*muškenum* steht nicht nur *ekallum*, sondern an gewissen Stellen auch *awilum* als deutlicher Gegensatz gegenüber ... Anders ausgedrückt, kann ich keine absolute Bedeutung des Wortes *muškenum* annehmen, sondern ausschliesslich die so eben nachgewiesene relative, also auch oder gerade dort, wo *muškenum awilum* gegenüber steht."

But he continues at once as follows: "Diese Anschauung lässt für mich nur eine Schlussfolgerung zu. Die komplementären Gegensatzpaare *ekallum* — *muškenum* und *awilum* — *muškenum* sind sachlich identisch oder ganz nahe verwandt. Dieser Schluss zieht einen weiteren nach sich. In oppositionellem Bezuge auf *muškenum* ist ein *awilum* ein Mitglied des *ekallum* genannten Kollektivs, worunter man sich vielleicht zunächst den Hof und die Spitzen der Zentralbehörden vorstellen darf. *awilum* bezeichnet somit den Angehörigen der oder einer Elitegruppe im Staate". And at p. 120 Kraus speaks of having reached a "Gleichung" *awilum = ekallum*.[70]

These are new departures, and they have to be considered carefully. If correct, the formula *awilum = ekallum* would inevitably lead to a monistic interpretation of *muškenum*, the very notion which Kraus has been exorcizing for a quarter of a century. If indeed *awilum = ekallum*, then there are no longer any different points of reference, to help distinguish different meanings of *muškenum*.

Needless to say, the consequences which would ensue cannot — by

70 In support of this equation Kraus quotes AbB iii 5: "[Was] meine Angelegenheit [betrifft], über welche du mir geschrieben hast: 'Hast du ... mit den Herren selbst (*itti awilema*) verhandelt?', (so) habe ich noch nicht mit dem Palaste (*itti* É.GAL) verhandelt." I do not find this compelling. All that the letter implies is that these "gentlemen" *(awile)* are conducting the business of the palace, but not that they *are* the palace.

themselves — serve to reject these new theses. But I fail to see that the first "Schlussfolgerung" is indeed derived from what preceded. For a number of reasons, the submission that the pairs *ekallum-muškenum* and *awilum-muškenum* are "factually identical or quite closely related" is open to doubt.

(a) The pairs *ekallum-muškenum* and *awilum-muškenum* are functionally different. To understand this, one ought to distinguish between two expressions which one finds used indiscriminately: these are "points of reference" and "Gegensatzpaar". A point of reference is something that provides extrinsic information which assists in arriving at a better comprehension of something being examined. The point of reference itself need not be connected with the object of examination, not affected by it nor affecting it. As for "Gegensatzpaar", the emphasis should be on the qualifying attribute "Gegensatz". It is not a matter of mere reference, — the persons, ideas, legal principles, etc. interact, collide, compete with each other, confine the partner, modify him.[71]

(b) Let us now apply these abstractions to the two pairs under discussion. It is not difficult to find that within each of the two the relation between the members is different. In the pair *ekallum-muškenum*, the former is a point of reference for the latter, but the latter does not tell us anything about the former. *ekallum* (the "palace") suggests for *muškenum* the meaning "Untertan", in conjunction with other considerations leading to the conclusion that the two are comprehensive: there is no gap between the two, and *muškenum* denotes the population at large, individually and collectively. This was, in essence, the theory of Kraus, to which I adhered.

(c) Altogether different, *awilum* and *muškenum*, in group (c) — only in CH — are a true "Gegensatzpaar". Between them, they split the free population into two parts, are mutually exclusive; as a result diverging rulings are given for identical situations.

(d) So incompatible are the two sets of pairs, that there is no ground for an equation of *awilum* and *ekallum*, based on no more than the association of each with *muškenum*.[72]

71 From other times and a different context, one is reminded of the Roman dictum, *concursu partes fiunt: Digesta Iustiniani* 32.80.

72 Altogether, the suggested equation reinforces my prejudice against employing the tools and methods of mathematics, when trying to

(e) A secondary, extrinsic consideration points in the same direction: We have noted the close relationship of *ekallum* and *šarrum*, quite generally,[73] but also in the association of each with *muškenum*: *ekallum u muškenum* has a close parallel in *šarrum u muškenum*.[74] Indeed, it could be said that these two pairs are "sachlich identisch oder ganz nahe verwandt". Hence, before one looks for any further link for *ekallum u muškenum* one should weigh the compatibility of such a link also with *šarrum u muškenum*. In our specific case, the result may be assessed as negative.

Outside the discussion of these theses of Kraus, but connected with (b) above, I wish to return to one point regarding the *muškenum*. The connection with the *ekallum*, as a point of reference, has provided for the *muškenum* the meaning "Untertan" (= subject). But, given the looseness of that connection, this interpretation need not be restricted: an examination of the "no-reference" occurrences of *muškenum* will not turn up any ground against the rendering "Untertan" in all these either. This allows us to simplify matters somewhat: we have now, it is submitted, a basic meaning "Untertan", common to LE (secs. 12, 13, /24, 34/, 50 [Tablet B]) and CH (secs. 8, 15, 16, 175, 176); this has to be modified only for the three blocks in CH, in which *muškenum* faces *awilum*.[75]

One more remark relating to the new theses of Kraus. Having declined to follow the first "Schlussfolgerung", one could plausibly decline to follow the second. But leaving this argument aside, I fail to see why and how vis-à-vis the *muškenum* "the *awilum* becomes a member of the collective called *ekallum*". Typically, the term *awilum* refers to an individual, equally typically the *ekallum* is a collective: it does not divorce, does not inflict (nor suffer) bodily injuries, does not

elucidate philological or legal problems (see already p. 137, note 22, above). On this point, apparently, I follow in the footsteps of Landsberger: see Kraus *1973:* 120.

73 See pp. 114f., above.

74 See p. 143, above.

75 Detailed pp. 134, 142, above. The actual translation of *muškenum* in this context is troublesome, not due to intrinsic difficulty, rather because one will almost inevitably become involved in anachronisms. In English one might consider "commoner" or "plebeian".

have to undergo medical treatment. Moreover, and from a different angle, the *ekallum*, however interpreted, does not refer to a class of persons, to a stratum of the population. Nor is it necessary to hold that the bureaucracy is decisively recruited from the *awilum* stratum of the population. Considerations of merit will have played a role.

But after all this has been said, one more observation. I do not see that the passages, to the examination of which the last pages have been devoted, are in any way essential for the basic edifice erected by Kraus. That edifice itself seems to me as valid as ever. In *1973*, I am with him from p. 92 to the top of p. 117. But then the sudden departure, the grounds for which I have not been able to comprehend.

Is all well in our understanding of *muškenum*? Any illusions one might harbour in this respect are dispelled by such texts as TCL 17, no. 76,[76] and sec. 15 of the edict of Ammi-ṣaduqa.[77] In both of them *muškenum* occurs at the side of more specific designations, and this seems to conflict with a wide, well-established general meaning of *muškenum*.[78] There is little purpose in offering what would be but questionable *Verlegenheitslösungen*.

76 Kraus *1958:* 225f.; *1973:* 122f.; *1984:* 66f.

77 Kraus *1984:* 178-179 offers improved readings (and a new numeration); see also the Kommentar, *ibid.*, pp. 239-248.

78 TCL 17 76 is easier to deal with. In the sequence *ša redim ba'irim u muškeni* one might conceivably render "eines Soldaten, Fischers und (anderen) Untertanen" (note, however, the well-founded doubts of Kraus *1973:* 101f., concerning "Oberbegriffe".).
But this won't do for Ammi-ṣaduqa 15. There we have a sequence [*š*]*a naši biltim ka*[*btim*] *rabi muškenim redim ba'irim u ilkim aḫim*. See *1973:* 102, improved by *1984, cit*.
Particularly puzzling is the insertion (between *naši biltim* and *redim*) of the triplet *kabtum rabum muškenum*. The first two are well-known: they denote well-to-do, upper class, influential etc. people (see Kraus *1984:* 245 for modern parallels). But in the present context they are difficult to understand. Kraus remarks: "... beide Wörter <sind>, wie ich schon früher betont habe [*1973:* 118], nicht literarisch-verschwommen, sondern 'bürgerliche' Vokabeln konkreter Bedeutung, die auch der 'Gesetzgeber' verwendet, wie unsere Stelle zeigt." Yes, but beyond the fact, significant in itself, that they are here, one would like to know what they mean. Kraus concedes that "allerdings geben unsere Quellen keine zur genaueren Bestimmung hinreichende Aufschlüsse." Somehow *kabtum rabum* look out of place (rather like "Grossgrundbesitzer" benefiting from relief enacted for poorer strata). Somehow, though, the *muškenum* seems

PARENTAL POWERS

This closes our discussion of *awilum* and *muškenum*, even though not quite. We have now to resume an examination of four sections in LE, which show the *mar awilim* (sec. 16),[79] *marat awilim* (secs. 26, 27/), and *mar muškenim* (sec. /24) in a state of dependence. The three last-mentioned raise the general question as to the extent of paternal, or parental powers. It is difficult to obtain a clear picture of these powers within the LE or within the laws of the ancient East generally. At any rate it is important that one dispense with notions derived from Roman *patria potestas*; these are entirely irrelevant to the rules — no doubt variated and far from uniform — obtaining in the East. It is unclear to what extent the age of the son or the daughter is a material factor. Does their legal dependence, such as it is, cease (or diminish) at a certain age, e.g., at puberty, or does it continue as long as they are living in the father's household, or perhaps as long as he is alive? Are the rules the same for son and daughter? One gets the impression that in the East parental powers were of a somewhat restricted nature. This is suggested by a number of provisions: in CH 168/169, disinheritance of a son requires judicial approval;[80] Deuteronomy 21:18-21 provides that the "recalcitrant son" *(ben sorer umoreh)* is to be put to death only after having been brought before the elders of the city.[81]

On the other hand, the possibility — encountered in many sources — that a person be sold, given into servitude or seized as a pledge on account of the debts of his father, has to be explained in terms of

attached to them, but in what fashion, to what purpose, eludes me. For a more sanguine approach to this triplet, see Gurney *1987:* 197; but I continue to worry about its unexplained insertion between *naši biltim* and *redim* (just noted).

79 It will be convenient to deal first with the three other sections.

80 According to CAD A/i 18a the section would apply only to the disinheritance of an adopted son, but there appears to be no warrant for this narrow interpretation. For the correct view see Driver-Miles *1952:* 349.

81 Even so, at stages of development earlier than those reflected in CH and Deuteronomy, or in some particular sphere of the law (e.g., that on sexual offences), there may have been domestic jurisdiction as well. See p. 284, below, on adultery. Cf. MAL, sec. 56 on seduction: "the father may treat his daughter as he pleases"; see also Genesis 38:24, where Tamar is to be burned at the command of her father-in-law, Judah.

paternal power and filial dependence. This is evidenced in LE by sec. /24, concerning the wrongful seizure of a *mar muškenim*.[82] Important functions are reserved for the parents with regard to the marriage of their children, especially the daughters. Although parents are often mentioned as taking a wife for a son, it is not clear that their consent was an *essentiale negotii*;[83] at any rate, as far as the daughter is concerned, LE 27/28 supports the view that she could not enter upon a marriage without the consent of her parents.[84]

THE MOTHER

LE 26 and 27/28 mention, at the father's side, also the mother of the girl.[85] Does this mean that the mother is accorded a say in the matter? The true import of the expression *abiša u ummiša* depends on that troublesome conjunction *u*: "Her father and her mother" is just as possible a rendering as "her father or her mother". This is underlined by the fact that the expression *abiša u ummiša* occurs in a variety of contexts, in which different interpretations may be necessary. In some instances alternation ("or") is clearly indicated, so in texts on adoption, in provisions dealing with the breach of the relationship.[86] It would make no sense to assume that these provisions would become operative only if the adopted son acted in contempt of both father and mother,[87]

82 See further CH 116, 117/; sec. 20 of the edict of Ammi-ṣaduqa; MAL 39, 48.

83 But see Falkenstein *1956:* 23ff. (text ITT III[2] 6444): a betrothal is faulted because of the lack of parental consent.

84 For both son and daughter parental support will often have been essential for covering the expense involved in getting married (the bride payment on the one hand, provision of a dowry, on the other). This would give the father *de facto* powers, but it is only the strictly legal aspect which is of interest.

85 See also Clay *1915*, text 28, secs. 6, 7; HL 28, 29 (*attaš annaš* = father [and] mother); cf. also Deuteronomy 21:18-21 (just mentioned in the text), and 22:15, on an accusation of prenuptial unchastity.

86 In CH 192, 193; Clay, *op. cit.*, sec. 4, 5; and in many documents of adoption.

87 Cf. the provisions on the ill-treatment of parents. CH 195 speaks only of a son striking his father. But Exodus 21:15 concerns one striking *aviw we'immo:* here the particle *we* presents the same problem as Akkadian *u*, but there can be no doubt that the rendering "or" is called for. Finally, see

or only if they both, acting in concert, wronged him.[88] On the other hand, whenever a private legal document mentions both father and mother as taking part in a specific transaction, cumulation ("and") is the only plausible interpretation.[89, 90]

However, the mere fact that a mother occasionally takes her place alongside the father cannot be regarded as proving conclusively that maternal consent was necessary. It is difficult to assume that patriarchal societies, which is what those of the ancient East essentially were, would endow a mother with the power of vetoing arrangements for the marriage of her daughter, arrangements made in accordance with the wishes of the father. Not only are things unlikely to have worked that way in fact, it is no less unlikely that a legislator would have laid down such a provision *de iure*.[91] *A fortiori* one cannot seriously consider the possibility that the consent of the mother alone would have sufficed. In view of all these considerations we should tentatively submit that in LE 26 and 27/28 the phrase *abiša u ummiša* is to be understood as an

the Athenian law, quoted by Aeschines (*Against Timarchos* 28): a man who beats his father or mother (τὸν πατέρα τύπτων ἢ τὴν μητέρα) must not address the assembly.

88 Note that in *ana ittišu* 7.3.23-45 the provisions concerning father and mother are kept separate.

89 So especially in all texts mentioning father and mother as taking a wife for a son, or giving a daughter in matrimony: see, as examples only, Schorr *1913*, no.3; for Nuzi see Saarisalo *1934:* 36f. (text 21); see also a Kassite document, IM 50097, published by Gurney *1949:* 135f.

90 The problem finds expression in *Mishnah Sanhedrin* 8.4. There Deuteronomy 21:18f. is interpreted as demanding cumulation: "(If) his father wanted, but his mother did not want, his father did not want, but his mother wanted: he does not become a 'recalcitrant son', unless both of them want ..." But it seems that the lengthy discussion of the case in *Mishnah Sanhedrin* is inspired by the desire to interpret the biblical provision in a very narrow fashion, practically to abolish it. Cf. *ibid.*, 8.1, limiting its application to a very short time, when the son is on the verge of puberty, but has not yet fully reached it. It is therefore much open to doubt whether the interpretation offered in *Mishnah Sanhedrin* 8. 4 is in accord with the intention of the biblical legislator.

91 Differently Korošec *1964:* 88, who moreover sees here a significant divergence from the CH: "Während nach dem CH der Brautvater allein das Mädchen verheiratete, verfügten in Ešnunna der Vater und die Mutter über die Hand ihrer Tochter (§§ 26-28); nur der Rücktritt vom Verlöbnis scheint dem Vater allein zugestanden zu sein (§ 25)." Cf. Korošec *1953:* 97.

elliptic formulation for "her father, or (after his death) her mother"; this would mean that legally the mother entered the picture only subsequent to the death of the father[92] or his being otherwise prevented from acting.[93] It is possible that in the exercise of her powers the mother may have acted with the assistance of some male member of the family.

Restricted Capacity

LE 16 ought now to be considered. This provides that a *mar awilim*, who is further described as *la zizu* (and similarly a slave) *ul iqqiap*. It will be convenient to start with the operative part, which we have rendered "shall not be given credit". The import of *qapum* (and the noun derived from it, *qiptum*, which does not occur in LE) is discussed by Szlechter, *1954:*70 ff.: his assumption that *qiptum* (prohibited by LE 16) was resorted to because already customary law forbade ordinary loans to such a *mar awilim* or a slave, has no support in the text itself, nor outside it.[94] Goetze's rendering "(not) to furnish a loan requiring security" is rather awkward, also legally not quite satisfactory;[95] much the best rendering seems to be that given by Kraus: "... wird nichts geborgt."[96] One may assume that the ordinary case concerns the

92 See CH 177, on the duties of the remarrying widow. In Schorr *1913*, no. 33, a mother, by herself, is giving away her daughter. In Nuzi a mother may be endowed with *abbutu* — "fatherhood", i.e. with the powers of a father: see Koschaker *1932:* 400; Korošec *1964:* 173f.; CAD A/i 50; AHw 6a. For dispositions by a mother see YOS vi 154 (discussed by Oppenheim *1955:* 72). A bride is given away by her mother in the Elephantine papyrus Cowley 18 (ca. 420 B.C.E.). See also, generally, Taubenschlag *1929:* 115ff. Differently, Finkelstein *1967:* 129: he seems to imply that any say a mother may have had ends with the death of the father (her husband).

93 See CH /29, on the duties imposed on the wife of a captive; CH 137 on those of the divorcee.

94 Szlechter's rendering of *qiptum* by *depositum irregulare* is not commendable. It is altogether better to dispense with technical Roman expressions in translating or explaining Akkadian legal terms.

95 Goetze thinks probably of the power of levying execution against a piece of land, not of "security" in the technical sense; see also Rabinowitz *1959:* 97. Korošec *1964:* 89 renders *qiptum* by "Darlehen".

96 *1958:* 163. Much in the same sense: Klíma *1956:* 440. Kraus *1984:* 179 has further honed his translation to "auf Borg geben" (sec. 17 of the Edict of Ammi-ṣaduqa); and see, there, also at pp. 208f., 252f., 396.

delayed payment of the price of commodities supplied, rather than a loan.[97] The difference between loan and *qiptum*, as we tend to see it, is that in the former there has to be the return of a chattel similar to that which has been furnished; in the latter there is to be the delivery of something different, the price. This is then a case of "Kreditkauf".[98] It has been noted that the section contains no explicit sanction, but Klíma suggests that the intention may simply have been to make it impossible to recover the sum which has been credited.[99] This seems plausible enough, but even so there remain some questions without answer: e.g., would a subsequent change (division of the estate, manumission of the slave) render the debt actionable, or was it altogether void? On the other hand, on the interpretation offered it would follow that there was no objection to cash transactions, with the *mar awilim la zizu* or slave as buyer. Of course, if big amounts were involved there might sometimes arise a suspicion of theft, but this is a different matter again, one which need not concern us at the moment.

In the present context the interest centres in the main on the phrase *mar awilim la zizu*. The verb *zazum* means, *inter alia*, "to divide, separate, share".[100] Hence, the literal rendering of *mar awilim la zizu* is "the son of a man (who is) not separated", or "has not been given a share". To express this more concisely we have used the term "coparcener". As for the import of the phrase, some scholars would regard age as the determining factor, i.e. for them the *mar awilim la zizu* is a minor.[101] We would doubt that, since credit transactions — of whatever nature — with minors are unlikely to have been of any importance. But even if one rejects (in the given case) age as a criterion, there still remains room for uncertainty and divergence of opinions. Some think of a son still living with his father,[102] others only of a son

97 The cognate *heqif*, in Tannaitic Hebrew, has the meaning "to agree to a delay in the payment of a price": see *Mishnah Shevi'ith* 10.1; *Tosefta Shevi'ith* 8.3.

98 See pp. 240f., below, on the close relation, in Babylonian law, of "Kreditkauf" and loan.

99 *Ibid.*: "dichiarare inesigibile il credito". One might also point to Ed. Ammi-ṣaduqa, sec. 17: *ša iqipu ul ušaddan*.

100 See CAD Z 76ff.; cf. *ibid.* 149, s.v. *la zizu*.

101 E.g., Szlechter *1954:* 38; Klíma *1957:* 169. Contrary to the view expressed above, Klíma regards as minor also the *mar awilim* of sec. 17/.

102 So Rabinowitz *1959:* 97, relying on *Tosefta Baba Bathra* 2.5: *ben šeḥalaq* — "(a) son who separated, took his share".

who after the death of his father has stayed in community of goods with his brothers.[103] Finally, there are those who cumulate both the possibilities and hold that the section may apply equally to a son living in the paternal household *(vivo patre)* and to an heir prior to the division of the paternal estate.[104] It is this last view that I should prefer, in the absence of any reason for limiting the scope of the section: *mar awilim* is less specific than either *marum* (= ben) — "son", or *aḫum* "brother", and may well include both.

ubarum, napṭarum, mudum

Before dealing with the rules concerning slavery, we may refer in brief to some further groups mentioned in the LE. Sec. 41 lists the *ubarum, napṭarum* and *mudum*. The meaning of all of these is uncertain.[105] In the same section mention is made also of the *sabitum* (usually rendered "alewife"), who occurs, together with the *tamkarum* — "merchant", also in LE 15. These are not classes, rather typical occupations. Both are well known and have been much discussed.[106] LE 15 is important in that it shows the *sabitum* engaged in business activities outside her usual sphere, the sale of liquor.

103 So Szlechter, *ibid.*, referring to MAL B, secs. 2, 3: *aḫu la zizute* — "brothers who have not separated, have not been given their share"; cf. also Goetze *1956:* 57f.; Korošec *1964:* 89. For a series of texts from Tell Ḥarmal, dealing with the division of estates, see Ellis *1974:* 133ff. A recurrent phrase is *zizu libbašunu ṭab* — "they are divided; their heart is satisfied".

104 Klíma *1957:* 169; Petschow *1961:* 269.

105 See Goetze *1956:* 109f. Subsequent efforts have had disputed results. Submissions by Finkelstein *1965:* 238 (seconded by Landsberger *1968:* 98ff., and further elaborated by Finkelstein *1970:* 252f.) have been termed "Irrweg" by Kraus *1976:* 165. His own efforts result in putting "wohlbegründete Unkenntnis an die Stelle unbewiesener Annahmen". Nor does CAD N/i 324b take the matter any further. On *ubarum* and *mudum* see Landsberger *1968:* 100.

106 For the *sabitum*, see Driver-Miles *1952:* 202ff.; Kraus *1958:* 161f. The *tamkarum* has been thoroughly examined by Leemans *1950*. See on both also the remarks of Goetze *1956:* 56.

SLAVERY

The importance of slavery in the society of Eshnunna is demonstrated by the fact that slaves — of both sexes *(wardum, amtum)* — are mentioned in many sections of the Laws. Nevertheless, we are very far from having a full picture of the institution. Captivity and birth from a slave woman will — as elsewhere — have been main causes of enslavement. But the LE (and CH) have nothing to say about this or about manumission.[107] Nor are there any provisions concerning the marriage of slaves, considered already in LUY 4, 5, and later in CH 175, 176.

The nature of a slave as a piece of property owned by his master is evident from a number of sections, especially from sec. 40; this lists *wardum* and *amtum* among chattels bought.

In our discussion of delicts we shall deal in greater detail with various offences perpetrated upon slaves. If a slave fell victim to a goring ox or to a vicious dog, in the circumstances described in secs. 54/55, respectively 56/57, a compensation of 15 shekels became payable. This ought not to be taken as representing the full value of the victim, or else the substitution of a suitable equivalent would have been a more likely provision (in the light, e.g., of LE 23/ and 49). Rather, 15 shekels are the fixed, uniform penalty for the culpable, but unintentional death of a slave.[108] Sec. 31 punishes the defloration of a slave girl with the payment of 20 shekels; here a much more pronounced penal element seems to be present.[109] In secs. 22, 23/ an *amtum* is the object of illegal distress.[110] Secs. 49, 50 deal with the possession of a stolen slave, respectively with the non-return of a fugitive slave, seized by an official. Sec. 49 provides as punishment that the delinquent give another slave; in comparison with CH 15, 16, this is rather lenient.

In all these cases the slave is the object or the victim of a delict. Secs. 33, 34/35 are the only ones in which a slave (woman) appears as a

107 See already Klíma *1953:* 228. On the double nature of the slave, at once chattel and human being, see further pp. 256f., below. Note also the observations of Sick *1984:* 102ff.

108 Discussed in detail, p. 289, below.

109 See Goetze, *1956:* 89, and the discussion, p. 281, below. In Ischali 326, the (unintentional) death of a slave woman is punished by a payment of 10 shekels.

110 See pp. 276ff., below.

wrongdoer, in that she attempts to pass on her child to a free person. These will be discussed in due course (pp. 165ff., below); here it will suffice to note that there is no mention of any punishment of the slave: possibly this was a matter left to the domestic jurisdiction of the master.[111]

Secs. 15 and 16 impose restrictions on the legal capacity of slaves. It may be noted that this is done in a roundabout fashion. In sec. 16, which has already been considered, the passive of the verb (*qapum* — "to credit") is employed; this is rather unusual, but thereby the draftsman manages to avoid mentioning the addressees of the section, and this in spite of the fact that the section is formulated as an apodictic command![112] Sec. 15 is ostensibly directed to the *tamkarum* and the *sabitum*, presumably because a slave is not considered a suitable subject, a suitable addressee. In effect this appears to be, in the main, a limitation of the slave's capacity to contract; however, it is difficult to arrive at definite conclusions, and that because of the absence of any sanction.

The actual import of sec. 15 remains in doubt. It is provided that a *tamkarum* or a *sabitum* is not to receive silver, barley, wool or oil from a slave or from a slave woman *adi ma-di?/ṭi?-im*. The phrase left here without translation is the key to the interpretation of the section, but widely divergent renderings have been offered for it. One school reads *madim* (from *madum* — "much"), another *maṭim* (from *maṭum* — "little").[113] For the time being one has to agree that the real import still eludes us.[114]

Finally, there are sections 51 and 52, containing police regulations concerning slaves. The former provides that a slave or a slave woman of Eshnunna, upon whom has been placed a *kannum*, a *maškanum*, or *(u)* an *abbuttum*, shall not go out of the gate of Eshnunna without his (her) owner.[115]

111 See, however, CH 282, on a slave who denies his master.
112 See pp. 103f., above.
113 See concerning both renderings, the notes on sec. 15, pp. 52f., above.
114 See Petschow, *1961:* 269; *1968a:* 135, note 2.
115 That is, without permission; for the use of *balum* — "without", in this sense, see e.g. CH 57, 59, 177; Driver-Miles *1955:* 180.

The discussion turns in the main on the exact meaning of the last term, *abbuttum*.[116] The opinion which is at present predominant sees in *abbuttum* a hairdo peculiar to slaves;[117] others hold that it is a mark incised or tattoed on the body of the slave;[118] a third group sees it as a peculiar object worn by slaves, such as a chain, or a metal tablet, or one of clay.[119] This controversy need not detain us. For our purposes it is sufficient to note that the section applies whenever a person bears some mark of being of servile status. Any of the three will be enough; we see no ground for following von Soden, who interprets *u* as cumulating, and thinks that a slave will bear all three marks simultaneously.[120]

Szlechter regards marking by *abbuttum* as a punishment, to be meted out only in accordance with a provision of law, or pursuant to a judgement. He sees sec. 51 as referring to a fugitive slave, one who has been marked in order to prevent a further escape.[121] There appears to be no warrant for these submissions. We agree that not all slaves were marked as such, but prefer to see this as a matter left to the master's discretion. There is no immediate, impelling public interest in the marking of a slave who has fled and has been recaptured. The slave's offence is not so much against the public order as against his owner: the loss would have been his, so the decision how to treat the slave ought to be his too. On the other hand, even if marking by *abbuttum* was indeed

116 For a survey concerning suggestions on all three terms, see Szlechter, *1949:* 401ff.; add Kraus *1947:* 180ff. On *kannum*, see Goetze *1956:* 129: "a piece of string which slaves wore around their necks"; AHw 438a: "Binde". But AbB i 39 has a slave's *kannum* made of copper (*ša* URUDU). On *maškanum* see von Soden *1949:* 372f.; AHw 627a: "Fessel"; Goetze *1956:* 128.

117 See CAD A/i 49b. See also AbB viii 71.

118 Szlechter *ibid.*; Driver-Miles *1952:* 306ff.

119 See the authors mentioned by Szlechter *cit.* p. 404; Goetze *1956:* 129, and objections raised by von Soden *1958:* 521f.

120 *1949:* 372f.: "Die Sklaven in Ešnunna hatten hiernach ausser ihrer Sklavenmarke noch eine Binde *(kannum)* und eine Fessel *(maškanum)* zu tragen." And cf. AbB viii 71, where *suḫarum šu ul kannum ul abbuttum* is rightly rendered "dieser Bursch (trägt) weder Sklavenfessel noch Sklavenhaartracht".

121 *1949:* 407, 412; *1954:* 40.

in some cases imposed by law, as a punishment, it would yet not follow that it was restricted to these.[122]

Some scholars have adduced CH 15 in comparison with LE 51.[123] There is indeed a basic similarity, but the situations are by no means identical. CH 15 concerns a person who has furthered a slave's escape *(wardam ... uštesi)*, and is to suffer capital punishment for his offence. In this case guilty knowledge is implied; consequently, it is immaterial whether the slave wore a distinctive mark. LE 51 does not concern the aiding and abetting of a fugitive slave. It appears to be addressed to the guards in charge of the city gate. It is their duty to hinder slaves from leaving — provided they are readily identifiable as such. The section is a *lex imperfecta*: no mention is made of the punishment which might be imposed upon the guard failing in his duty.

Divergent interpretations have been offered for sec. 52. Szlechter sees here a provision concerning a fugitive slave, who has been recaptured and brought back to Eshnunna, by a *mar šiprim*, a messenger.[124] However, there is in the section nothing that refers to an escapee; in making his suggestion Szlechter may have been influenced by his assumption, which we do not accept, that marking by *abbuttum* always bears a punitive character. In the view of Goetze,[125] the section deals with a slave who comes to Eshnunna in the suite of a foreign envoy: the authorities will prevent the slave from leaving the city without the permission of his master, provided that the precaution has been taken of marking him in one of the customary ways. However, this would be a rather peculiar situation, one unlikely to be taken care of in a police regulation. The final phrase, *ana belišu naṣer* — "... shall remain in the custody of his owner", is also strange: nobody would expect anything other than that the slave remain with his master. Perhaps it ought to be regarded as an explanation, or consequence, of the preceding provision concerning marking: "... (thereby) he is safe for his owner."[126] This too

122 Szlechter points to *ana ittišu* 7.3.23ff. However, this passage concerns the enslavement of a person hitherto free. The father is granted power to shave the adoptive son who has denied him, to put the *abbuttum* on him, to sell him. But there is no need to regard the marking by *abbuttum* as constituting an additional punitive element, over and above enslavement.

123 Klíma *1953:* 234; Goetze *1956:* 131.

124 *1954:* 40; see also Miles-Gurney *1949:* 187.

125 *1956:* 129, following San Nicolò *1949:* 262.

126 See also CAD A/i 48b.

would be somewhat unusual; there are no other instances where explanations of this kind are attached to the provision laid down. For the time being the exact import of sec. 52 remains then in doubt.

UPBRINGING OF CHILDREN

Scanty as well as obscure are some sections concerning the upbringing of children. There are three sections, 32 to 34/35. They have indeed this common element, but actually they deal with a number of unrelated legal questions. The first concerns the breach of a contract, where a father has handed over his son for nursing and upbringing, but has then failed to furnish the nurse with the necessary means of maintenance (food and clothing). This section will be considered in detail in our discussion of contracts (pp. 252ff., below).

The two following sections differ from sec. 32 in that they concern slave children. The interpretation of sec. 33 depends to a considerable extent on the verb ending the introductory part of the protasis. Regarding this we have already noted a divergence between the two tablets: A iii 7 reads *[i]t-ta-di-in*, but in B ii 16 the last sign of the version of A is missing, and we have only *it-ta-di*. The version of B has usually been regarded as a mistake of the scribe, and it is not categorically denied that this may indeed be the correct explanation.[127] According to this view the slave woman had handed over her child to a free woman *(marat awilim)*, and had done so in fraud of her owner — who was thereby to be deprived of his property, the child. The apodosis upholds the claim of the owner, who has "seen" — that is has recognized — the child of his slave woman: he can take it back.[128] It has been stressed that the section does not mention any penalty being imposed upon the free woman (we have already noted that the slave woman may have been left to the discretion of her master); yet, on the facts stated, the case would be one of theft, since the *marat awilim* could hardly have been unaware of the identity (and the servile status) of the woman from whom she had

127 Note, however, that in writing this word the scribe has already passed beyond the end of the line; an omission is therefore likely to have been conscious rather than accidental.

128 CF. CH 280: ... *bel wardim u lu amtim lu warassu u lu amassu utedi* — "... the owner of the slave or the slave girl identifies his slave or his slave girl (sold abroad)" (CAD I/J 31b).

received the child — if indeed there had been a direct handing over. To say that "in the context ... the legislator is exclusively concerned with the ownership of the child",[129] is not quite satisfactory — in view of the gravity of the offence committed, and especially because the ruling, upholding the owner's title, could in any case have hardly been in doubt. So the section, stating the obvious, would be almost devoid of purpose. Also it is to be noted that the supposed "giving" in sec. 33 lacks any further definition, contrary to what one finds in the section preceding (*ana šunuqim ana tarbitim* — "for suckling, for upbringing"), and in that following (*ana tarbitim* — "for upbringing").[130]

In view of all this it may perhaps be warranted to consider a different possibility, for which one may rely on the working principle which accords tentative preference to the *lectio difficilior*. The version of B would then be the original one, which A "corrected", brought into line with the repeated occurrence, in secs, 32 and 34/35, of forms of the verb *nadanum* — "to give". If this is right, *ittadi* would be Gt of *nadum* — "to throw", and *marša ittadi* would mean "she abandoned her son". We should then interpret *marša ana marat awilim ittadi* (literally, "she threw her son to a free woman") to mean "she abandoned her son in such a manner that a free woman would find him".[131]

Admittedly, this is not the simple and immediate sense of the passage, but there are some arguments which can be adduced in favour of this interpretation. First, the absence of any sanction against the free

129 Goetze *1956:* 95.

130 But Szlechter *1954:* 39 finds a different significance for this omission: "La loi ne reconnaît pas à l'esclave la capacité de donner en adoption son enfant; la remise de l'enfant est dépourvue d'effets juridiques." Too simply, CAD N/i 49a, sees here an "elliptical usage" and renders "gives her child (i.e. *ana tarbitim* for rearing) to somebody's daughter".

131 For *maram nadum* — "to neglect, abandon a child", see C. Bezold, *Babylonisch-assyrisches Glossar*, 1926, p. 191b. See also AHw 706b (publ. 1967), *nadum* 12b: "jmd. preisgeben, verwerfen"; CAD N/i 78bf.: "to reject a person, to abandon, disregard someone". One text deserves attention, because it demonstrates how easily *nadum* and *nadanum* can take each other's place in the eyes of the scholarly beholder: TIM 2: 104, line 10, is adduced in AHw and CAD s.v. *nadum*, but Cagni, publishing the tablet as AbB viii 104, renders *ṣuḫaram tadima* by "hattest du mir einen Burschen 'gegeben'". For *ana X nadum* see AbB viii: 21 *ana Abi-maraṣ nadiaku* — "ich bin dem A. preisgegeben". A biblical parallel is Psalms 22: 11: *'alekha hošlakhti mereḥem* — "upon thee I was cast from the womb."

woman, who brought up the child, would now be explained: she has not acted in collusion with the mother, rather has saved a foundling. Secondly, we have now a factual situation quite different from that in the following sec. 34/35. Finally, the suggested statement of facts reveals a true legal dilemma, a conflict of interests between two persons, each of whom may with some justification expect the support of the law. On the one hand, there is the master, arguing that the act of his slave woman, who was bent on cheating him *(usarir)*, cannot derogate from his rights; on the other hand, one may assume, the woman argues that the foundling is the finder's, who saved its life.[132]

It would have been fascinating to have the details of such a controversy. The verdict in favour of the owner of the slave woman (and consequently owner also of her child) will cause no surprise; early legal systems tend to give decisive weight to the right of ownership, to the exclusion of considerations conflicting with it. Nothing is said about any duty of the owner to reimburse the woman for the expenses which she will have incurred. It must remain an open question whether this is a further instance of lack of completeness, or rather that the silence of the section is to be understood as implying a negative regulation, in other words that there was no such duty.[133]

In sec. 34/35 the facts are not free from complexity, but the difficulties of interpretation concentrate in the apodosis, again because

132 See Yaron *1959b:* 160ff., and *1963d:* 137ff., on the acquisition of rights over persons saved in time of famine.

133 Roman law deals with the problem of the abandoned slave child in three texts: *Codex Iustinianus* 8.51.1. (224 C.E.); *Codex Theodosianus* 5.9.1. (331), and 5.9.2 (412). The first upholds the claim of the owner, if the child of his slave woman has been abandoned against his will, or without his knowledge ("si invito vel ignorante te partus ancillae ... tuae expositus est"); in the two later constitutions the owner's knowledge precludes vindication. LE 33 corresponds to C.I.8.51.1, since the owner's lack of knowledge is evident from the fact that the slave woman is said to have acted fraudulently.
The question concerning reimbursement, which for LE had to be left open, is for Roman law answered by C.I.8.51.1: the owner of the child is bound to repay what has been rightly spent *in alendo eo vel forte ad discendum artificium;* the reference to the teaching of an occupation implies that considerable time may have passed, just as in LE 33: *inuma irtabu* — "when he had grown up". There is no duty of reimbursement if the child is claimed from the person who stole it.

of the conjunction *u*. A slave woman hands over her child,[134] *ana tarbitim* — "for upbringing". I would see in this "handing over for upbringing" the essential difference from the preceding section. But there are also some other divergences to be noted: there is a change of all the persons acting. Where in sec. 33 there was (a) slave woman *(amtum)*, (b) her master *(belum)*, and (c) a free woman *(marat awilim)*, we have now, in sec. 34/35 (a) a slave woman of the palace *(amat ekallim)*, (b) the palace *(ekallum)*, and (c) the recipient of the child, described as *muškenum*.

Concerning the consequences which ensue, we are told (i) that the palace will recover the child (end of 34/); (ii) that the recipient shall?/may? "replace" *(iriab)* an equivalent to the palace (sec. /35). The two provisions are linked by *u*; this means that from the point of view of language two interpretations are equally possible: (a) the palace recovers the child, or (i.e. unless) the recipient renders its equivalent; (b) the palace recovers the child, and (moreover) the recipient has to render an equivalent.[135] Scholarly opinion is sharply divided, with the balance in favour of (a).

Goetze *1948* rendered sec. /35 by "also he who adopted the child ... shall recompense" etc., i.e. in accordance with interpretation (b). This met with the categoric objection that "*u* means 'or', not 'also'"; hence — "the palace may take the child from the *muškenum* or he may keep the child and give his equivalent to the palace".[136] From the point of view of language, this interpretation was certainly possible, but by no means compelling. As for its substantive legal merits, no attempt was made to detail these; nevertheless, it soon gained the adherence of other

134 The text, suddenly very detailed, specifies "her son or her daughter"; see pp. 88, 113, above.

135 The verb *rabum* — "to replace" refers usually to compensation. But LE 23/, CH 8, 265, show that it is wide enough to give expression also to a penal element.

136 Miles-Gurney *1949:* 185. We have discussed the problem posed by the conjunction *u* (see pp. 38f., above), and can only repreat that in the LE there is no way for distinguishing between cumulation ("and") and alternation ("or"). For the former see particularly sec. 31 *u amtum ša belišama* — "and the slave woman (remains) her owner's indeed"; sec. 38 *u aḫušu šamam ḫašeḫ* — "and his brother wants to buy". In both instances the use is similar to that of sec. /35, and in neither can there be any doubt as to the correct interpretation. There is then no basis for the assertion that *u* must always be rendered "or".

authors.[137] Following suit, Szlechter *1954:* 39f. stressed especially the difference between an ordinary *amtum* and an *amat ekallim*, holding that the latter could enter into a contract concerning her child which was not entirely devoid of effect, since by rendering a substitute the recipient would be able to repel the claim of the palace for the return of the child. One may entertain some doubts: there is no proof for the contention that the slave woman of the palace was, vis-à-vis the palace, endowed with legal capacities or powers in excess of those of an ordinary *amtum* vis-à-vis her private owner. In his standard, *1956* edition Goetze adhered indeed to his original rendering ("also" etc.), but in his commentary he fell into line, writing that "the law upholds the right of the adoptant against the claims of the palace. All the new father has to do is furnish a child of equal value to the palace" (p. 95). Aware of the difficulties involved, Goetze would restrict the rule, to make it apply only where "the adoptant proved that he acted in good faith"; but in the conditions prevailing in small townships it is rather unlikely that anyone receiving the child from its mother would be unaware of her status. Finally, if the option were that of the person who took the child, one would expect a simpler formulation, putting first things first: the "taker" might render the child's equivalent, or (if he failed to do so) the palace would recover the child.

Altogether then I tend to give preference to the contrary opinion, expressed by San Nicolò,[138] and should hold — in the sense of interpretation (b) — that in sec. 34/35 there is a cumulation of two provisions: not only will the palace take back the child, but it will moreover exact an equivalent child as a penalty. In other words, the case is treated as one similar to theft. One should not be misled by the use of contractual terminology, *ana tarbitim ittadin* — "she gave for upbringing", *lequ ša ... ilqu* — "the taker who took". This does not allow any conclusion as to the legality or the effect of what has taken place, no more than the use of the verb *šamum* — "to buy", in LE 40, CH 7. A right of the palace defeasible at the discretion of private

137 See Klíma, e.g., *1953c:* 148, and note 39, there; Korošec *1953:* 97. Similarly Petschow *1961:* 271.

138 *1949:* 261. San Nicolò is followed by Böhl; Diakonoff; Lipin.

persons would be rather extraordinary, acceptable only on the basis of really compelling evidence.[139]

Even though we have denied the legal efficacy of *ana tarbitim nadanum* in the specific circumstances of sec. 34/35, the meaning of the phrase requires consideration. The corresponding phrase *ana tarbitim lequm* — "to take for upbringing", occurs in CH 188;[140] as to the exact import there are differences of opinion. David defines *tarbitum* as "Pflegschaftsverhältnis, nicht Adoption im eigentlichen Sinne".[141] On the strength of CH 188, 189, he sees the teaching of a handicraft as the main purpose of such a relationship. Driver-Miles argue in detail in favour of full adoption.[142]

The LE do not contribute to the solution of this controversy. On the contrary, they show that matters are actually even more complicated. It emerges that one must distinguish between a non-technical *ana tarbitim nadanum*, not concerned with any change of status, and the technical use of the same phrase, where the creation of a new status relationship is involved.[143] The former is present in LE 32, where a man gives his son[144] to be suckled and brought up.[145] It seems certain that no personal relationship between the child and its nurse is envisaged, no more so than in CH 194. All that the section is concerned with — we have seen — is the father's neglect to provide for the maintenance of his child; in the end, if the penalty is paid, the child is to return to its father. On the

139 Secs. 33 and 34/35 deal only with the substantive aspects of the case. It is a necessary implication that the claimant, whether a private person (as in sec. 33) or the palace (as in 34/35), will have to prove his claim, in particular that the child is indeed that of his slave woman. For disputes which turn on the status of a person (is he free or slave) see ARM VI 40; ARM XIII 141; AbB i 129.

140 The abstract noun *tarbitum* — "upbringing", is used concretely, as designation of the child adopted, in CH 185, 186, 189, 190 and 191.

141 *1927:* 34.

142 *1952:* 392ff.

143 This variation of import is facilitated by the wide range in which the verb *nadanum* is employed. Often it refers to a transfer of ownership (especially, but not only, in conjunction with *ana kaspim* — "for silver"), often it does not, as in LE 36/37, and *passim* in CH.

144 Klíma *1950b:* 280 has suggested that the section may refer to a foundling, but there seems to be no warrant for this.

145 For further references see Driver-Miles *1952:* 393, note 2; Szlechter *1954:* 109.

other hand, a technical import must be postulated for the phrase *ana tarbitim nadanum* in sec. 34/35. There the transaction between the slave woman of the palace and the recipient of the child must have been aimed at the creation of a permanent relationship, the affiliation of the child. In this respect it is immaterial whether one adheres to the opinion of Miles-Gurney, or to that of San Nicolò (which we incline to prefer). According to the former, such a relationship has indeed come into being, at least in an inchoate fashion, and it will be perfected if the adoptant *(lequm)* is prepared to furnish a suitable substitute; according to the latter, the mere attempt of creating such a relationship is countered with the imposition of a penalty.

CHAPTER SIX

MARRIAGE AND DIVORCE

LE AND CH

There is in the LE no exhaustive, or at least systematic, treatment of the law concerning marriage and divorce; by contrast, the discussion in CH is much more detailed. For example, the LE do not deal with childlessness (CH 144-147), nor with illness of the wife (CH 148/149). Of delicts connected with marriage, the LE consider rape (subsequent to betrothal) and adultery, but not incest (CH 154-158). A wife's liability to be seized for the debts of her husband does indeed emerge from sec. /24 (comparable to CH 116), but there is nothing that corresponds to the detailed provisions of CH 151/152. On the other hand, for each of the sections in LE (but one) there is a correspondence in CH.[1] When encountering difficulties, one may therefore occasionally wish to rely on the Code; this is legitimate, as long as it is done with proper caution.

CONCLUSION OF MARRIAGE

Although the relevant provisions in the LE are few, they make it possible to discern at least the main outlines of the institution. One gets also a fairly clear notion as to how marriage came about and how it ended; some of the details even take us beyond the information

1 The following correspondences may be noted:

LE 17/	—	without correspondence
LE /18	—	CH 163/164
LE 25	—	CH 160, 161
LE 26	—	CH 130
LE 27/28	—	CH 128, 129
LE 29	—	CH 133-135
LE 30	—	CH 136
LE 59	—	CH 137

supplied by the CH. The first step toward marriage consisted of informal negotiations: the young man (or someone on his behalf, e.g., his father) "asked" (*šalum* — sec. 27/) for the consent of the father of the bride. As a rule there followed the handing over of the "bride payment" (*terḫatum* — secs. 17/18, 25, and 26), effecting betrothal (better: "inchoate marriage"[2]). The emphasis of the texts is on the unexpected: mishaps might occur to upset plans. Death might intervene (sec. 17/18), or the father of the bride might have second thoughts (sec. 25). For all their prominence in the laws, these were relatively exceptional cases. In the normal course of events, the bridegroom would formally demand his wife ("claim at the house of the father-in-law" — *ana bit emim šasum*, [sec. 25]); a formal marriage contract (*riksatum* — sec. 27/28) might be entered upon;[3] certain ceremonies would often take place (*kirrum* — "marriage feast", sec. 27/28). Finally, the marriage was completed by the "taking" (*aḫazum* — secs. /18, 27/28, 59) of the bride,[4] and by her entry into the house (*ana bitim erebum* — sec. /18) of the husband. The marriage relationship might be adversely affected by the absence of the husband (secs. 29, 30); death (sec. 17/18) or divorce (sec. 59) would necessarily terminate it.

The preliminary negotiations were largely informal, and in themselves of little legal significance.[5] But their positive issue, i.e., that the father of the bride give his consent to the proposed union, was indispensable.[6] In sec. /27, the absence of parental consent is the main defect derogating from the legal import of the relationship of the couple living together in the man's house.

Legally, the parties to the proceedings are the bridegroom and the father (or the parents) of the bride. In the LE the bridegroom appears to be acting on his own, but CH presents a more complicated picture:

2 See Driver-Miles *1952:* 249ff.
3 The question whether the contract had to be in writing was discussed by Greengus *1969:* 505ff. See further p. 201, below.
4 Concerning the exact import of *aḫazum*, see the discussion by Landsberger *1968:* 85ff.
5 Differently Westbrook OBML, chapter 2, who envisages a preliminary executory betrothal contract, which precedes the giving of the *terḫatum*. It is not clear what the purpose of such an agreement would be, nor how it would function. The evidence for its existence is precarious.
6 We have already discussed the problems arising out of the reference, in LE 26 and 27/28, to both father and mother; see pp. 156ff. above.

sometimes the bridegroom acts by himself (as in secs. 159, 160, 161), on other occasions his father is acting for him (so in secs. 155, 156, 166).[7] It seems then that he could — in law — act independently, but was in fact often assisted by his father. The bride, on the other hand, was object rather than subject.[8] In an early patriarchal society she would, as a rule, have little say in the choice of her mate — at least in case this was her first marriage.[9]

BRIDE PAYMENT *(terḫatum)*

Before we enter into a detailed discussion of the various sections, some remarks concerning the bride payment *(terḫatum)* may be in order. It is typical of an ancient collection of legal rules that there is no general statement on the *terḫatum*; rather, it is mentioned only in connection with extraordinary occurrences. In sec. 17/18, where death has caused the failure of the marriage, the disposal of the *terḫatum* is itself a main purpose of the ruling; in the two other sections, 25 and 26, its payment is an essential preliminary part of the facts. The LE do not give us any details concerning the substance of the *terḫatum* brought by the bridegroom. It seems that the *terḫatum* consisted usually of a sum of silver (sec. 17/: *kaspum ... itar* — "the silver shall return"); this would not preclude an agreement for the substitution of some other kind of property, or an arrangement that the bridegroom work for the father of the bride.[10]

The nature of the *terḫatum* (and also of its biblical counterpart, the *mohar*) has been much discussed, and various theories have been propounded for its interpretation. Koschaker views Babylonian marriage as "Kaufehe" (marriage by purchase), with the *terḫatum* as the

7 Similarly in MAL: in sec. 30 the father of the bridegroom acts, in sec. 31 the bridegroom himself.

8 See already Koschaker *1917:* 119.

9 But see p. 220, below, on second marriages. See also Schorr *1913,* no. 1 for a marriage contracted by a woman on her own. For the practice in demotic documents and in the Talmud, see Yaron *1961:* 46.

10 Nothing is said about anything akin to the *biblum* (provisions for the marriage feast? See Driver-Miles *1952:* 250) mentioned in CH 159-161; cf. also Mal 30, 31, where the terms *biblu* and *zubullu* are synonyms; they have a wide meaning, including both silver payments and various gifts in naturalia.

price paid for the bride.[11] This approach has met with opposition on the part of several scholars. M. David pointed to differences in the terminology of marriage and sale.[12] In the opinion of Driver-Miles (*1952:* 261), the *terḫatum* is a mere gift, made in order to ingratiate the bridegroom with the family of the bride and to gain their approbation. Slightly different is the definition of *terḫatum* and *mohar* as compensation gifts.[13] It has also been suggested that the origins of *terḫatum* are to be found in the sphere of evidence: according to this view it served, in the beginning, to prove that the union was a lawful marriage, not a mere concubinage, and was retained even after the introduction of written marriage contracts.[14]

It is not our intention to go into the details of this controversy, rather we shall be content with some general remarks. First, it should be taken into account that the bride payment may have changed its nature in the course of time. Marriage will have occasioned the transfer of property from the family of the bridegroom to that of the bride (*terḫatum, mohar,* etc.), but also *vice versa* from the family of the bride to the bridegroom (dowry: *šeriktum, mullugum, šilluḫim,* etc.). It will probably be correct to assume that in most ancient systems of law compensation payments to the family of the bride represent the earliest stage, with counter-gifts as yet relatively insignificant. In biblical law, in ancient Greece and in early Rome, one finds payments which are functionally similar to the Babylonian *terḫatum*. Later these payments come into collision with the custom, which had developed, that the bride bring a substantial dowry with her; this dowry might then become the predominant element and will often have included the bride payment which had been given to the father at an earlier stage of the proceedings. Far-reaching changes may result: the bride payment may lose its primary functions, or some of them, and may eventually degenerate into a mere fiction. This has happened in Roman *coemptio* and in Talmudic law; in both the bride

11 *1917:* 137. Later Koschaker took pains to qualify his views: there was indeed a link with notions of sale, but a wife was never actually "purchased" like a chattel: *1950:* 235. See further the detailed remarks of Landsberger *1968:* 93ff.

12 *1934:* 11f.; but see Furlani *1935:* 379f.

13 Burrows *1938:* 13.

14 van Praag *1945:* 152.

payment is purely symbolic, and the wife is "acquired" *nummo uno*, or by one *peruṭa*. In Talmudic law the *mohar* undergoes the metamorphosis of becoming a fund to provide for the wife in case of termination of the marriage (by the death of the husband, or also by divorce, provided she does not bear the blame for it).

Although the payment of a *terḫatum* will have been the rule, it appears that this was not an indispensable step on the road to marriage. This is clear from CH /139/140, dealing with the dissolution of marriages which had been contracted without the payment of a *terḫatum*. For Eshnunna the same is necessarily implied by sec. 27/: a *terḫatum* was not rendered in that case, but it was not for that reason that the marriage was voided. In the absence of a *terḫatum* there would simply be no legal tie prior to the marriage itself, that is to say the various effects of betrothal, in the sphere of contract (LE 25, CH 159-161, HL 29, 30) and delict (LE 26, CH 130, Deuteronomy 22:23-27), would not ensue.[15]

Even after the *terḫatum* has been paid, most ancient Near Eastern systems of law leave room for retraction by either party, subject (in the main) to pecuniary consequences only. We shall return to this topic when discussing LE 25.[16]

Death of a Childless Wife (CH 163/164)

We should now return to one point which has been mentioned, namely the custom of returning the *terḫatum* to the bridegroom, so that it forms part of the dowry *(šeriktum)*. In the time of Hammurabi this custom seems to have been widespread, but not yet prevalent. The state of the law is reflected by CH 163/164:

> *šumma awilum aššatam iḫuzma mari*^{meš} *la ušaršišu sinništum ši ana šimtim ittalak šumma terḫatam ša awilum šu ana bit emišu ublu emušu utteršum ana šerikti sinništim šuati musa ul iraggum šeriktaša ša bit abišama šumma emušu terḫatam la utteršum ina šeriktiša mala terḫatiša iḫarraṣma šeriktaša ana bit abiša utar*

15 See pp. 190ff., 278ff., below.
16 See pp. 190, below.

Driver Miles (*1955:* 63) offer the following translation, which can be taken as representing the dominant interpretation of the passage:

> 163: "If a man has married a wife and she has not provided him with sons, (and) that woman has then gone to (her) fate, if his father-in-law renders to him the bride payment[17] which that man has brought to the house of his father-in-law, her husband shall bring no claim to the dowry of that woman; her dowry belongs to her father's house."
>
> 164: "If his father-in-law does not render the bride payment to him, he shall deduct the full amount of her bride payment from the dowry and shall render (the residue of) her dowry to her father's house."

It will be useful to go into the details of this section, since a correct understanding of it may be relevant to the interpretation of LE 17/18. The customary translation of CH 163/164 is hardly satisfactory, since it leaves us with a text which is excessively and unusually loquacious. It contains superfluous advice on methods of accounting. Actually, one could cut out more than half the section (27 words out of 49!) without omitting anything of substance. The following abridged version, leaving out the end of 163/ and the beginning of /164, would be quite sufficient:

> *šumma awilum aššatam iḫuzma mari*[meš] *la ušaršišu sinništum ši ana šimtim ittalak ina šeriktiša mala terḫatiša iḫarrasma šeriktaša ana bit abiša utar*
>
> "If a man has married a wife and she has not provided him with sons, (and) that woman has then gone to (her) fate, from her dowry the full amount of her bride payment he shall deduct, and (the residue of) her dowry to her father's house shall render."

It is the kind of matter which would not escape the attention of Koschaker. He suggests that sec. 164 may have been added by Hammurabi: it includes also what is already provided in sec. 163, which is then altogether dispensable.[18] Hardly a very satisfactory

17 For the sake of uniformity, "bride payment" is substituted for Driver's "bridal gift", as a rendering of *terḫatum.*

18 "... der neben ihm entbehrlich scheint" (*1917:* 87, note 6).

explanation, since the addition of /164 would then be devoid of purpose. It has also been pointed out that sec. /164 endows the husband with a power of retention (or deduction);[19] this is so, but then this purpose would have been fully achieved also by the shorter version proposed above. The correct solution seems to be that proposed by van Praag:[20] he points to three well known Old Babylonian marriage contracts, which record the return of the *terḫatum* to the bridegroom (or to his father) — at the time of the marriage.[21] Under this practice, the *terḫatum* retained the function of an earnest, and served as means for fixing the pecuniary consequences in case the one or the other of the parties did not live up to his undertaking.

The Code of Hammurabi, dealing with the death of the wife in absence of issue, provides for two possibilities: it rules first (sec. 163/) on the case where the *terḫatum* has been returned to the bridegroom at the time of the marriage, then (sec. /164) on the case where it has remained in the hands of the bride's father. This interpretation is supported also by the fact that the return of the *terḫatum* is not in any way made obligatory. In both the parts of the section the return (or non-return) of the *terḫatum* belongs to the protasis, is part of the *res gestae*, and as such precedes the operative provisions. Both parts of the section are now meaningful: one might have thought that the location of the *terḫatum* (in the hands of the husband, or in that of the bride's father) might in some way influence its final destination, or perhaps even that of the dowry — ***beati possidentes!*** Section 163/164 shows that that is not so: the result reached in the end is the same in both cases. The new custom, under which possession of the *terḫatum* vests in the husband immediately on the consummation of the marriage, has not improved his legal position: in case the wife dies, he will still have to return the *šeriktum*. Incidentally, one sees that — contrary to the view of Koschaker — it is the second part of the section (/164) which preserves the *antiquum ius*,[22] and provides for a

19 Driver-Miles *1952:* 252.

20 *1945:* 135f.

21 HG III (1909), texts 9, 10, 483. The last-mentioned document is Schorr *1913*, no. 209. All the three are given in full, with detailed discussion, by Driver-Miles *1952:* 253ff.

22 San Nicolò *1950a:* 442, comes to the same result by comparing CH 163/164 with LE 17/18; Klíma *1957:* 169 still terms sec. /164 "the younger provision of Hammurabi".

mutual refund by way of set-off. Sec. 163/164 should then be rendered as follows:

> "If a man has taken a wife and she has not provided him with sons, (and) that woman has (then) gone to the fate:
>
> (i) If his father-in-law had returned to him the bride payment, which that man had brought to the house of his father-in-law, her husband shall not claim the dowry of that woman; her dowry belongs to her father's house indeed.
>
> (ii) If his father-in-law had not returned the bride payment to him, he shall deduct the full amount of her bride payment from her dowry, and shall return (the residue of) her dowry to her father's house."

DEATH PARTED THEM (LE 17/18)

We return now to the LE, to consider two sections concerning the failure of the marriage, secs. 17/18 and 25. Sec. 17/18 is of a complex nature.[23] It begins with an introductory passage, which relates — as a preliminary factual occurrence — that the bridegroom had brought a *terḫatum* to the house of his father-in-law. This introduction has to be read in conjunction with each of the two subsections which follow (the first occupies the rest of 17/, the second all /18); (i) "if one of the two went to the fate ..."; (ii) "if he took her and she entered to his house ..."

It will be recalled that in Tablet A sec. 17/18 is vitiated by a mistake of the scribe: due to a homoioteleuton he has omitted the apodosis of subsection (i) and the protasis of subsection (ii).[24] This matter has already been discussed in detail and there is no need to return to it; we shall henceforth concentrate on the fuller version of Tablet B.

The introduction is straightforward and does not call for comment. The same may be said also of subsection (i) as a whole: it provides for the case that *ina kilallin išten* — "one of the two", i.e., either the groom or the bride, happen to die before the marriage: the silver (i.e., the *terḫatum*) will revert to its owner. In other words, repayment will be made to the bridegroom, or — if it is he who has died — to his

23 See p. 101, above.
24 See pp. 24f. above.

family. We have already noted that this specific case is not considered in CH, but there is no reason to doubt that the same common sense solution would have applied under it too.[25]

A number of difficulties hinder our understanding of subsection (ii) = sec. / 18. The protasis of subsection (i) — we have seen — is made up of two parts, the introduction and the statement concerning the death of "one of the two". But the unfolding story of subsection (ii) consists of three stages, each of which, in the neatness typical of scribe B, occupies one complete line: B i 13 (the introduction common to both the subsections) tells of the payment of the *terḫatum*, B i 16 brings the important next step, the consummation of the marriage ("... he took her and she entered his house"). The remaining, last line of the protasis, B i 17, reverts to the common topic of both subsections, death, leading up to the one-line apodosis, in B i 18, setting out the pecuniary consequences.[26]

No problems arise in text or interpretation of lines 13 and 16. Line B i 17 presents difficulties of reading. While there is no doubt about the end of the line, speaking of the death of the wife ("... the bride went to the fate"), there are divergences in the reading of some signs at the beginning of line 17. Indeed, over the years there emerged what can be described as a *consensus fere omnium*, and it is this which is expressed in the translation offered above "(and) *either the marrier or*". Combining the two parts of the line, one obtains that subsection (ii) — like (i) — deals with two possible deaths, that of the groom or the wife.[27] My problems and misgivings will be set out after a detailed survey of the various contributions.

The *ed. princeps* gave for the disputed signs the reading *lu-ú a-aḫ-ḫa-ru-ú*. Until 1964 this reading was generally followed, with only some minor reservations and variations.[28] There was less agreement on the actual rendering: all did indeed proceed from the same basic notion, considering *aḫḫarum* to be somehow connected with the idea

25 Compare MAL 31, which is somewhat more complicated. See the discussion in Yaron *1963c:* 116f.

26 The apodosis, another example of extreme conciseness, is intact but not easily comprehensible.

27 So first in CAD A/i 192b, to be discussed at once.

28 Goetze *1956* reads *ù(?) a-aḫ-ḫa-ru-um(?)* — "but soon afterward"; he does not account for the switch from *lu-ú*, not questioned by anyone, to the doubtful *ù*. Von Soden *1958:* 519 reads *lu-ú a-aḫ-ḫa-ru-ma!*

of "lateness", but beyond that there were notable divergences. Goetze, and some scholars following him,[29] would regard the word as an adverb of time, more or less the equivalent of *warkanum(ma)* — "afterward, thereafter" etc., which occurs several times in CH. Others interpret it as an adjective, meaning roughly "delayed, being in delay".[30] However, amongst those following the latter view, there were further divergences concerning the exact import of "being in delay": the proposals included delay in the payment of the *terḫatum*;[31] in the restitution of the dowry;[32] finally, in the consummation of the marriage.[33] For the beginning of line 17, there seems to be no good reason to doubt the reading *lu-ú*, but even so the import of the particle is uncertain, and depends decisively on what follows. There are two possibilities. One can either take *lu* (with Goetze *1948* and Szlechter *1954*) as a particle of emphasis ("verily"); or else one can see it as the conjunction "or". This has been first suggested by von Soden *(ibid.)*; in his view, *lu* introduces an alternative to the occurrence mentioned in line 16; in other words, the beginning of line 17 would itself belong to the introductory, preliminary part of the protasis: consummation — or delay of it.[34]

For all the differences set out, these were all interpretations of basically the same text. An entirely new departure came in 1964, with the publication of CAD A/i: a new reading was offered, namely *lu-ú a-ḫi*(!)-*za*(!)-*n*[*u-u*]*m* ⌜*lu*⌝ *kallatum* — "(if) either the bridegroom or the bride (should die) ..."[35] The addition of the groom broadened the scope of the provision considerably.

29 See notes on sec. 17/18.
30 Proposed by von Soden *1949:* 370.
31 See Böhl *1949/1950:* 100.
32 Szlechter *1954:* 20.
33 Von Soden *1958:* 519: "Entgegen meiner früheren Vermutung möchte ich jetzt *aḫḫaru* nicht im Sinne von 'mit einer Zahlung rückständig' verstehen, sondern im Sinne von 'mit dem Vollzug der Ehe rückständig'." See also his AHw 20a.
34 In CAD A, *cit.*, *lu* is followed by a second *lu* (preceding *kallatum*): "either ... or". This will be discussed at once.
35 The reading is customarily attributed to Landsberger, who adduces it *suo nomine* in *1968:* 73. His reading is *lu-ú a-ḫi-za-nu lu-ú kal-la-tum*. Note the minute differences. Gone are not only the exclamation marks, but also the square brackets (whole and half); gone is also — *u*]*m*, — ending *aḫizanu-um*. The omission may have been conscious (not enough room for *lu-ú*?).

The reading *aḫizanum* — "marrier"[36] prevailed soon. It was accepted by Bottéro,[37] Klíma,[38] Petschow,[39] Finkelstein,[40] and Kraus.[41] Dissent, if any, was very restrained, implicit rather than explicit. Goetze used the third (1969) edition of ANET to accept the correcting reading *šir* ("carcass") in LE 53, but failed to take cognizance of *aḫizanum*. Von Soden refers specifically to B i 17,[42] but refrains from offering a reading. In his Czech translation (*1979:* 116) Klíma abandons *aḫizanum* and reverts to the earlier version, rendering "nato nevěsta odešla za osudem" — "thereupon the bride went to the fate". Lastly, Westbrook comments, rather resignedly, that "the difficulties detailed below arise from the reading *aḫizanum* ..., which adds an element not in CH 164, namely the death of the husband. From the legal point of view, the earlier reading was more satisfactory, but one has to make the best of the evidence as it stands".[43]

Yes, but how does it really stand? It is a question which I may ask, but which I am not entitled to answer, since this is not within the sphere of the historian of law. But there are two points which should be mentioned: (a) In *1956:* 60, years before *aḫizanum* was brought into the picture, Goetze remarked that the first third of B i 17 was "written over an erasure and therefore hard to read"; (b) Finkelstein *1970:* 249, note 34, asserts that "Landsberger's reading of *a-ḫi-za-nu* rather than *a-aḫ-ḫa-ru-um* (?) ... is confirmed by collation". *Ibid.*, p. 245 he tells of having "conducted a seminar in the fall of 1966 on the Laws of Eshnunna where certain new readings and interpretations were proposed, which prompted Mrs. R.S. Ellis to undertake a collation of the original tablets during her stay in Baghdad in the winter of 1968." He further observes: "If the results were not always conclusive, this was due to the poor state of the surface of text A at many points, which has been rendered even less legible by a thick coating of preservative

36 The term is first used by Westbrook OBML; it is a good choice, because "marrier" is as rare and quaint as *aḫizanum*.
37 *1965/1966:* 92.
38 *1966:* 254; also 1970: 453, note 37.
39 *1968a:* 136f., 139.
40 *1970:* 249.
41 *1973:* 52, 54.
42 AHw 1239b (publ. 1976), s.v. *šimtu*.
43 OBML chapter 5, note 20.

covering the entire surface."[44] In such circumstances, how reliable can a collation of an admittedly difficult detail be? I can again only put the question.[45]

I am aware that all these deliberations leave us neither here nor there. So let us for the moment put aside the doubtful part of B i 17, and turn to the apodosis. Here, incidentally, Tablet A re-enters the picture, and the text of both tablets is identical and certain. In spite of this, there are considerable divergences in the interpretation. The apodosis consists of six words, forming three sentences. It reads *mala ublu ul ušeṣṣe wataršuma ileqqe*. We have rendered this, with deliberate equivocation, as follows: "whatever (one) has brought, (one) will not cause to go forth; its *excess* only (one) will take". Wishing to arrive at an interpretation which will be more meaningful and comprehensible, one has to consider and determine four points: (i) Who is the subject of *ublu* — "brought"? It could be either the husband (H), or the wife (W): the reference would then be either to the *terḫatum* (brought by H), or to the *šeriktum* (brought by W); (ii) Who is the subject of *ušeṣṣe* — "will cause to go forth"? It might be a surviving spouse, or in his/her place the head of his/her family. (iii) Who is the subject of *ileqqe* — "he will take"? Here apply the same considerations as under (ii); finally, (iv) returning to *ušeṣṣe*: What is the exact import of this verb?

Let us consider the last point first. The verb *šuṣum* (the causative form of *waṣum* — "to go forth") has several widely divergent translational equivalents; as a result it does not convey conclusive information on the identity of the subject. "Causing to go forth" may refer to two greatly different acts: (1) that someone having some object (or person) in his possession lets it go, sets it free, relinquishes it,

44 *1970:* 245, note 6. Ostensibly this refers only to Tablet A, but one would like to know whether the protective coating was not applied also to Tablet B?

45 As far as I know, the results of the collation by Mrs. Ellis were not published in a detailed and coherent fashion. This is certainly deplorable, if one bears in mind that it was the first collation ever, 20 years after the publication of the LE, and that apparently there has been none in the 20 years which have passed since. So far we have had only the scattered, brief remarks in Finkelstein *1970* (and once, referring to LE /28, in *1981:* 20, note 1). In our immediate context one would wish to know what Mrs. Ellis read in all the left side of B i 17, — up to *kallatum*.

expels it; or (2) that some person other than the possessor obtains the object from him, deprives him of it, exacts it, recovers it. As an example for (1) one may refer to *ana ittišu* 7.3.3: there the divorcing husband is the subject of *ina biti ušeṣišu* (sic!) — "from the house he will cause her(!) to go forth". On the other hand, in passages concerning the redemption of persons *šuṣum* refers usually to the act of the redemptor.[46, 47] The same verb occurs also in the context of lease, with the tenant as subject (see CH 42, 44). When discussing LE/18, scholars have as a rule preferred rendering (2); accordingly, *ul ušeṣṣe* would mean "he will not recover". This rendering is not objectionable, but one should bear in mind that rendering (1) is equally possible; using it we should obtain "he will not cause to go forth" = "he will not relinquish".

As for the subjects of the three verbs, the main interpretations which have been put forward can be arranged in two groups. Some authors have held that the husband (H) is the subject of all of them;[48] to some extent they may have been influenced by a reluctance to admit inexplicit changes of subject.[49] Others have felt less hesitation on this account: here we find a switch from wife (W) to her father, or family (WF),[50] or also from H to WF.[51] All these views call now for a somewhat more detailed discussion.

We have seen the provisions laid down in CH 163/164. In the view of Goetze *1956:* 63 "the ruling of the LE is different; there is no equalization of claims, and nothing is returned to the father-in-law". If

46 Cf. Yaron *1959b:* 165, note 15. And see CAD A/ii 378b (on LE/18).

47 The same applies also to the Hebrew cognate *hoṣi'*; the comparable range of Hebrew *hešiv* may be noted: it may have to be rendered "to hand back" or "to take back"; see Yaron *1959a:* 323.

48 Goetze in *1950* (ANET) and *1956*; Szlechter *1954:* 20; Lipin *1954:* 49; Böhl *1949/1950:* 100. Von Soden *1949:* 370 renders: "was er (der Gatte) (dem Schwiegervater) gebracht hat, wird er nicht hinausbringen (d.h. die Zahlung wird nicht zurückgängig gemacht); was darüber hinaus überschüssig ist, wird er (selbst) nehmen". But see later his abridgement, *1958:* 519: "... dann wird er was er brachte nicht nehmen ..." There is no further interpretation. See also CAD A/ii 501b.

49 See pp. 95f., above.

50 San Nicolò, in a private communication mentioned by Miles-Gurney *1949:* 177, note 5; cf. also San Nicolò *1950a:* 442. Klíma *1953:* 194; cf. *1957:* 169.

51 Yaron *1963a:* 6f.; so also Bottéro *1965/1966:* 92, 97.

one may paraphrase this — each side is to hold on to what it has: the father to the bride payment, the husband to the dowry. From an abstract legal point of view, this is certainly one of the possible solutions, in the situation brought about by the death of the wife (the sole possibility considered by Goetze).[52] However, and more concretely, this solution is without foundation in the wording of the section. One would have to assume that the draftsman has failed to make himself understood, and there seems to be no justification for such an assumption.

The following rendering is given by Szlechter: "... et si après que la jeune femme est décédée, il (le *mar awilim*) est en retard (pour la restitution de la dot) il ne fera pas sortir autant qu'il apporta, il devra prendre seulement le reliquat." Here too then the husband is the subject throughout. In his commentary[53] Szlechter points to the analogy of CH 163/164; he explains LE / 18 as meaning that the husband is bound to restore the *šeriktum*, and will then recover the *terḫatum*. However, should he be in delay with the restoration of the dowry, he will have a claim only to that part of the *terḫatum* which is in excess of the dowry. This is rather different from Goetze's view: where Goetze would let the husband keep the excess (of the dowry), Szlechter makes him recover the excess (of the *terḫatum*). For a number of reasons Szlechter's interpretation cannot be accepted. First of all, there is an unwarranted transposition of *aḫḫarum* — "en retard": whatever the alleged *aḫḫarum* mean, in the section it precedes the death of the wife and must not be taken out of its context. Also, Szlechter's suggestion depends on the assumption that the *terḫatum* was greater than the *šeriktum*. This would be rather atypical, and in disagreement with both CH / 164 and the Old Babylonian marriage contracts which have been mentioned.

Father and daughter figure in the rendering proposed by San Nicolò: "he (the father-in-law) shall get back not what she brought in,

52 In the practice of the Elephantine documents, the dowry (which here too included the bride payment [*mohar*]) would remain with the surviving husband; see Yaron *1961:* 70. Under Talmudic law, the husband is the sole heir of all the property of his wife, also of her dowry; it is different only if the return of the dowry has been expressly stipulated in the marriage contract, for the case that she die without issue: see *Palestinian Talmud, Kethuboth* 33a.

53 *1954:* 48f.; cf. *1978:* 154f.

but (only) his surplus"; similar is the interpretation given by Klíma.[54]

My interpretation of the apodosis was eclectic: it followed that of Goetze in assigning *mala ublu* to the groom; on the other hand, I agreed with San Nicolò that the "taking of the excess" *(ataršuma ileqqe)* could be only the act of the wife's father (or a successor of his). These two assumptions led almost necessarily to a third, that *ul ušeṣṣe* had to be rendered "he shall not return, shall not relinquish", again with the wife's father as subject. This gave for the apodosis the following import: "whatever he (H) has brought, he (WF) will not (have to) relinquish; its excess indeed he (WF) will take."

It was easy to attribute *mala ublu* to the groom: after all, he was mentioned expressly as the one who brought the *terḫatum* (and the same verb *wabalu* was used). But one might bear in mind that there was also another "bringing", namely that of a dowry by the wife.[55] Landsberger *1968:* 73 objects to the introduction of the dowry, which he regards as a kind of exegetic *deus ex machina*. But the dowry is there alright, albeit implicitly: the reference to *watrum* involves necessarily a comparison of two entities; one is the *terḫatum* — the other has to be the *šeriktum*.

The interpretation of the apodosis emerged from the factual situation which existed at the time of death: The groom had brought a *terḫatum* some time ago, at the time of the marriage the bride had brought with her a dowry *(šeriktum)*. These two had now to be set one against the other.

It will be noted that I differed from San Nicolò and Klíma on two points: the subject of *ublu* and the rendering of *ušeṣṣe* ("relinquish" instead of "recover"). But the divergence concerned only matters of

54 *1953, cit.* Rather different, not in substance but in wording, is Klíma's comment in *1957:* 169: the husband is obliged to return the difference between the *terḫatum* ... and the value of her dowry, brought by his wife from her family. This reformulation may be in response to the objection put forward by Goetze *1956:* 64, note 11, that "the text of the section ... does not mention the father-in-law". But to avoid Goetze's criticism Klíma is paraphrasing too freely: *ileqqe* cannot be rendered "obliged to return". Actually Goetze's objection is adequately met by the fact that 17/18 is only one section, and that the second provision has to be read in conjunction with the first, introductory passage. Just as for Goetze *mala ublu* is a reference to *terḫatam libilma* of the introduction, another reference may be to the father-in-law, who is also mentioned there.

55 For the use of *wabalu* for such a bringing, see CH 138, 149.

language, and the actual result was the same. I was guided by the assumption that *mala ublu* referred to the *terḫatum*; but this was not unavoidable. So San Nicolò's interpretation might actually have been the correct one.

Going by a different way, I have yet — with San Nicolò and Klíma — arrived at a solution which is identical with that laid down in CH / 164. It is submitted that from the point of view of method there can be no objection to being guided by CH in this matter. Quite obviously, CH and LE need not — and do not — arrive always at identical solutions. But where there is obscurity, such as in the interpretation of LE / 18, one may take the clear ruling of the CH as a starting point, and see whether it will suit the text to be interpreted. This is the more admissible when one is concerned with family law: one may assume that matters like the *terḫatum* were regulated in the various cities and states more or less similarly — by a kind of common law, which would change only very slowly. Also, in view of the fact that CH introduces a new rule on this matter (by providing, in 163/, for the possibility that the *terḫatum* had been returned at the time of the marriage), one may assume that the *antiquum ius*, as reflected by the second part of the section (/ 164), goes back to earlier times. It would therefore be surprising to find in the LE a ruling altogether different.

The protasis should now be considered again, in the light of the conclusion that the apodosis provides for a set-off of *terḫatum* and *šeriktum*, and further for the refund of the latter's excess.

The three variant proposals based on the notion of "being in delay" must all be rejected. The one suggesting delay in the payment of the *terḫatum*, because it is not known (and altogether unlikely, save in the most exceptional of circumstances) that the payment of the *terḫatum* was postponed until after consummation. It is objectionable also for a further reason: the suggested ruling, by distinguishing between sums already paid (which [WF] would be allowed to keep) and sums overdue (which H is released from paying), would improve the position of a person who had been neglectful of his obligations.[56] Delay in the

56 See further Böhl *1949/1950:* 100, note 19: there it is suggested that the bridegroom, even though granted relief, would have to pay interest on the outstanding sum, up to the time of the wife's death. This suggestion is based on the assumption, now generally abandoned, that LE 18A is part of the preceding section. But cf. pp.33f., above.

restitution of the dowry has already been discussed and found unsatisfactory. There remains the suggestion that the reference is to a delay in the consummation of the marriage: in objection to this it has been pointed out that prior to the marriage itself there is no possibility of making deductions from the dowry, since that is given to the bridegroom only at the time of the marriage, or possibly at some later date.[57]

All the differences of opinion which have been set out in detail found expression prior to the emergence of the reading *aḫizanum*, in 1964. We return to it once more, proceeding now on the assumption that *aḫizanum* is indeed the correct, true reading. Obviously, one must remain faithful to one's text, and there is no point in devoting one's efforts to the interpretation of something that does not exist. Nor ought one, on the other hand, rest content with having established what the text is. It is disconcerting to see that nobody has confronted the problems of legal substance arising from the reading *aḫizanum*.

We must ask how death of the *aḫizanum* can be integrated with death of the *kallatum*, how one is to understand the apodosis as a whole, intended to provide an answer for both the cases. Some minutiae (e.g., the identification of the respective subjects of the three verbs, — *wabalum*, *šuṣum*, *lequm*) can be adjusted, without an excess of difficulty. But the main finding, set out when death of the *kallatum* was the only topic, remains unaffected: LE / 18 provides for a set-off of *šeriktum* (dowry) and *terḫatum* (bride payment). A protasis can contain a cumulation of related cases, but a single apodosis provides only one solution. On this basis, it is generally (and plausibly) accepted for LE / 18 that a set-off applies equally consequent upon the death of the marrier or his wife.

At first glance it may seem very satisfactory to treat both parties to the marriage (or their successors) in an identical fashion: "equality is equity". Indeed, equal treatment is fair as long as both parties are in an equal or near-equal position. This is the case as long as the

57 See Petschow *1961:* 269, note 21. On delayed dowries, generally, see Yaron *1963b:* 27ff. Hallo *1964:* 95ff. speaks of a dowry as handed over many years before the time agreed for consummation. But his case rests on treating the relevant document, Schorr *1913*, no. 1, not as a contract of marriage but as a (preliminary) "contract to marry". There seems to be no warrant for this (and see p. 173, note 5, above.)

marriage has not yet been consummated (sec. 17/): marriage is as yet "inchoate", and while the death of a prospective spouse may be a harrowing experience, concretely "nothing" has happened. It may be assumed that the survivor will be able to revert to the situtation which existed prior to "inchoacy", and pick up the thread again. Hence *kaspum ana belišuma itar* — "the silver to its owner indeed shall return".

Where death of a spouse is subsequent to the consummation of the marriage we find a much-changed situation. Death of the wife leaves the husband more or less where he was prior to the marriage. It follows that mutual restitution (effected by way of set-off), as laid down in CH / 164, is an adequate and plausible provision: the widower can now contemplate a fresh start. By contrast, the death of the marrier leaves his widow in a position of inferiority. She is no longer a virgin (and that in a society which sets much store by virginity). As a widow, her prospects in the marriage market are greatly impaired. In circumstances so unequal, a ruling based on "equality" becomes a travesty of justice; what was seen as *summum ius* turns into *summa iniuria*.[58]

Is this analysis not tainted by anachronism, does it reflect Old Babylonian attitudes? I would assert that it does. Widows (and other wives whose marriages had been disrupted in a variety of circumstances) constituted a problem which Old Babylonian society was aware of and wished to alleviate. This "notion of care" (or "Versorgungsgedanke", as Petschow aptly calls it) is reflected in various provisions of the CH.[59] Even within LE one can point to secs. 29 and 30 (which permit a second marriage of an absentee's wife), and sec. 59 (protecting a divorcee-mother). The death-of-*aḫizanum* part of LE / 18 stands by itself.

Summa summarum: I do not succeed in reconciling that death-of-*aḫizanum* ruling with Old Babylonian attitudes. Nor is it satisfactory

58 In such a situation, Talmudic law achieves better results by enlarging the rights of the survivor (widower and widow) at the expense of the family of the deceased: the widower is heir to his wife (*Mishnah Baba Bathra* 8.1), hence there is no restitution of the dowry (subject to the exception mentioned p. 185, note 52); the widow does not inherit, but is entitled to the sums specified in her marriage contract *(kethubah)*, or alternatively to maintenance and accommodation. See in detail Yaron *1960:* 174ff.

59 See Petschow *1965b:* 160f.; *1968b:* 7.

to treat it as an exception to a wide tendency: one would wish to have an explanation for such an exception. Even so, I resist temptation to argue against the reading *aḫizanum*: as long as Assyriologists insist on it, — so be it.

THE REJECTED GROOM (LE 25)

In sec. 17/18 the marriage failed because of an occurrence beyond human control. We turn now to consider the case, dealt with in LE 25, where the marriage fails because of the wilful refusal to allow it to take place. It will be noted that the section (as also the corresponding LI 29) deals only with refusal on the part of the bride's father. The other possibility, refusal by the bridegroom, was to a considerable extent taken care of by the very payment of the *terḫatum*. Its recipient, the father of the bride, could — in case the bridegroom refused to consummate — sit pat and do nothing; he did not need the intervention of the law on his behalf. But refusal by the father (or family) of the bride necessitated the exaction of the sum which the groom had originally paid, and also (in LE) the exaction of an equivalent penalty. This had to be provided for by the law. It is only in CH 159 and HL 30 that an increased desire for completeness causes refusal by the bridegroom to be expressly regulated.

We see then that the parties retain a power of retraction *(poenitentia)*. At a price they can abandon the inchoate relationship which has come about with the payment of the *terḫatum*. Note that the texts listed treat both sides equally, hence equitably. The bride-father has to return double, the groom — *sub silentio* or expressly — forfeits what he has paid.

Near Eastern unanimity and equity on this matter is broken by MAL 30.[60] It tilts to the male side, and shows the father of the groom in full control of the situation. He is entitled to proceed with the family's claim to the bride, and will succeed over the opposition of her father. In so holding MAL may adumbrate the stand taken by Jewish law in Talmudic times. Once betrothal *(eruśin, qiddušin)* has taken place, the relationship created thereby, though not yet a complete marriage, is terminable only by death or divorce, just as consummated

60 See Cardascia *1969:* 164ff.

marriage.[61] And divorce, be it remembered, was in Talmudic law a male privilege. Biblical law is altogether silent. It follows that a definite answer cannot be given to the question whether — in assessing the rules probably obtaining under it — one is to be guided by the general Eastern picture or by the Talmud. While, on the whole the first possibility seems to be preferable,[62] MAL 30 diminishes certainty.

We return to LE 25. All the difficulties in the interpretation of the section are concentrated in the protasis. The apodosis states simply that "the father of the daughter the bride payment he received shall twofold return". The protasis, on the other hand, is complicated and not in all respects clear. There are several items in need of elucidation: (i) What is the meaning of *ana bit emim issi*? (ii) What is the meaning of *emušu ik-ši-šu-ma*?[63] (iii) What — if any — is the legal import of a further factual statement, *marassu ana* [*šanim* (or *ibrim*) *i*]*ttadin* — "he gave his daughter to [another (or: a friend)]"? Let us consider these one by one.

The absence, until recently, of any known parallel to *ana bit emim issi* has hampered the correct interpretation of the phrase. In the course of his work on the LE Goetze has offered three different translations. In *1948* and *1950* (ANET) he rendered it by "calls at the house of (his) father-in-law".[64] This is slightly misleading, because of its very literalness: English "to call at" equals "to visit", but more than a mere visit is implied here. In *1949:* 118 he suggested "enters (??) the house of his father-in-law";[65] this was obviously but an attempt to render *ad sensum*, with accuracy disclaimed by the question-marks. Finally, in *1956* a very definite rendering was given: "offers to serve in the house of (his) father-in-law".

61 This is implied in many Talmudic texts, and spelled out expressly in Maimonides, *Personal Status* 1.3.
62 In passing one may note I Samuel 18:19: "But it came to pass at the time when Merab Saul's daughter should have been given to David, that she was given unto Adriel the Meholathite to wife." However, it is not clear whether the *mohar* had already been given, formalizing the relationship. The case is of doubtful significance also because royalty is involved: might could all too easily supplant right.
63 Concerning the reading (*ikšišuma* or *ikšisuma*), see notes on sec. 25.
64 So also CAD E 154b.
65 Followed by Klíma *1953b:* 235.

To arrive at this result a *tour de force* was necessary. Goetze himself pointed out (p. 77) that a phrase *ana bit X šasum* was known also from other sources, that it meant ordinarily "to raise claims against the house of X", and that the interpretation suggested by him for LE 25 was different. The postulated neutral "to initiate a claim" would hardly furnish the necessary link between "to raise a claim" and "to offer services".[66]

More conservative renderings of the phrase have also been proposed, such as "von jemandem eine Leistung fordern",[67] and "intenter une action contre ..." or "faire une demande vis-à-vis de ..."[68] *ana bit X šasum* was examined in detail in Kraus *1958:* 57ff.; he arrived at the following paraphrase: "einen seiner Dienst- oder Leistungspflicht nicht genügenden (Lehns)mann durch die Repressalie der Wegführung von Familienmitgliedern behördlich zur Pflichterfüllung zwingen wollen". This was rather too exact. Kraus recognized (p. 59, note 1) that his interpretation was not suitable for LE 25: he would resolve the difficulty by expressing doubts that the verb in LE 25 was indeed *šasum*, and the phrase there related to the one he was discussing. But in the light of new material he has accepted that *ana bit emim issi* is indeed connected with *ana bit X šasum* of the other passages, and that a satisfactory common denominator is available in Landsberger's rendering "von jemandem eine Leistung fordern".[69] The

66 Goetze *1956:* 81 points to the parallel provision in LI 29, "if a son-in-law enters (I.IN.TU) the house of his father-in-law"; he suggests that there too the meaning is "to enter into a work contract". But this is again not very likely, since the section continues "and makes his betrothal gift (NÍG. MUSSA)".

67 Landsberger, as quoted by Koschaker *1950:* 251, note 42. And see there the correct interpretation of LE 25 offered by Koschaker, without the benefit of supporting evidence: "nach Zahlung des Brautpreises die Braut verlangt".

68 Szlechter *1954:* 22, 46; *1978:* 126, 151. Cf. Bottéro *1965/1966:* 92: "faire 'réclamation'".

69 Kraus *1974:* 112: "Der von mir einmal zu Unrecht geleugnete Zusammenhang mit dem bekannten Ausdrucke *ana bit* NN *šasum* war schon von Koschaker [see note 67, R. Y.] definitiv bewiesen worden; den praktischen Sinn der Phrase *ana bit emim šasum* hat Landsberger daraufhin bestimmt als an die Familie eines Mädchens, für das der Brautpreis bereits bezahlt war, gerichtete Aufforderung des 'Bräutigams' zur vereinbarten Auslieferung der 'Braut'." See also YLE, p. 124.

contents of this "Leistung" are not defined more exactly, nor is such a definition implied in the phrase itself: all will depend on the circumstances of the particular case, and on the parties involved in it. Where, as is often the case, an authority raises claims against a citizen, this will indeed in the ordinary course of matters concern his feudal duties. But where a son-in-law claims from his *emum*, this concerns the giving of the bride.

Evidence relieving the phrase *ana bit emim issi* of its isolation has emerged with the publication of two Old Babylonian texts, U. 16900 F,[70] and BM 80754.[71] In the first text, from Ur, a man who has lent silver complains to the god Nana against the recalcitrant debtor. The gist of the matter is the following: an impecunious suitor borrowed silver to pay his debt (presumably his bride's *terḫatum*, or part of it). He has already a son and a daughter, but the loan has not yet been repaid. More than that, when sued by the lender, the borrower has on oath denied his indebtedness. In these circumstances, all that the disappointed creditor can do is to invoke divine wrath and vengeance upon the head of his adversary. Here it will suffice to quote, with some minor deviations from Gadd's transliteration and translation, lines 5-12 of the text:

> *kaspam ula išuma iṭḫiam ina kaspija ḫubullišu uppil ana bit emim issi maram u martam irši libbi ula uṭib kaspi šalmam ula uterram*
>
> "Since he had no silver, he came to me; with silver of mine he settled his debts. He claimed at the house of the father-in-law. He got a son and a daughter (but still) did not content my heart; my silver in full he did not return to me ..."

This passage may be taken as disproving definitely the interpretation which Goetze has offered for LE 25. In his view, *ana bit emim issi* — "he offered to serve" etc. indicates a situation comparable to the undertaking of Jacob, when he declares his willingness to work seven years for Rachel (Genesis 29:18). To be sure, there is nothing

70 Gadd *1963:* 177ff. See my discussion of this document, *1965:* 23ff. Landsberger *1968:* 74f. made similar use of U.16900 F.

71 Finkelstein *1967b:* 127ff. The text was republished by Kraus, as AbB vii, no. 188.

objectionable or unfeasible, in either law or fact, in such an arrangement, but it is just not present in LE 25. It is certain that in U. 16900 F no such offer can be expressed by the phrase *ana bit emim issi*, since we are told in so many words that it is silver which the rascally groom brought to his creditor, the father-in-law.

After U. 16900 F, the poorly preserved letter BM 80754 was disappointing. It is written by one woman to another. That much is clear, but not much more, — as the widely divergent interpretations offered by Finkelstein and Kraus show. A key passage (in line 6) is read by Finkelstein *ana PN mariki ana bit emim issima*, "I called PN your son to the *bit emim*".[72] Kraus suggests for the third word the reading *mari*; he concedes that *ma-ri-ki* was originally written, but contends that KI was (incompletely) erased by the scribe.[73] He translates, "für meinen Sohn PN habe ich die Familie des Schwiegervaters angesprochen." The interpretation of Kraus has the advantage of being closer to the meaning established in LE 25 and U. 16900 F. *šasum* is on behalf of the groom (even though not by himself). Finkelstein proposes a complete inversion of the use of the phrase: it refers not to an act by or for the groom, rather an act against him. But Kraus readily admits that he is not able "die Gesamtlage, auf welche der lakonische Brief sich bezieht, zu rekonstruieren."

Finkelstein takes BM 80754 as starting point for a detailed discussion, on the one hand, of the term *ana bit emim šasum*, on the other hand of the terms *bit emim* and *bit emutim*. Concerning the first, it is his central submission (*1967b:* 131) that *"ana bit emim šasum* is an idiomatic phrase, none of the components of which may be separated from it and translated literally". With this we agree entirely, but it does neither prevent us, nor absolve us, from enquiring into the genesis of the phrase. At the end of his paper, Finkelstein renders *šumma awilum ana bit emim issi* by "if a man 'announced his wedding'". Here we should object not so much to "wedding", rather to "announce"; one must remember that in the comparable idiom *ana bit*

72 "I performed *ana bit emim šasu* for your son PN." At the end of his paper (p. 135) Finkelstein renders, as approximate meaning, "I requested that PN, your son, be wedded formally (to my daughter)".

73 One may note that both the eminent Assyriologists were working from the original. Kraus read the letter on two separate occasions, in 1971 and 1973; he asked also for further collations (*1974:* 111, and 114, note 1).

X šasum the verb means "to claim, demand".[74] And in particular, in LE 25 the contrast with what follows, namely the rejection of the groom by the girl's father, calls for a more pregnant rendering. Therefore we translate "claimed consummation", seeing in this claim the most important, most prominent demand a groom would make at his father-in-law's.[75] Incidentally, "claimed consummation", or "demanded consummation" suits BM 80754 perfectly, whereas "announced" does not. Finkelstein himself, aware of this, renders "I requested that PN, your son, be wedded formally (to my daughter)". But "announce" and "request" are miles apart, and we cannot have the one here, the other there.

We are in accord with Finkelstein's remarks concerning *emutum* and *bit emutim*, and especially with his rendering of the latter term by "bridal, nuptial chamber" (pp. 131f.). We are less happy when he throws together the abstract *bit emutim* and the rather more concrete *bit emim*: "... both these terms may denote the 'wedding' as well as the 'nuptial chamber'. And while *emutum* by itself means 'marriage (alliance)' and *emum* any male relation by marriage, when either term is preceded by *bit* the phrase then denotes the 'nuptial chamber' or the 'wedding ceremony and festivities'" (p. 135). As far as *bit emim* goes this statement is too general and sweeping. When one examines the texts adduced, the evidence is somewhat scant. In one Old Babylonian version of Gilgameš, P IV 26, the rendering "wedding" is quite possible, but by no means necessary. CAD E 156 gives "wedding (lit. house of the bride's father, where the wedding takes place)", and there is no need to go beyond the literal meaning.[76] I do accept Finkelstein's rendering *bit emi* — "nuptial chamber" in Middle Assyrian Laws, sec. 32, but one has to remember that this is about 500 years later than LE, and consequently of little immediate relevance to our discussion. More important than the texts adduced are some others, passed over, in which the rendering of *bit emim* by "wedding" is altogether out of

74 In his paper Finkelstein does not mention *ana bit X šasum*.

75 I accept Finkelstein's criticism (p. 131) of my earlier rendering "he claimed at the house of the father-in-law", — not so much as "stilted and vague", but as overliteral. I certainly did not, at the time, recognize that the phrase was an idiom.

76 Another Old Babylonian text is adduced by Finkelstein (p. 133) — CT 46, Pl. 23: IV, 27ff. In both line 27 and 30 *e-mi* is restored, and one can hardly be sure that *emutim* is impossible.

question: so in LE 17/, CH 159, 160, 161, 163/, all of which refer to the bringing of the *terḫatum* (well in advance of the actual wedding!) to the house of the father-in-law, and similarly in MAL 30, concerning the bringing of the *biblum*.[77]

Let us now return to LE 25. It ought to be stressed that the introduction to it differs from that to secs. 17/18 and 26. These two mention the payment of the *terḫatum* as the decisive preliminary occurrence, the *conditio sine qua non*, which provides the background for the subsequent development and the actual provision laid down in each of them. Sec. 17/18 has been discussed in detail and there is no need to return to it. Sec. 26 lays down the death penalty for an outsider who, after a *terḫatum* has been paid, without the consent of the parents of the bride forcibly cohabits with her. The recital of facts in sec. 25 begins at a later moment, when the bridegroom — immediately before the time agreed upon for the wedding —claims the bride from her father, demands consummation. For this we have indeed a biblical parallel in the story of Jacob. Having completed his term of service, he claims his wife.[78, 79] As often as not, considerable time might pass between betrothal, effected by the payment of a *terḫatum* (or part of it), and consummation; there would therefore be room for a formal *šasum*, a formal claim that the marriage be consummated. The proper time for this would be after the completion of the period of betrothal, if beforehand agreed upon, but at any rate not before the bride payment had been rendered in full, as evidenced by U. 16900 F and Genesis 29:21.[80] The proximity of the formal claim to consummation may be the reason why so far it has escaped notice; the two would almost coincide, and the stress would naturally be on the predominant element, on consummation. It follows that only in special circumstances will the claim become independently visible. In

77 MAL 30 is discussed by Finkelstein (p. 130) for a different purpose, to show that the reference need not be to the father-in-law personally.

78 Genesis 29:21. Incidentally, it may be noted that the betrothed is here called *iššah* — "wife", just as in Deuteronomy 22:24, CH 130, 161.

79 Cf. II Samuel 3:14. In altogether different circumstances David — using language reminiscent of Genesis 29:21 — claims (the return of) his wife Michal. Note that the intervening marriage of Michal (with Palṭi ben Laish) is simply disregarded. See further p. 209, note 123, below.

80 This need not exclude the possibility that the parties, in very exceptional circumstances, might agree on a postponed rendering of the *terḫatum*. For stipulated delays see Cassin *1969:* 127f.

LE 25, and also in BM 80754, this happens precisely because consummation has altogether failed to take place.[81] In the story of Jacob the formal claim has to be mentioned, as leading up to the fraud perpetrated by Laban. In the text from Ur, U. 16900 F, one may assume that the claim is mentioned as the immediate consequence of the one fact all-important in the eyes of the petitioner, the payment made *(ḫubullišu uppil)* — and that with his silver! Note that in this case there is no reference at all to consummation; the writer continues at once with the birth of children to bring it home that a long time has passed.

Summing up, one ought to stress one point: *ana bit emim šasum* implies necessarily that the agreed *terḫatum* has already been paid, since only this founds the claim.[82] It is this mention of the claim which prepares the ground for the reference to the *terḫatum*, in the apodosis of LE 25, and there is no need to rely for it on the phrase which follows, *emušu ik-ši-šu/su-ma*, as Goetze does, *1956:* 78f. He derives the hypothetical *ikšiš* from *kašašum*, and renders the phrase as a whole by "his father-in-law takes him in bondage".[83] This suggestion depends to a decisive extent on the interpretation given to *ana bit emim issi*: an offer of the bridegroom to serve can be meaningfully followed by the acceptance of that offer on the part of the father of the girl. However, once that interpretation of the introductory phrase is rejected, that suggested for the following one can hardly be upheld. Its parallel in CH 160 (and 161) is not — as Goetze suggests — the introductory statement concerning the payment of the *terḫatum*, but rather the phrase *abi martim marti ul anaddikkum iqtabi* — "the father of the daughter said 'I shall not give thee my daughter'". This agrees with the interpretation offered for *ikšišuma* by a number of authors:[84] they derive it from a verb *kašum*, which is rendered

81 The corresponding section CH 160 refers instead, somewhat vaguely, to the payment of the *terḫatum*. This may perhaps be due to the fact that the immediately preceding section concerns refusal by the bridegroom.

82 See already Koschaker *1950:* 259: "auch wäre ein *šasum* des Bräutigams ... vor der Leistung der *terḫatum* nicht denkbar".

83 See also Goetze *1949:* 118: "... accepts him into servitude."

84 See von Soden *1949:* 370, AHw 463b; Landsberger *apud* Koschaker *1950:* 259 ("ab-, zurückweisen"). This view is followed also by Klíma *1953b:* 236; Korošec *1953:* 29 ("zavrnil" = "has rejected"); Szlechter *1954:* 22: "l'a offensé"; Bottéro *1965 / 1966:* 92: "l'a repoussé". Cf. CAD E 154b.

"Unrecht tun, ungerecht behandeln". This may again not be quite reliable, since AHw shows that such a verb is rather poorly attested.[85] Nevertheless, while the lexical aspect remains in doubt, one can yet be fairly confident that the meaning of the verb under discussion is to be found within the proposed range of "to wrong, to injure, to reject". This seems to be indicated also by its place in the sequence of events recorded in the protasis, between the bridegroom's claim and the father-in-law's action, making the marriage finally impossible.

This brings us to the third and final item to be considered. What, if any, is the actual import of the statement that the girl has been married off to some third person? It would have been of interest to know which word was written in the break, in line 27. The restorations *ana* [*šanim* — "to another", and *ana* [*ibrim* — "to a friend", have been proposed; possibly *ana* [*ibrišu* would be more exact, in the light of CH 161.[86] As to the import of this final part of the protasis, it has been suggested that it is "rechtlich überflüssig".[87] I concur, at any rate as far as the apodosis actually before us is concerned. To arrive at the provision laid down in it, *terḫat imḫuru tašna utar* — "... the bride payment he received he shall twofold return", the marriage to an outsider is irrelevant and may be disregarded.

But there is more to it. Reference has also been made to corresponding provisions outside the LE, namely LI 29 and CH 161. In these sections a further sanction is laid down, a prohibition of the marriage of the girl to the KU.LI=*ibrum*, the "friend", or "fellow" of the bridegroom.[88] Goetze *1956:* 81f. contents himself with stating that

85 Finkelstein (p. 135, note 1) asserts that "the verb demanded in the context is *nakaru*, in the form *ikkiršu*, with or without enclitic *-ma.*" But he admits that "to attain such a reading one would have to assume some serious corruption after IG" (= the first sign).

86 So already von Soden *1956:* 34.

87 Koschaker *1950:* 259. Similar results are reached by Szlechter *1954:* 47.

88 It has been suggested that the prohibition was *in personam*, directed against a particular "friend" of the bridegroom, who may have had some specific function in the marriage ceremonies: San Nicolò *1950b:* 117, note 1; in greater detail, van Selms *1950b:* 65ff. Wider is the approach of Greengus *1966:* 68, who thinks of "one of the groom's companions, a member of his peer group". Szlechter (p. 47) seems to think in terms of a general prohibition, speaking of "la défense de donner la fille à un autre qu'à celui qui a apporté la *terḫatum*". See also CAD I/J 5. At p. 7a much stress is put on the "institutionalized relationship between free persons of

"this has no analogue in the LE", but Szlechter *1954:* 47 is led to far-reaching conclusions. He juxtaposes Sumerian law (alleged to be represented by LI 29) and LE 25. In the former the marriage with a KU.LI is prohibited, but no penalty is laid down (only the *simplum* of the bride payment has to be returned); in the latter there is a penalty, but no prohibition of giving the daughter to another. Both these provisions are amalgamated in CH 161, having both penalty and prohibition.

This seems rather heavy a load to put upon an *argumentum e silentio*. I should perhaps be willing to follow suit, were it not for the fact that LE 25 is followed by three sections in each of which the operative part, the apodosis, takes account of, and regulates, part only of the situation. Sec. 26 says nothing about the fate of the girl who has been raped; /28 provides for the punishment of one of two adulterers, but does not mention the other; sec. 29 does not tell us who will be entitled to keep the child to whom the wife of a prisoner of war gave birth in his absence.[89] It will not do to import into the LE, in one case almost as a matter of course, the solution laid down in CH, but see a strong contrast, a substantial difference, in another.[90]

the same status and profession" (echoed by Greengus in the passage just quoted). This may be somewhat exaggerated, and at any rate such a technical import need not always be present. So it is rather pedantic to render *ana alti ibrišu alaku* (Šurpu IV, 6) by "have intercourse with the wife of a person of the same status". Adultery does not depend on the identity of status of the two males in the triangle.
For similar problems, concerning the import of *tappau* ("neighbour, comrade"), see MAL 18, 19, and the discussion by Cardascia *1969:* 131ff. On the use of biblical *re'a* in a similarly general, indefinite sense, see Yaron *1970:* 552f. The broad, non-technical view of these terms is supported also by Petschow *1973:* 27, note 43.

89 We have dealt with this phenomenon of incompleteness: see p. 87, above.

90 Note, morever, that the reading and consequent interpretation of LI 29 are in doubt. See Civil *1965:* 3; followed by Wilcke *1968:* 153ff.; Petschow *1968b:* 14, note 47. In their view, LI 29 actually provided for the return of double the bride payment, just as LE 25 and CH 160, 161. Endorsing Civil's reading, Finkelstein *1969a/1969b* submits that double payment is provided for also in LUF 12. It seems then that Szlechter's distinction between Sumerian law and later Old Babylonian practice relating to the "rejected bridegroom" can no longer be maintained.

Was then the marriage of the girl to the *ibrum* prohibited in Eshnunna? Possibly it was, but the section is silent, and we do not really know. We have to be content with *non liquet*.

IS SHE A WIFE? (LE 27/28)

Sections 26 (on rape) and 27/28 (on adultery) will be considered in detail in the chapter on Delicts.[91] Here we have to deal with the introduction, very detailed and complex,[92] to sec. 27/28. For adultery to occur, the woman involved in the act must be an *aššatum* — "wife". It is on this preliminary but crucial question, "is she a wife or is she not?", that the attention is focused. Two sets of facts are presented: the first results in a negative conclusion: she is not a wife, (hence cannot be guilty of adultery); the second is positive: she is a wife, hence she qualifies as a partner to the crime of adultery.

Not only the structure of the section is complex; there is also the cumulation of various factual elements which makes for complication.[93] There is the preliminary element, the absence of parental consent, apparently essential for a girl's (first) marriage. Whatever happened took place *balum šal abiša u ummiša* — "without asking her father and?/or? her mother". Typically, the case may have been one of elopement, proceeding from collusion between the girl and her abductor. This may be regarded as a mitigated, diluted form of *Raubehe*. The LE do not inform us what remedies were available to the girl's father for this infringement of his rights and authority.[94] Lack of parental consent might indeed be due also to other situations: the father may have been absent (e.g., in the circumstances envisaged in secs. 29 and 30), or he may have been incapacitated. But these would be exceptional cases, in which the exercise of parental authority (including the power of consent) might have temporarily passed to some other member of the family, the mother of the girl, or her brother.[95]

91 See pp. 278ff., below.
92 See pp. 102f., above.
93 See p. 91, above.
94 Compare Exodus 22:15-16.
95 On parental consent, see the discussion pp. 155f., above.

Cohabitation was apparently suffered to continue, active steps to separate the woman from her "taker" are not mentioned. On the other hand the couple, and especially the groom, did not achieve reconciliation with the girl's parents, by means of *kirrum u riksatum* fixed for them.[96] A rider adds that the time factor is irrelevant. The mere passage of time cannot overcome the original defect in the relationship of the couple, the continuing absence of parental consent. There is no change in the status of the girl: even if she should dwell in the man's house for a year, she has not become an *aššatum*.

But what is the meaning of *kirrum u riksatum*? Opinions differ on both the terms. In rendering *kirrum* by "marriage feast" we follow Landsberger *1968:* 76ff., against "libation", proposed by Greengus *1966:* 65. The "drinking party", as Landsberger terms it, may be taken to have habitually accompanied the marriage ceremony. *riksatum* (plural of *riksum*) is derived from the verb *rakasum* — "to bind". In a legal context it is usually rendered "contract", "Vertrag".[97] It was widely held to refer to a document, but this is disputed by Greengus *1969:* 505: "The Old Babylonian marriage contract ... did not have to be in writing in order to have legal validity. The extant Old Babylonian marriage documents do not prove the necessity of written marriage contracts since the writing down of these records was occasioned not by marriage but by the pressure of related transactions for which more durable proof was desired." The evidence adduced by Greengus is impressive. Speaking of CH he remarks that when it "intends to prescribe the writing of a document, it does so unambiguously and employs for unmistakable clarity terms like *ṭuppum*, *kanikum*, and *kunukkum*."[98] This is so. But in LE there is no such reference to writing (which need mean no more than that the Laws lag behind reality). In view of this, one is on less certain ground in asserting that *riksatum* in LE 27/28 does not imply writing; and the same hesitation will be in place vis-à-vis CH 128, to be discussed at once: we shall suggest that it is

96 Note the use of *šakanum* in this context (but also in others, e.g. CH 123). While consent of both parties is necessarily implied, the transaction presents itself as formally unilateral: it is the groom who "sets" or "fixes" the contract. If, in the context of LE 27/28 this is significant, it might imply that obligations of the groom were the main, possibly the only topic dealt with at that late stage.

97 AHw 985a.

98 *Ibid.*, p. 507.

directly dependent on LE 27/ (or a similar text).

One more detail remains: how is one to understand the ambiguous particle *u*? Does it entail a cumulation of feast and contract, or is the provision content with either of the two? Before attempting an answer, one has at least to include also sec. /28, the positive reverse of 27/, in which the phrase recurs: if there had been *kirrum u riksatum*,[99] the woman is an *aššatum* (wife of the man she had eloped with); her intercourse with an outsider will amount to adultery. The interpretation of *u* ("and"?/"or"?) depends then on the intention of the promulgator (or, if that be uncertain, on the inclination of the judge/s). If the broad issue of correcting past faults, of regularizing the relationship of abductor and abductee was a main consideration, they would be content with either *kirrum* or *riksatum*. If they were to view the case in the narrow context of a capital charge of adultery, they might possibly wish to decide the other way.

Summing up, I suggest that LE 27/ may have its roots in an actual case. The girl taken without parental consent was subsequently accused of adultery, in cohabiting with a male other than the one with whom she had eloped. The legally relevant facts, either not disputed or else established in the course of the proceedings, were as follows: (i) the woman had been subject to parental power; (ii) for whatever reason, a *post factum* regularization of their relationship had not been achieved; (iii) they had lived together for a considerable period (at least one year). The legal question to be decided: was the woman, in the circumstances set out, an *aššatum*, in other words, did her intercourse with a male other than her abductor constitute adultery? The answer is negative.

Sec. /28, we have just seen, complements 27/. It admits the possibility of post-elopement regularization. If this has taken place, she is an *aššatum*, and the rest follows.

Let us note again the essentially narrow limits of LE 27/28: *kirrum* and/or *riksatum* are mentioned only as a possible corrective for a vitiated union. In ordinary circumstances the status of *aššatum* comes into being by the rendering of a *terḫatum*. Scholars have speculated on a variant to LE 27/: suppose there had been belated parental consent plus prolonged cohabitation — but no contract or ceremony;

99 Or *riksatum u kirrum*, as in /28. The inversion shows that no argument can be based on the sequence.

would this have been regarded as sufficient for declaring the woman an *aššatum*? Some scholars reject such a possibility.[100] I would prefer to hold (with Koschaker *1951:* 113, note 26), that such an informal mode, in comparison with which MAL 34 and Roman *usus* (as a means of *conventio in manum*) have been mentioned, remained possible in Eshnunna. The passage of time cannot overcome the absence of parental assent, but it can heal defects of form. In such situations the time element may also have been significant. Maybe the reference to a period of one year is connected with such a situation.

Against the background suggested for LE 27/28 it may be of interest to have a close look at CH 128 and 129, two sections which may have been connected with LE 27/28.[101] It is submitted that the compilers of the CH had before them LE 27/28 (or a text closely similar). But they dealt with the two subsections in a very different manner, and separately. We shall do likewise. CH 128 reads as follows:

> *šumma awilum aššatam iḫuzma riksatiša la iškun sinništum ši ul aššat*
>
> "If a man has taken a wife, but has not fixed her contract, that woman is not a 'wife'."

When one compares this with LE 27/, one is at first glance more impressed by difference than by similarity: CH 128 is a much briefer text (11 words for 28 in LE). Many of the details set out in LE 27/ are missing altogether. Why then suggest a direct connection? — Because of two unusual features common to both the sections: (a) they offer a definition of status; (b) that definition is a negative one, declaring that in the circumstances a woman is not an *aššatum*. The CH, we have had occasion to note,[102] is not much concerned with brevity of expression; here too, the trimming down of LE 27/ was not undertaken for purposes of style, but rather to fashion something entirely

100 See San Nicolò *1949:* 260; followed by Klíma *1950b:* 281f. Szlechter *1954:* 50 sees in LE 27/ a far-reaching innovation, abolishing an informal mode of concluding a marriage, which had previously been lawful.

101 Landsberger *1968:* 89 refers to LUY 11 (= F 8) as a kind of "Urform" of LE 27/ and CH 128.

102 See pp. 89ff., above.

new, free of the complexities inherent in the original.[103] The reference to (lack of) parental consent and the rider concerning the passage of time were cut out altogether; so was the mention of a *kirrum*. With these specifics, out went also the background of elopement. In this manner the compilers created a simple provision, insisting on a contract as requisite for a valid marriage. It is in this fashion that CH 128 has been generally understood, and rightly so. That they made secondary use of early material is not relevant to the interpretation of CH 128.

LE /28 was discarded altogether. No positive counterpart then for *ul aššat*. CH 129 offers a broadly couched provision on adultery. It reads as follows:

> *šumma aššat awilim itti zikarim šanim ina itulim ittaṣbat ikasušunutima ana me inaddušunuti šumma bel aššatim aššassu uballaṭ u šarrum waradsu uballaṭ*
>
> "If a wife is caught lying with another male, they shall bind them and into the water they shall cast them; if the wife's husband lets his wife live, then the king shall let his slave live."

Nothing to remind one of LE /28. The language is altogether different; also, the approach to the substance of punishment is much more detailed.[104] The formulation of the section may be that of the compilers, or they may have taken it from some other source at their disposal.

I find support for my contention that LE 27/28 (or a similar text) is perceivable in CH 128 also in a further consideration. When one compares two sets of provisions, in LE and CH, on sexual misbehaviour (committed or alleged to have been committed), the results are the following: LE 26 deals with rape; 27/28 with non-commission, respectively commission of adultery (subsequent to elopement). CH 127 concerns unproven allegations against a priestess or "a man's wife" *(aššat awilim)*; CH 129 concerns adultery (generally); 130, rape;

103 But note Sauren *1986:* 71. He regards the detailed version of LE 27/ as the later one!

104 See already Sauren, p. 72: "La décision du CH montre un état plus évolué."

131-132, further allegations against an *aššat awilim* (and questions of proof).[105] Note that in LE 27/ the negative definition *ul aššat* is the logical finale of an unfolding story. The independent CH 128 (and its concluding statement *ul aššat*) are alien to the topic of sexual misbehaviour, an intrusion into an otherwise fairly coherent set of provisions. CH 128 is where it is only because it was originally part of a section dealing with adultery.

Very astute and close to the mark were some early observations of Mahler.[106] He started off by stressing that CH 128 must be related to the sections which precede and follow. Patently mistaken was his interpretation of *riksatum* as a "Willensäusserung" of the woman, and of the phrase *riksatiša la iškun* as indicating that "ihre Einwilligung (oder Zustimmung) nicht erfolgt ist". This led him to hold that the underlying situation was one of rape: the section viewed this as a "Vergewaltigungsakt", and decreed that "die Frau daher nicht eine Ehefrau ist." Yet all these faulty submissions culminated in the statement, "begeht sie also irgendein unzüchtiges Delikt, so unterliegt sie nicht den in den folgenden Paragraphen ausgesprochenen Gesetzesbestimmungen." Had LE 27/28 been available, Mahler would not have failed to come up with the correct solution.[107]

CH 128, in its actual location in the Code, allows a rare glimpse into the doings of Hammurabi's anonymous Tribonian: how he (and associates?) went about their task, collected, selected, adapted, rewrote, rearranged — or else failed to do so. It should not have been difficult for the compilers to do what Driver-Miles did, namely relocate sec. 128. Had they done so, — they would have deprived us of an interesting insight.

105 Note that in both CH and LE the sections on sexual misbehaviour are followed by sections concerning the absentee husband.

106 *1927:* 147ff.

107 A glance at Driver-Miles *1952* may be instructive. In the Preface to the book they note that it was written in the early 1940's, well prior to the discovery of the LE. Even so, CH 128 presented a problem to them; this is shown by the deft transfer of CH 128, from its actual setting to a more suitable place, at the beginning of the discussion of marriage: they consider CH 128 at pp. 245-249, the set on sexual misbehaviour at pp. 275-284. Petschow *1965b:* 148 suggests that CH 127 and 128 are linked by "das Stichwort *aššatum*"; I prefer another possibility which he mentions, "das die Anordnung von einer oder mehreren Vorlagen beeinflusst ist" (p. 159).

THE ABSENTEE HUSBAND (LE 29, 30)

We turn now to the problems arising out of the husband's absence from the matrimonial home. Some of these are considered in sections 29 and 30. The former deals with the case of a man who is for a long time detained in a foreign country, as a result of enemy activity.[108] If his wife was in the meantime married to someone else, and gave birth to a son, the returning captive will get back his wife. In the latter section the absence is malicious, motivated by hatred of "king and country". It should be noted that the scope of each of the sections is exactly delimited, and that they provide only for two specifically defined situations. Nothing is said about ordinary absence, *voluntatis suae arbitrio*,[109] e.g., for the purposes of trading,[110] or for compelling personal reasons, e.g., to escape the pressure of creditors.[111]

Again, with regard to sec. 29, one ought to note the very narrow formulation of the apodosis: its only concern is to provide that the returning captive is entitled to get back his wife. Contrary to the corresponding sections in CH, LE 29 does not say in what circumstances a captive's wife was permitted to enter upon a second marriage.[112] The "long time"[113] is mentioned only for a negative purpose: it does not affect the rights of the first husband; it is because of this irrelevance of the time factor that such a vague description is sufficient. CH 133 and 134 lay down criteria for the permissibility of a second marriage: it is prohibited as long as there are means of subsistence in the husband's house (133), permitted if there are not (134). However, it must remain an open question whether this distinction was applied also in Eshnunna; in the section itself there is no indication either way. Nothing is provided in LE 29 concerning the

108 Two cases are distinguished, but the differences are not at all clear. See the discussion by Goetze *1956:* 84ff.; also Szlechter *1963:* 182.

109 Cf. *Codex Iustinianus* 7.43.10 (291 C.E.)

110 The case is not considered in CH either, but it may be the topic of MAL 36.

111 A possibility mentioned by Szlechter *1965:* 295.

112 Inexact is Szlechter *1954:* 62f., stating that the LE allowed "l'épouse du prisonnier de guerre de se remarier si la captivité était longue". In the same vein also *1978:* 161. On all the questions concerning the captive husband, see also Szlechter *1963:* 181-192.

113 Restored, but likely to be correct. A specific time does not appear to be mentioned.

child borne out of the second union: will it stay with its father, or will it rather follow the mother on her return to the first husband? And, since nothing is said about the child, to what purpose is it mentioned at all? Perhaps as part of the *res gestae*, an actual occurrence. A more substantive interpretation is also possible: it might have been argued that the birth of a child had endowed the second union with additional effect, in excess of the first one. The ruling that she has to return to her first husband rejects such a contention. The claim of the first husband prevails; no account is taken of the wishes of the wife.

It is usually taken for granted that the child will remain with its father — on the strength of CH 135.[114] This involves a further assumption, namely that the second marriage of LE 29 was contracted under the circumstances set out in CH 134. If the wife was in the wrong in remarrying, we have the parallel of MAL 36: there it is provided that the husband claiming the wife will also take the child. Incidentally, the rule of CH 135, protecting the interests of the father, involves the separation of the child from its mother, possibly a matter of considerable personal hardship. There is no reason to assume that CH 135 was intended to be *ius cogens*, binding law. It merely informed the parties of the decision to be expected, in case the matter was litigated. Nevertheless, one may assume that the parties concerned were free to arrive at such arrangements as they considered desirable.

In none of the sources which we have considered is there a reference to a "Verschollenheit" of the absentee husband, the uncertainty *ubi sit et an sit*.[115] It has been suggested that the LE presume the dissolution of the first marriage as a consequence of the disappearance of the husband,[116] and this has even been turned into a presumption of death;[117] there seems to be no warrant for these views. In CH and MAL maintenance or non-maintenance of the wife is the all-important consideration; LE is silent altogether. It is submitted that if a wife had full information of the whereabouts of her husband, more

114 Klíma *1953b:* 235, note 56; Goetze *1956:* 87. Szlechter, *1954:* 63, refers also to MAL 45.

115 A faint suggestion of something akin to "Verschollenheit" may be present in the word *ḫalqu* (MAL 45, line 73), usually translated by "lost, missing" (see LE 50). But too much weight ought not to be given to a single word, used *obiter* in the course of the narration of facts.

116 Szlechter: *1954:* 64.

117 See Szlechter *1963:* 186.

than that, even in the unlikely case that she were in actual contact with him, this would not in itself deny her the liberty of remarrying. If the husband failed in his duty to maintain his wife, there would be no objection to the union — at least *pro tempore* — of his wife with another. The law would not intervene on the husband's behalf, even though he might still have a claim to get her back, when he returned home (CH 134-135). MAL 36 imposes a time limit: after the passage of five years the husband's claim would fail. One may sum up: LE, CH and MAL envisage that in certain situations the wife of an absentee captive can enter upon a new union without fearing punishment. The basic consideration may have been a practical one: in the great majority of cases the absentee would never return. Abstract principles, for example ideas concerning the inviolability of the marriage tie and the desire to protect it from interference, will not have played a significant rôle; at any rate, they were not allowed to prevent solutions based on common sense and the need of facing reality. Only if related to some concrete factor would principle prevail. So if the unexpected happened and the first husband turned up: LE 29 and CH 135 regarded him who was *prior tempore* as *potior iure*, and resolved the conflict situation in a way giving preference to past ties over the present ones. Similarly, principle is activated when a wife enters upon a second marriage under less than compelling circumstances, that is although she does not lack maintenance in her husband's house: she is to die the death of an adulteress, being thrown into the water (CH 133).

LE 30 and CH 136 appear to be closely connected,[118] and render the same decision. The husband's malicious absence,[119] in breach of his duties as a citizen, is punished by his being deprived of any claim to have his wife return to him; it is interesting that misbehaviour in the public sphere causes here the extinction of private rights. Neither LE nor CH mention the passage of any period of time, so one must hold that that was not considered relevant: remarriage could probably take place at once.[120] However, it seems likely that the rule applied only in

118 See already pp. 89ff., above.

119 There seems to be no ground for assuming that "hatred" had to find expression in some overt act prior to the flight. So Szlechter *1965:* 295.

120 One may contrast this with LI 18 and CH 30. Land subject to feudal services is finally lost after an absence of three years, and passes to him who has borne the burden.

case the woman entered upon a second marriage. While the fugitive husband is definitely displaced by the competitor who took the woman, there is no evidence of an intention of the legislator to treat desertion by the husband as terminating the marriage *ipso iure*, automatically.[121, 122] Nothing is said about the circumstances which made possible the return of the fugitive husband. He may have patched up his relations with the ruler. A revolutionary situation, where yesterday's "outs" have become today's "ins" is not envisaged. Had such a situation arisen, the issue presented in LE 30 would have been resolved by the factual "Machtlage", not by legal niceties.[123]

An exhaustive discussion of the rules concerning the absentee spouse, as given by other ancient systems of law, would take us outside the proper limits of this book. But some brief, general remarks may be in order. Very intricate and not yet well understood are the provisions of MAL 36 and 45, into the details of which we shall not go.[124] The Bible does not deal with the problem. On the other hand, the attitude of Talmudic law is unequivocally negative: lack of maintenance or absence of news concerning the fate of a spouse, however prolonged they be, do not affect the marriage tie.[125] Talmudic

121 Differently Klíma *1953b:* 235, who speaks of *capitis deminutio*; the use of the technical Roman term does not make for greater clarity.

122 Cf. the marriage of David's wife Michal to Palṭi ben Laish (I Samuel 25:44). If this be related to rules of law, it may reflect provisions similar to LE 30, CH 136. Being a political fugitive, David loses the protection of the law: his wife can be married off to another. For this argument see already Genesis Rabba 32.1; and cf. *Babylonian Talmud, Yevamoth* 76b. For early Rome, see Dionysius of Halicarnassus 8.41.4.

123 We have already noted David's successful demand for the return of Michal (II Samuel 3:13-16). The "Machtlage" had changed, as poor Palṭi had to realize.

124 See Driver-Miles *1935:* 250ff., Szlechter *1963:* 188ff.

125 Talmudic law, proceeding from Exodus 21:10, regulates in considerable detail the wife's rights to maintenance. See *Mishnah Kethuboth* 4.4; 5.8, 9. Provision is also made for the maintenance of the wife out of the property of her absentee husband: *Mishnah Kethuboth* 13.1, 2; *Tosefta, ibid.* 13.1. But a failure to maintain will not affect the marriage tie, and the woman is in no circumstance entitled to enter upon a new marriage. A court might bring pressure to bear upon a neglectful husband, to make him divorce his wife (*Palestinian Talmud, Giṭṭin* 50d), but against an absentee husband the intervention of the authorities would be of little meaning.

marriage ends only in two ways, by death or by divorce.[126]

For early Greek law we have the evidence of Homer: "Verschollenheit" is at the very centre of the Odyssey. It is a typical case: the whereabouts of the hero are not known to his wife, nor is it known "whether he be alive or dead" (4.110). The competition of the suitors eager to marry Penelope occupies a considerable part of the narrative, and there is no suggestion or implication that her remarriage would have been anything but completely lawful.[127] It is evident that Penelope was entitled to treat her union with Odysseus as dissolved.[128] But, since she persisted in waiting, the marriage lasted: her reunion with her long-missing husband is but its continuation, not a new marriage. In later times, similar rules are reflected in *Stichus*, a comedy by Plautus.[129]

A theory, according to which marriage was terminated by "Verschollenheit" and that *ipso iure*, irrespective of the wishes or the behaviour of the spouse who stayed at home, has been put forward for classical Roman law.[130] This doctrine has gained wide adherence, but a meticulous examination of the sources has led me to conclude that it is without foundation.[131] There was no *ipso iure* dissolution, and as long as the spouse who remained at home elected to treat the marriage

126 See *Mishnah Qiddushin* 1.1: "And she (the wife) acquires her freedom by a bill of divorce or by the death of her husband." One may again speculate whether biblical practice is to be envisaged as conforming with the approach of LE, CH and MAL, or one has rather to be guided by a *Rückschluss* from the Talmud. Cf. pp. 190f., above, on a similar problem in the context of betrothal.

127 This is the more certain since the narrator is hostile to the suitors and would not have failed to mention a wrong of theirs, especially in the sphere of marriage. Rather the main complaint against them is that they waste the property of Odysseus (or of his son, Telemachos) by their perpetual feasting and merry-making.

128 In *Odyssey* 18.269ff. Penelope is not granted permission to remarry, in case of her husband's "Verschollenheit". The text speaks of the possibility of widowhood, and marriage after Telemachos has grown up; cf. p. 221, note 176, below.

129 This may be relevant to Greek law, in view of its Greek model (the comedy is based on Menander's *Adelphoi*), and in view of the fact that the action takes place at Athens.

130 Levy *1927:* 145-193, especially at p. 162.

131 Yaron *1963e:* 62ff.

as existing, exist it did. It would be terminated, retroactively, by intelligence of the missing spouse's death, intelligence considered as sufficiently reliable to constitute proof that death had indeed occurred. It could also be terminated by a declaration of divorce, the reception of which by the absentee was not regarded as essential.

DIVORCE (LE 59)

Divorce is the last topic to be considered in this chapter. It is dealt with in one section only, LE 59; poorly preserved, it is well on its way to becoming a veritable *crux interpretum*. Attempting to elucidate its meaning, Assyriologists and legal historians alike have put forward widely different restorations of the text, and have been wont to change their opinions from time to time. In spite of all these efforts agreement is as remote as ever. One of the authors comments, in a rather resigned fashion, that "before we obtain a deeper knowledge of the Eshnunna legal practice it remains hardly possible to understand this provision in a satisfactory way".[132] One still has to try.

The protasis, in this instance the relatively simple part of the section, mentions three factual elements. First there is a condition precedent, the birth of sons (=children?[133]); by bearing children the wife has considerably strengthened her position within the family. "The main purpose of marriage is the perpetuation of the family. To a wife who fulfils this purpose the law accords special protection."[134] Next there are two culpable acts of the husband: his divorcing the mother of his sons, and his taking another wife. The import of the cumulation of these two acts is not clear to me. Would the provision not apply in case the husband did not remarry? This is unlikely; my hesitation *vis-à-vis* the "second wife" is due to the fact that such a provision would be easy to avoid: faced with the dire consequences threatened by LE 59, a divorce-minded husband would finesse, by

132 Klíma *1957:* 171.
133 See Driver-Miles *1952:* 338. On the corresponding problems of interpreting Hebrew *ben* and Latin *filius* cf. Yaron *1960:* 228ff.; *1968:* 60ff. For a strict interpretation of *marum*, see Falkowitz *1978:* 79; rightly rejected by Westbrook OBML.
134 Goetze *1956:* 145; see also the literature quoted there.

refraining (for how long?) from a fresh attempt at matrimony. If LE 59 was to have a meaning, it would have to apply to divorce as such. It would then seem that here, as before in LE 25, the third person constitutes an element which is "rechtlich überflüssig".[135]

It has been suggested that the divorce of a wife who had given birth to children was invalid. Especially forceful is the formulation of Goetze *1956:* 146 who holds that "the divorce was wilful and illegal, therefore invalid".[136] It is a conclusion a lawyer would have hesitated to reach. In fact, the section says nothing about illegality. More than that, even if divorce were illegal, one has to bear in mind that an illegal act is not necessarily void: often *quod fieri non debet factum valet*. Ample proof for this maxim is available, in *leges imperfectae* (where the act in contravention of the law is valid, and no sanction of any kind is laid down) and *leges minus quam perfectae* (act punishable, but valid). In this respect, comparison with post-classical Roman law may be useful: there, under the impact of Christian doctrine, divorce (except for some specific causes) is severely penalized, but it is none the less valid; the legislator refrains from declaring it a nullity.[137] The same appears to be true also of LE 59: it sets a high price for divorce, a price that might — if the law was effectively enforced — have greatly restrained its incidence, but the section contains nothing that in any way supports a theory of prohibition of divorce.[138] This cannot be merely a question of unclear formulation. The LE knew very well how to express curt and definitive prohibitions: see secs. 15, 16, 51. A prohibition of divorce would probably have read quite simply: *aššassu*

135 A very similar formula occurs in a deed of gift from Susa, MDP XXIV, no. 380: "... *izzibši aššatam šanitam iḫḫazma* ..." — "he divorces her, takes another wife"; cf. Koschaker *1936:* 231, note 3, who inserts "oder", regarding the cases as alternatives. In LE 59 *-ma* (in *izimma*) precludes this interpretation. The question troubling us will not arise for those (the great majority of authors) who make the second wife figure in the apodosis. We shall later set out our reasons for not following this view.

136 Goetze may have misunderstood remarks of Koschaker *1951:* 115. But see, in the same vein, David *1950:* 165: "A marriage from which children are born cannot be dissolved by divorce without well-founded reasons." For conflicting views of Klíma see *1952:* 542 and *1957:* 171.

137 See Kaser *1975:* 175f.; Yaron *1964:* 542ff.

138 The approach advocated here has been suggested, e.g., by van Praag *1950:* 81; Korošec *1954:* 368; Szlechter *1954:* 52.

ul izzib — "he shall not divorce his wife".[139] There are indeed in ancient Eastern laws provisions expressly prohibiting divorce, so in case of marriage subsequent to rape,[140] similarly also in case of a false accusation of prenuptial unchastity.[141] The mere wrongful dismissal of a *mater liberorum*, however displeasing to the legislator, does not belong to this category.

To sum up: there appears to be no justification for holding that the divorce mentioned in LE 59 was anything but fully valid.

On the whole, there has been little comment on the protasis. The husband is the subject of all the three verbs occurring in it, *wullud* — "he caused to bear, begot", *izib* — "he divorced", *itaḫaz* — "he took, married". The differences of opinion are centred on the apodosis, and there — naturally enough — on the gap in its middle. This gap is certainly a complicating factor, but it is quite possible that the interpretation of the section would have been difficult even if the text had been complete. The protasis introduced three persons, clearly and distinctly: the husband as subject, and two women as objects of divorce, respectively of marriage. In the apodosis, on the other hand, there is no noun designating any of the persons acting.[142] There are merely three verbs (in actual fact only two, since the second is missing, due to the gap); these verbs may have either masculine or feminine subjects,[143] and may therefore *prima facie* refer to any of the *dramatis personae*, that is to the husband (H), to the mother of his children (W_1), to her rival, the second wife (W_2) — or even to some other man (M) or woman (F). Note that logically the second (missing) verb and the third one are inseparably connected, since the second stands in a

139 Cf. the wording of CH 148/, forbidding the dismissal of a wife who has been attacked by a certain illness.

140 Deuteronomy 22:28-29 (probably also MAL 55). In case of divorce in contravention of Deuteronomy 22:29, the Babylonian Talmud (*Makkoth* 15a, *Temurah* 5a) imposes upon the husband the duty of taking back his divorcee. It is characteristic of the unlimited power of divorce granted to the husband by Talmudic law that the validity of the forbidden act is not questioned. But it is not impossible that a different view may have been taken in biblical times.

141 Deuteronomy 22:13-19.

142 On the absence of an express subject from the apodosis, see pp. 94f., above.

143 See p. 41, above.

relative clause qualifying the subject of the third. The phrase *warki* ... *ittallak* means "he?/she? shall?/may? go after ..."; the relative clause inserted between these two words, *ša i* ..[..]., tells after whom, or after what, the subject of *ittallak* goes. Yet even so there still remains room for divergences of opinion and interpretation, since the subject of *ittallak* may be either the subject or the object of the verb in the relative clause: to take as example one of the many restorations which have been suggested: *ša ira[mm]ušu* may mean either "whom he?/she? will love", or "who will love him".[144]

The suggestions which have been made for the interpretation of the apodosis can be arranged in the following groupings, notwithstanding minor differences in philological details: the apodosis concerns (i) the future of H and that of W_2; (ii) only the future of W_2; (iii) only the pecuniary position of W_2; (iv) only the future of H; (v) the future of H and that of W_1.

The *editio princeps* (Goetze *1948*) assigned *innassaḫ* — "he?/she? shall be torn out" (the first verb) and *ittallak* (the third) to H, but did not attempt a restoration of the verb in the relative clause, in the middle of the apodosis.[145] Suggestions for a full restoration and interpretation were first offered in three papers, all published in the course of 1949.[146] They all proceeded from the *editio princeps*, and arrived at substantially the same result, even though differing in the minutiae of restoration. Von Soden suggested *ša i-ra-a[m-m]u-ši*, taking H to be the subject of the verb, present tense of *ramum* — "to love", with a feminine object indicated by the suffix *-ši*; he rendered the final passage of the apodosis, "der (Frau) nach, die er liebt (=whom he loves), wird er gehen".[147] Both the restoration and the

144 On the question whether LE 59 extends beyond A iv 32, see pp. 78, above, 221f., below.

145 So also van Praag *1950:* 81. David *1949:* 14, also *1950:* 165, note 60, attributes *innassaḫ* to H, but does not deal with the remainder of the apodosis.

146 Von Soden *1949:* 373; Miles-Gurney *1949:* 188; San Nicolò *1949:* 260.

147 Koschaker *1951:* 112, note 24a, quotes Böhl's suggestion *ira[mm]ušu*, with masculine object. In *1956:* 34, von Soden still upheld his original suggestion *ira[mm]uši*. In *1958:* 522 he accepted the ending *-šu*, yielding to the insistence of Goetze (*1956:* 144: "what I saw on the original tablet excludes a final *-ši*"). This change need not affect the essence of von Soden's interpretation: with W_2 as subject, "whom he loves" becomes "who loves him".

interpretation have been followed by many scholars.[148] Miles-Gurney (who restored *i-t*[*a-aḫ-z*]*u*) and San Nicolò *(i-ḫ*[*u-uz-z*]*u)* resorted for their suggestions to forms of the verb *aḫazum* — "to take, marry"; here too H was the subject: he will go after the woman (W_2 or possibly F) he has taken, or will take.[149] Landsberger *1968:* 102 suggested *warki ša i-iḫ-*[*ha-zu*]*-ma ittallak* — "er folgt der (Frau) mit der er in Hinkunft verheiratet sein wird (in ihr Haus)".[150]

Koschaker *1951:* 104ff. relied on the restoration proposed by von Soden, but from this starting point he arrived at a very different interpretation of the apodosis. In his view it deals throughout with W_2: she is expelled from the matrimonial home (the house of H), loses all that she has brought with her,[151] but is allowed to enter upon a marriage with some *extraneus* (M), "will go after the man who will love her".[152] The substitution of a masculine suffix, suggested by Böhl (who restored *ša ira*[*mm*]*ušu*), would not force Koschaker to abandon the substance of his interpretation: only the final passage was affected thereby, and had to be rendered, "she will go after the man she will love".[153]

148 Goetze *1950:* 163 (ANET); Klíma *1950b:* 278, *1979:* 119; Böhl *1949/1950:* 105; Korošec *1953:* 36, 97; Lipin *1954:* 58; Falkowitz *1978:* 79; Haase *1979:* 25f; Borger *1981:* 38; Saporetti *1984:* 47; Westbrook OBML.

149 Diakonoff *1952:* 219, note 10, would restore *i-zi-bu-ši-ma* — "whom he has divorced": the husband is driven from his house to follow W_1, whom he has divorced. What is the purpose of driving both the spouses from the house?

150 This is in essential agreement with the views of the authors just mentioned. Landsberger remarks: "Die Ergänzungen von San Nicolò und von Miles-Gurney sind zwar grammatisch unmöglich, treffen aber sachlich das Richtige." See, however, Finkelstein *1970:* 255: "Landsberger's suggestion for the much-disputed verb in line 32, *i-iḫ-*⌈*ḫa-zu*⌉*-ma* is not supported by collation of the traces, except for the *-ma* which is certain. The best reading, in terms of the context and as best fitting the traces, is *i-*⌈*ra-am-mu*⌉*-ma.*" AHw 952a persists in reading *warki ša i-r*⌈*a!-am!-mu*⌉*-šu.*

151 Page 113: "Sie ist aus dem Hause ihres Mannes ausgewiesen mit Verlust ihres Eingebrachten ..."

152 Page 112: "nach demjenigen (Manne) der sie (*ši*) liebt (besser 'erwählt', noch besser futurisch 'erwählen wird'), wird sie gehen."

153 For criticism of the view of Koschaker see San Nicolò *1954:* 503; Landsberger *1968:* 102.

In the view of Szlechter the purpose of LE 59 is to regulate the pecuniary position of W_2. He takes up Koschaker's suggestion that W_2 is to be taken as the subject of *innassaḫ*, and interprets this to mean that she is denied any share in the property which had been H's during his first marriage. In the break he would restore *ša i-r[a-a]š-š[u-]ú*; the final part of the apodosis is then rendered by "à l'avenir ce qu'il acquerra elle suivra" (*1954:* 33, 62). In paraphrase, this is explained to mean that the second wife and her children shall be entitled to inherit the property acquired in the course of the second marriage. However, there is in the section no mention of the issue of the second marriage, and it is also unlikely that W_2 would be established as H's heir. No support has been forthcoming for Szlechter's restoration and interpretation.[154]

In the standard *1956* edition Goetze sees the apodosis of LE 59 as devoted exclusively to H. He would restore *ša i-ma[-aḫ-ḫa-ru]-šu*, and renders the whole provision as follows: "he shall be expelled from (his) house and whatever (property) there is and will go after him who will accept him". The desire to retain the same subject throughout seems to have been given considerable weight, and the result is no doubt grammatically and stylistically smooth. From a legal point of view, we shall see, it is less satisfying.[155]

I come now to my own proposal, according to which the second part of the apodosis concerns W_1.[156] In our examination of the apodosis as a whole, it appears useful to deal with the first verb *(innassaḫ)*, and with the last one *(ittallak)*; once one has arrived at a satisfactory interpretation for these two, one will obtain a clear meaning also for the verb in the damaged relative clause, which we leave to be considered last.

I agree with those authors who hold that the husband is the subject of *innassaḫ*: he will be driven from his house and property. The objections raised by Koschaker and Klíma are not decisive; the latter remarks that "it is not easy to punish the husband in such a radical

154 See Goetze *1956:* 143, note 8 and 144; von Soden *1956:* 34.
155 See Klíma *1957:* 170ff.; von Soden *1958:* 522; Szlechter *1958b:* 189. CAD A/i 320a refrains from accepting Goetze's restoration, but follows generally his interpretation, rendering: "he (the divorcing husband) will have to leave for anybody who [will ...] him."
156 See Yaron *1963a:* 9ff.; so also Bottéro *1965/1966:* 96.

way".[157] Koschaker is less specific, but finds fault with the fact that the law — contrary to the interests of the children — would deprive them, especially the younger ones, of their natural protector, their father. Discussing the various pertinent provisions of the CH, Koschaker states quite generally that "nirgends kommt das Gesetz auf den Gedanken bei verbotener oder auch nur missbilligter Ausübung seines Scheidungsrechts den Mann aus dem Hause zu entfernen und so die Einheit der Familie, die es doch aufrechterhalten will, zu zerstören".[158] The views of both these scholars fail to carry conviction, since they disregard a considerable amount of relevant material, which supports the dominant attribution of *innassaḫ* to the husband. First of all, there is CH 137, depriving the husband, who divorces his wife after she has given birth to children, of half his property; this is left to the wife for the children and for herself. This is a provision of essentially the same nature as LE 59. Half is admittedly different from the whole, but the difference is in the main one of quantity, not of principle.[159] Nor will it do to set CH 137 aside, and that because it concerns the marriage of a hierodule, to which special rules are said to apply, and which is believed to be of lesser cohesion.[160] If so, why the greater penalty in case of divorce? Moreover, one ought to take into account also the evidence of several marriage contracts which provide, for the eventuality of divorce by the husband, that he is to lose all his property.[161] Indeed the documents go beyond LE 59, in that the birth of children is not made a condition for the penalizing of divorce. While caution is indicated in the use of private documents for the interpretation of a text of different nature, such as the LE, they can yet not be dismissed

157 *1957:* 171.
158 *1951:* 107.
159 Note that the children remain with their mother.
160 These are the arguments of Koschaker *1951:* 106, note 8.
161 See, e.g., Schorr, *1913,* no. 4 (= HG III]1909, text 2), a document concerning marriage with two women, one of whom is to be wife-in-chief: ... *u H ana* W_1 *u* W_2 *aššatišu ul aššati atti igabima ina bitim u unutim iteli* — "should H say to W_1 and to W_2 his wives, 'thou art not my wife', — he shall forfeit house and property". Cf. also HG, *ibid.*, text 5, and the Old Assyrian document Eisser-Lewy, no. 4. For the interpretation of the last mentioned see further CAD E 416b. All the documents referred to (and others) are considered by Szlechter *1954:* 55f.

as irrelevant.[162] One may broaden the basis of the argument by pointing to similar penal provisions in a relationship which is in some respects comparable to marriage, namely adoption. There, wrongful disowning of the adoptee (which corresponds to wrongful divorce) is often said to be punishable by depriving the adoptive parent of his property. Moreover, in this case one can point to a text akin to the LE, namely the so-called Sumerian family-laws contained in *ana ittišu* 7.3, lines 34-39: *šumma abu ana marišu ul mari atta iqtabi ina biti u igarum iteli* — "if a father says to his son 'Thou art not my son', he forfeits house and wall".

We may then sum up: there is textual support for the view that the husband is the subject of *innassaḫ*, and no serious objection has been raised which would compel us to abandon it.

Our attention turns now to the third verb, *ittallak*. We have noted that some authors would attribute it to the husband, others to the second wife. In objection to those scholars who make H go after the woman he loves or marries,[163] Koschaker points out that *warki ... alakum* — "to go after", would show the husband in a position of dependence for which it is difficult to find an explanation.[164] Goetze too holds that the husband "goes after" someone, becomes dependent on him; only he follows not a wife, but some outside person "who will [accept] him".[165] However, Klíma seems to be right in observing that this "must be assumed to be a pure recommendation for the expelled husband, thus a very curious phenomenon in a legal work of that time".[166]

It appears then that in LE 59 too there is a change of subjects in the apodosis, an occurrence for which other examples have already been

162 For early Roman law see Plutarch, *Romulus* 22.3: a husband wrongfully divorcing his wife forfeits his property; half goes to the wife, half is consecrated to Ceres. But the rule is "vielumstritten": Kaser *1971:* 62, note 16.

163 Or, more exactly, "will love" (von Soden), or "will marry" (San Nicolò); see, however, Koschaker *1951:* 107, note 11, pointing out that for the couple H-W_2 one would expect the praeteritum rather than the present.

164 *Ibid.*, pp. 108f.

165 See *1956:* 143: "In Old Babylonian society nobody can exist in isolation, and least of all a man who has been deprived of his property and is now penniless. He has compelling reasons to attach himself to another 'house' from which he can expect ... protection ..."

166 *1957:* 171.

adduced.[167] The final clause, *warki ... ittallak*, lays down a grant of "Freizügigkeit", that is to say of a woman's power to go and be married to whomsoever she pleases. Against this background, a restoration based on *ramu*, giving expression to the woman's volition, appears the most plausible. Taking account of the remarks of Finkelstein,[168] we adopt the restoration *ša irammu-ma* — "(after) whom she will love".[169] The important question remains the reading of the sign immediately preceding the break; on this there are the conflicting statements of Goetze and von Soden.[170] Even if it should be thought that there is room for doubt on this point, it ought to be remembered that the restoration and the resulting interpretation offered by Goetze do not lead to a conclusion which is satisfactory from the legal point of view.

Hence, the proposed reading of the second part of the apodosis is *warki ša ira[mm]uma ittallak*, to be rendered "she may go after whom she will love". Phrases which may be compared with this occur in CH 137, 156, 172: *mut libbiša iḫḫassi* — "a husband of her heart may take her".[171] In MAL 36, 45, the corresponding phrase is *ana mut libbiša tuššab* — "she may dwell with a husband of her heart".[172] On more detailed comparison it can be seen that there is full correspondence between the supposed *ša irammuma* of LE 59 and *mut libbiša* of the other sources. The extent of a woman's possibilities is the same in all of them: after the lapse of her first marriage,[173] or its frustration, the choice of the "master of her heart" is granted to her, but having made that choice she "goes after him", is dependent on him; only he can

167 See pp. 95f., 184, above.

168 See note 150, p. 215, above.

169 In substance, this does not differ from von Soden's often repeated *irammu-šu*.

170 Goetze *1956:* 144: "The second sign is hardly *-ra.*" Von Soden *1958:* 522: "*ra-* statt- G.s *ma-* scheint mir nach der Photographie sicher."

171 See already Koschaker *1951:* 112; cf. also *ana ittišu* 7.3.4-5.

172 Close to the suggested wording in LE 59 are some biblical texts. See Jeremiah 2:25: ... *ki ahavti zarim we'aḥarehem elekh* — "for I have loved strangers, and after them I will go"; Hosea 2:7 ... *elkha aḥare me'ahavay* — "I will go after my lovers"; see also *ibid.*, verse 11.

173 Because of divorce (CH 137), incestuous carnal knowledge by the father of the bridegroom (CH 156), death (CH 172), or absence of the husband (MAL 36, 45).

"take her", not she him, as Koschaker stresses, discussing the relevant sections of CH. Coming to the verb, one sees full correspondence between LE (using *alakum* — "to go") and MAL (*wašabum* — "to sit, dwell"), with the wife as subject; in CH the husband is the subject of *aḫazum*, the wife its object. Even so, there is no substantive difference between the sources: all the sections quoted deal with a woman's capacity of choosing her spouse, or getting married.

Incidentally, one may note that there is no reference to parental control, — such as there is in secs. 26, 27/28. Once the daughter is given in marriage, parental control has terminated. If the union is dissolved, by death or by divorce, the woman is free to make her own decisions. So also in secs. 29 and 30, where the husband is absent.[174]

All that has been said so far could apply equally to the first wife, who has been divorced by her husband, or to the second one (as suggested by Koschaker and Klíma). Of these two possibilities, the first appears to be the one indicated. We have maintained above that there need be no doubt concerning the validity of the divorce; we continue along this line of thought by denying any doubt concerning the validity of the second union.[175] In these circumstances, there is no good reason for granting W_2 the right to marry again, some outsider, M. If one takes the passage as referring to H, indicating that W_2 will follow him into his new surroundings, this would be legally irrelevant and superfluous.

We submit, in conclusion, that the person who is granted power to remarry is W_1. The reason for stressing this power of hers can be established by adducing, in the first instance CH 137, and also CH 177. The former restricts, by implication, the divorcee's power to remarry: being left with half the property of the husband, and also with the children, she has to devote herself to the task of bringing them up: only afterwards is she allowed to marry again. CH 177

174 For Talmudic law, see *Mishnah Kethuboth* 4.2: After the father has given his daughter in marriage, he has no authority over her. In a different context, note Numbers 30: 2-17: the vow of a young girl, living in her father's house, can be annulled by the father, that of a married woman by her husband. By contrast, the vow of a widow or a divorcee is not open to paternal intervention (verse 10). Lapse of her status as a married woman has not re-established the father's authority.

175 Cf. also Szlechter *1954:* 57.

permits the remarriage of a widow, the mother of small children, only with the consent of the judges and after an inventory has been drawn up.[176] LE 59 is apparently more liberal: the mother who has been wrongfully divorced is free to remarry at once.[177] One may assume the existence of provisions designed to safeguard the interests of the children, even though no mention is made of them.

Our discussion of LE 59 has not progressed significantly beyond what was said already in YLE, some 20 years ago. I have paid careful attention to some observations of Westbrook (in OBML, chapter 4), but cannot accept them. I still do not see a true role for the "second wife" within the framework of the section. The phrase *warki ša irammuma ittallak* remains another major point of disagreement. I cannot perceive its function, if applied to H (and W_2): it is fairly pointless. As applied to W_1 it corresponds to widespread practice (and suffice it to mention CH 137 once more); in particular it resolves problems which might have arisen in the context of the fact that property is left in the hands of the divorcee.

I have left for a kind of postscript the suggestions of Landsberger *1968:* 102, adding to sec. 59 the first three words of A iv 33. He reads as follows: *wa-ar-ki ša i-iḫ-⌈ḫa-zu⌉-ma it-ta-la-ak* / [DA]M-*sú (=aššassu)* É *(=bitam) te-re-de*; Landsberger regards *te-re-de* as "Versehen für *iredde*", and translates: "er folgt (der Frau), mit der er in Hinkunft verheiratet sein wird (in ihr Haus); seine (erste) Gattin erbt das Haus".

As ever so often, Landsberger's suggestions found swift and wide

176 See also Homer, *Odyssey* 18. 269f.: In case Odysseus die, Penelope is allowed to marry again, but only after Telemachos has grown up: "But when thou shalt see my son a bearded man, wed whom thou wilt ..." For comparable conditions imposed in Roman wills, see *Digesta* 35.1.62.2.

177 The right of the divorcee to enter upon a new marriage is a main purpose of divorce, and as such would not require special mention. Nevertheless, documents of divorce often contain references to that right. See *ana ittišu* 7.3.4-6: *mut libbišu iḫḫussu ul iraggumši* — "a husband of her heart may take her, he (the former husband) will have no claim"; similarly also in Schorr *1913*, no. 7. Of later times, see Liverpool 8: *ašar ṣebatu tallak* — "she (the divorcee) may go wherever she wishes" (quoted CAD Ṣ 120a). For similar clauses in Aramaic documents, see Yaron *1961:* 64, note 2.

acceptance, — by Kraus,[178] Finkelstein,[179] von Soden,[180] Szlechter;[181] various translators followed suit.[182] It was disconcerting that nobody seemed to be troubled by the unique mistake *terede*, postulated by Landsberger: there is in all LE (and CH) not a single finite feminine verb-form.[183] It was left to Falkowitz to come forward with an explanation of sorts: he took *terede* to be an Assyrianism.[184]

I do admit the possibility, but not likelihood, that LE 59 extends into line 33. But this is about all. I am not convinced that *terede* is adequately accounted for (a) as a mistake, or (b) as an Assyrianism. If the draftsmen had wished to go into details of property devolution, they would preferably have brought it up at once after *inassaḫma*; also, as in CH 137, property would have passed to the children rather than to their divorcee-mother.[185]

178 *1969:* 53: "Seine Frau übernimmt das 'Haus'."

179 *1970:* 255: "Landsberger's reading [DAM-*š*]*u* [*sic!* See Finkelstein's note 53: "Thus, since only the end of ZU is preserved at the beginning of the line."] É *te-re-de* is almost certainly correct, and ... is the logical conclusion of sec. 59 rather than the beginning of sec. 60."

180 AHw 966a: "(verlassene Gattin) *bitam terede.*"

181 *1978:* 147, 160f. Szlechter's reading is slightly different: [*u*] *bitam te-re-de*. True to his view that all of the apodosis concerns W_2, he extends this to the addition.

182 Klíma *1979:* 119; Haase *1979:* 26; Borger *1981:* 38.

183 See p. 41, above.

184 *1978:* 80; amongst other arguments Falkowitz relies on my remarks regarding *alšu u belšu* (YLE, pp. 73ff.; cf. in this edition, pp. 115ff.). There is a notable difference between explaining an isolated phrase and explaining a feature of grammar which is in direct conflict with the usage of LE (and CH). Falkowitz is followed by Westbrook OBML and by Sauren *1986:* 81.

185 The radical reconstruction of A iv 33-37 by Sauren *1986:* 76ff., and its incorporation in sec. 59, have already been mentioned: see p. 80.

CHAPTER SEVEN

PROPERTY AND CONTRACT

INTRODUCTION AND CLASSIFICATION

"Property and Contract" is a wide and somewhat vague heading. Under it we shall discuss rights of a pecuniary nature, but excluding those rights which originate in the sphere of the law of persons (adoption, marriage, etc.), as well as those originating in delicts. It may be stressed again that these distinctions and classifications are merely a matter of convenience; there is no wish to suggest that anything of the kind was present, even only in a hazy fashion, to the mind of those who made and administered law at Eshnunna. This reservation applies in particular to the distinction between two kinds of wrong, that of breaking an undertaking (a contract), as against one in which no agreement is involved (a delict).

In the LE property and contract are at very different stages of development. The idea of ownership had taken root very early. A free person will usually have a variety of chattels in his possession; they are his, "belong" to him. He is sensitive to interference and will be anxious to resist it, to protect his "rights". Society will be willing to assist the owner in his endeavour. By the time of the LE these basics were long-established. In its substance, the protection of ownership may even have been more clear-cut and emphatic than in later times, when secondary considerations (such as the desire to protect a purchaser in good faith) may also have played their part.

Contract was in its infancy. While it was unavoidably based on agreement, its legal efficacy was tied to performance, at least part-performance by at least one of the parties.[1] This is not different from what one finds elsewhere in the ancient Near East (and beyond it). Meaningful progress in the sphere of contract will be a major achievement of Roman law. It is especially the emergence of consensual

1. See p. 252, below, on sec. 9.

contracts (sale, hire, partnership and mandate) which is significant: in these the legally binding effect follows at once from the mere agreement of the parties, does no longer depend upon performance or the observation of forms.

Irrespective of these differences, the LE deals with matters of property and contract in an equally fragmentary and incomplete manner. Much is presupposed, and more is simply omitted. Comparing them with the CH (also by no means complete and systematic), one notes the absence of provisions, e.g., on the tenancy of land (CH 42-52), on the laying out of plantations (CH 60-65), on partnership and agency (CH U, 100-107). Such a central topic as the law of sale is in the LE considered only with regard to some isolated, marginal points. The rules concerning the taking of pledges are only vaguely indicated by the provisions penalizing unlawful distress (LE 22, 23/24).

Property and contract are touched upon in sections 1-5, 7-16, 18A-24, 32-41; possibly also in the fragmentary and altogether obscure sec. 60 (to which we shall make no further reference). Several of these sections are discussed elsewhere: secs. 15, 16, 33, 34/35 in the chapter on "Classes and Persons";[2] secs. 12, 13, 22, 23/24, 40 under "Delicts".[3] The remaining sections may be considered under the following headings: (i) Regulations concerning prices and hire: 1-4, 7-8, 9A-11, 14;[4] (ii) Sale: 38, 39, 41; (iii) Loan: 18A-21; (iv) Liability for the breach of a variety of undertakings: 5 (negligence in carriage by boat), 9 (non-performance of agricultural services), 32 (non-payment for services rendered), and 36/37 (loss of property deposited).

Prices and hire

The considerable number of regulatory sections, as well as the prominent place accorded to them at the head of the LE, testify to the desire of the authorities to intervene in the economic process, to supervise and restrain its excesses. The basic aim will have been the wish to keep prices from rising, and to fix maximum rates of interest. But the wages laid down for agricultural workers may well be minimum wages.

2 See pp. 158ff., 162ff., 165ff. above.
3 See pp. 268ff., 275ff., below.
4 Other sections of a regulatory nature are 18A, fixing the rate of interest; 33 and 41, concerning particular cases of sale.

More difficult is the interpretation of the sections on the hire of wagons and boats; the meaning of these depends on the intentions (hidden from us) of the regulator: is it desired to protect the rights of the owners of such vehicles, or those of the public using them? A definite answer cannot be given, but on the whole the latter possibility seems to be the more likely one.

The desire to fix maximum prices reflects inflationary tendencies; at least in a mild form these seem to have been present in the ancient East, no less so than in later times elsewhere. Regulatory provisions occur also in the CH[5] and HL,[6] and there are also other sources testifying to the preoccupation of the authorities with problems of this kind.[7] It is a different question altogether whether these steps met with an appreciable measure of success, or rather remained mere pious wishes.

Sections 1 and 2 give a list of maximum prices for some basic commodities. It is not intended to enter here into a detailed examination of these; rather we may refer to Goetze *1956:* 24ff. and Szlechter *1954:* 65f. The prices laid down are rigid, and no allowance is made for possible seasonal fluctuations, such as are usual for agricultural produce.

The sections on hire deal in the main with the needs of an agricultural economy: the hiring of boats, wagons, and various agricultural workers. The object of sec. 9A is uncertain.[8] Quite obscure is sec. 14, the only one of these sections not connected with agriculture. Various suggestions have been put forward, but have not yet met with acceptance.[9] For the time being, it seems best to follow Goetze in leaving the matter open.

Concerning the sections on hire, one may note that there is no distinctive terminology, no attempt to separate the hire of services from that of chattels, or — in other words — the hire of persons from that of

5 The stress is on hire: see especially secs. 215/216/217, 221/222 /223, 224 (fees of physicians), 228 (fee of a builder), 234 (calking of a boat); 239, 242/243, 257, 258, 261, 268-277 (hire of persons and of various objects).
6. See the detailed lists of prices in secs. 176B-186.
7. See Szlechter *1954:* 65, note 1; Petschow *1968a:* 135.
8. See, however, Szlechter *1959:* 498; also note on the section, p. 49, above.
9 For details on the various suggestions see notes on sec. 14. CAD I/J 17b, A/i 20b would make sec. 14 refer to the work of a fuller; but this may be doubted, in view of the fact that the hire amounts to 20 percent of the object's value.

other movables, animate or inanimate. In legal Akkadian the verb *agarum* (which incidentally does not occur in the LE) applies both to the act of hiring services and to that of hiring chattels; the noun *idum* (Á) denotes the remuneration payable for any of the two. It has been reasonably concluded that Babylonian law and practice envisaged a comprehensive "hire of movables";[10] it is only the lease of land which is kept separate. This comprehensive approach may have been facilitated by the fact that the various services were in the great majority of cases performed by unfree labour, so that the worker was the object of the agreement rather than a party to it. When the contract is with a free worker, he too — in imitation of the wording of the prevalent case — does not "let his services", but is hired "from himself" *(itti ramanišu)*.[11] It is for this reason, to make it relate to the ordinary case, that we prefer to render the introduction to section 9, *kaspam ... ana* $^{aw.}$*agrim [li]dinma* by "give silver ... for a hired man",[12] rather than "to a hired man". From the point of view of language, both renderings are equally possible.[13]

Szlechter *1954:* 68f. has advanced the interesting thesis that in Eshnunna there obtained a double monetary system, the one in silver, the other in grain, in barley. "L'orge est une véritable monnaie, ayant un pouvoir libératoire au même titre que l'argent, autrement dit un pouvoir libératoire absolu." In this, it is submitted, Szlechter goes too far. True, while sec. 1 gives prices in terms of silver, sec. 2 states rates of exchange in terms of barley. True also that in the sections on hire grain is the prevalent means of payment;[14] but this is sufficiently explained by the agricultural background. In many parts of the world it is even at present not unusual for agricultural workers to receive all or part of their remuneration in kind; this may answer also the assumption of Korošec,[15] who suggests that the LE may reflect the transition "von der Natural- zur Geldwirtschaft".[16]

10 See Lautner *1936:* 4, and literature mentioned there.
11 Cf. Lautner, *ibid.*, pp. 2f.
12 Cf. LE 26, where the *terḫatum* is brought *ana* — "for" a man's daughter.
13 Szlechter *1954:* 106, note 29, moves in the same direction, but rather too cautiously.
14 Secs. 3 and 7 mention silver as an alternative means of payment.
15 *1964:* 87.
16 Cf. also CH 51, 111: these sections provide for the payment of debts of silver in grain, but only in specific situations.

Szlechter relies also on the duality of the rates of interest (sec. 18A: 20 percent on loans of silver, 33 1/3 percent on barley), which in his view confirms the co-existence of two monetary systems. We disagree, and submit that it is just this duality which militates against his suggestion. If these were indeed corresponding means of payment, there would be no justification for the very different rates of interest. Barley is mentioned in sec. 18A merely as an example for the loan of fungibles other than silver; we may assume that the same increased rate would apply also to the loan of other commodities, e.g., oil or wine.

SALE

We come now to the few sections on sale. The emphasis on performance, noted above, leads of itself to the identification of sale and conveyance. As long as the chattel has not been handed over, nothing of legal import has occurred. In case of advance payment, of all or part of the price, one may assume that a recalcitrant seller would have to return double the sum he had received. This is made likely by the provision, albeit *in impari materia*, laid down in sec. 25.

LE 38 deals with the case where "one of brothers", or "one of partners" *(ina atḫi išten)*[17] wishes to sell his share. It has been plausibly suggested that the property in question is part of the family estate.[18] A restrictive interpretation of the section has been proposed by Korošec, who speaks of "ungeteilte Erbgemeinschaft";[19] I am not sure that this is indeed called for. In principle a power of pre-emption might be admitted even after partition has taken place:[20] *zittum* need not be

17 According to Goetze *1956:* 107, note 1, *atḫu* — "persons who are mutual brothers" implies that there are at least three partners. This is not necessarily so; see MDP XXVIII no. 425 (quoted by Szlechter *1954:* 92), a document dealing with two persons only, described as *atḫu*. Against Goetze see also Hirsch *1969:* 120, note 13. Goetze remarks further that "if there were only two persons involved, one would say *aḫum aḫam*"; but this, meaning "one another", denotes reciprocity or action of the one upon the other, and would not suit the context.

18 San Nicolò *1949:* 261; Klíma *1948:* 329; Korošec *1951:* 85; Haase *1965:* 146f.

19 *1951: ibid.; 1964:* 89.

20 Cf., in a different context, *Babylonian Talmud, Baba Bathra* 107a: "Brothers who have divided are heirs."

restricted to mean "ideal share", prior to the division of the estate, it can equally refer to what a party has already received as his share. For a reliable answer one would first of all have to establish the exact import of *atḫu*, that is to say whether it necessarily denotes a specific legal relationship, in excess of that which exists permanently between brothers.

The brother's desire to acquire the property is mentioned already in the protasis (*u aḫušu šamam ḫašeḫ* — "and his brother wants to buy"); in other words, his power of pre-emption is presupposed by the draftsman. The true purpose of the section is to regulate the payment due, just as in the properly regulatory sections which we have been discussing. The amount payable is expressed by means of the enigmatic phrase *qablit šanim umalla*, which constitutes all of the apodosis. The verb *mullum* means "to fill", that is "to pay (in full)".[21] The phrase *qablit šanim mullum* is not a freak, it occurs also in another Old-Babylonian text;[22] this suggests that it is an idiom or technical term. In any case, little will be gained by dissecting the phrase into its component parts, *qablitum* ("middle, half"), *šanum* ("other"), and the verb *mullum*. The phrase as a whole is as yet obscure and the translations which have been offered for it differ widely.

Goetze *1948* rendered *qablit šanim umalla* — "he shall pay half of (what) an outsider (would have to pay)". This rendering has been followed by an impressive array of scholars[23] — a remarkable fact,

21 Cf. LE 5. See further the edict of Ammi-ṣaduqa, sec. 10: *mišlam umallu* — "they will pay half"; see also MAL 4 (*šurqam mullu* — "to pay in full for a theft"), 50, 52, C 3 (*napšate mullu* — "pay for a life"). Incidentally, *mullum* does not occur in the legal part of CH.

22 VAB vi 208 (quoted by von Soden, *1949:* 372) = CT xxix 9b (Goetze, *1956:* 107) = Frankena, AbB ii 136. Frankena renders *ad sensum* "bereit ... zu übernehmen", commenting: "dies offenbar die Bedeutung des Satzes, dessen eigentlicher Sinn unklar ist." See Hirsch, *ibid. qablitum* is mentioned, in the context of sale of land, in a number of Old-Assyrian texts. See especially Schaeffer, no. 22 (published by Garelli *1964:* 124ff.), where the object is a neighbouring house, and rights of pre-emption may again be involved. Note Garelli, *ibid.*, pp. 127f.

23 E.g., San Nicolò, *ibid.*; von Soden, *1956:* 34 (hesitating in AHw 598b, 887a: "Sinn ... unklar"); not clear to me is his rendering, *1949:* 372, "ich will das 'Mittlere' des anderen (durch meinen Verzicht) auffüllen"; Korošec, lastly *1964:* 89; Bottéro *1965/1966:* 94.

since Goetze himself abandoned this interpretation already in *1950:* 163a.[24] Actually, that rendering and the ensuing interpretation are unlikely to be correct. The usual term for "half" is *mišlum.*[25] One would like to know why in the technical phrase under discussion a different noun, *qablitum*, is substituted for it? Is it not perhaps that in the present context a different translation is called for (even though it is admitted that "half" may in another context be a correct translational equivalent of *qablitum*)? More important is another objection: such an arrangement would be grossly unfair to the brother who wishes to sell. Korošec *(ibid.)* suggests that the legislator wishes to lend his support to the continuation of the family partnership, but even this does not explain why the seller should be made to lose half his property.[26]

Goetze *1956* offered a rendering which was the converse of the earlier one, but no less open to objection: the apodosis was now translated "he shall (also) pay the price for the half of the other, i.e. the (third) associate". This is but a free paraphrase, and brackets might have been used more liberally. Goetze proceeds here from the assumption that the section refers at least to three persons; on this we have already voiced our hesitation. As to the purpose and actual import, Goetze suggests that "the legislator wants a situation precluded in which one member of the partnership dominates the relationship by buying out his associates. When any partner increases his share by buying an additional share he, although paying in full, must cede proportional parts of the purchase to the other associates without receiving payment from them. The principle expressed

24 There Goetze leaves the phrase without translation (note 12: "This expression, not yet fully understood, seems to imply a preferential treatment.")

25 See CH 199, /220 (*mišil šimišu išaqqal* — "half his price he shall weigh out") 238, 247 (... *inaddin* — "... he shall give").

26 So also, with even greater emphasis, Haase, *1965:* 148: "Der Grund ... könnte in dem Bestreben zu sehen sein, den Zerfall von wirtschaftlichen Einheiten und die Abwanderung von Vermögen aus der Familie zu verhindern. Wenn der Verkaufende nur die Hälfte dessen bekommen durfte, was er vom Käufer zu erhalten hatte, so wird er sich den Verkauf an einen Dritten überlegen." But the loss of half the value would effectively discourage also sale to a brother, and the situation would be entirely frozen, which will hardly have been desired. And see already Szlechter *1954:* 26, note 99.

should, of course, be generalized so as to cover any number of associates". Hardly a very plausible regulation: it would penalize the buyer who would have to pay at least twice the value of what he was actually receiving; would he not be rather reluctant to buy? Also, such a rule would be going far beyond what is necessary for its postulated purpose: it would have been sufficient to make provisions offering the other associates an opportunity to participate in the transaction, if they wish to do so. This is then altogether too complicated a solution and unlikely to be correct.[27]

Szlechter's interpretation of LE 38: "Le frère qui se propose de vendre sa 'part successorale', peut être astreint à la vendre à l'un de ses frères par préférence à un tiers, contre une indemnité équivalente à la valeur de sa part." This makes sense,[28] but is — unfortunately — not related to the text and the translation. His translation is: "... il paiera (litt. il indemnisera pour) la moitié (c'est-à-dire la part) de l'autre (frère)".[29] But this would involve an unusual amount of "elegant variation". Why should the draftsman switch from *zittum* to the uncommon *qablitum* (which might even be inexact, in case there were more than two brothers)?[30] Why, furthermore, describe the partner wishing to sell his holding by *šanum*, an expression which elsewhere refers to a third person, an outsider (LE 26, 29, 30, 59)? Also Szlechter does not take account of the letter AbB ii 136, where the impersonal *šanum* could not possibly be understood to refer to the addressees of the letter.

Different altogether are the suggestions put forward by Diakonoff *1952:* 218. He regards the seller as the subject of the apodosis, which is taken as imposing upon him the duty of giving preference to his brother, over others: "he (the seller) must satisfy him in preference before others (?)". Whatever the attraction of rendering *qablit šanim* by "before another", or "against (?) the other", — it is much open to

27 See the doubts expressed by Petschow, *1961:* 272; Haase, *ibid.*, p. 146.

28 Note the Talmudic rules of pre-emption (albeit, in different circumstances). The price is equal to that paid by the outsider. *Babylonian Talmud, Baba Meṣi'a* 108b.

29 See also *ibid.*, note 99, and p. 91; substantially identical in Szlechter *1978.*

30 Szlechter himself feels compelled to rely on explanatory glosses.

doubt whether the very concrete *mullum* can be rendered in an abstract fashion by "to satisfy, prefer".[31]

Over the years, four different translations have been offered by CAD, all of them unsatisfactory. CAD Ḫ 135a renders "he shall pay (him) in full for the other half (of the common property)". It seems that this is in agreement with Szlechter, — and open to the same objections.

CAD Z 139b renders "he must compensate him (also) for the property (chattels, stores etc.) held by the brothers in common". I am not quite sure what this is meant to convey. Also, even if we suppose that "in common" is a suitable paraphrase of *qablitum*,[32] we have to note that *šanim* is left altogether without translation or explanation. M/i 182a renders "he pays for the half of the other (partner)", which returns us to Goetze *1956*. Finally Q 6a has "he may match any outsider's offer". This has the advantage of being easy to understand. The trouble is that "offer" does not connect up with anything they adduce s.v. *qablitum*.

It is submitted that the correct interpretation is that offered already in *1949/1950:* 103 by Böhl: he renders *qablitum* by "het gemiddelde", that is, "the average".[33] A power of pre-emption, granting a privileged position to a very limited number of persons, might be unfairly exploited, in an attempt to obtain the object for a small price. According to Böhl, the buyer would have to pay the average price which an outsider might be willing to pay. If not ready to do so, he would forfeit his power of pre-emption. There might be room for disagreement in a particular case, but we are given a simple criterion which would safeguard the interests of each of the parties.[34]

31 One might refer again to the Old Assyrian parallel (see note 22): it shows clearly that *qablitum* is something delivered by the buyer (or on his behalf).

32 Cf. the Old Assyrian use of *bari* ("between") in the sense of "common" (AHw 107a); and see Kutscher *1954:* 241f.

33 Similarly also Lipin *1954* and *1963*. Comparable is the rendering *ad sensum* by David *1949:* 16: "de redelijke prijs (?)" — "the reasonable price". Böhl's approach was taken up again by Leemans *1981/82:* 60ff. Leemans sees excessive subdivision of land as underlying LE 38; but it is not necessary to restrict the section to this particular situation.

34 The postulated semantic development of *qablitum* from "middle" to "average" causes no difficulty; see, e.g., in post-biblical Hebrew *benoni*

For Böhl's rendering there is an interesting parallel, in both language and substance, in a late Syriac text, — some 2,500 years after the LE! Jesubocht, sec. 5m, has been rendered as follows: "Was nun die Häuser und Felder des Verstorbenen betrifft, die er von seinem Vater und seine Witwe von ihm geerbt hat, so darf sie, bis sie sich wieder verheiratet, darin wohnen und von den Erträgnissen sich nähren. Wenn sie sich aber gezwungen sieht sie zu verkaufen, muss sie dieselben zu einem mittleren, angemessenen Preise *(b^{e}-ṭîmē meṣ'āyē wa-triṣē)* an den Bruder ihres Gemahls verkaufen."[35]

The section which follows, LE 39, is straightforward in its wording, yet not in all respects clear. It tells of a person who became impoverished *(iniš)*, and sold his house. He is granted the power to redeem his house whenever the buyer, in turn, wishes to sell it.

Several questions arise. First, is the reference to the plight of the owner-seller, his lack of means, a material part of the facts of the case?[36] I am inclined to an affirmative answer; *prima facie* this would reduce the incidence of redeemability, in that the provision would apply only to weak strata of the population.[37] This leads to another major question: will redeemability be determined by objective criteria, or will it rather be established subjectively, by the owner's express reservation, in the document of sale, of a power to redeem. Such a rule would make for a greater degree of certainty: nothing is left to chance, all is declared. Nor would it involve any measurable handicap for the impoverished seller: there is little difference between the impact of his latent, *ex lege* right to redeem, and the patent mention of this right in the document. Still, apparently no document has turned up containing such a reservation.[38]

If express reservation was not required, could the owner nevertheless waive his power, by inserting a suitable statement to that effect in the document? Westbrook objects: "If a right designed to protect

> *ben* ("average" > "between"). Aramaic *meṣi'a* can be translated by both "middle" and "average".

35 "Corpus juris des persischen Erzbischofs Jesubocht", Sachau *1914:* 104/105. The work is supposed to have been written in the late 8th century C.E. (see *ibid.*, p. IX).

36 Goetze compares Hebrew *makh*, in Leviticus 25:25, 35, 39, 47.

37 So Westbrook *1985b:* 109.

38 Reservation of redemption occurs in "famine sales", mainly of children, but this is a very different topic; see Yaron *1959:* 155-176.

persons with weak bargaining power could be excluded by a contractual clause, it would stultify the law entirely."[39] The point is well taken. But is it really compelling? The impecunious seller might find it easier to sell, might also obtain a better price, if able to transfer unencumbered title.

Westbrook relies entirely on one objective test for the seller's plight, and consequent redeemability, namely on the price he received: "If it was far below the normal price, it is a sure sign that the sale is made under pressing economic circumstances."[40] This too is not as simple as it may look. How far below the normal would the price have to be, to trigger redeemability? A further possible complication: in a given case, the "normalcy" of the price might itself be a matter of contention.

No time-limit for redemption is mentioned, but the occasion to exercise the power depends on the buyer's intention to alienate the property. As long as the buyer holds on to it, he is secure in his possession.[41] It is probable, however, that the parties were free to make different arrangements. For such a case, Moran refers to Khafajah text 82.[42] There it is provided that the owner may at any time redeem the field he sold, but only with money of his own *(umi kasap ramanišu iraššu eqlam ipaṭṭar).* The editor, Rivkah Harris,[43] remarks that "this clause is meant to exclude outsiders from acquiring the fields cheaply. The field has obviously been undersold and the buyer wishes to protect himself against the possibility of a third party robbing him of his profit". Such a provision would not have been easy to supervise, and would therefore have been of doubtful efficacy. The legal notion underlying it may have been one that was widespread in ancient systems of law: the ownership in property acquired with a third person's money vests in that third person, not in the actual buyer.[44] Consequently, repurchase of the field with money belonging

39 *Ibid.*, p. 114, note 37.
40 *Ibid.*, at p. 109.
41 This is very different from the biblical provision: there, it will be remembered, land within the confines of a city is redeemable only within one year, but that at the discretion of the seller; Leviticus 25: 29-30. For ruses to prevent redemption, see *Mishnah 'Arakhin* 9.4.
42 *1957:* 220.
43 *1955:* 96f.
44 See Taubenschlag *1955:* 324, note 16. Also Petschow *1954:* 125ff.

to an outsider would not result in true redemption, merely in the substitution of a new alienee for the earlier one.

If the previous owner, for lack of funds, failed to exercise his power of redemption and the property passed into the hands of a third person, would he have a further chance, at the time of subsequent alienations, in other words, was redemption a continuous liability? I tend to think that it was, or else provisions concerning redemption would have been all too easy to circumvent, by the simple device of a fictitious transfer, following immediately upon the true original sale. Even so, "continuous" need not mean eternal: at some time the power to redeem must terminate. Unfortunately, LE 39 does not enlighten us on this.

We are equally in the dark when it comes to the price payable at the time of redemption. Nothing is said about it.[45] Szlechter *1954:* 96 would fix it at the price paid originally by the buyer, but the examples which he adduces — dealing with the redemption of persons, and with the recovery of property given as a pledge — are not exactly to the point. Rigid adherence to the original price might have some important drawbacks. Not only would it fail to take into account possible changes in the value of the land, it would also discourage development of the property by the buyer. As Szlechter himself observes (*ibid.*, note 25) documents dealing with the redemption of land do not state that the sum paid is identical with the original price. Westbrook *1985b* too has come out strongly in favour of the equality of original price and redemption price. This would have been easier to live with concerning agricultural land than concerning built up areas.

We have already had opportunity to mention LE 41, the contents of which are quite obscure (see p. 160 above). The apodosis is the more easily intelligible part: in it the alewife *(sabitum)* is enjoined to sell beer at the current price. This is then essentially another regulatory section. Even here, however, there remains room for doubt: the suffix *-šum* may be rendered either by "to" or by "for". Hence, *inaddinšum* is either "shall sell to him",[46] or "shall sell for him".[47] The interpretation of the factual situation underlying the protasis may depend on this

45 See already San Nicolò *1949:* 261.

46 So Miles-Gurney *1949:* 186; Szlechter *1954*; CAD A/i 310b.

47 So Lipin; Goetze *1956*; Bottéro. Landsberger *1968:* 99f. dwells on the difficulties inherent in each of the two interpretations.

minute difference. In Szlechter's view, the persons mentioned there (that is the *ubarum*, the *napṭarum*, and the *mudum*) wish to sell beer in retail, and the *sabitum* is instructed to supply the beer to them at the proper market price, that is, at the maximum permissible (as is the case also in the other regulatory sections).[48] This is a relatively simple interpretation, but there appears to be nothing to connect the classes mentioned with the sale of beer; also one would like to have a reason for the designation *šikaršu* — "his beer"? Miles-Gurney *1949:* 186 suggest that the *ubarum* etc. may have had to furnish beer as part of the rent of immovables; this seems rather far-fetched, even though they can point to some cases where beer is used for such a purpose. Goetze thinks of a case where one of those mentioned wishes to sell his beer ration. The *sabitum* acts on his behalf and will have to see that he gets the proper price; here then the purpose would be to achieve a decent price, not to restrict it. This last solution is the most complicated of the three, and the situation would be quite peculiar and inherently improbable: if anything of the kind ever happened, the matter would hardly have gained the attention of the legislator. In these circumstances, I prefer to join San Nicolò *1949:* 261, in admitting that I do not understand what this section is about.

LOAN

Loan is dealt with in four sections, 18A-21. Of these, only sec. 18A is straightforward; it fixes, we have seen, the rate of interest for loans of silver at 20 percent (per annum), that of barley at 33 1/3 percent. These rates are given in CH, sec. L; they are those current also in actual practice, though deviations are not unknown.[49] The other sections are difficult to understand, and that because of the use of technical terms, which have as yet no parallels in other sources. Our suggestions will consequently be in the main of a hypothetical nature.

Sections 19-21 deal with different types of loan, one *ana meḫrišu* (19), and one *ana panišu* (21); in sec. 20 the key phrase is illegible. It

48 Szlechter mentions the possibility that the reference may be to a minimum price, for fiscal reasons. On sec. 41, see also Landsberger, *ibid.*, and Finkelstein *1970:* 253f.

49 See Leemans *1959:* 77f.; Simmons *1959:* 83f.; Reschid *1965:* 22ff.; see also Greengus *1986:* 194f.

has already been noted (pp. 111f., above) that LE 19 probably derives from a different source, a fact which adds a further element of uncertainty, in that it furnishes a possible reason for divergences of wording.

The main sentence of LE 19 is simple: *awilum ... ina maškanim ušaddan* — "a man ... at?/from ? the threshing-floor will collect".[50] This man is qualified by the relative sentence *ša ana meḫrišu inaddinu* — "who will give *ana meḫrišu*".[51] Note that the object lent is not specified. But payment on the threshing-floor suggests that it refers to grain. LE 19 differs from the sections following it, also in that it contains no reference to a payment of interest. Goetze and Szlechter, each in his own way, see therein the clue for the rendering of *ana meḫrišu*; in the former's view (*1956:* 67) it concerns a loan "'in (terms of) its equivalent', i.e. recording in the deed not the amount actually lent, but the amount to be repaid"; the latter holds that the loan was in truth gratuitous, i.e. he sees "the equivalent" as referring to the quantity of grain actually handed over.[52] I should prefer the view of Goetze, also since Szlechter himself points out (p. 72), that the use of a particular terminology does not conclusively prove the true nature of a type of loan: interest could easily have been deducted in advance, at the time of the loan, or else the document could mention an amount larger than that actually given. Others see in *ana meḫrišu* a reference to the status of the borrower, translating it by "an seinesgleichen, einem Ebenbürtigen". I do not think that this rendering is necessary: in LE / 35 *meḫeršu* is the "equivalent" of a slave-child, regarded as an object rather than a person. Also, I fail to see the relevance of the identity of status of lender and borrower; that might — in very particular circumstances — have some bearing on the payment of

50 So, essentially, Goetze *1948, 1950*; Szlechter. Goetze *1956* renders "shall be made to pay (the debt) on the threshing floor" (followed by Loewenstamm *1957:* 197b, "he has to repay"); this reflects the mistaken passive rendering of *ušaddan* (and see already Hartmann *1956:* 440; Moran *1957:* 220). Note the rather similar rendering of the relative clause (but correct on *ušaddan*!) by Landsberger *1968:* 74, quoted in text.

51 But note the translation in Kraus *1984:* 197: "Ein Mann lässt sich das, was er an seinesgleichen hergeliehen hatte, auf der Tenne (zurück)geben". The switch in the rendering of *awilum ša*, from subject to object, departs from the usual, but is not necessarily wrong.

52 Szlechter *1954:* 79; so also Korošec *1964:* 89.

interest (see Deuteronomy 23:21), but then interest is not considered in LE 19.[53]

Proceeding from the same premise of equality of status, Landsberger (*1968:* 74) renders: "Jemand, der seinem Standesgenossen (eine Leistung in Gerste) zu leisten hat, (dieser) hat sie auf der Tenne einzutreiben." This is not only awkward German; it is just as awkward Akkadian (though one might find comparable constructions in Mishnaic Hebrew). While we are in principle ready to admit change of subject as a possibility, in the present case *awilum* would altogether remain without a verb of its own. Landsberger continues with the following comment: "Dem Leistenden [sind] keine Transport- und Lagerungskosten aufzubürden, gleichgültig, was der Titel der Leistung (Feldabgabe, Schuld) ist. *ana meḫrišu* (für *ana awilim*) dürfte keine stilistische Floskel sein, mit anderen Worten: Der Palast vom Untertanen, der Eigentümer vom Feldpächter, sind berechtigt, Ablieferung an einer ihnen genehmen Stelle zu stipulieren." Landsberger, if I understand him correctly, sees as the main (though implicit only!) purpose of LE 19 a difference in the duty incumbent on the borrower: if lender and borrower are of equal status, the borrower is not bound to bear incidental expenses of transport and storage; but his superiors (the palace, or the lessor of land) may so stipulate. This reads into the text quite a lot, leaning too heavily on a mere *argumentum e contrario*. Also, the stress on the primary, local import of *ina maškanim* — "on/from the threshing-floor" seems exaggerated. A transferred interpretation, in terms of time, seems preferable; so already Petschow *1968a:* 137: "Fälligkeit".

What then was the actual purpose of the section? Possibly, the fixing of the date for repayment, in case this has not been specifically laid down in the document of loan. This may be important especially where the payment of interest, adjusted to the duration of the loan, is not stipulated. The provision guides the calculations of the parties in a transaction of this type.[54]

53 The rendering "ein Ebenbürtiger", and the like, is that of von Soden *1956:* 33, *1958:* 520, AHw 641a; Kraus *1958:* 48, *1984:* 197; not quite clear is CAD M/ii 58a, "lending out against a corresponding commodity."

54 Korošec *1951:* 88 sees a distinctive feature of the loan *ana meḫrišu* in its being a "Bringschuld", i.e. that the debtor is obliged to seek out his creditor. This is indeed a general principle of the law of obligations, but

LE 20 is particularly difficult: in it the complexity of the content is aggravated by the poor state of preservation of the tablet. The apodosis is simple: it envisages payment in grain, at the time of the harvest *(ina eburi)*.[55] The rate of interest is 33 1/3 percent, that is to say the rate already fixed in sec. 18A.

The protasis consists of two parts, an introduction setting out the basic facts *(šumma awilum ... iddinma)*, followed by a qualifying statement *(še'am ana kaspim i-te-x-[x)*; it is with this qualification that the legislator will wish to deal.[56] Each of these parts has its difficulties. Of the introduction, only the words quoted were certain: someone "gave" (= lent) something; two questions remained. The object lent was in dispute (but this, we shall see, seems to have been resolved): Goetze and many others held that the object was silver.[57] A minority, represented by Korošec[58] and Szlechter[59] held that the loan had been one of barley. YLE (pp. 157 ff.) followed the minority. The other question arose from the end of line 10: the phrase describing the type of loan, or its purpose, was and remained illegible, and the numerous suggestions put forward were but conjectures.[60]

The obscurities in the first part of the protasis need not prevent the interpretation of the second part, which is essentially separate. Here the main problem was presented by the last word, read by Goetze *1948* as *i-te-wi-š[um]*, and rendered there "expresses ... for him".[61] The translation shows that Goetze derived *itewiš[um]* from *awum* — "to speak", but von Soden (*1949:* 370) objected that in that verb *a* does not

it hardly finds expression in LE 19: *ušaddan* (just as *ileqqe* in secs. 20, 21) refers to an act of the creditor; subject to the doubts just noted, *ina maškanim* points also to the place of the debtor.

55 We take *ina eburi* to mean much the same as *ina maškanim* of LE 19.

56 See pp. 100f., above, on the components of protases.

57 San Nicolò *1949:* 260: "Gelddarlehen, dessen Rückzahlung in Getreide zugesagt ist"; Böhl *1949/1950:* 100; Leemans *1950:* 14; Loewenstamm *1957:* 197; von Soden *1958:* 520; AHw 267a; Bottéro *1965/1966:* 102; Petschow *1968a:* 137, note 4.

58 *1951:* 88: Korošec speaks of grain as "in schwerer Not zur Verpflegung entliehen"; see also *idem 1953:* 92, 95. This is based on the reading *i-te-pi-i[r*, suggested by von Soden in *1949*, but since abandoned (see below). For the view of Korošec, see further *1964:* 89.

59 *1954:* 20, 76; *1978:* 123, 172.

60 See the notes on sec. 20, p. 56, above.

61 Goetze was followed, e.g., by Böhl *1949/1950:* "bepaald heeft", and by Szlechter *1954:* 20: "soit stipulée".

change into *e*; therefore he looked for other readings. First *(ibid.)* he suggested the reading *i-te-pi-i[r]*? (from *eperum* — "verpflegen, in Verpflegung geben"), later (*1956:* 33) he mentioned as a further possibility the reading *i-ṭe$_4$-pi-š[um]* — "er ihm (Korn) hinbreitet" (from *ṭepum*).

Goetze *1956* still adhered to his reading, but — possibly in deference to von Soden's objection — he now derived *i-te-wi* from *ewum* — "to equal" (p. 159, glossary), and rendered the phrase by "he has equated for him(self) barley to silver".[62] Thereupon von Soden *1958:* 520 abandoned his previous attempts, accepted Goetze's reading and derivation, dissenting only from the actual translation: he insisted that *ewum* — here as elsewhere — can only be rendered "to become" ("werden"). This yielded "wenn es (i.e. das Darlehen) zu Korn für Silber ihm wird".[63] The end result of von Soden's strenuous efforts to arrive at a faithful rendering of the phrase is hardly convincing. Tortuous and twisted, in German as well as in Akkadian, it might with difficulty be acceptable for a literary text, but it will not do in a section of law. The wording is rather curiously impersonal (how did the silver "become" grain?), and all too complicated; von Soden's interpretation would be better suited to a simpler formulation, such as *kaspum še'am itewišum*.[64]

However, these niceties of language apart, there is broad agreement between all the scholars following Goetze as to the actual import of the section. A person lent silver but "translated" the loan into terms of barley. He did so in order to profit from the considerable difference in the rate of interest: the maximum rate for silver is much smaller, 20 per cent only.[65] One may entertain some doubts: this would be all too easy a

62 Goetze himself stresses that for such a phrase "an occurrence cannot be quoted at present" (*1956:* 67, note 19).

63 See also in AHw 267a.

64 This would also be more in tune with the parallel which von Soden *1958:* 520 adduces from the Old Babylonian epic of Zu: *umu namrum da'ummatam liwišum* — "when the light turned into darkness for him": Nougayrol *1952:* 92:68.

65 Goetze *1956:* 67 mentions as a further possibility speculation on the rise of the price of barley. This is not likely, since the debt is payable at the time of the harvest, when prices are lowest. Different again is the interpretation offered by Bottéro, *1965/1966:* 102: if a debtor wishes to repay a loan of silver by means of grain, he has to pay interest at the increased rate usual for loans of grain. This would be a very harsh provision.

way for the circumvention of the maximum rate of interest. All a lender would have to do is to turn the loan of silver into a fictitious loan of naturalia, and thereby he would become entitled to a higher rate. One may take for granted the desire of lenders to circumvent restrictions imposed by law;[66] consequently, the effectiveness of provisions limiting interest is always in doubt. But, effective or not — one finds it difficult to believe that a law taking the trouble of restrictively fixing rates of interest would actually expressly condone practices of this kind.

Szlechter holds that the loan was one of grain, but formulated in terms of silver, so that the lender be able to benefit from the anticipated seasonal decline of the price. To protect the debtor, the law wishes to foil this device. Szlechter sees the section as "une autorisation légale permettant au débiteur de se libérer en orge bien que les parties aient convenu, au moment de la conclusion du contrat, que le remboursement du prêt devrait s'effectuer en argent".[67] Similarly, Korošec sees LE 20 as having been enacted "um Wuchergeschäften entgegenzuwirken" (*1964:* 89).

This was the state of the discussion when I worked on YLE. I continued with a detailed, comparative examination of the underlying possibilities. First of all, a matter of terminology had to be disposed of: jurists are accustomed to define as loans only transactions which involve the undertaking to return fungibles of the kind received. Whenever one kind of object is given but another is to be rendered, they will tend to regard this as a case of barter or sale. They will speak of "Pränumerationskauf" when the consideration for a sum of silver given is to consist of some other commodity, to be rendered at a subsequent date; of "Kreditkauf", when in consideration for some commodity given, silver is to be paid sometime later. However, there are a number of factors limiting the usefulness, indeed the validity of these distinctions, where Babylonian law is concerned. For one thing, sale and loan appear as closely intertwined, functionally. Sale is a cash trans-

66 Plautus, *Curculio*, lines 509-511, has this to say about money-lenders: "The people have passed bills without number against you, and once they pass them, you smash them; you always find some loophole. To you laws are like boiling water that soon grows cold." (Transl. P. Nixon, *Loeb Classical Library*.)

67 Szlechter *1954: 78; 1978:* 272f.

action, the simultaneous exchange of some object for silver.[68] No instrument had been developed, within the framework of sale, for the separation of the two, that is, for the postponement of performance by either the seller or the buyer. Loan is the solution for this difficulty: every case of "Pränumerationskauf" or "Kreditkauf" is construed as a loan. There are different possibilities. "Pränumerationskauf" is a loan granted by the buyer: either a loan of silver, to be converted into a price at the time the object (barley, oil, wine, etc.) is handed over; or else a loan of the commodity, construed (fictitiously) as having been handed over and returned at once for the period specified. Conversely, "Kreditkauf" would be a loan granted by the seller, either of the silver he is to receive in due course, or of the commodity he has already supplied, fictitiously thought of as returned prior to the payment of the price. Of these constructions, that of money loans will probably be prevalent, but the other is equally possible. The actual formulation in a given case may depend on the interests of the stronger party to the transaction (often the buyer), who may wish to profit from expected fluctuations of the price. If an increase is foreseen, it would be to the benefit of the buyer to regard the transaction as already perfected, and the commodity as loaned; if a decline of the price is expected, he would wish to stipulate that he will get the commodity at *maḫirat illaku*, the price current at the time of actual delivery. *Pro tempore* the transaction would be construed as a loan of silver.[69]

Within the sphere of loan proper we have already alluded to two important factors which may — in a particular case — influence the formulation of the transaction, and may incidentally lead to confusion in our legal classifications. First, there are considerable differences in the rate of interest for silver and naturalia. This is not a peculiarity of Old Babylonian law; one finds the same situation in other sources. In Neo-Assyrian documents of loan, the rates usually stipulated are 25 percent per annum for silver, 50 percent for naturalia.[70] In Ptolemaic Egypt the maximum rate of interest for money loans was 24 percent per annum;[71] in loans of naturalia the interest usually amounted to 50

68 See Koschaker *1917:* 138: "Man kann direkt sagen, dass für das juristische Denken des Babyloniers Kauf und Barkauf identisch waren."
69 See on these questions San Nicolò *1922:* 76ff., and earlier authors quoted there, p. 78, note 5.
70 Kohler-Ungnad *1913:* 459ff.
71 Taubenschlag *1955:* 343.

percent. In post-classical Roman law, interest on money was limited to 12 percent (the *centesima*), but the lender of naturalia was permitted to take up to one half.[72] Justinian fixed the standard maximum rate for money at 6 percent, but permitted 12 percent for loans of commodities (*specierum fenori dationibus* — *Codex Iustinianus* 4.32.26.2, of 528 C.E.).

Actually, the divergence may be even much greater than appears at first sight. Whereas the rates for money are yearly ones, there is every reason to assume that the rates for naturalia envisage a much shorter time, until the next harvest.[73] However, the picture must not be distorted: if grain is lent late in autumn and returned (with interest), say in June or July, this means in effect that for several months the lender will have the grain on his hands — until the season comes for lending it again. During that time he will have to store it, and will have to bear the expenses and the potential losses this may involve. This may indeed be at least a part-explanation for the great difference in rates.

If one disregards possible fluctuations in price, it appears that the creditor might profit considerably from disguising a loan of silver as one of grain. This is, in essence, the interpretation offered for LE 20 by Goetze and those following him. That it is practicable and not inherently unlikely is shown by the occurrence of such a case in the *Codex Iustinianus*, 4.32.16 (about 240 C.E.): A borrower complained that a loan of money had been disguised as one of grain, in order to evade the restrictions on interest. Note that he is given a remedy.[74]

A second approach to the problem disregards the differences in the rate of interest, and concentrates on the fact that prices of commodities were often subject to very considerable seasonal fluctuations. If grain

72 *Codex Theodosianus* 2.33.1 (325 C.E.): "Quicumque fruges humidas vel arentes indigentibus mutuas dederint, usurae nomine tertiam partem superfluam consequantur, id est ut, si summa crediti in duobus modiis fuerit, tertium modium amplius consequantur. ... quae lex ad solas pertinet fruges: nam pro pecunia ultra singulas centesimas creditor vetatur accipere."

73 See also the detailed discussion, with examples, by Billeter *1898:* 302ff.

74 "Cum non frumentum, sed pecuniam fenori te accepisse adleges, ut certa modiatio tritici praestaretur, ac nisi is modus sua die fuisset oblatus, mensurarum additamentis in fraudem usurarum legitimarum gravatum te esse contendis, potes adversus improbam petitionem competenti uti defensione."

was lent at a time when prices were high, it might be profitable for the lender to have the loan appear as one of silver, repayable in grain at the low prices current at the time of the harvest. That might be so even if he had to forego the higher rate of interest. This is the situation reflected in a considerable number of documents, usually classified under the heading of "Fruchtwucher".[75] However, in an actual case it might often be difficult to distinguish between "Fruchtwucher" and "Pränumerationskauf".

One may ask why actually the law would endeavour to prevent "Fruchtwucher"? There was no objection to genuine "Pränumerationskauf". In cases which in reality are "Fruchtwucher", it is still to be assumed that the calculations correspond to the market prices current at the relevant times, i.e. when the grain is given, respectively returned. If these were true sale and purchase transactions by the creditor, in other words if he sold grain when it was scarce (and highly priced), and bought other grain when it was abundant (and cheap), the law would not intervene; why should it in the case of "Fruchtwucher"? The need to restrict the rate of interest may have been the decisive consideration: the customary rate (of one third) gives the lender sufficient profit, and he must not be allowed to increase it by resort to fictitious transactions. Genuine sale would be in a different category; but it is doubtful whether it was practicable on any considerable scale, since the small peasantry would have lacked the necessary funds.

Outside the sphere of cuneiform law, one might refer to *Babylonian Talmud, Baba Meṣi'a* 74b (bottom), where steps are taken to prevent "Fruchtwucher": "Our Rabbis taught: A man may say to his fellow, 'Lend me a kor of wheat', and determine (the amount due in) money: if it became cheaper he renders wheat unto him, if it became dearer he renders money." In view of the Talmudic prohibition of interest, this seems rather rigorous a stand to take, and later it was endeavoured to change the import of the text.[76] The Talmudic provision is then a close

75. See San Nicolò *1922:* 79, note 6a, and the documents and literature mentioned there. See also HG VI(1923) text 47. A further instance may be MAH 16. 161 (in Szlechter *1958:* 20f.)

76 *Ibid.*, 75a: "But did he not determine (the amount in money)? — R. Shesheth answered: It is meant like this; in case he did not determine (the amount), if it became cheaper, he takes his wheat; if it became dearer he renders money."

parallel to LE 20, as interpreted by Szlechter and Korošec.

In conclusion, one may again point out that the majority view fails to assign any actual purpose to the section. Apart from this significant shortcoming, one may say that each of the conflicting views on LE 20 can find support in the factual and legal background, as emerging from all the sources which have been adduced. It follows that our enquiry has failed to provide a decisive answer: that can only be found within the section itself, to the renewed examination of which we return now.

The uncertainties of the dominant interpretation of the second part of the protasis are largely due to the fact that the alleged phrase *X ana Y ewum* is a *hapax legomenon.* The question therefore arises, whether *i-te-wi-š[um]* is indeed the correct reading of the last word of the protasis, that is, the last word in A ii 11. Goetze's copy confirms *i-te*, but it shows an erasure in the lower part of the third sign; of the last one there are only the poor remains of what appears to be a sign beginning with two horizontal wedges. On this basis, the reading *i-te-pu!-u[š]* might be considered, to be confirmed (or disproved) by collation. This would give *še'am ana kaspim itepu[š]*, a phrase the interpretation of which will cause no difficulty: "he made barley into silver", that is, converted barley into silver. *X ana Y epešum* is well known, and means "to make X into Y", "to change X into Y", to endow X with new attributes. Occurrences at Boghazköi, Nuzi and Alalakh, it is true, are all concentrated within the sphere of the law of persons ("to make someone son, father, brother, king", etc.).[77] However, an idiom closely similar to the proposed *še'am ana kaspim epešum*, and *in pari materia* with it, is found in a much later source, in Mishnaic Hebrew. There we have several times the phrase *'aśah X damim* — "to make X (some commodity) money". Here it will suffice to quote one relevant text, *Mishnah Baba Meṣi'a* 5.9: "... Moreover Hillel used to say: A woman may not lend a loaf of bread to her neighbour unless she makes it money *('ad šeta'aśennu damim)*, lest wheat should rise in price and they be found partakers in usury."[78]

77 See CAD E 230bf.; AHw 227a.

78 Compare *Baba Meṣi'a* 74bf., quoted above. Here, as there, we find extreme precautions against the taking of interest: the lender must derive no profit from the loan. See also *Mishnah Pesaḥim* 7.3; *Temura* 5.5; *Tosefta Baba Meṣi'a* 6.9; *Palestinian Talmud, Baba Meṣi'a* 10c.

The above analysis led me to come down on the side of Korošec and Szlechter:[79] the comparative survey resulted in the conclusion that *še'am* was likely to be the correct restoration of the alleged gap at the beginning of line 10. It was therefore gratifying to find the reading *še'am* proposed by Landsberger *1968:* 74 and supported by collation.[80] Thereby, LE 20 received an interpretation which was more meaningful than that allotted to it by the dominant view. It emerged as a provision against "Fruchtwucher", unparalleled in any ancient Near-Eastern source known at present. It is only in Talmudic law of the Tannaitic period, almost 2000 years after Eshnunna, that the matter is tackled again.

The last of the sections on loan, LE 21, is well preserved, yet its import is by no means clear. Goetze wished to interpret the key phrase *ana panišu* as meaning the opposite of *ana meḫrišu* (of sec. 19). However, it is doubtful whether there is any connection between the two; even if there were, this would give little comfort, since the meaning of *ana meḫrišu*, we have seen, is also quite uncertain. It is likely that secs. 19 and 21 come from different sources, so that the one cannot be used to explain the other.[81]

Goetze renders *ana panišu* by "in terms of its initial (amount)". Loewenstamm *(ibid.)* would connect LE 21 with the preceding section 20, but this too is not very probable, since there is nothing in the wording of the sections to support this view. Szlechter *1954:* 74 mentions CH, sec. L, *šumma (tamkarum) kaspam ana ḫubullim iddin*, and suggests that *ana panišu* is a substitute for the well-known term *ana ḫubullim* — "for interest". Such a mechanical equiparation is methodically unsound, and does not warrant any conclusion as to the import of the phrase in LE 21. In effect, Szlechter disregards the phrase altogether and treats LE 21 as if it were ruling on an ordinary loan of silver.

However, we have already been informed (in sec. 18A) of the permissible rate of interest for silver, and it will not be satisfactory to regard sec. 21 as a mere repetition, devoid of any purpose of its own. Yet this is, in effect, the interpretation given to it so far. There must be

79 No reliable restoration can be suggested for the end of the first part of the protasis (end of line 10).

80 See Finkelstein, *1970:* 250.

81 Pace Loewenstamm *1957:* 196f.

some more specific situation, some problem for which the section is meant to supply the solution. Such a situation was indeed suggested by Landsberger *1968:* 74: "Wenn (aber) jemand Geld als Vorschuss (auf die Ernte) gibt." This is not plausible, and that because of two reasons: (a) the apodosis speaks of a return of silver, not a rendering of grain; (b) in case of prepayment on account of the price, the question of interest would not arise.[82]

A suggestion of mine is also far from certain. One should note that there is no reference to the date of payment; this had been a material factor in the preceding sections. The simplest, literal rendering of *ana panišu* would be "before him", i.e. "at his disposal".[83] Quite tentatively it may then be suggested that *ana panišu* refers to a situation where silver has been put at the disposal of the borrower, but has not yet been actually taken by him.[84] The question arises whether interest is payable in these circumstances. An affirmative answer is given, and it may be possible to explain it. An individual lender who had agreed to keep silver at the borrower's disposal, would forego the opportunity of lending it to someone else: hence he ought to be indemnified. It is different if the lender is an institution disposing of large sums.

For all their differences, secs. 19 to 21 have one feature in common: in each the apodosis refers not to the borrower's duty to pay, but rather to the rights of the lender: he will collect, he will take. In this instance the language of the law does not follow that predominant in documents. These refer typically to the borrower's undertaking to pay. While the actual result is the same, one wonders what may have caused the departure from contractual formulation.[85]

DISTRESS

What are the ways and means to make a debtor pay his debt? On this important matter we have only the indirect and incomplete information that can be derived from LE 22 and 23/24, dealing with unlawful

82 See already the remarks on "Pränumerationskauf", pp. 240f., above.

83 Szlechter *1954:* 75 mentions that the phrase *ana panišu* occurs regularly in Neo-Assyrian and Neo-Babylonian documents of loan. It does not follow that at the time of the LE, a thousand years earlier, the phrase need have had the same import.

84 So already Kunderewicz *1966:* "do dyspozycij"; Haase *1979:* 22, note 6.

85 And see already note 54, above.

distress.[86] It is a necessary implication that in case the creditor's claim was well-founded he was entitled to seize the debtor's dependents, free and unfree, and hold them until the discharge of his debt. *A fortiori* he would also be entitled to seize other property belonging to the debtor,[87] subject, probably, to specific rules exempting from seizure certain kinds of property.[88] The taking of a distress *(niputum)* seems to have been a very frequent occurrence; the theme recurs again and again in Old Babylonian correspondence.

The creditor or claimant proceeded by way of self-help, based — it seems — on custom and practice; at any rate deeds of loan do not provide for it, in case of non-payment, nor is there anything to suggest the need for authorization by a judicial body.[89] Distress seems in the main to have been a means of pressure, to induce the debtor to fulfil his obligations. It is also possible, as has been suggested, that work done by the distrainee would be credited to the debtor; however, there would be the cost of maintenance, and interest might also continue to accumulate. Hence, in case the debt was a considerable one, the idea of working it off was not always practicable.

BREACH OF CONTRACT

We come now to the last part of this chapter, the four sections dealing with liability arising out of the breach of contracts. Two of these, secs. 5 and 36/37, deal with damage incurred in the course of the execution of a contract; the others, sec. 9 and 32, concern the failure of one of the parties to perform his share of the transaction.[90]

In both secs. 5 and 36/ the person liable (in the one case a boatman, in the other a depositee) has to pay the *simplum* only, i.e. he has to make good the loss actually incurred. There is then nothing inherent in the situation that would call for the imposition of a penalty.[91]

86 See in detail pp.275ff., below.
87 So ARM IV 58 tells of a seizure of donkeys.
88 Cf. CH 241; Deuteronomy 24:6.
89 Cf. Driver-Miles *1952:* 210.
90 Another failure to perform, in sec. 25, has already been discussed in detail. See pp. 190ff., above.
91 In BM 105347 (Falkenstein *1956:* 99ff.) the owner of a boat which had been sunk denies having let it. One may presume that in this manner he wishes to increase the compensation due to him.

THE NEGLIGENT BOATMAN

Sec. 5, in its rather terse formulation, would appear to deal only with the relationship between a carrier (*malaḫum*—"boatman") and the owner of the object/s carried. The corresponding sections in the CH (236, 237) are more detailed, and discuss also the three-cornered case where the boatman is not the owner of the vessel. The boatman is liable towards each of his contrahents, for damage resulting from his negligence. The law does not create any relationship between the owner of the vessel and the owner of the goods transported.

It has been duly noted that the boatman's liability under LE 5 depends on his being negligent — *egum.*[92] Prior to the publication of the LE it had been widely held that the notion of negligence as determining liability was an innovation of Hammurabi;[93] this view is then no longer tenable.[94]

Szlechter *1954:* 101 mentions the possibility that under a contract the carrier may assume full liability, independent of his being guilty of negligence. There is indeed no reason why such an agreement should be unfeasible; however, the documents which he mentions refer all to the boatman's responsibility vis-à-vis the owner of the vessel, not the owner of the goods being transported. A converse stipulation, i.e. contracting out of liability for negligence, would be equally possible, but does apparently not occur in the contracts.[95]

LOSS OF A DEPOSIT

Section 36/37 concerns the loss of property which had been deposited. No mention is made of a remuneration of the depositee, probably because the point is immaterial in the context of the circumstances set out in the section: liability or absolution would not depend on it. Generally, I agree with Szlechter (p. 82) that the absence of remuneration need not be regarded as an inherent trait of the contract of deposit. As for negligence — it is doubtful whether that notion plays

92 See Goetze *1956:* 38f.; Szlechter *1954:* 101.
93 See, e.g., San Nicolò *1931:* 184f.
94 For further remarks and references on LE 5, see Petschow *1973b:* 233ff.
95 For a detailed discussion of the carrier's liability in Greek and Roman law, see Brecht *1962.*

any part here: it might indeed appear to be suggested by the use of the D-form *ḫulluqum* (in 36/), in contradistinction to the impersonal forms *ḫaliq* and *ḫalqu* (in /37), but this is not altogether a safe indicator.[96] It seems then rather that we are here within the sphere of liability for results.[97]

The first part of the section, 36/, makes the depositee liable in case there is no evidence showing that the house has been burgled. It does not follow that if there had been evidence to that effect he would necessarily have been absolved. Comparison with /37 suggests that for absolution there were some further requirements. It must be borne in mind that under sec. 36/ the depositee is condemned to make good the loss, and it is sufficient to set out the elements which are essential for that purpose. One may assume that to clear himself the depositee would at least have had to swear to his innocence of fraud.

The second part of the section deals with a set of facts resulting in the depositee's absolution of liability (*mimma elišu ul išu* — "he shall not have anything upon him"). There is, however, a measure of uncertainty concerning those facts. In order to solve the problems arising, Goetze and von Soden have — independently of each other — had resort to that radical means, emendation of the text.[98] Goetze *1956:* 13, 100, holds that "the *lu* before *imqut* at the beginning of sec. 37 lacks motivation"; "the context[99] suggests that house-breaking must have been mentioned". Therefore, postulating a homoioteleuton, Goetze conjectures *lu <ippališ lu> imqut* — "was either <broken into or> collapsed". This conjecture, we have noted, gains in importance because of the implication of a mistake common to both tablets, A and B.

Von Soden *1956:* 34 would emend the text by inserting *lu* after *imqut*, obtaining *lu imqut <lu> itti buše awil maṣṣartim ša iddinušum ḫuluq bel bitim ḫaliq* — "(the house) either collapsed <or> with the goods of the depositor, which he had given to him, loss of the owner of the house was incurred". At first sight this may appear as an attractive

96 See the discussion by Szlechter *1954:* 83, and note 10 there.
97 See also Bottéro *1965/1966:* 103. See further pp. 264ff., below.
98 See the discussion p. 23, above.
99 That is to say, the facts set out in sec. 36/ (my note, R.Y.).

suggestion: by assuming that /37 actually deals with two different, independent cases, von Soden would neatly disentangle what looks like a mixture of facts unrelated to each other — the collapse of the house and loss of property belonging to the owner. However, collapse and "joint loss" are not logical alternatives; and, what is more important, von Soden fails to take account of CH 125: there too "joint loss" is but one of several elements, not a separate case.

A third view, represented, e.g., by Goetze *1948*, Böhl, Korošec and Szlechter, refrains from any addition to the text; *lu* has then to be understood not as expressing alternation, but as a particle of emphasis: "if the house of the man indeed fell down".[100] In our transliteration of the text we have adopted the reading *luqqut* — "plundered, robbed" (instead of *lu imqut*).[101] Either of these two proposals seems preferable to the suggestions of Goetze *1956* or von Soden *1956:* emendation of a text should be a last resort, after all other attempts at interpretation have failed, or have had to be rejected as unsatisfactory. In our view, then, /37 deals only with one case, the plundering of the depositee's house. To be free of liability, the owner must have incurred loss of his own; he must swear that that was so, and also that he had not behaved in a fraudulent fashion.[102]

The sections of CH dealing with deposit, 122-126, have been the subject of searching enquiry by Koschaker.[103] It is of great interest to check his submissions in the light of LE 36/37. Koschaker attributed to Hammurabi the introduction of formal requirements in bringing about the contract of deposit or in proving it (secs. 122, 123). Nothing of the kind is mentioned in LE: however, this is hardly an argument of

100 Rather similarly also CAD B 353b, except that the particle *lu* is not reflected in the translation.

101 Proposed by Landsberger *1968:* 99; followed, CAD L 101b. See notes on the text, pp. 65f., above.

102 Note the Roman rules in a comparable legal relationship, the loan of chattels *(commodatum).* Ordinarily, a borrower will not be liable in situations of *force majeure*; it will be different, if having opportunity to save some chattels, he preferred his own to that of the lender. See *Digesta Iustiniani* 13.6.5.4: "... proinde et si incendio vel ruina aliquid contigit ... non tenebitur, nisi forte, cum possit res commodatas salvas facere, suas praetulit." See also *Pauli Sententiae* 2.4.2.

103 *1917:* 7-45; see the comments and criticisms of Driver-Miles *1952:* 233ff.

great weight, since the point is not relevant to the matter in issue. In his criticism of the way CH 125 is formulated — mentioning both loss of property belonging to the depositee and negligence on his part — Koschaker came to the conclusion that it reflected reformulation at the hands of the compilers of the Code. An earlier law, so he postulated, absolved the depositee of liability in case of "joint loss"; otherwise he had to pay. The CH injected the notion of negligence (*egum*), and omitted the case of non-liability, hence the confused formulation. It so happens that the first half of Koschaker's "earlier" law is actually identical with LE / 37; thus, his view is vindicated as remarkably acute and exact.[104]

Another relevant text, considered by Goetze *1956:* 104, is Exodus 22:6ff., dealing with theft of property deposited. Three possibilities are envisaged: (i) the thief has been apprehended: he has to pay double; (ii) if the thief has not been apprehended, the depositee swears to his innocence: (iii) if convicted, the depositee has to pay double.

Goetze then arranges these rules in the sequence Exodus-LE-CH, regarding the biblical text as the archaic of the three. I am not sure that this is necessarily so. Exodus deals with the possibility of dishonesty on the part of the depositee; in the LE this is present only by implication, but the actual ruling may well have been the same. The depositee who shrinks from swearing that he did not behave fraudulently, or whose oath is for some reason not accepted at its face value, would probably have fallen under the rules applying to theft. Concerning the doctrine of "joint loss", — I am not satisfied that it constitutes an advance in legal thought. It is artificial, and in a given case it may well have led to results which were not just. As for the oath, that is imposed both in Exodus 22:7 and in LE / 37. Its absence in CH 125 is not due (as Goetze seems to imply) to any advance in legal thought or legal machinery: there is no room for an oath in a section which in any case makes the depositee liable for the loss which has been incurred. In Sec. 125 CH does not consider the depositee's possible bad faith, as can be seen by comparison with CH 124: the depositee who has denied receiving the deposit has to pay double the value of the chattel deposited.

104 Stressed already by Goetze *1956:* 104.

HARVESTER'S FAILURE TO PERFORM

Of the two sections concerning nonfeasance (failure to perform), the one, LE 9, deals with failure to supply the service which had been agreed upon and (at least partly) paid for; the other, LE 32, concerns the failure of the employer to live up to his part of the contract, failure to pay.

The facts of LE 9 are as follows: A man has paid in advance 1 shekel of silver,[105] for the services of a harvester. This amounts to the hire payable for a harvester for 15 days, under LE 7; alternatively, the period already paid for may be even longer, if one applies the general rate of pay fixed for hired labour in LE 11. I agree with Szlechter *1954:* 104 that the agreement was probably not for a fixed time, rather for the harvest as a whole. It appears that advance payment on account of the hire is an essential prerequisite: it is only through performance by one of the parties (in the given case the employer) that a legal tie is created. This important principle may have been of wider application.[106]

When the time of the harvest duly arrived, the undertaking was not honoured, the harvesting was not carried out. The section provides for the payment of 10 shekels, a rather stiff, tenfold penalty. According to the interpretation suggested above (p. 226) a question of impossibility to perform (e.g., because of illness or death) could hardly arise: we do not regard the undertaking as a personal one on the part of the harvester, but as generic, entered upon by a person who undertakes to supply the man (or, more frequently, a number of men) who will actually perform.[107]

105 This sum is probably mentioned only as an example: Szlechter *1954:* 106.

106 Lautner *1936:* 55 speaks of the creation of a "Rechtswirkung des Vertrages durch das Mittel der Empfangshaftung". Differently Szlechter *1954:* 106f.: "A défaut d'un versement préalable, la sanction stipulée en cas de defaillance du mercenaire était néanmoins valable." At any rate, LE 9 would provide no criterion for such a case.

107 Compare, for Roman law, Kunkel *1956:* 215.

Non-Payment for Services of a Wet-Nurse

In LE 32 the facts are straightforward, and the difficulties concentrate in the apodosis. A man has given his son (to a wet-nurse) to be suckled and brought up, but has then failed to provide the proper rations of food, oil and clothing,[108] for a period of three years. This may mean one of two things: either that failure was total and immediate — he gave nothing at all; or else, that he furnished supplies for part of the time, and only later neglected his duty. From the point of view of language both interpretations pass muster,[109] but I should consider the second situation as inherently more likely. The period of suckling and upbringing mentioned seems to have been customary for arrangements of this kind.[110] Nothing is said of a failure to pay the hire, and this may well have been included in the rations to be given.

It is generally held that LE 32 imposes upon the father, who neglected to provide for the maintenance of his son, the payment of 10 minas (= 600 shekels) of silver. This will indeed not be exacted from him, but his claim to have his child returned to him will depend on his paying up, to the amount mentioned. Now one ought to realize that 600 shekels of silver would be an enormous amount, quite out of proportion to the circumstances described; how could one possibly account for it?[111] Goetze and Szlechter do indeed stress that a penal element is obviously present, but even this cannot be accepted as a sufficient explanation — within the framework of a legal text which does not impose on any delict a penalty in excess of one tenth of that sum, i.e. 1 mina. Within the sphere of non-delictual obligations, 10

108 No quantities are mentioned: these may have been customary, or else specifically set out in the contract. Cf., however, CAD E 165b, speaking of allowances "stipulated by law"; there seems to be no warrant for this.

109 *šalas šanatim la iddin* can be rendered either (a) "three years he did not give (the rations)", or (b) "he did not give (the full rations) for three years".

110 Goetze *1956:* 94 refers to *ana ittišu* 3.3.45-50: *ana mušeniqti iddinšu / ana mušeniqtišu šalaš šanati ipra piššatam udannin* — "He gave him (his son) to a wet-nurse. He guaranteed to his (i.e., the son's) wet-nurse (rations of) food, oil (and) clothing for three years." See also the documents quoted by Goetze, note 11, there.

111 For a detailed discussion of the difficulties inherent in the accepted interpretation of LE 32, see already Lipin *1954:* 35f.

minas of silver would be equivalent to the hire of a wagon, with oxen and driver, for 1800 days (LE 3), or to that of a harvester for approximately 24 years (LE 7)! Why should the legislator have reacted in so ferocious a manner in a case like this, treating it not as a mere breach of an undertaking, but as a most heinous delict? Szlechter suggests that the real intention of the legislator may have been that the child remain with the nurse.[112] If so, why the circumlocution? Would he not have simply said *ana marišu ul iraggam* — "he shall have no claim to his son" (cf. the wording of LE 30)? Surely this would have been no less effective a preventive threat than the reference to an imaginary, quite unrealistic sum.

There is room also for some other objections. First, it ought to be noted that in sec. 32 the term *ma-na* is not otherwise defined; this is contrary to the ordinary usage of the LE. Apart from sec. 1, where *manum* is a unit of weight of commodities, we have *ma-na kaspam* (KÙ. BABBAR) — "mina silver", in LE 31, 42, 43, 44/45, 46, 47A, 54/, 56/.[113] In LE 42, it is true, *ma-na* occurs three times without definition, but this is given in the first case and the last,[114] and repeating it throughout would have been tedious and pedantic.[115] It is therefore likely, we submit, that in sec. 32 the reference is not to silver.[116] Can it be to some other metal?[117] Here too, a negative answer seems to be indicated, though for the opposite reason: whereas the amount of silver would be excessively large, that of another, baser metal would be too small (e.g., 10 minas of copper would be equivalent to only 3 1/3 shekels of silver). Besides, silver is the only metal mentioned in the LE as a means of payment, so one would wish to have a very good reason for a sudden divergence.

112 *1954:* 108; but see also his note 37, there.

113 So constant a term is *mana kaspam* that some translators have, without compunction, added "silver" to their translation of LE 32.

114 "If a man bit and severed the nose of a man, *1 ma-na kaspam isaqqal* — 1 mina silver he shall weigh out ... a slap in the face — *10 šiqil kaspam išaqqal* 10 shekels silver he shall weigh out."

115 In the poorly preserved section 48, "silver" may have been mentioned at the beginning of the section, as suggested in CAD D 29a.

116 A determined effort to explain a payment of 10 minas silver is made by Sick *1984:* 73. It does not solve the riddle.

117 MAL have minas of *annakum* (tin) as means of payment: see secs. 5, 7, 21, 24, E.

While there is no mention of a metal, a reason for the payment is given: it is *tarbit marišu* — "(the cost of) upbringing his son". Such a statement is equally unusual. There is no parallel for it in the LE, in any case in which a fixed sum is payable. It is only where that sum is *incertum*, has yet to be established, that such a description is given: see sec. 22.[118] In sec. 32 one would expect a multiple of the value of the goods which have not been delivered.

I wish to note that Professor Kraus has (in private conversation) expressed doubts about the reading *ma-na*; it has been queried also by San Nicolò *1949:* 260. So a collation might be of interest.[119]

Finally, one may note two instances of litigation due to the non-payment of the wages and/or rations of a wet-nurse. Schorr *1913:* 241 tells of payment subsequent to litigation, but sums or quantities are not given. The arrears seem to have accumulated over two years. More interesting is UMM H 24.[120] Here too rations were in arrear for two years. The decision gives the wet-nurse 12 minas of wool (at LE prices this is equal to 2 shekels), 48 qa of sesame oil (= 4 shekels) and 5 shekels silver. The grand total of 11 shekels may — or may not — have involved a penal element, but nothing reminiscent of the alleged 10 minas of LE 32.

118. Unfortunately, that description is itself not quite certain: see pp. 276f., below.

119 An interesting suggestion has been put forward by Eichler *1987:* 78. Instead of *ma-na* he would read ⌜GÍN KÙ.BABBAR⌝ — "(10) shekels of silver". If correct, this would resolve a very troublesome crux.

120 Szlechter *1963b:* 127ff.

CHAPTER EIGHT

DELICTS*

TERMINOLOGY AND CLASSIFICATION

Within the laws of Eshnunna, and at the present stage of our knowledge of Old Babylonian procedure, a distinction between crime and tort, the one part of public law, the other the sole concern of the parties themselves, would serve no useful purpose. There is little likelihood that any distinction of this kind ever occurred to the ancient legislator. Consequently, we have decided to include under the general heading of "Delicts" all those cases giving rise to penal provisions, which are not connected with contract.[1] It is even open to question whether one is justified in separating those obligations which have their origin in the breach of a contract.

Delicts, in this wide sense, occupy a prominent place in the LE, being dealt with in 21 sections. To classify these, the customary division into delicts against property and delicts against the person will not be of much help. Szlechter uses it, but runs into difficulties, in the main because of the double nature of the slave, at once chattel and human being. He observes, quite rightly, that the slave is considered as the

* I have read a typescript of R. Westbrook's forthcoming *Studies in Biblical and Cuneiform Law*, devoted mainly to delicts. Westbrook's very original work, bold in concepts and the use of sources, relates to many of the topics discussed in this chapter. I have not taken note of it here: the proper assessment of the views expressed in it must be postponed to a more suitable occasion.

1 In this we follow the practice of Szlechter (*1954:* 110ff. = *1978:* 197ff.), and the approach advocated by Nörr *1958:* 1, and accepted also by Renger *1977:* 65-77. More dogmatic is the line taken by Haase *1963b:* 55ff. See lastly also Sick *1984:* 221, distinguishing between "staatliches Strafrecht" and "privates Bussrecht"; further, *ibid.* 241, between "öffentliches Strafrecht" and "Anwendung von staatlich gesetztem und reglementiertem Privatrecht".

property of his master; consequently, whenever a slave is injured, this is viewed as an act against an object belonging to an *awīlum* (*1954*: 117). Having made this statement, he at once transfers, rightly again, the killing of a slave to the sections on delicts against persons. The Laws fix separate, more lenient sanctions where the victim of a delict is a slave, but do not consider the case as essentially different.

Guided to a considerable extent by the Laws themselves, one may divide the various delicts into five groups, four of which form more or less compact entities within the text. Only the first has to be collected from all over the LE. These groups are then the following: (i) Theft and related offences: secs. 6, 12, 13, 34/35, 40, 49, 50; (ii) False distress: 22, 23/24; (iii) Sexual offences: 26, 27/28; 31; (iv) Bodily injuries: 42, 43, 44/45, 46, 47, culminating in unpremeditated homicide, 47A; (v) Damage caused by a goring ox, and comparable cases: 53, 54/55, 56/57, 58.

Before considering the various delicts in any detail, we wish to deal with two preliminary questions. First we shall survey the sanctions laid down; secondly, we shall consider anew a problem examined by Nörr *1958*, and formulated by him as follows: To what extent do the Laws take into account the subjective element of guilt, as against the objective one of the result ("Erfolg") ensuing from the deed?

SANCTIONS

Sanctions are relatively simple. In the great majority of cases they are of a pecuniary nature, consisting in the payment of a quantity of silver. Ordinarily the amount is fixed by law, and ranges from 10 shekels to 60.[2] In one instance (sec. 22), it is *incerta pecunia*, an amount which remains to be determined by the court.[3] Terminology is surprisingly uniform: in penal contexts the verb used is always *šaqalum* — "to weigh out" (17 loci). In two further instances *šaqalum* occurs in breach of contract, visited with a stiff penalty: sec. 9 (tenfold) and sec. 32

2 10 shekels: secs. 6, 12, 13, 42, 47. 15 shekels: secs. /55, /57. 1/2 mina (= 30 shekels): 42, 44/45. 2/3 mina (= 40 shekels): 47A, 54/, 56/. 1 mina (= 60 shekels): 42. In secs. 31, 43, 46, the figure is disputed, either 1/3 mina (= 20 shekels) or 2/3 mina. For details, see notes on the text of these sections.

3 See pp. 276f., below.

(obscure, see discussion, pp. 253ff.). Interestingly enough, CH is less consistent in its usage: occasionally, *šaqalum* is used in non-penal contexts,[4] on the other hand *nadanum* is used with reference to penalties.[5]

A number of sections envisage penalties in kind. So sec. 23/ which provides for the return *(rabum)* of two slave women for the one whose death had been caused; sec. /35 imposes the duty of giving an equivalent child, in addition to the one taken wrongfully. Similarly, sec. 49, penalizing one found in possession of a stolen slave or a stolen slave woman, provides for the "bringing along" *(redum)* of a further slave or slave woman. Note that from the point of view of the aggrieved party the result is the same in all three cases: his property has been doubled. From the point of view of the offender, sec. 23/ differs: since he is unable to return the object of transgression, he has to return double. In all three instances, penalty in kind allows a better approximation to the actual value of the slave misappropriated.

In two other sections dealing with theft, secs. 40 and 50, a sanction is not specified.[6] The legislator is content with defining the circumstances as amounting to theft; the consequences are assumed to be known. A provision *sui generis*, we shall see, is that laid down in sec. 53. There is no penal sanction, in the proper sense of the term: rather it is desired to distribute the loss equitably between the owners of both the oxen.

Some severe offences are punishable by death. The death penalty occurs in each of the groups of offences, with the exception of group (iv), the causing of bodily injury. Punishable by death are nocturnal burglary or entry (secs. 12, 13); the causing of death, in some specific circumstances (secs. /24, 58);[7] some sexual offences (secs. 26 [rape of a betrothed girl], /28 [adultery]). Specific modes of execution are not

4 E.g., secs. 9, 119 (2 times), 278, 281 (2 times).

5 So in secs. 5, 8, 106, 107, 112, 126, 259, 260. Contrast, in largely corresponding provisions, *šaqalum* (LE 54/55) and *nadanum* (CH 251/252).

6 Klíma *1956b:* 7, note 4 holds that sec. 50 imposes the death penalty, but I see no basis for this.

7 Note that LE has no general provision concerning murder, comparable to LUY 1. Less severely than in LE 58, in other cases unintended, yet culpable homicide is punished by a payment of 2/3 of a mina silver (secs. 47A, 54/, 56/); in case the victim is a slave, the penalty amounts to 15 shekels (/55, /57). Compare Ishchali, no. 326, lines 4-5.

laid down in the LE (unless such a specific mode was contained in the very fragmentary sec. 60, the contents of which are altogether uncertain).[8]

Szlechter (*1954:* 110f. = *1978:* 197f.) has drawn attention to differences of formulation in the "capital" sections. In secs. /24 and 26, the formulation is *din napištim ... imat* — "(it is) a case of life ... he shall die". Szlechter holds that in these cases the death penalty was avoidable, by way of composition between the offender and the offended (the *muškenum* of sec. /24, or, in sec. 26, the father of the raped girl); only in the absence of settlement was the culprit put to death. Sec. 58 reads *napištum ṣimdat šarrim* — "(it is a case concerning) life: decree of the king". Derivation from a royal decree serves to explain an unexpected ruling that negligent homicide should be punishable by death (this, one may add, would not necessarily exclude composition).

However, the interest focuses on the phrase *imat ul iballuṭ*, in secs. 12, 13, and /28. It is clearly a very emphatic expression. Szlechter derives from it, cumulatively, that (i) the death penalty was mandatory,[9] and (ii) the offended party could resort to immediate self-help.[10] These suggestions are attractive, but not sufficiently so. From the point of view of method it is hardly legitimate to attach to one phrase two quite different implications (mandatoriness of the penalty and immediacy of the retribution).

Let us examine a common element: all these are cases of *flagrans delictum*, referring to a person caught "in the very act". This is supported by the use of *naṣbutum* — "to be seized, caught", which recurs in all three sections. In 12 and 13, what is basically a minor offence (visited with a penalty of 10 shekels) has become greatly aggravated when it occurs at night-time. The owner of the house (or the land), in fear of his life, reacts violently, the intruder is killed, the

8 On modes of execution in Babylonian law see Szlechter *1962:* 166f. From the use of the term *din napištim* (LE /24, 26) and *napištum* (LE 58), Szlechter would deduce that execution was by way of cutting the throat *(égorgement)*. This seems questionable.

9 So also Landsberger *1968:* 72: "kann/darf nicht begnadigt werden"; Sick, *1984:* 150.

10 Szlechter *1978:* 197 drops self-help.

killer absolved.[11] In sec. /28, concerning adultery, moral outrage takes the place of apprehension.[12] Incidentally, the power to react immediately and extremely would be strictly limited in time: once the moment of danger or excitement has passed, only the ordinary judicial process will continue to be available to the aggrieved party.

Did rules of this kind obtain at Eshnunna? We do not know: comparison with sources remote in time and place does not furnish a sound basis for conclusions, and in particular I do not see that *imat ul iballuṭ* helps in any way. In situations of the kind described, the paramount question is whether the reaction was justified or justifiable. *imat ul iballuṭ* does not connect up.

As a matter of language, the idea of excluding composition, of making the death penalty mandatory would fit better the emphatic element in *imat ul iballuṭ*. But here another question arises: what would account for such a stringent attitude? The protection of life (and property) does indeed call for the severe punishment of nocturnal intrusion; nevertheless, this is not a particularly heinous offence, so why not allow the parties to settle the case, if they are ready to do so? This question is made more cogent by the fact that in this sphere the law would anyhow have to be set in motion by the aggrieved party. As for adultery (sec. /28), one may ask what distinguishes it from the rape of an inchoately married girl (in sec. 26): why should the death penalty be mandatory in the one case, subject to composition in the other? Also, one has to bear in mind that adultery is expressly pardonable in CH 129, HL 198, MAL 15; there is little reason to assume that the LE were more severe.

11 Compare Exodus 22:1f.: If a thief is found killed when breaking in, "he has no blood" *(en lo damim)*; if the sun shone upon him, "he has blood" *(damim lo)*; as in LE 12, 13, a distinction is made according to the time of the occurrence: if he was killed at night, his death is not to be avenged. For a provision in the Laws of Solon, see Demosthenes, *Against Timocrates* 113; in XII Tables 8:12: "Si nox furtum factum sit, si im occisit, iure caesus esto". The phrase *iure caesus esto* declares the killing of the nocturnal thief to have been "lawful", not subject to punishment; for a parallel, in a different context, see Livius 1.26.9.

12 In Roman law, the *lex Iulia de adulteriis coercendis* (of 18 B.C.E.) permits a father to kill his married daughter's paramour, if they had been caught *in flagranti*, provided he kills his daughter too: "... pater eum adulterum sine fraude occidat, ita ut filiam in continenti occidat" (Collatio 4.2.3). See also *Digesta Iustiniani* 48.5.24 pr.

A further remark concerning *imat ul iballuṭ*: apparently, the phrase is isolated within legal Akkadian. As far as I can see it does not occur outside the LE. In a non-legal context see ARM X 32:30 *amat ul aballuṭ* — "I shall die, shall not live"; in the Bible, Isaiah 38:1, 2 Kings 20:1: "... Thus says the Lord: set thy house in order, for thou shalt die, not live."

Having failed in our attempt to assign a substantive import to *imat ul iballuṭ*, we might look again at the stylistic aspects of the phrase. For all its apparent isolation, *imat ul iballuṭ* is a precursor of a frequent detail of biblical style, a particular form of parallelism. Parallelism, quite generally, is probably the best-known peculiarity of biblical style. It is defined as "correspondence, in sense or construction, of successive clauses or passages, esp. in Hebrew poetry".[13] A meticulously exact parallelism is achieved by the pairing of antonyms, one of which (usually the second) is negated. In this manner the antonyms become synonyms. For our purposes, the best example of a "negated antonym parallelism" is furnished by *imat ul iballuṭ* itself. The verbs *matum* and *balaṭum* are a true "Gegensatzpaar", turned into synonyms by the simple expedient of inserting *ul; imat = ul iballuṭ*.

The phrase is quite emphatic, but being unable to establish its target, we ponder another possibility: emphasis may be but an unavoidable side-effect; the true purpose may be to refrain from too curt, too abrupt one-word decrees of the death penalty. The verb *imat*, by itself, conveys all that has to be said; *ul iballuṭ* adds nothing, nor indeed does it diminish from the gravity of what is being decreed — but somehow the phrase as a whole is now in a better concert with the usual style of the LE. One may point also to LE 26 (and /24) where *din napištim* precedes *imat*, and provides the desired padding. In LE 58, *ṣimdat šarrim* may have an import of its own — but it also cushions the one-word decree: *napištum*. CH uses a different terminology: the expression commonly indicating the death penalty is *idak* — "(he) shall be killed". Sometimes it is padded by a preceding *awilum šu* — "that man" (so, e.g., in secs. 3/, 6, 7, 16 [*bel bitim šu* — "that owner of a house"], 19); on other occasions *idak* stands all by

13 *The Shorter Oxford Dictionary*,1986, p. 1509b.

itself (so, e.g., in secs. 8, 14, 15). Matters of style carry less weight in CH than in LE.[14]

The LE do not provide for any corporal punishment other than the death penalty. There are no cases of mutilation, such as occur in the CH, nor is there anything comparable to the compound punishments particularly frequent in the MAL.[15]

TALION: AN EYE FOR AN EYE

It has been noted that the LE do not know the principle of talion, which has the offender suffer bodily harm identical to that which he has caused. Some attempts to find vestiges of it have indeed been made. So by Klíma, who would see in sec. /24 an exceptional case, which shows the application of that principle at least in a symbolic fashion.[16] Haase *1963b:* 73 includes LE 58 under the heading "Echte Talion", but does not state his reasons. Klíma's suggestion concerning LE /24 has been considered and rejected by Szlechter *1956:* 490f.; we concur. It is characteristic of a regime of talion that meticulous attention is paid to the exactness of retribution.[17] This may even occasionally lead to results which will appear to us as somewhat grotesque; so e.g., in CH 209/210/, MAL 55. In Eshnunna a number of serious offences are punishable by death; among these are two instances of homicide, in secs. /24 and 58. It follows that there is in these cases identity (or near-identity) of offence and punishment. However, this is purely coincidental, and will not furnish support for an otherwise not evinced system of talion.[18] The matter is well put by

14 Different, yet comparable one has, in biblical Hebrew, the doubling of the verb *moth yamuth* (or *moth yumath* [passive]). This emphatic phrase is quite common, in texts imposing the death penalty. This too may be a matter of style rather than of legal substance.

15 See, in great detail, Haase *1963b*, cit.

16 Klíma *cit.*, pp. 7f. Nörr, *cit.*, p. 11, note 41, speaks of "Abwandlung des Talionsgrundsatzes"; but at p. 15, note 52, he describes the LE as "nicht mehr von der *lex talionis* beherrscht".

17 Note the worries of a reader of *Time* magazine, May 7, 1979: "If some of our courts see it as fair and just to execute murderers, then, logically, it would follow that it is fair and just to steal from thieves and rape rapists. I can't imagine what would be done with pot smokers, or pornographers."

18 This also against Petschow *1968b:* 18, note 64.

D. S. Jackson: "... the term talion is rightly applied only when non-fatal bodily injuries are involved, and where the offender is punished by suffering the same injury as he inflicted. Thus, the death penalty for murder is not an example of talion."[19]

Is talion no longer known in Eshnunna, or is it not yet known there? This is a question on which scholarly opinion is sharply divided. What seems to be the dominant view on talion is concisely formulated by Driver-Miles, who say that "talion was a fundamental principle of early law and was only gradually replaced by a system of fixed composition" (*1952:* 408). It would follow that the LE represent a more advanced stage of the law than CH (and the Bible).[20]

Dissenting opinions have been voiced by a number of scholars, who regard talion as the later stage.[21] It is pointed out that the Laws of Ur-Nammu, preceding the LE and CH by centuries, are based on a system of fixed penalties, in silver.[22] It is even possible that talion may have been introduced by Hammurabi himself. On the whole it is this view which seems preferable. The dominant opinion may to some extent reflect the fact that within modern systems of punishment talion is no longer an overt guiding principle. To the present-day observer it appears as "primitive, archaic, barbaric". One may readily

19 *1973:* 281, note 1.

20 So indeed David *1949:* 27: "hoger stadium der ontwikkeling"; also e.g., San Nicolò *1949:* 261: "in CH dafür *noch* (my italics, R. Y.) vielfach ... Talionsrecht"; Goetze *1956:* 261: "The CH and the Covenant Code ... both *retain* (my italics, R. Y.) the *ius talionis*"; in a footnote he adds: "the archaism in the laws of Hammurabi is remarkable". Korošec *1964:* 205 speaks of talion as "noch angewendet" in CH. More complicated is the view of von Soden *1956:* 32: he speaks of "Wiedereinführung der Talion durch Hammurabi". Kramer *1963:*84, referring to LU, writes: "... even before 2000 B.C. the law of 'eye for eye' and 'tooth for tooth' had already given way to the far more humane approach in which a money fine was substituted as a punishment." See also Klíma*1966:* 247.

21 Loewenstamm *1957:* 194; Finkelstein *1961:* 98. A paper devoted entirely to this topic is Diamond *1957:* 151ff. And again Finkelstein *1981:* 59, and note 13, there.

22 The recent publication of LUY 1, where the death penalty is imposed for homicide, has renewed the dispute. See lastly Yaron *1985a:* 136ff., against Haase *1983:* 246. For a talionic interpretation of LUY 1, also Sick *1984:* 306.

accept all these attributes as perfectly correct,[23] but they should not be allowed to distort the true perspective. Talion is not primary, original: on the contrary, it cannot be disputed that within the sources at present available pecuniary penalties constitute the earlier system.[24, 25]

GUILT AND ERFOLGSHAFTUNG

We come now to the second preliminary question, that concerning the element of subjective guilt ("Schuld"), as contrasted with (absolute) responsibility for results ("Erfolgshaftung"). There is in the LE no express reference to the intention to cause harm, to premeditation, nothing that could be compared with such provisions as CH 206/, Exodus 21:14, or (in great detail) Numbers 35:16-21. Nevertheless, there are data which point to the conclusion that the question of "fault" was present to the mind of the legislator. This emerges from the fact that with regard to some delicts knowledge, of a specific formal type, concerning the danger, is a condition precedent of liability.[26]

23 Note the very different evaluation of talion by Cardascia *1979:* 175f.: "Sur un plan strictement rationnel, on conviendra que le talion est la seule peine qui soit pleinement justifiable. Il est la *seule peine équivalant exactement à l'infraction* (author's italics, R. Y.) ... D'autre part, le talion est une sanction dont *la valeur éthique dépasse celle de bien d'autres* (author's italics, R. Y.), les peines pécuniaires, en particulier."

24 Remarkable is the speech which Thucydides (3.45.3) puts in the mouth of Diodotus, in opposition to the proposed execution of the Mytilenaeans, subsequent to their revolt against Athens (427 B.C.):

> "All men are by nature prone to err, both in private and in public life, and there is no law which will prevent them; in fact, mankind has run the whole gamut of penalties, making them more and more severe, in the hope that the transgressions of evil-doers might be abated. It is probable that in ancient times the penalties prescribed for the greatest offences were relatively mild, but as transgressions still occurred, in course of time the penalty was seldom less than death. But even so there is still transgression." (Tr. C. F. Smith, *Loeb Classical Library.*)

25 It may be noted that Diamond finds support for his view as to the historical sequence also in the way English criminal law developed in the course of the Middle Ages.

26 Cf., in the sphere of contract the reference to negligence in LE 5.

Our main source on this point are the provisions concerning the goring ox, etc.; here one has to distinguish between sec. 53 and secs. 54/55, 56/57 and 58. In the first there is no mental element and liability is absolute. Contrary to this, in the latter sections there is a pronounced mental factor: liability depends on a formal warning having been tendered to the owner, drawing his attention to the dangerous circumstances. The disregard of this warning constitutes gross negligence,[27] and this justifies the punishment of the owner, in case damage (the sections mention only death) has ensued.

Sexual intercourse cannot take place unintentionally. Rape (sec. 26) involves the use of force (or at least the threat of its use) against the uncomplying woman, hence it is necessarily premeditated.[28] Ordinarily this will be the case also in adultery. The LE (and so also the CH) do not deal with the possibility that the male accused of the offence may himself have been the victim of mistake or deception, but it is difficult to believe that such a defence would not have been admissible.[29]

Rather more complicated are the provisions on bodily injuries. Sec. 42 deals with five possible injuries, some of which can hardly have been caused without intention. The first concerns the biting off of a man's nose: in this very peculiar case both negligence and accident seem to be excluded, but it may still be questioned whether intention was a material element. More significant may be the last case, that of *meḫeṣ letim*, commonly rendered "slap in the face"; if this is correct, intention must be implied: it is the insult rather than the bodily injury which is the main point.[30] It is therefore difficult to agree with Nörr (p. 9) that the section takes into account only what he calls the exterior result of the deed. The other provisions concern the destruction of an eye, a tooth, an ear; here it is not possible to rule out cases of accident or negligence, and it would not be quite justified to transfer an implication of intention from one example to the other. This is so in

27 Cf. Nörr *1958:* 12.

28 In LE 31 consent or otherwise of the slave woman will have been immaterial.

29 Cf. MAL 13, 14, 23, where knowledge is an express element of the offence. And see p. 283, below, on the possible deception of the man concerning the status of the woman.

30 See pp. 286f., below.

spite of the fact that the payments (30 shekels for tooth and ear, 60 for nose and eye) seem reasonably well coordinated: we cannot be sure that in these injuries intention was regarded as material in assessing the sum payable. The same goes also for sec. 43, imposing the payment of 2/3 of a mina (= 40 shekels) for the severing of a finger. Little that is useful can be derived from sec. 44/45: a penalty of 1/2 a mina silver is imposed for breaking an arm or a leg. The injury is said to have resulted after *awilum awilam ina* [ ] *iskimma* — "a man had knocked down a man in a [?]". Goetze derives the verb *iskim-ma* from *sakapum* and this is accepted by both the dictionaries. The difficulty concentrates on the qualifying term *ina x*: Goetze read *ina ik/g-x-x*, for which *ina ik[-ki-im]* might be a possible restoration.[31] Under *sakapum*, AHw 1011a leaves all the break blank, while CAD S 70b departs in an unexpected direction, reading *ina suqim* — "in the street", — hardly a qualifying circumstance.[32]

For LE 46, Haddad 116 clarifies the nature of the injury: it concerns the breaking of a collarbone.[33] The penalty, 1/3 of a mina or 2/3, was long in contention. Haddad 116 would settle the dispute in favour of the lesser sum. In sec. 47, Haddad 116 supplies the reading *ina ši-gi-èš-tim*, describing the circumstance of the occurrence, but the meaning of the phrase is uncertain. Al-Rawi's rendering "in a brawl" yields a good sense, but it derives little support from his reference to AHw 1127a;[34] also, the nature of the injury remains unknown.[35]

Sec. 47A, preserved only in Haddad 116, deals with homicide *ina risbatim* — "in (the course of) a brawl".[36] The section has a close, but more elaborate parallel in CH 206/207/208.

31 For *ikkum* — "mood, (bad) temper", see CAD I/J 59; AHw 369b. But neither of the dictionaries does so restore.

32 Despite the comparable *suqam ina alakišu*, in CH 250; there the context is different, and the place of the occurrence may have been significant.

33 For *kirrum* (or *kerrum*) see CAD K 410b, AHw 468a.

34 S.v. *šaggaštum*; the rendering there "Mord, Tötung", is too remote.

35 Goetze read *i-še-el*, but notes (*1956:* 120) that a verb *šelum* is not known elsewhere. The reading *ik/q-te-el*, in Haddad 116, has not added to the understanding of the text (so Professor F. R. Kraus, in a private communication).

36 See AHw 988b.

To sum up: it is difficult to assess the mental element in secs. 44/45ff.: in sec. 44/45 the qualifying phrase is unknown. In 47 its interpretation is not yet certain. Only in 47A both the text and its meaning are definite. A mental element is indeed present, but it falls short of intention. In the parallel CH 206/207/ the defendant is allowed to clear himself by swearing *ina idu la amḫaṣu* — "knowingly (i.e. intentionally) I did not strike (him)".[37] We are here midways between mere accident and premeditation, comparable — in case death ensues — to the modern case of manslaughter, as distinguished from murder. The lenient treatment meted out to the offender may reflect the agony of the moment;[38] another reason may be in the victim's possible contribution to the situation.[39]

Various elements are discernible in the provisions concerning false distress. The condition precedent, the falseness of the distress, is established by the oath of the complainant, the alleged debtor. It seems then that a mistake on the part of the distrainor would have been dismissed as irrelevant: the person distraining acts at his own risk. If that is so, LE 22 is entirely within the range of "Erfolgshaftung". In sec. 23/24 there is the additional factor that the distrainor *uštamit* — "caused [the distress] to die". This, as Nörr (pp. 10f.) rightly notes, excludes natural death, but it does not necessarily imply that the causing of death was intentional.[40] Note that the corresponding CH 116 dispenses altogether with the causative form of the verb, but takes care to describe the circumstances in a clearer fashion, speaking of death *ina maḫaṣim u lu ina uššušim* — "through beating or ill-treatment".

Finally, there are theft and related offences; here too the circumstances are not uniform. Disregarding sec. 6 (because of the uncertainty of its import), we have on the one hand secs. 12, 13, 34/35, 50, on the other hand secs. 40, 49. In the former intention is implied, in

37 But note that after swearing he still has to pay medical expenses.

38 So already Nörr *1958:* 10.

39 So Haase *1961:* 223.

40 The verb *šumutum* — "to cause death" signifies causation, not "fault", as Szlechter *1954:* 118, 121 insists (repeated Szlechter *1978:* 207f., 210). Note especially secs. 54/55, 56/57, 58, where ox, dog and wall are the respective subjects of the verb. In these cases *uštamit* cannot be related to the owner, to indicate a guilt of his.

the latter it may be absent. Secs. 12 and 13 concern burglary, respectively unlawful entry: the death penalty imposed in case the offence occurred at night seems to exclude instances of accidental or negligent trespassing. In sec. 34/35 knowledge of the servile status of the child's mother will hardly have been deniable. The abuse of official powers, dealt with in sec. 50, was necessarily conscious. Secs. 40 and 49, concerning the unaccounted for possession of stolen property, are different: in these instances it is likely that liability was imposed irrespective of any subjective guilt of the accused.[41] The mere fact that he has failed in establishing the identity of his predecessor in title or possession will be enough to render him liable.

In conclusion it may then be said that in many offences a subjective mental element emerges as a material factor, though as a rule this fact does not find expression in the wording of the provision. In other cases there is pure "Erfolgshaftung". But it may be well to remember that the two approaches, at first sight in conflict with each other, co-exist also in modern criminal law, where recently the so-called "crimes of absolute liability" have even been on the increase.

THEFT AND RELATED OFFENCES

We have now to deal with the various offences, following the classification already proposed above. First, then, theft and related offences. True to the typical lack of system and completeness in the LE, there is no general provision concerning theft; rather the attention of the Laws is focused on some exceptional cases, the inclusion of which within the scope of theft might have been queried. Nor do we have any clear ruling as to the sanction, but sec. 49 may allow some tentative conclusion. There it is laid down that a person seized in possession of a stolen slave has to furnish a further slave.[42] Since there

41 See Westbrook-Wilcke *1977:* 113: "The multiple damages system applies, in principle, to the purchaser, albeit innocent, of stolen goods as much as to the thief."

42 Cf. a constitution promulgated by Constantine (*Codex Iustinianus* 6.1.4 pr, 317 C.E.): "Quicumque fugitivum servum in domum vel in agrum inscio domino eius susceperit, eum cum pari alio vel viginti solidis reddat." There is a close affinity between "fugitive" and "stolen": see *ibid.*, 6.1.1 (286 C.E.): "Servum fugitivum sui furtum facere ... manifestum est"; and see pp. 272f., below, on LE 50.

appear to be no qualifying circumstances, the sanction may perhaps be generalized; if so, it would follow that the penalty for theft consisted in the payment of an equivalent amount, or rather primarily in the rendering of an equivalent object.[43] It seems that the sanctions laid down for theft in the various laws of the ancient Near East were far from uniform. On the one hand, there is the mild, restrained approach in LE, and also in LI and in biblical law,[44] on the other hand there is the considerably more severe attitude reflected in CH, HL and MAL.[45] However, it should be noted that the duty of rendering an equivalent is imposed in addition to the duty of returning the stolen object itself. If this has been destroyed, or otherwise lost, double payment may have been the rule. This is suggested by sec. 23/, even though that section does not deal with theft but with the death of a slave woman wrongfully distrained.

The interpretation of LE 40 is hindered by the elliptic formulation of its protasis. It has already been suggested that the facts of the case were probably similar to those set out in commendable detail in CH 9.[46] A purchaser must take care to have sufficient proof available, or else he may find himself accused of theft. This would apply to any purchase; Goetze's rendering of *šimam mala ibaššu* by "any other valuable good" is not quite exact.[47] The phrase means "a purchase,

43 Cf. the deliberations of Szlechter *1954:* 115ff. We agree that the death penalty for theft is unlikely within the framework of the LE, and also that there is, on the other hand, no reason to assume that in Eshnunna theft went unpunished. His distinction between theft and the receiving of stolen property seems immaterial.

44 See LI 12. In biblical law double restoration is imposed in cases of ordinary theft (Exodus 22:3, 6). A more severe attitude may be reflected in some narratives in Genesis. See 31:32 on the theft of Laban's idols by Rachel, and Ch. 44 (verses 9, 10, 16 and 17) on the "theft" of the silver cup belonging to Joseph.

45 See, e.g., CH 6, 7, 8, etc.; HL 57, 58, etc.; MAL 3, 4, 5. Pecuniary penalties are very heavy, and in some cases mutilation and even capital punishment is laid down. For a detailed discussion see Westbrook-Wilcke, *cit.*, 111-121.

46 See pp. 92, 140, above.

47 But so also Korošec *1954:* 369: "ein wirtschaftlich wertvoller Gegenstand"; see further Loewenstamm *1957:* 193.

however much it be", and does not imply anything as to value.[48] Also, "valuable good" would be rather too vague, and the exact scope of the section insufficiently defined. Note that LE 40 does not specify any particular mode of proof, such as a document of sale or witnesses.[49] With CH 9, it is to be assumed that the claimant will be obliged to prove his own title (or at least prior possession). Otherwise an intolerable situation would have arisen, where anyone could arbitrarily challenge the possessor and put him into the jeopardy of being condemned as a thief.[50]

Several documents from the kingdom of Eshnunna illustrate LE 40 and 49. One is IM 51105,[51] a letter addressed to Nanna-marsin, a high-ranking official in Šaduppum (= Ḥarmal): he is ordered to send (to Eshnunna?) two persons who have been named as sellers in a litigation against two persons found in possession of lost cattle. The document is quite straightforward and we can content ourselves with giving (with some minor changes) Goetze's rendering of the essential part (lines 4 to 21): "Cattle belonging to Badidum were lost and they seized them in the hand of Dukunum and Šarrum-Adad, the *tamkarum (ina qati D. u Š-A. tamkarim iṣbatušunu<ti>ma).* This is what they said: 'There are the sellers who sold to us *(nadinanu* [[*um*]] *ša iddinunaši ibaššu).* Warad-Sin, son of Ša-ilum, and Luštamar, son of Sin-x, who sold to us, dwell in Šaduppum.' Having heard (this letter), send Warad-Sin and Luštamar here, so that they may answer their opponent ..."[52]

The litigation is then as yet in its early stage. The accused possessors try to clear themselves by naming their sellers. For the moment, the dispute turns into an interim trial between the possessors and the

48 So already Kraus *1958:* 75: "irgend etwas (Ver)käufliches"; Bottéro *1965/1966:* 94: "toute marchandise qui soit". The phrase *šimam mala ibaššu* is essentially the equivalent of *mima šumšu* — "whatever its name", in CH 7, 122; the two phrases are juxtaposed by Goetze *1956:* 114f.

49 CAD K 168a goes beyond the actual wording of the text, in rendering "... he cannot establish (the identity of) the seller by witnesses."

50 On unproven allegations of theft, see also Yaron *1966a:* 510ff.

51 Goetze *1958:* 54f., text no. 28.

52 Too much is being read into the end of the text, in CAD A/ii 159a: "... send PN and PN_2 here so that they can pay damages to their adversary in court."

alleged sellers. The owner will await the outcome, and will then pursue his case against the loser. Note that there is no mention of the alleged sale having been recorded in writing.

The second text dealing with a case of theft, NBC 8237,[53] introduces us to a later stage of the proceedings. Here the accused has tried to extricate himself by claiming to have received the chattels from an associate of his who has in the meantime fled the country, going to Babylon. This will not do: the accused is condemned to pay 24 shekels. Unfortunately, the text reveals neither the nature nor the value of the chattels in issue. However, since 24 shekels is not a round sum, it may be assumed to be in some relation to the value of the stolen property. It is also to be noted that the sentence does not impose the rendering of an equivalent, rather is couched in terms of silver *(pecuniaria condemnatio)*, possibly because no object suitable to satisfy judgement was available to the accused. There is a proviso which might eventually benefit the convicted possessor: should the absentee return, he will be seized and tried for theft. The essential part of the text, lines 1 to 7, reads as follows:[54] "Sin-eribam, the son of Ilima-aki, they seized in (possession of) stolen property belonging to Ilšu-naṣir *([i]na šurqim ša Ilšu-naṣir iṣbatuma).* He spoke thus: 'There is (someone) who sold[55] to me (namely) my associate *(ša iddinnam tappi ibašši);* (but) he has fled to Babylon'. The judges caused him to seize litigation and fined him 1/3 mina 4 shekels silver ...".[56]

Some details can be deduced from these two documents. The occurrence in both, with slight variations only, of the defendant's plea *ša iddinu ibašši* — "there is (someone) who sold", suggests that this may have been an almost stereotype formula, employed whenever it

53 Simmons *1960:* 28f., text no. 60.
54 Adhering to the translation of Simmons, with some changes.
55 Simmons: "gave".
56 Two other relevant documents, UCBC 847 and 863, are too fragmentary to be considered here with profit. Both are from Ishchali, and have been published as nos. 91 and 107 in Lutz *1931.* The former has been much discussed, with little concrete result: see Christian *1933:* 147; Koschaker *1936:* 211; and especially Miriam Seif *1938:* 37. Further rich documentation is adduced by Westbrook-Wilcke *1977:* 114ff. For more material on "disputes arising from thefts of cattle in which the accused declares himself innocent and lays a charge against others", see Gurney *1983:* 39.

was desired to shift responsibility to a third person. With regard to *ṣabatum* — "to seize", two distinct usages are to be noted. The verb may refer to the lost or stolen chattel, which is being discovered in the hands of an unauthorized possessor;[57] or else it may refer to the accused being seized.[58] Note that in NBC 8237 *ina šurqim ṣabatum* means "to seize in (possession of) stolen property". The phrase does not imply that the accused was apprehended in the course of committing theft: this is obvious from his being allowed to name a previous possessor.[59]

Note that neither LE 40 nor CH 9 fix a period within which a claim can be brought. AbB vii 108 concerns a dispute concerning a slave, whom the defendant claims to have purchased from the claimant 15 years earlier [a break in the tablet hides the claimant's reply]. Over so long a period difficulties of proof might have arisen. It is easier to establish early ownership (or possession) than to prove transfer, unless the buyer has been careful in guarding his documents. The longevity of claims of theft is typical for early legal systems, which tend to prefer the rights of the owner.[60]

Let us now consider LE 50.[61] The section refers to the duty of officials to bring to Eshnunna fugitive slaves or stray cattle, which they may have seized in the exercise of their duties.[62] If the official kept the slave (or animal) in his house (Tablet B specifies: for a period in excess of one month), he will be liable to an accusation of theft on the part of the authorities.[63] Note that no distinction is made between

57 So in IM 51105; also in LE 33. In CH, see, e.g., secs. 9, 19, 253; in MAL, sec. 1 (?); cf. further CAD Ṣ 12b, 41a. See also AbB i 76, line 7f.: *mimma ina qatišunu ul ṣabit* — "nothing was seized in their hands".

58 So in NBC 8237; LE 12, 13, /28, 49; CH 22, 23, etc. CAD Ṣ 8f., 40.

59 For remarks on IM 51105 and NBC 8237, see also Petschow *1975*: 248.

60 See Kaser *1971:* 137, 419.

61 See pp. 27f., above, on divergences between tablets A and B. On LE 50 see Szlechter *1970:* 82-86.

62 See ARM XIII, 26 and 118. The former reports the flight of two slaves of the palace and efforts made to capture them; the latter tells of instructions to seize fugitive slaves. In Roman law see *Digesta Iustiniani* 1.15.4, on the duties of the *praefectus vigilium:* "... fugitivos conquirere eosque dominis reddere debes."

63 See *Digesta Iustiniani* 11.4.1 pr: "Is qui fugitivum celavit fur est."

ordinary theft and misappropriation of property found. One ought to pay attention also to the fact that the section is addressed to a well-defined group of persons: would the same period of delay be granted to officials in the city of Eshnunna itself? And would the same rule apply to ordinary citizens who had seized fugitive slaves or stray cattle? At first sight one might assume that in these cases a more stringent attitude was taken and the duty to deliver the find was immediate, or at any rate lay within a much shorter period;[64] but one cannot be sure, in view of LI 12, a provision of general application, which also tolerates a delay of up to one month.[65]

Sections 12 and 13 concern unlawful entry into a field, respectively into a house.[66] The interpretation of the term *ina kurullim* (in LE 12), giving some further detail concerning the circumstances in which the accused was apprehended, is not quite certain.[67] Goetze *1956:* 52f. arrives at the proportion *eqlum: kurrulum* (LE 12) = *bitum: bitum* (LE 13). This is very probably correct, but then the second *bitum* of LE 13 is also vexing; at any rate it becomes likely that a place is indicated. In view of AHw's "Getreideschwade, Garbe" for *kurullum*, one should tentatively follow Goetze *1948,* rendering *ina kurullim* by "in the crop". This might mean that the provision of LE 12 would apply only if the culprit was caught within the planted part of the field.[68]

64 Note AbB viii 71: Two days ago the writer's "boy" *(ṣuḫarum)* has been seized in Appaz; he is detained in the house of Nurum-liṣi. That boy wears neither *kannum* nor *abbuttum*. The writer asks that the boy be handed over to someone he is sending to fetch him. We do not know how the young fellow came to be detained, nor in what capacity N.-l. was holding him. The reaction of the owner was very swift.

65 Cf. *Digesta Iustiniani* 11.4.1.1, fixing a period of 20 days for the return of a slave. On concealment of fugitive slaves see also Mitteis *1891:* 396ff.; Taubenschlag *1959:*108, note 849.

66 The text specifies *ša muškenim* — "of a *muškenum*"; see p. 136, above.

67 For various suggestions see the notes on sec. 12, p. 50, above.

68 CAD Ṣ 40a renders "with the (stolen) sheaf"; so also, with some hesitation, Bottéro *1965/1966:* 91. This might *per se* be possible (see the similar construction in LE 49); but it is difficult to square this rendering with the corresponding situation in sec. 13 (unless one accepts the suggestion of Landsberger *1968:* 72; but this we have rejected, see notes on sec. 13, p. 51, above).

It is then submitted that LE 12 and 13 (as also their parallels in other Near Eastern sources, LI 9, CH 21, HL 93) deal with a situation where actual theft has not yet been committed. There is no reference at all to anything stolen; one may, therefore, assume that the culprit was apprehended before he had had opportunity to carry out his intentions. This is supported also by the fact that the penalty consists in the payment of a fixed sum, not related to the value of anything stolen. It is this very fact, that theft had not yet been committed, which necessitated the creation of a special offence. Even so, it is somewhat unexpected that entry into a field and into a house are treated in an identical fashion.[69]

LE 12 and 13 introduce a distinction which is absent from LI and HL: if the illicit entry took place at night, it was punishable by death.[70] Nocturnal entry has already been considered in detail in our discussion of sanctions.[71]

LE 34/35, concerning the wrongful acceptance of a child of a slave woman belonging to the palace, has already been considered in detail (pp. 167ff., above), and there is no need to return to it. If the interpretation which has been offered is correct, this provision too would support the assumption that the penalty for ordinary theft consisted in the duty of rendering an object equivalent to that stolen.

The last section to be considered within this group of offences is LE 6; it punished by a penalty of 10 shekels the seizure *ina nullani* of another man's boat. The interpretation of the section depends entirely on the meaning of the phrase *ina nullani*, but that is as yet quite uncertain.[72] In Goetze's view, the relatively small penalty excludes outright theft; with Miles-Gurney *1949:* 181 and San Nicolò *1949:* 258, he is willing to regard the case as one of *furtum usus*, theft committed by unauthorized use. Goetze takes *ina nullani* to denote an attenuating circumstance, some kind of emergency. Nevertheless, since there

69 See already Szlechter *1954:* 117. For Roman law, see *Pauli Sententiae* 2.31.35, *Digesta Iustiniani* 47.2.21.7.

70 In CH 21 there is no room for such a distinction, in view of the stringency of the section imposing in a general fashion the death penalty for breaking in, that is, even if it took place in day time.

71. See pp. 259f., above. Note further that under XII Tables 8.9 the nocturnal harvesting of another's field constitutes a capital crime.

72. See notes on the section, p. 47, above. See further Goetze *1956:* 36f., 40; Szlechter *1954:* 132.

was an invasion of the rights of another person, this has to be atoned for by the payment of the penalty mentioned. Others would see in *ina nullani* a reference to the illegality of the action.[73] This view seems to be supported by the texts accumulated in the dictionaries.[74]

Illegal distress

We come now to cases of illegal distress, provided for in LE 22, 23/24. This topic too is treated in a typically incomplete fashion; especially we are not told about the consequences of the illegal distress of free persons. One hears only, in sec. /24, that causing their death is a capital offence. Note that CH 114, the section corresponding to LE 22, is formulated in a wider fashion, omitting any qualification of the status of the person taken in distress. It has been suggested that in Eshnunna there was no punishment for the unlawful distress of a free person, as long as death was not caused.[75] This is doubtful since it disregards the unsystematic character of the Laws, which does not allow us to treat every omission as a negative regulation. Nor do we know, whether unlawfulness of the seizure was an essential element of liability.

It appears that the conditions in which a *neputum* might be kept could be rather harsh ones. See, e.g., UET 5, no. 9: "Zu Aḫu-kinum sprich: folgendermassen (hat) Awil-Amurrum (gesagt): Seit du auf die Reise gegangen bist, ist nach deiner Abreise Imgur-Sin hierhergekommen und hat erklärt: 'Ich habe ein Drittel Mine Silber von ihm zu bekommen.' Dann hat er deine Ehefrau und deine Tochter als Schuldhäftlinge weggeführt. Komme her, und bevor deine Ehefrau oder deine

73 Klíma *1948:* 328; Böhl *1949/1950:* 98, note 9; Korošec *1954:* 370. A variant is offered by Szlechter *1954:* 132: he would see LE 6 as concerned with a case of illegal distress, akin to that provided for in secs. 22, 23/24 (to be discussed at once). There appears to be no warrant for this suggestion: the rendering "de façon illégale" does not indicate a connection with distress, in the absence of a more explicit reference; note that the technical term *nepum* — "to distrain" is not used in LE 6. See also Petschow *1968a:* 133f.: "widerrechtliche Ingebrauchnahme *(furtum usus)*".

74 AHw 803a; CAD N/ii 333ab.

75 Szlechter *1954:* 127f. Critical of Szlechter also Sick *1984:* 36ff., in his detailed discussion of LE 23/24.

Tochter im Gewahrsam infolge langen Eingesperrtseins stirbt, befreie deine Ehefrau und deine Tochter, bitte."[76]

The factual background of the provisions on unlawful distress has been examined by Szlechter in great detail.[77] In his view the situation dealt with is not distress which has been illegal from the outset, but rather distress turned illegal by the detention of the person distrained even after the discharge of the debt, especially where the debt has been discharged by the work rendered by the distress at the home of the creditor. This may indeed be a typical possibility, but there is in the wording of the situation no clear indication which would justify the narrow interpretation proposed by Szlechter.[78] His linguistic submissions are open to doubt: even if *la* may be rendered "no more, no longer", this is not the ordinary meaning of the particle.[79] What is clear is only that "at the time of the distraint, there is no debt outstanding"; the phrase *(la) išu* "does not imply that there had never been an outstanding debt",[80] — nor does it necessarily imply the opposite, that there had been one.

The sanction laid down in LE 22 for the distress of the slave woman has been the subject of contention between Goetze and von Soden. In the opinion of the former, the convicted distrainor has to pay silver *mala taḫḫi amtim* — "in full compensation for the slave woman" (*1956:* 73f.). Von Soden has repeatedly insisted on reading *mala idi amtim* — "as much as is the hire of the slave woman";[81] but Finkelstein *1970:* 250, relying on the collation by Mrs. Ellis, has rejected the reading *idum* (Á).

76 Kraus *1959/1962:* 28f.

77 Szlechter *1954:* 127ff. See also his *1956b:* 273ff.

78 For an alleged case of wrongful distress made after payment of a debt, see ABPh, no. 47. See further Leiden 1006 = AbB iii 67: "Zu Belanu, den Marduk am Leben erhält, sprich: also sagt Šamaš-tappašu: Gemäss der Feldurkunde der Tochter des Marduk-gamil bist du entschädigt worden. Annatum, ihr Landpächter, hat dich gerade bezahlt. Warum hast du einen Schuldhäftling genommen *(ammini niputam teppi)*? Ich habe den Schuldhäftling zurückgegeben." We do not know what the relationship between the writer and the recipient was, which made this swift, direct intervention possible.

79 Szlechter mentions that LE 22, 23/24, CH 114 use the *t*- form *(ittepe)*, while in CH 115 the G-form *ippi* is used, but the import (if any) of this difference is uncertain.

80 Both quotes from Jackson *1984:* 416.

81 *1949:* 370; *1956:* 33; *1958:* 520. Endorsed by Landsberger *1968:* 74.

Goetze's case was to a considerable part based on the supposed parallel occurrence, in LE 53, of the noun *taḫḫum* — "value" (of the dead ox), in contradistinction with *šimum* — "price" (of the surviving one). However, a distinction of this kind, between "price" (defined as "the amount actually paid for some specific good") and "value" ("the abstract amount which one might realize for some specific good"), would appear to be of little purpose.[82] But there is no need to argue the point in detail any more, since the reading *taḫḫum* in LE 53 has been abandoned.[83] This means that the alleged *taḫḫum* of LE 22 would become a *hapax legomenon* in the language of the Babylonian collections of laws: itself a ground for hesitation and close scrutiny.

While Goetze's *taḫḫum* is unlikely to be correct, it may yet in substance be close to the mark, if the reading proposed by CAD *mala* š[ÁM] *amtim*[84] is accepted.[85] Payment of a variable sum (the actual value, or price) constitutes an advance over fixed penalties — which might in a given case be too large or too small.[86]

LE 23/24 fixes the penalty in case the unlawful detention has terminated in the death of the distress, caused by the distrainor. First the death of a slave woman who had been distrained is considered, and — we have seen — the surrender of two slave women is provided for. Where the distrainor has caused the death of the wife or the son of a *muškenum*,[87] he is himself liable to the death penalty. We have already had occasion to remark on the inverted sequence, in sec. 23/24, slave — free person, contrary to what is usual.

One can now see that the provisions on illegal distress of a slave-woman, as set out in LE 22 and 23/, are in line with those concerning

82 Goetze *1956:* 138, in his discussion of LE 53, dispenses with it tacitly.

83 See p. 76, above.

84 "(Silver) to the amount of the price of the slave-woman": CAD M/i 148a.

85 Taken up lately by Eichler *1987:* 76, note 21.

86 One may compare the much richer material of CH. There one finds fixed penalties or the surrender of an object equal to that destroyed: *X kima X iriab* (or *inaddin*); see secs. /231, 245, 246, 263. It is only when a fraction is payable that one finds the simple circumscription *kaspam mišil šimišu (šimiša) išaqqal (inaddin)* — "silver, half its price he shall weigh out (give)" (secs. 199, /220, 247), respectively *ḫummušam šimišu* — "one fifth its price" (secs. 225, 248).

87 See pp. 141, 143f. above.

theft. One should realize that the provisions are essentially identical, that they vary only because of the different factual data. Congruent with the probable rules concerning theft,[88] LE 22 provides for the payment of the value of the illegally distrained slave-woman (in addition to her return to her owner, — implicit, but unavoidable). In 23/ death makes return impossible; in lieu the law provides for the rendering of two (equivalent?) slave-women. In material terms, and from the point of view of the owner, the outcome is the same. From the point of view of the offending distrainor, — the penalty or punishment imposed on him equals that which he would have suffered if he had stolen the slave-woman.

SEXUAL OFFENCES

Sexual offences considered in the LE are rape and adultery.[89] Note that the LE, just like LI and LU, do not deal with incest, a topic considered in some of the later collections.[90] These provisions may reflect a growing tendency to intervene in matters traditionally left in the hands of the family (or its head).

Sec. 26 imposes the death penalty for forcible cohabitation, without the consent of her parents, with a girl for whom a *terḫatum* had been paid. The protasis has then three elements qualifying the act of cohabitation, and we have to ask whether they are all material.

The payment of the *terḫatum*, effecting betrothal, is certainly an essential part of the facts. Near Eastern laws known to us do not regard rape *per se*, of an unattached woman, as a capital delict. The typical "unattached" woman is a girl who has not yet been betrothed (a "virgin"): it is she who is discussed in various collections of laws, but the same lenient attitude (or even more so) would apply also to a woman who had been attached but no longer was so, i.e. the widow or divorcee.

The rape of a virgin, prior to betrothal, is considered in MAL 55, which orders talion to be executed upon the wife of the ravisher. He is

88 For these see LE 49, and pp. 268f., above.
89 See the detailed discussion in Finkelstein *1966:* 355-372.
90 See CH 154 to 158, and Driver-Miles *1952:* 318ff. Cf. HL 189, 190. In the Bible, provisions on incest are concentrated in Leviticus, 18: 6ff., 20: 11f., Deuteronomy 27: 20, 22f.

to marry the girl he has raped, and may not divorce her. If the father of the girl does not agree to the match, he is entitled to receive compensation. Deuteronomy 22:28-29 also sees the solution in the marriage of ravisher and ravished, with divorce prohibited.[91] It is likely that a similar solution would have applied also in Eshnunna.[92] Betrothal has created a personal tie, violation of which by an outsider is a capital crime: so also in CH 130, Deuteronomy 22:23-27.[93]

The absence of parental consent to the act of cohabitation seems also to be material. If they had agreed, this would have amounted to a breaking off of the betrothal, with the consequence laid down in LE 25: repayment of double the bride money. Would parental indulgence subsequent to the rape absolve the ravisher of the severe punishment in store for him? Szlechter *1954:* 124 answers in the affirmative, but I

91 This rather lenient attitude may reflect traces of "marriage by capture" ("Raubehe") which may have occasionally occurred, and in which early society might acquiesce. See especially the remarks of Korošec *1938:* 294, on "Raubehe" in Hittite law, referring to HL 28 and 37; see, however, the doubts expressed by David *1934:* 38ff., note 39; Friedrich *1959:* 94f.; Fiorella Imparati *1964:* 210f.
Sometimes, as is only to be expected, abduction of the girl would provoke violent reaction on the part of hèr family: see HL 37, and Genesis 34: 25-31, on the avenge of the rape (or seduction) of Dinah.

92 Of non-Oriental sources see the Laws of Gortyn, col. ii, lines 2-16, imposing penalties determined by the status of the victim and of the culprit. In Roman law rape is closely connected with abduction *(raptus)*; both, it seems, became criminal offences only in imperial times. For post-classical times the tone was set by Constantine, in a constitution of 320 C.E. (*Codex Theodosianus* 9.24.1). This law, harsh in the extreme, may reflect Church influence (see Biondi *1954:* 483: "La legislazione va quasi di pari passo con la Chiesa nella repressione"; and see the sources adduced by him). Constantine laid down that anyone connected with the crime was to die, so also the woman if she consented to being abducted. If abducted against her will, she was yet to forfeit any claim to the inheritance of her parents. Parents who failed to prosecute were to be deported. Th. Mommsen remarks that "unvernünftiger ist der Strafluxus wohl niemals aufgetreten als in dem constantinischen Entführungsgesetz" (*1899:* 702, note 5); for more details see Eger *1914:* col. 250; Rein *1844:* 394ff.

93 Note the extraordinary leniency of HL 28: even the taking of another man's bride, without the consent of her parents, is settled by an indemnity.

would prefer to leave the matter open. Logically, the situation at the time of cohabitation should be decisive, but one cannot be sure that this view was taken in Eshnunna.[94] In addition, there is the outraged bridegroom to be taken into account: his personal sphere has been invaded and he may consequently also have had a say in the matter.

Contrary to the two former qualifications, it does not appear that the force used upon the bride constitutes a material factor. In principle, the claim of the ravisher that the bride was a willing partner to his act would not — even if proven — mitigate his crime and punishment. Her consent would become important only when her own fate came to be decided: force used upon her absolves her of punishment;[95] consent, actual or implied by the circumstances, renders her equally guilty; the case would probably have been regarded as adultery.[96] Nevertheless, in one particular context such broadening of the circle of guilt might provide the male offender's escape hatch: under CH 129 and HL 198, guilt of the female partner raises the possibility of pardon by the husband, and consequential pardon of her paramour by the king. This has been mentioned, and will be discussed at once, in detail. But LE 26 concentrates solely on the male offender (the rapist), hence it is uncertain whether the idea of "interdependent pardon" would have applied in Eshnunna.

None of the sources dealing with the rape of a betrothed girl rules on the question whether the bridegroom is still bound to his undertaking.[97] In other words, the question whether he is entitled to recover

94 Note that condonation of adultery is widely permitted. See generally the remarks of Finkelstein, *1966:* 371f., on tendencies towards leniency in the treatment of this crime. And see further, p. 283, below.

95 See CH 130, Deuteronomy 22: 25-27; cf. HL 197, MAL 12. And compare the story about Joseph and Potiphar's wife (Genesis 39: 7ff.). After failing to seduce him, she accuses him of having attempted to rape her. To make her charge stick, she had to "cry with a loud voice" (verses 14, 18). *Codex Theodosianus* 9.24.1 demands that the girl "vicinorum opem clamoribus quaerere".

96 Seduction of a girl not yet betrothed is considered in MAL 56 and Exodus 22:15-16. Exodus envisages marriage; if the father of the girl refuses his consent he is nevertheless entitled to compensation equivalent to her *mohar*. The decision of MAL may have been similar: the father is entitled to compensation, and is given power "to treat the girl as he pleases".

97 See Goetze *1956:* 83.

the *terhatum* in case he refuses to complete the marriage, is left without reply. On general grounds I should think that he is not, just as he would not recover in case his wife had been ravished at some later date, subsequent to consummation. However, the relationship between the ravished wife and her husband is first considered only in Talmudic law.

LE 31 is straightforward. The defloration of a slave girl is punishable by a payment of 20 shekels. No mention is made of the use of force. From the legal point of view, consent of the girl seems to be altogether immaterial;[98] it would not diminish the penalty imposed upon her ravisher or seducer.[99] It might perhaps influence her treatment at the hands of her master, but in this the law takes no interest.

Note that LE 31 concentrates on the pecuniary aspects of what has happened. Defloration of a virgin slave girl is an offence against her master, diminishes the value of his property.[100] Since it does not depend on a possible legitimate tie of hers with a third person (to whom she may be "inchoately" married, with the consent of her master) the scope of LE 31 is actually broader than that of LE 26. On the other hand, the emphasis on defloration would exclude the case where the victim had no longer been a virgin. One possible explanation is that in such a case her owner has incurred no actual loss.

98 Defloration of a slave girl without the consent of her owner is dealt with also in LUY 8 (F 5): cf. Finkelstein *1966:* 355; Szlechter *1967b:* 106f. A trial for this offence is recorded in a Sumerian text 3N-T403 + T430, adduced by Finkelstein, p. 359. See also Landsberger *1968:* 47ff. The fine imposed amounts to half a mina silver.

99 So already Finkelstein, *1966:* 360: "... her sexual violation, whether by rape, seduction, or even by her own solicitation, is exclusively considered as a tortious invasion against her owner ..."

100 It has already been noted that the sum payable is rather high: see Goetze *1956:* 89. In comparison, Goetze adduces sec. /55 (15 shekels payable when a slave is killed by a goring ox), and concludes that "a slave girl was considered more valuable than a slave". This is questionable; it is contradicted e.g. by Ishchali no. 326, which sets the penalty for the death of a slave at 15 shekels, that of a slave-girl at 10. The high sum in LE 31 is accounted for by the different circumstances, which justify vindictive damages. Miles-Gurney *1949:* 184 (also Klíma *1953b:* 232, note 43) think of a continuous offence ("presumably the man has taken her to his house"), but there is no warrant for this: the verb *ittaqab* should be given the same rendering and import as in sec. 26.

The final provision, *amtum ša belišama* — "the slave woman (remains) her owner's indeed" is necessary, in view of the practice, which we have noted, of terminating such affairs by way of marriage; or else it might have been thought that by paying up the ravisher-seducer had acquired his victim.[101] This is not the case: the owner is in a position similar to that of the father who has refused consent to the marriage of his (unbetrothed) daughter who has been raped or seduced: he gets the penalty but keeps his slave.

Adultery is an offence for the punishment of which most ancient legislations have provided. In the East this crime is dealt with, apart from Eshnunna, also in CH 129, HL 197, 198, MAL 14, 15, 23, and in the Bible, Leviticus 20:10, Deuteronomy 22:22.[102, 103] All these sources

101 As here, Petschow *1968b:* 6, note 16. Compare and contrast Exodus 21:36 (p. 297, below).

102 The earliest provision on adultery occurs in the Ebla text TM.75. G.2420, lines 575ff. (Sollberger *1980:* 146). The matter is settled by composition. (Note that the import of two subsections, lines 581ff., is uncertain.)

Another provision on adultery is LUY 7 (= F 4); see Finkelstein *1966:* 369ff.; Petschow *1968b:* 4f.; Szlechter *1967:* 106, 111f. The wife suffers death, the paramour is absolved. With Finkelstein one has to assume that he managed to satisfy his accusers that he was ignorant of the married status of the woman. See also MAL 13, 14, 23, on the requirement of guilty knowledge.

Note that both Finkelstein and Szlechter (contrary to Gurney and Kramer, who first published the text) refuse to regard the expression DAM.GURUŠ as reference to a specific status of the offended husband. Rather they treat it as equivalent to DAM.LÚ = *aššat awilim*: see Szlechter, p. 111 and Finkelstein p. 370, note 44:

> "I doubt that the use of GURUŠ here has any special implication from the juridical point of view, since it is hardly conceivable that the ruling either in LUY 7 (= F 4) or LUF 11 [both references adjusted, R. Y.] would have been different had the woman been denoted simply as DAM.LÚ. The resumption in line 7 with LÚ — who can be no other person than the GURUŠ in line 1 — would seem to bear this out. I suspect that the term was used here simply because the GURUŠ-class constitutes the largest sector of the population under the Ur III kings — in part, at least — corresponding to the *muškenu* of the post-Ur III period. In these two rules, therefore, it may be tantamount to saying 'anybody, someone, fellow', etc."

envisage the death penalty for both the offenders. However, in all of them, except in the Bible, the husband is expressly endowed with a wide measure of discretion regarding his wife; he may be content with a lesser punishment, or may even allow her to go unpunished altogether. But by being lenient toward his wife, he has also been lenient toward her paramour: he too will remain alive, and moreover his punishment must not exceed that of the woman. By decreeing equal treatment for both the *adulterii rei* the law prevents effectively a conspiracy of husband and wife, directed against an "innocent" male.[104]

Leviticus and Deuteronomy decree the death of both the offenders, and a possibility of pardon is not mentioned. True, in actual practice the decision whether to prosecute would ordinarily have remained with the aggrieved husband, who could agree to composition.[105] Even so, there is another problem: once the husband had set the wheels of justice moving, did he retain any power over them, a discretion to stop them again? No definite answer can be given, and one must bear in mind also a possible discrepancy between theory and practice.

From LE 27/28 it emerges that adultery is committed only if the woman involved is an *aššatum* — "wife".[106] We have already gone into the intricacies of LE 27/28, giving negative and positive definitions of that status.[107] However, we have submitted that these definitions may

We agree entirely (over the objections of F. Yildiz *1981:* 96, note 38). What makes these remarks particularly interesting is the fact that in the context of LE and CH both Szlechter and Finkelstein insisted on the strict separation of *awilum* and *muškenum*. Note also Korošec *1968:* 287: "Die Möglichkeit, dass der Ausdruck GURUŠ ... als pars pro toto allgemein den Mann kennzeichnet ist nicht von der Hand zu weisen."

103 For the Greek and Roman world see Erdmann *1934:* 268ff.; Mommsen *1899:* 688ff.

104 Cf. Driver-Miles, *1935:* 39. In Gortyn the accused could demand that his accuser swear that there had been no deceit; col. ii, lines 36-44: "si vero se dolo malo deceptum dicat, deprehensor ... illum sane in adulterio deprehensum nec dolo malo deceptum esse iurato" (tr. M. Guarducci). For Athens see W. Erdmann, *op.cit.*, p. 292. In Roman law, cf. *Digesta Iustiniani* 48.5.33 pr: "... lex parem in eos qui deprehensi sunt indignationem exegit et severitatem requirit."

105 So Loewenstamm *1962:* 55ff. (Hebrew), relying on Proverbs 6:32-35.

106 Cf. *Digesta Iustiniani* 48.5.6.1 "... adulterium in nupta committitur ..."

107 See pp.200ff., above.

have arisen out of an actual occurrence; if that is so, it would follow that the circumstances set out there need not be the only ones in which a woman might be called an *aššatum*. The specific questions up for decision in LE 27/28 seem to have their root in the fact that no *terḫatum* had been given, as is necessarily implied by the lack of parental consent. Had a *terḫatum* been given, the bride would at once be called an *aššatum*, even prior to the consummation of the marriage. This is shown by CH 130 (and 161). CH 130 proves, by implication, that in Babylon cohabitation of an outsider with the consenting bride would have been regarded as adultery. The situation will have been the same also in Eshnunna.

Of all the Eastern sources on adultery, LE /28 is the only one to deal solely with one of the offenders — by general consent with the woman. This dominant opinion is not necessarily wrong, but it ought to be pointed out that a different interpretation is at least equally possible. It has already been noted that in the official Akkadian of the Old Babylonian period there is no difference between the masculine and the feminine of the third person singular: *imat ul iballuṭ* means "he/she shall die, he/she shall not live". The dominant approach has been determined by the desire to preserve the identity of subjects. It is admittedly more in accordance with our "Sprachgefühl" to render "the day in the lap of a man she will be seized, she shall die" etc., than to render "she will be seized, he shall die". But we have already seen that unindicated changes of subject do occur in the LE (see pp. 95f., above). The question which of the two adulterers is the one more likely to be meant should therefore be considered on legal grounds; however, it ought to be said at once that conclusive results cannot be obtained.

Arguments against the dominant view, hence by implication in favour of attributing the punitive provision to the male partner, are at least two: (i) The dominant view leaves us without any ruling concerning the fate of the woman's accomplice. One may guess that he would also suffer death, yet nothing is said about it. If, on the other hand, the section applies to the male offender, the adulteress would be dealt with by the husband himself, or by his/her family. (ii) A comparison with the provisions concerning rape may also be suggestive. CH 130, MAL 12, Deuteronomy 22:25-27, all stress that the woman suffers no punishment; HL 197 does so by implication. In LE 26, we have seen, death is decreed for the ravisher, but no mention is made of the girl: the law concentrates on the man only.

I submitted, in conclusion, that the punishment for adultery, laid down in LE / 28, might refer to the male offender.[108] The woman will have been left to the domestic jurisdiction of the husband, or his father;[109] custom may have given a say in the matter also to her family.[110]

The question whether the principle limiting the punishment of the male offender to that of the woman was applied also in Eshnunna must remain unanswered. It would, of course, not arise for those scholars who hold that *imat ul iballuṭ* denotes mandatory death penalty, but we have already dissented from this view, which would impute to the LE a more severe attitude than that which we find in CH, HL and MAL. Also there is no reason to assume that in Eshnunna the discretion of the husband was more restricted than that which he enjoyed elsewhere. But even so, in the absence of any reference to this point, one should not postulate a consequential royal pardon for the male.

Bodily injuries

Bodily injuries are dealt with in secs. 42-47A. The LE concern themselves only with injuries inflicted by free men upon free men. There are no distinctions relating to the status of either party, the offender or the offended. Consequently, the provisions are much simpler than those of the CH. There we have, first of all, the well-known distinction between *awilum* and *muškenum*, with very different sanctions laid down. Special note is taken also of injuries to slaves (CH 199, 213/214, 219/220).[111] More than that, with regard to *let awilim maḫaṣum* — "to slap a man's face", CH enquires whether

108 This suggestion has found little echo. Only Petschow, *1968a:* 138, note 1, declared the subject "strittig".

109 Cf. Genesis 38:24.

110 Cf., for Roman law, Dionysius of Halicarnassus, 2.25.6.

111 Injuries to slaves are singled out in the HL, secs. 8, 12, 14, 16, 18; biblical sources do not deal with injuries to a *servus alienus* (except for the slave killed by a goring ox). Exodus 21:26-27 grants a slave his freedom if his eye or tooth has been destroyed by his master.

the slapper and the slapped were social equals and grades the punishment accordingly. And in case the slap was administered by a slave to an *awilum*, "they shall cut off his ear" (sec. 205).[112]

The import of these differences between LE and CH need not be the same throughout. In line with our detailed discussion,[113] we should suggest that there was in Eshnunna no legal distinction between *awilum* and *muškenum*; there will, however, have been separate treatment for injuries to slaves, even though the Laws do not preserve these provisions.

As to the actual contents of secs. 42 to 47A, we have already mentioned them when discussing intention. Here we shall be content with some supplementary remarks. Sec. 42 starts off with the rather exceptional case of biting off a nose, but Goetze is able to point to a parallel in LUF 17 and HL 13, 14.[114] The destruction of an eye is dealt with in all the major texts treating of bodily injury: CH 196/, /198/199; HL 7, 8; Exodus 21:24, Deuteronomy 19:21. So is the destruction of a tooth: CH 200/201; HL, *ibid.*; Exodus, Deuteronomy, *ibid.* On the other hand, the injury to an ear finds a parallel only in HL 15, 16.[115] The section ends with *meḫeṣ letim*, that slap in the face to which so much attention is paid in CH 202-205.[116]

112 For mutilation as a punishment, see also CH 194, 195, 218. And see already p. 262, above.
113 See the conclusion, p. 148, above.
114 Goetze would so render also *nefeš* of Exodus 21:23, Deuteronomy 19:21. His suggestion has been cooly received: see Loewenstamm, *1957:* 194f.
115 It occurs also in our times. I noted randomly an Australian case where a motorist's ear was bitten off in a brawl over a parked car (*The Times*, 28.8.1969). A Cambridge student was charged with biting off an ear, causing grievous bodily harm (*The Times*, 30.10.1984).
116 As a further parallel, Goetze mentions HL 9, but there are divergent renderings for this section. For further references see AHw 546a. Note also UCBC 756 (first published by Lutz *1930:* 379ff.) The document was re-edited by San Nicolò *1932:* 189ff. It is a protocol of a trial for a slap in the face. The defendant denied the charge, but refused to take an oath. He was condemned to pay 3 1/3 shekels of silver (one third of the sum imposed in LE 42). See also Sick *1984:* 248, and note 1134.
In later times the "slap in the face" is the insult *par excellence* mentioned in the famous passage Matthew 5:39. Talmudic law distinguishes further

LE 42 and 43 do not state anything concerning the circumstances in which the delict was perpetrated; in our discussion of intention we have had to rely on the nature of the various injuries. LE 44/45 imposes the payment of 1/2 a mina of silver for the breaking of an arm, respectively a leg. Qualifying circumstances are given in 44/ (poorly preserved, on Tablet A only). Their import eludes us. The penalty imposed is equal to that payable for the destruction of a tooth, or to half the penalty for the destruction of an eye.

In HL the breaking of an arm or a leg is treated as equal to the destruction of an eye (see secs. 7, 8, compared with secs. 11, 12); so also in CH / 198/199, the breaking of a bone (GÌR.PAD = *eṣimtu*). One might be tempted to regard the relatively lesser penalty in LE as due to qualifying circumstances. However, this is uncertain, especially — but not only — when one compares different collections of laws. The reference to other comparables might produce rather different results. So one might follow the knocking out of a tooth (or teeth?) through the sources. Basically the penalty seems rather high: in LE 42 it is fixed at 1/2 a mina silver (i.e., half the amount payable for the destruction of an eye). In CH / 201 the penalty exacted for a tooth is 1/3 of a mina (one third of that payable for an eye under CH / 198). In the HL, three stages can be discerned, as follows. Secs. 7 and 8 tell of a change in the penalty: "If anyone blinds a free man or knocks out his teeth, they would formerly give 1 mina of silver, now he shall give 20 shekels of silver ..." 8: "If anyone blinds a male or female slave or knocks out his/her teeth, he shall give 10 shekels of silver." Significantly, while the penalties are lowered, the equality of eye and tooth is maintained. That the Hittites themselves were not altogether pleased emerges from the fact that in the end they abandon this equality, in a later version (given in KBo VI 4): "If anyone blinds a free man in a quarrel, he shall give 1 mina of silver... If anyone blinds a slave in a quarrel, he shall give 30 (?) shekels of silver... If anyone knocks out the teeth of a free man, in case he knocks out 2 teeth or 3 teeth, he shall give 12 shekels

between an ordinary slap, and one inflicted with the back of the hand; this is considered as even more insulting, and draws double damages (*Mishna Baba Qamma* 8.6; *Tosefta, ibid.*, 9.31: "since it is *makkah šel bizzayon* — a blow of contempt"). For Roman law see Aulus Gellius, *Noctes Atticae* 20.1.13.

of silver. If it is a slave, he shall give 6 shekels of silver."[117] All this goes merely to show that a comparison of numbers is often unprofitable and devoid of purpose.[118]

In LE 46 a man hit *(imḫaṣ)* another, breaking his collarbone. Goetze *1956:* 121 sees here premeditation, a case of "battery". The import of *maḫaṣum* has been examined by Nörr *1958:* 9, who comes to the negative result that the verb, by itself, reflects merely the exterior act of hitting, dealing a blow. In view of this one cannot, with Goetze, speak of an "aggravating circumstance which results in a stiffer penalty".

In sec. 47, a man is made to pay 10 shekels for having inflicted an injury of unknown nature, in circumstances which even the parallel version in Haddad 116 has not fully clarified.[119] Since the injury is unknown to us and may be of a relatively trivial nature, one cannot be sure that the circumstances in which it occurred were alleviating ones (as suggested by Goetze, p. 121).

Strictly speaking, sec. 47A, concerning unpremeditated, yet culpable killing, goes beyond bodily injuries. But the topics are closely related, as shown by comparison with the parallel section 206/207/208 in CH. This starts off, innocently enough, with a case of mere wounding, in course of a brawl. Once the attacker has on oath cleared himself of intent, he is let off with payment of medical expenses. Even if death has ensued, the sums involved — higher in LE (2/3 a mina silver) than in CH (1/2 a mina) — are on the moderate side.

The enquiry into numbers, just condemned, acquires some meaning if they reflect some recurring patterns or ratios. In the LE, we have culpable, but unintentional killing of a free person punished by a penalty of 2/3 a mina silver (= 40 shekels): so in sec. 47A, also in

117 The translations are those of Goetze, *1950b:* 189. The rendering of Friedrich *1959* shows one discrepancy: while Goetze uses the plural ("teeth") throughout, Friedrich has the singular ("Zahn"), switching to the plural only in the last passage ("2 Zähne oder 3 Zähne").

118 See also Finkelstein *1981:* 24, note 6. But we shall at once offer some more positive remarks about ratios of penalties.

119 *i-še-el* (A iii 41) or *ik/q-te-el* (Haddad 116: 8). Neither is known from another source.

two sections still to be examined, sec. 54/, death caused by a gorer-ox, and 56/, death caused by a vicious dog. This is no more than an identity of numbers, which we are wont to shrug off. But when one notes that the death of a slave is visited with a payment of 15 shekels, in /55 and /57,[120] this leads one to think that the lives of free persons and of slaves are assessed in a ratio of 8:3. This assumption is clinched by the abstract, general statement of Ishchali 326:4-5, *mar awilim 2/3 mana kaspim warad awilim 15 šiqil kaspim* — "a son of a man 2/3 a mina of silver, a slave of a man 15 shekels of silver".

The closest parallel to LE 54/55 is furnished by CH 251/252: for the fatal goring of a free person *(mar awilim)* 1/2 a mina silver is payable, for a slave *(warad awilim)* 1/3 a mina. The ratio is 3:2. The actual span between free and slave is much greater in LE than in CH: 25 shekels in the former, only 10 in the latter. Differently put, under CH the life of free persons (in terms of silver) is worth less, that of a slave more!

CH 251/252 retains an early dichotomy *awilum-wardum*, such as can be traced also in CH 116 and 229/231/.[121] Transition to the trichotomy *awilum-muškenum-wardum* may give rise to problems. There are none in 196/199 and 200/201 (two sections which Scheil has divided into six): these are in the main parallel to LE 42. There is essential correspondence between the *awilum*-victim of LE 42 and the *muškenum*-victim of CH /198/ and /201. Both codes have fixed tariffs, amounts of silver payable for a particular injury. The retribution for injuries to an *awilum (mar awilim)* is talionic; the introduction of talion may have been a primary purpose of the new system. So in 196/197 and in 200/. For the destruction of a slave's eye, or for the breaking of his bone, CH /199 provides for payment of half his price (so also in CH /220). Finally, sec. 200/201 deals with knocking out of a tooth: wittingly or not, compensation for a slave's tooth is not mentioned.

Four sections, CH 202 to 205, deal with the slap in the face. The first and last result in corporal punishment. A *mar awilim* slapping his equal had to pay 1 mina silver (a very sharp increase!); *muškenum* slapping

120 Sec. 47A has no provision on the killing of a slave. As already noted, the slave does not figure in the block 42-47A.

121 With important variations: in both death of a free person is punished by death; the death of a slave results in the payment of 1/3 a mina silver (116), respectively in the rendering of "slave like slave" (/231/; also in 219/).

muškenum costs 10 shekels (sec. 204): the figure equals that laid down in LE 42.

The actual impact of Hammurabi's *Dreiklassengesellschaft* varies. The provisions just discussed (talionic, but also pecuniary) indicate a harsher reaction to injuries inflicted upon an *awilum*. The *muškenum* is only relatively affected; in absolute terms, his position as a victim remains what it had been prior to his being set up as a distinct class. By contrast, in the provisions which follow, the division of classes is super-imposed without change at the top. The old sanctions are now restricted to a limited group, the *awilum (mar awilim)*. As a whole, then, these sets have become more cramped, but also more lenient.

In CH /207/208, death resulting from a brawl is visited by a penalty of 1/2 mina silver in case the victim was a *mar awilim*; the life of a *muškenum* is compensated by only 1/3 mina (the sum paid for a slave gored to death: /252). In CH /207/208 there is then no room for the slave-victim.

This omission must have been conscious. Two solutions were within easy reach. They could have retained the structure, e.g., of sec. 251/252, fixing for all free victims a uniform compensation of 1/2 a mina. Or else they could have increased the liability for the death of an *awilum*, say to 1 *mina*. Either of the solutions would have left room for the slave-victim (very important in a provision of general nature).

If neither road was taken, this looks like a deliberate and authorized decision: there emerges the intent to lower — for the greater part of free victims — the penalty for culpable homicide. For the *mar awilim*, note that a deliberate physical insult (sec. 203) was to be twice as costly as his death, caused without premeditation.

CH 209/214 deals with abortion and ensuing death. Mere abortion (209/, /211/, /213/) is punished by the payment of 10, 5, 2 shekels. This span is much wider, and the resulting pattern (which recurs in 215/216/217, on fees for medical treatment) is better.

More complex is the case with fatal outcome. An earlier Sumerian law, in UM 55-21-71,[122] but also MAL 50 and Exodus 21:23, call uniformly for the death penalty, a severe sanction for the probably unintended death of the pregnant free woman. At first glance, CH is in

122 See Civil *1965:* 4f. For the latest discussion of the abortion texts, see Otto "Leben um Leben ...", to appear in *Biblica* 70 (1989).

line with the other sources. In truth, the death penalty is decreed only if the victim was a *marat awilim*. Further complication is introduced by vicarious punishment: it is the offender's daughter who is to be killed. What if he had no daughter? This question has given rise to many speculations. It has been suggested that absence of a daughter would have re-activated direct liability of the perpetrator. Perhaps so; but it is equally possible that with meticulously exact retribution not feasible, pecuniary compensation should take its place. A combination, then, of two elements: one clearly restrictive, the other possibly so.

For the *marat muškenim* a payment of 1/2 a mina would suffice (/212/); for a slave-girl, it is again 1/3 a mina (/214).

Hammurabi's men had mastered the art of introducing change discreetly. Not wishing to be regarded as "soft on delict", they salute the *antiquum ius*, then deftly restrict its application.

Provisions on medical fees (CH 215/216/217), and on liability for operations that failed (CH 218, 219/220) have no parallel in other cuneiform laws. Their examination might take us too far.

THE GORING OX AND COMPARABLE CASES

One last group of delicts remain to be considered, those concerning the goring ox (secs. 53, 54/55), the vicious dog (sec. 56/57), and the sagging wall (sec. 58).[123] The first of these, sec. 53, stands apart, in that it deals with a case where an ox gored and killed another ox; the other sections deal with the death of a human being, free (54/, 56/, 58) or slave (/55, /57).

Section 53 provides that the owners of oxen should divide between them the price of the live ox and the carcass of the ox killed. Oriental law has here arrived at a unique solution, which is at once ingenious and equitable. There is a live ox, the price of which can be divided,[124] and there is the carcass, to be disposed of in the same

123 For discussions of this group of sections see also Yaron *1966b:* 396ff.; Haase *1967:* 11ff. After the publication of YLE, see especially Jackson *1974:* 55-93, Finkelstein *1981*, and Sick *1984:* 119ff.

124 Goetze *1956:* 138 assumes that the goring ox was to be destroyed, slaughtered. This has been doubted already by Moran *1957:* 221. If every first gorer had to be destroyed, the case of LE 54/55 could not have arisen. Haase, *op. cit.*, pp. 14ff. deals in great detail with the import of the

manner. The solution laid down may have its roots in the practice of the courts, a kind of Solomonic kadi justice, giving little thought to abstract considerations. If one were nevertheless to look for underlying principles, these might have been the one or the other of two. First, a desire to divide the loss which has been incurred between two persons who may be equally guilty, or else equally blameless.[125] We have to note that the ruling follows entirely from the result, the "Erfolg"; it does not take account of any fault on the part of either owner, nor of the rôle played by either ox. Secondly, the actual circumstances may often have been unknown and incapable of being ascertained.[126] In the absence of proof, one might have held with some formal legal justification that the owner of the dead ox would not succeed in pressing his claim. But there might also be a different approach, formulated as a rule of Talmudic law some 2000 years after the LE. Under this rule, "money which is in doubt, is to be divided [without an oath]".[127]

LE 53 is probably the closest parallel, known so far, between a rule in an ancient Near Eastern legal text and a biblical provision;[128] the similarity became even more accented when the reading *širum* ("flesh, carcass") was substituted for *taḫḫum* ("value"). The same case of ox killing ox is dealt with in Exodus 21:35, which reads: "And if a man's ox gored his fellow's ox and it died, then they shall sell the live ox and divide the silver of it; and the dead [ox] also they shall divide."

provision concerning the "price" *(šimum)* of the surviving ox. He favours the view that actual sale is envisaged, but I can see nothing precluding an agreement between the parties, leaving the ox with its owner, provided he is willing to pay half its value. The purpose of the section is the fixing of a modus for calculating the amount due, and actual sale is not unavoidable. As here already David, *1949:* 24. The price achievable may have been affected by the fact that the ox was an (incipient) gorer.

125 Finkelstein *1981:* 23 uses the term "loss distribution".

126 Cf. Daube *1961:* 259.

127 E.g., *Babylonian Talmud, Baba Qamma* 35b, *Baba Meṣi'a* 2b.

128 See Loewenstamm *1957:* 195. Landsberger *1968:* 102 says of LE 53 that it is "haargenau identisch mit der Regelung die das Bundesbuch trifft"; and see Jackson *1974:* 74; Finkelstein *1981:* 19: "The specific wording of the biblical rules of the goring ox is so close to that of the cuneiform antecedents that any explanation of the resemblances other than one based on some kind of organic linkage is precluded."

Anyone looking at the two texts without preconceived notions will see at once how closely similar they are, not only in the actual solution proposed but even in the mode of formulation. The identity of the very peculiar ruling laid down in both the sources makes it virtually certain that they are connected with eath other, probably since both borrowed from a common fount, Oriental legal practice.

An essentially negative stand was early taken by David.[129] Indeed, I do agree that biblical law has its own "principles, methods, and aspirations";[130] yet it does not follow that it did not make use of, and build upon, rulings which are evidenced in a variety of sources, but may have been widely used, common to Eastern practice. David's approach was at once taken up and elaborated by van Selms.[131] He sees LE 53 as "proclaimed for the small kingdom of Eshnunna alone", and denies that it could have influenced the Book of the Covenant. This is a wrong formulation of the question in issue. There is no ground for regarding LE 53 as an innovation or invention of the lawgiver in Eshnunna. It is merely his reception of a rule which I assume to have been of wide application, throughout the ancient East. At any rate, this seems to me the only possible explanation for the identity of rules which David, van Selms (and some others) fail to account for.[132] From this starting point, even though for opposite reasons, I cannot agree with Westbrook's statement: "Codex Eshnunna exists as a school text and in some form must have reached the Israelite cultural sphere, since Exodus 21:35 ... is virtually a translation of CE 53."[133] So far, no remnant of the LE has been found outside the borders of Eshnunna. Its emergence, many centuries after the destruction of the city, in the "Israelite cultural sphere", is less than plausible.

My own suggestion, that the biblical provisions concerning the goring ox (and in particular Exodus 21:35) may have been derived

129 See *1949:* 24, note 63. See also his paper *1950:* 149ff.

130 Hence, I concur also with Finkelstein *1981:* 5 that "the biblical author ... transposed these laws into a distinctly different framework and in effect transformed them ..."

131 *1950:* 321ff. Against van Selms see also Jackson *1974:* 81.

132 David's approach is specifically rejected by Finkelstein *1981:* 18, note 10: "Strangely, the plainly contrary indications of the evidence are ignored rather than confronted and refuted."

133 *1985a:* 257.

from a common Near Eastern legal tradition and practice, has won the approval of Petschow,[134] but also the posthumous strictures of Finkelstein.[135] He objects especially to my assumption concerning the existence of "customary laws and practices common to the ancient Near East". However willing to renounce my own assumptions for better ones of others, I have yet to see these. In any case, Finkelstein refrains from committing himself: "There is, in short, no certain way at present of explaining the verbal identity between sources that are perhaps as much as five hundred years and as many miles apart. But the fact of this identity is incontrovertible and compels us to postulate an organic linkage between them even if this linkage cannot be reconstructed. With this I consider the subject of the interdependence of sources to have been paid its sufficient due for our present purposes."[136]

Indeed, for our reasoning to be valid, there is a basic question which must be answered. Is the solution reached in LE and Exodus truly peculiar and extraordinary?[137] Is it not the sort of ruling which might in any case be expected, and could well have been reached in both independently, without the need of assuming any connection? A brief examination of the provisions laid down in non-Oriental systems will justify the approach which is being advocated here.

The relevant provisions in the Laws of Gortyn are unfortunately rather obscure, but it seems at least certain that they contained nothing that is comparable with the ruling of LE 53.[138] On the other

134 *1973a:* 17, note 11; see also the cautious remarks ot Jackson *1974:* 82.

135 *1981:* 18, note 10. Finkelstein's dissatisfaction with my loose use of the term "positive law" (Preface to YLE, p. 11, above) was justified: "proper law" would have been more suitable. Most of our other differences could, I believe, have been settled over a cup of coffee. Unfortunately, the opportunity for such a conversation never presented itself.

136 *Ibid.*, p. 20.

137 See the comments of Jackson, *cit.*, pp. 77f.

138 See Margherita Guarducci, *Inscriptiones Creticae* IV (1950), no. 41, coll. i-ii (= P. Cauer and E. Schwyzer, *Dialectorum Graecarum exempla epigraphica potiora* [1923], no. 161). Guarducci (p. 93) paraphrases the contents in Latin as follows:

> "Quadrupedis dominus, qui iniuriam passus sit, quadrupedem integrum habeat a quo damnum illatum sit; si tamen noluerit quadrupedem accipere ab altero domino, iste simplum ei pendeat... Si quis bestiam vulneratam non egerit vel mortuam

hand, the solutions laid down in Roman law are quite certain: two possibilities are envisaged. If the surviving ox has been the "aggressor", its owner is liable; if not, he is not bound to make good the damage or part of it. This may be good legal logic, but it is a far cry from the equitable ruling of LE and Exodus. The relevant text is *Digesta Iustiniani* 9.1.1.11, where Ulpian quotes from the republican jurist Quintus Mucius Scaevola, as follows:

> "Cum arietes vel boves commisissent et alter alterum occidit, Quintus Mucius distinxit, ut si quidem is perisset qui adgressus erat, cessaret actio, si is qui non provocaverat, competeret actio: quamobrem eum sibi[139] aut noxam sarcire aut in noxam dedere oportere."[140]

Because of the very simplicity of their formulation, LE and Exodus leave some essential points without regulation. We have postulated that it will often have been impossible to establish what actually happened, but the question of proof must have arisen at least concerning the basic fact that the surviving ox had indeed gored and killed the dead one.[141] More important is another matter: the underlying assumption seems to be that the two animals involved in the incident were originally of roughly the same value. If in a particular case there should happen to be considerable differences, the principle laid down might not work in a satisfactory manner, or would require some adjustment.[142] Also, nothing is said about the

> non attulerit (scilicet ut domino alterius bestiae damnum demonstret), vel (ipsi domino) non ostenderit, cum scilicet neque agere neque afferre potuerit, ex lege neutiquam agendum esse praecipitur."

See also Plato, *Nomoi* 11, 936 D-E.

139 Th. Mommsen: "[eum sibi] cuius esset is qui adgressus erat tum tibi ..."

140 "Noxam dedere" refers to the limitation of the owner's liability by handing over the animal which (or the slave who) had caused the damage. Cf. Kaser *1971:* 630ff.

141 This is the decisive element in a Nuzi litigation (JEN 4, no. 341); the case is quoted in full by Finkelstein *1981:* 21, note 5.

142 Where I merely put a question, Greenberg *1968:* 60f. takes a more definite stand. He views Exodus 21:35 as paradigmatic, and quotes Goetze *1956:* 138 that "it is the intention of the legislator to divide the loss as evenly as possible". He continues: "Should there be a disparity in their values ... the principle derivable from this paradigm must be applied ... the two

place where the encounter between the two animals occurred. The solution might be rather different, according to its happening on public domain, in the field of the claimant, or in that of the defendant.

All these questions, and many others, are considered in Talmudic texts in great detail. The simple statement of Exodus (which is also that of the LE) served as the basis for an elaborate superstructure, taking into account, and providing for, a great variety of possibilities. This process of interpretation may not always have been confined to merely supplementing the actual lacunae, many as they were, of the ancient provision, but may rather have involved substantial changes. The early formula providing for the division of the two oxen, the live and the dead one, is in *Mishnah Baba Qamma* 1.4 (at the end) elaborated into "payment of half the damage from the body (of the live ox)". The compensation is restricted to half the damage, but the owner of the live ox may have to surrender it (or its value) altogether, in case the dead animal had been the more valuable one.[143] This means in effect that liability is limited by two factors: compensation will not exceed (i) half the damage, (ii) the full value of the surviving ox. If one reckons up the loss sustained by each of the parties, this solution may again be the most equitable one, but it is open to question whether the Talmudic ruling does indeed reflect correctly the intention of the ancient provision. There, the basic principle of limitation would rather appear to be that liability should not exceed half the value of the surviving ox. A more detailed examination of the Talmudic rules would be out of place here.

One other question concerning LE 53 still remains to be considered: What was its scope? The wording is quite general, so one might think that it applied to every case of ox goring ox. This is one possibility, but not necessarily the only one. If one reads the section

owners divide the loss equally — or, in other words, the gorer's owner is liable only to half-damages." I hesitate to follow this, the equitable solution provided for in the Talmud (as we shall see presently). Is one justified in carrying it back over 2000 years? And see also Jackson, *ibid.*, p. 76.

143 See the ruling in *Mishnah Baba Qamma* 3.9. Haase *1967:* 15 assumes that it is the stronger (and consequently more valuable) animal that kills the weaker (and less valuable). Not necessarily so: vicious disposition may also play a significant part.

in conjunction with the one that follows, it may seem likely that in LE 53 "the owner of the killing ox was not aware of the animal's vicious disposition; this is shown by the completely different tenor of sec. 54".[144] This could then be another example of the lack of completeness in the LE (and CH);[145] that phenomenon can be demonstrated in the immediate context of the present discussion: remember that LE 53 is missing in CH, and that on the other hand CH 250 has no parallel in LE. I have no explanation for these omissions.[146] It shows merely that CH, even though more systematic than LE, did not aim at comprehensiveness.

But I am now less sanguine when it comes to importing into LE (or CH) the provisions of Exodus 21:36, which read as follows: "Or if it was known that the ox was a gorer beforetimes, and its owner did not guard it, he shall fully replace ox in place of ox, and the dead (ox) shall be his." True, this is a logical continuation of Exodus 21:35;[147] *non sequitur* that it can be properly read into the LE, as a kind of omitted LE 53A. It is one thing to adduce a biblical text to help clarify the meaning of a cuneiform provision;[148] it is something different, and doubtful, to import into Old Babylonian law a whole section, in reliance on a source so much later. This does not mean that Exodus 21:36 would be out of place in the world of LE or CH. But we should remind ourselves that we are dealing with texts, not with mere possibilities.

The following three sections apply where the death of a human being has been caused — by a goring ox, a vicious dog, or a sagging wall. These sections differ from LE 53 in an important feature. In all of them liability for the fatal occurrence depends on the owner's prior knowledge of the special danger inherent in his property. Moreover, that "knowledge" of the owner has to be of a formal

144 Goetze *1956:* 138.
145 Amply discussed, pp. 86f., above.
146 Nor am I convinced by those offered by Finkelstein *1981:* 24: I see no *a priori* difficulty which prevents the inclusion, in CH, of a provision akin to LE 53, nor to the inclusion in LE of one akin to CH 250.
147 Immaterial to the present discussion is the suggestion that Exodus 21:35-36 constitutes a later addition to the text: see Daube *1947:* 85f. and *1961:* 260f.; Jackson *1974:* 86 comes to the rescue of verse 35, but follows Daube with regard to verse 36.
148 See p. 41, note 80, above.

nature: *babtum ana belišu ušedi* — "the ward (authorities) have had (it) made known to its owner".[149]

The three sections continue with the statement that the owner, though forewarned, did yet not take the necessary measures: *kalabšu la iṣṣur* — "he did not guard his dog"; *igaršu la udannin* — "he did not strengthen his wall". In LE 54/ the verb describing the owner's failure to act is uncertain.[150] However, while the lexical aspect remains in doubt, the actual meaning is hardly in question; it is sufficiently determined by the related sections within the LE, and by the parallels in CH and Exodus.

One would like to know the exact import of these statements concerning omissions on the part of the owner of the chattel — omissions occasioning the damage. Are they merely a connecting link between the official warning and the fatal outcome *ikkimma uštamit* — "it gored and killed", etc. (as the case may be), or do they rather have a substantive import of their own? In other words, would the owner be allowed to plead that he had taken reasonable steps to forestall the danger and that the fatal event was not the consequence of his own neglect, but rather of circumstances beyond his control, and that he should therefore be absolved of liability?[151] No definite answer is offered here, but on the whole it would seem more likely that notions of "Erfolgshaftung", strict liability for the results, would prevail, and that because of the prior official warning.[152]

149 The same element of formal knowledge recurs in CH 251/ and Exodus 21:29.

150 Goetze *1956:* 136 reads *pa-ši-ir*, but notes that this causes philological difficulties; these he proposes to solve with the help of the parallel provisions in CH 251/, Exodus 21:29. Note that there is also a formal discrepancy: CH has two finite verbs (*ušarrim* — "he did [not] dehorn"; *usanniq* — "he did [not] tie up"); more important is the fact that finite forms, not the stative, are used in LE 56/, 58. Von Soden, *1949:* 373, suggested the reading *ú-ši-ir*, deriving this from *šurrum* (the verb employed in CH 251/); he has been followed by Szlechter, but not by Goetze (p. 136, note 8). Von Soden himself has on a later occasion (*1956:* 34) mentioned the possibility of a scribal mistake, and would read *u-<še>-ši-ir* — "(nicht) in Ordnung bringt".

151 This possibility is preferred by Haase *1967:* 48.

152 Cf., for Talmudic law, *Mishnah Baba Qamma* 4.9; *Tosefta, ibid.*, 5.7. The texts reflect conflicting opinions. Some are willing to examine the steps

The LE contain no provision corresponding to CH 250 and Exodus 21:28, concerning a man killed by a first gorer. The CH and Exodus agree in absolving the owner of personal liability, even though the latter source orders the stoning of the ox.[153] One may assume with a fair degree of probability that the rule obtaining in this matter at Eshnunna was similar to that recorded in CH 250. Goetze would explain the omission of this case by asserting that the "LE never include cases in which there is no punishment".[154] This is not quite exact, in view of LE 30 and /37, both of which arrive at solutions negating a claim. In this context one ought also to note that all the ancient Eastern sources, LE, CH and Exodus, deal only with the causing of death. Lesser injuries caused by a goring ox are regulated only in Talmudic law: see *Mishnah Baba Qamma* 3.8.

Now to the case of the vicious dog; this occurs only in the LE. CH and Exodus omit it altogether, probably because it was in no way different from the leading stock example of the goring ox. In LE the consequences are identical for both ox and dog killing a man.[155] We

taken by the owner, and would absolve him if he has taken proper precautions; cf. also Philo, *De legibus specialibus* 3.145. Absolute liability of the owner is implied in a dictum of R. Eliezer (about 90 C.E.), that *en šemira ela sakkin* — "there is no guarding except the (slaughterer's) knife"; cf. also Josephus, *Antiquities* 4.8.36, and the Septuagint to Exodus 21:36. Even this view does not impose upon the owner a duty of having the goring ox slaughtered, but makes the owner liable irrespective of the circumstances.

153 The stoning of the ox, decreed in Exodus, constitutes a new element, and must not be read into LE and CH. See in particular the full discussion by Finkelstein *1981:* 26ff.

154 *1956:* 140. And see already van Selms, *cit.*, p. 326.

155 Of later times, one may note *Mishnah Baba Qamma* 7.7, which lays down a general prohibition of breeding dogs, unless they are chained. For Greek provisions concerning dogs, see Plutarch, *Solon* 24.1. In Rome, the aedilician edict contained detailed provisions regarding death or injury caused by a dog. See the quotation by Ulpian, *Digesta Iustiniani* 21.1.40, 42:

> "Ne quis canem [or any other wild animal] qua vulgo iter fiet, ita habuisse velit, ut cuique nocere damnumve dare possit. Si adversus ea factum sit et homo liber ex ea re perierit, solidi ducenti, si nocitum homini libero esse dicetur, quanti bonum aequum iudici videbitur, condemnetur, ceterarum rerum, quanti damni datum factumve sit, dupli."

follow Goetze in rendering *kalbum šegum* by "vicious dog".[156] Some scholars prefer "rabid dog";[157] this, while ostensibly more exact, is open to question.[158] Note that the owner's fault, from which his liability derives, is that although officially warned, *kalabšu la iṣṣur* — "his dog he did not guard". Now, once it is known that a dog is rabid, immediate destruction of the animal is the only possible remedy. That would have been as obvious in ancient times as it is now. If the text is content with less, this shows rather conclusively that the peril inherent in the situation was one for which "guarding" the dog could be regarded as sufficient.

As a last case we have to consider that of the sagging wall, provided for in LE 58. The case is not mentioned in our other sources. As parallel to LE 58, CH 229/ has been referred to,[159] but there are some significant differences. The provisions in CH deal with a rather more specific case: they concern the shoddy construction of a house and the builder's liability in case his fault has resulted in the death of one of the occupiers.[160] In LE the responsibility is the owner's, and toward the public at large. So I am not sure that this is a useful comparison.

There are interesting differences between secs. 54/55, 56/57, on the one hand, and sec. 58, on the other hand. Where the death of a free man *(awilum)* has been caused by ox or dog, the law imposes a penalty of 40 shekels of silver; but death through the collapse of a sagging wall is defined as *napištum* — "(a case concerning) life", a capital case. Relative to the former provision, the latter one has with good reason been called "étrangement sévère".[161] Death of a slave,

156 So also Bottéro, and most recent translations; CAD K 69a; AHw 1208b (ambiguous: "wild sein, rasen"). "Beisswütig" is the felicitous rendering of Sick *1984:* 120, 123.

157 Strongly in favour of rendering *šegum* by "rabid" is Driver *1972:* 57. See also AHw 424b ("tollwütig"); CAD N/ii 54a; Borger.

158 Adamson *1977:* 140: "No associated symptoms are mentioned, so that rabies cannot justifiably be incriminated as the cause of death." On *kalbum šegum* see also ARM III 18: 15f.: *kima kalbim šegim ašar inaššaku ul ide* — "like a vicious dog, where he will bite I do not know." It is characteristic of the vicious dog that it bites unexpectedly.

159 See Nörr *1958:* 14, 17.

160 Or else in damage to property: see sec. /232.

161 Korošec *1953: 96.*

caused by ox or dog, is punished by a payment of 15 shekels, but it is not considered in the context of the sagging wall. This omission deprives us of a valuable means of comparison. The conflicting rulings laid down have attracted the attention of scholars and various suggestions have been put forward which would account for the discrepancy.

In the view of Goetze *1956:* 140 "more caution can be expected from people who have to deal with potentially dangerous animals whose behaviour contains an element of unpredictability ... on the other hand, the danger inherent in a sagging wall is predictable and therefore always preventable". Actually, two different explanations are combined here: the first part refers to caution on the part of potential victims, whereas the second one seems to refer to prevention of damage by the owner of the wall, the accused.

Goetze's first passage is echoed by Haase.[162] He suggests as reason for the divergence that everyone should keep distant from animals belonging to someone else. He finds support for this view in the fact that sec. 58 imposes the death penalty upon the knowing owner. The more lenient punishment in sec. 54/ may be due to the contribution of the victim, his lack of care;[163] such a contribution should not be assumed in sec. 58. So far Haase, whose suggestions fail to convince. A dangerous animal — a vicious, but unguarded dog would be the best example — may come quite suddenly upon the unsuspecting victim, who will consequently have little opportunity to beware.[164] On the other hand, the sagging wall is a stationary danger; in view of the warning issued by the ward authorities it is probably also a notorious one. The person who approached it and was killed can more easily be regarded as "contributor" than he who was set upon by a goring ox or vicious dog. To sum up: the attempt to explain the divergence of sanctions as due to the behaviour of the victim leads to no result.

Finkelstein *1981:* 22 sees the sequence goring ox — vicious dog — decrepit wall as an attempt "to illustrate negligent wrongs in a series

162 *1961:* 224; see also his *1967:* 51, note 203, in reply to reservations in Yaron *1966b:* 405.

163 Finkelstein *1966:* 364, note 30 also suggests contributory negligence.

164 The animal is "wont to move and cause damage" — *Mishnah Baba Qamma* 1.1.

of situations of increasing gravity". However, an attempt to distinguish between ox and dog founders on the exactly equal treatment of the two cases in 54/55 and 56/57. It is true that the ox is a valuable asset, the decrepit wall is not. But I fail to see this difference as an "extenuating circumstance" working in favour of the owner of the ox. The law would wish to counteract, not encourage, an owner's unwillingness to dispose of the dangerous beast.

More promising may be the approach of David *1949:* 25f., followed by Nörr *1958:* 13: there is indeed no difference in the guilt of the owner. The decisive fact is that in secs. 54/55 and 56/57 death has been caused by a creature with a "will" of its own, independent of the will of its owner.[165] Against this it could be argued that one does not find in LE or CH a recognition of an animal's volition.[166] Even in Exodus, where the animal is put to death, this does not absolve its owner.[167] The owner's fault, the true ground for his liability, consists in his not having prevented the fatal happening, although forewarned. In this respect there is no appreciable difference between ox, dog, and wall.

It seems possible that the difference of sanctions may have its root in a difference of origins. The provisions concerning the goring ox, in LE 54/55 (and probably also those on the vicious dog, LE 56/57) reflect the long established practice of the courts, a kind of Eastern *ius gentium.*[168] This view is supported by the recurrence of related provisions in CH and Exodus. By contrast, in LE 58 a specific source is mentioned: *ṣimdat šarrim* — "decree of the king". It is likely that here we have before us an example of the proper law of Eshnunna itself, its *ius civile.*[169]

The ruling in the case of the sagging wall may have been laid down after a particularly outrageous occurrence, possibly for the punish-

165 See also Finkelstein *1981:* 22.
166 Haase *1967:* 50, note 202, attributes this to lack of completeness.
167 The admissibility of compensation in this case is sufficiently accounted for by the absence of premeditation.
168 As this term is defined by Gaius, *Institutiones* 1.1: "... quasi quo iure omnes gentes utuntur."
169 Again in the parlance of Gaius, *ibid.*: "... quasi ius proprium civitatis."

ment of the offender in that case itself,[170] and was then recorded for application also in future instances.[171] Royal intervention could well have been of a more drastic nature than the "normal" practice of the courts.

170 A principle like *nulla poena sine lege* will hardly have been formulated at that early time. Compare, in biblical law, Leviticus 24:10-23 and Numbers 15:32-36. Both passages concern offences proclaimed or defined for the punishment of acts already committed.

171 Incidentally, the assumption that the section proceeds from an actual occurrence would also explain why no provision is made for the case of a slave killed by a sagging wall.

BIBLIOGRAPHY

I. Translations of the LE [Akkadian text indicated by asterisk]

Artzi *1951* — Artzi, Pinchas. *"šene osafim mišpaṭiyim millifene tequfath Hammurabi", Bulletin of the Israel Exploration Society* 16 (1951) 30-37

Böhl *1949/1950* — Böhl, Franz Maria Theodor de Liagre. "Het Wetboek van Bilalama, Koning van Esjnunna", JEOL 11 (1949/1950) 95-105

Borger *1982* — Borger, Rykle. "Der Codex Eschnunna", in TUAT I, 1. Lief., (1982) 32-38

Bottéro *1965/1966* — Bottéro, Jean. "Antiquités assyro-babyloniennes", in *École pratique des hautes études, IVeme section, Sciences historiques et philologiques, Annuaire* (1965/1966) 89-105

Bouzon *1981* — Bouzon, Emanuel. *As leis de Eshnunna*, 1981;*

Diakonoff *1952* — Diakonoff, Igor Mikhailovich. "Zakony Bilalamy Tzaria Eshnunny", *Vestnik Drevnei Istorii* (1952, no. 3) 213-219

Goetze *1948* — Goetze, Albrecht. "The Laws of Eshnunna Discovered at Tell Ḥarmal", *Sumer* 4 (1948) 63-91;* [with autograph]

Goetze *1950a* — ____ "The Laws of Eshnunna", in ANET, 1st ed. (1950) 161-163

Goetze *1955* — ____ "The Laws of Eshnunna", in ANET, 2nd ed. (1955) 161-163

Goetze *1956* ____ *The Laws of Eshnunna*, 1956 [AASOR 31, 1956, for 1951-1952];* [with autograph]

Goetze *1969* ____ "The Laws of Eshnunna", in ANET, 3rd ed. (1969) 161-163

Haase *1963a* (or Haase I) Haase, Richard. "Die Gesetze von Ešnunna", in *Die keilschriftlichen Rechtssammlungen in deutscher Übersetzung* (1963) 9-16

Haase *1979* (or Haase II) ____ "Die Gesetze von Ešnunna", in *Die keilschriftlichen Rechtssammlungen in deutscher Fassung*, zweite, überarbeitete und vermehrte Auflage, 1979, pp. 20-26

Klíma *1979* Klíma, Josef. "Zákony z Ešnunny", in *Nejstarši zákony lidstva* (1979) 115-119

Korošec *1953* Korošec, Viktor. "Zakonik mesta Ešnunne in Lipit-Ištarjev zakonik", *Slovenska Akademija Znanosti in Utmenosti, Razred za zgodovinske in družbene vede, Razprave* II, 1953

Kunderewicz *1966* Kunderewicz, Cezary. "Zbiór praw z Esznunny", in *Czasopismo Prawno-Historyczne* 18 (1966) 9-29

Lipin *1954* (or Lipin I) Lipin, Lev Aleksandrovich. "Drevneishie Zakony Mesopotamii", *Palestinskij Sbornik* 1 (1954) 14-58

Lipin *1963* (or Lipin II) ____ "Zakony iz Eshnunny", in N.V. Struwe, *Chrestomatia po Istorii Drevnevo Vostoka* (1963) 190-194

Mendelson *1952* Mendelson, Isaac. *"ḥuqe Ešnunna", Ḥoreb* 11 (1952) 157-164

Saporetti *1984* Saporetti, Claudio. "Le leggi di Ešnunna", in *Le leggi di Mesopotamia* (1984) 41-48

Szlechter *1954* (or Szlechter I) Szlechter, Émile. *Les lois d'Ešnunna*, 1954;*

Szlechter *1978* (or Szlechter II) "Les lois d'Eshnunna", RIDA 25 (1978) 109-219;*

YLE Yaron, Reuven. *The Laws of Eshnunna*, 1st. ed., 1969;*

II. Texts, Literature, Abbreviations

AASOR *The Annual of the American Schools of Oriental Research*

AbB *Altbabylonische Briefe*

i F. R. Kraus, *Briefe aus dem British Museum*, 1964

ii R. Frankena, *Briefe aus dem British Museum* (LHI *und* CT 2-33), 1966

iii R. Frankena, *Briefe aus der Leidener Sammlung* (TLB iv), 1968

iv F. R. Kraus, *Briefe aus dem Archive des Šamaš-Ḫazir in Paris und Oxford* (TCL 7 *und* OECT 3), 1968

v F. R. Kraus, *Briefe aus dem Istanbuler Museum*, 1972

vi R. Frankena, *Briefe aus dem Berliner Museum*, 1974

vii F. R. Kraus, *Briefe aus dem British Museum* (CT 52), 1977

viii L. Cagni, *Briefe aus dem Iraq Museum* (TIM II), 1980

ix M. Stol, *Letters from Yale*, 1981

x F. R. Kraus, *Briefe aus kleineren westeuropäischen Sammlungen*, 1985

xi M. Stol, *Letters from Collections in Philadelphia, Chicago and Berkeley*, 1986

ABPh	Ungnad, Arthur. "Altbabylonische Briefe aus dem Museum zu Philadelphia", ZverglRw 36 (1920) 214-253
Adamson *1977*	Adamson, P. B. "The spread of rabies into Europe and the probable origin of this disease in antiquity", *Journal of the Royal Asiatic Society* (1977) 140-144
AHDO	*Archives d'histoire du droit oriental*
AHw	von Soden, Wolfram. *Akkadisches Handwörterbuch*, 1959-1981
Al-Rawi *1982*	Al-Rawi, Farouk N. H. "Assault and Battery", *Sumer* 38 (1982) 117-120 [Edition of Haddad 116]
Alt *1934*	Alt, Albrecht. *Die Ursprünge des israelitischen Rechts*, 1934
ANET	*Ancient Near Eastern Texts Relating to the Old Testament*, ed. J. B. Pritchard, 1st ed. 1950; 2nd ed. 1955; 3rd ed. 1969
AO	*Der alte Orient*
AO	Tablets in the Musée du Louvre
Arch. Or.	Archiv Orientalní
ARM	*Archives royales de Mari.*
Artzi *1984*	Artzi, Pinhas. "Ideas and Practices of International Coexistence in the Third Millennium B.C.E.", *Bar-Ilan Studies in History* 2 (1984) 25-39
B	Letters from Mari, in the Louvre
Bengtson *1962*	Bengtson, Hermann. *Die Staatsverträge des Altertums* II, *Die Verträge der griechisch-römischen Welt von 700 bis 338 v. Chr.*, 1962
Billeter *1898*	Billeter, Gustav. *Geschichte des Zinsfusses im griechisch-römischen Altertum bis auf Justinian*, 1898

Biondi *1954*	Biondi, Biondo. *Diritto romano cristiano*, vol. III, 1954
Bi. Or.	*Bibliotheca Orientalis*
Birot *1980*	Birot, Maurice. "Fragment de rituel de Mari relatif au *kispum*", in *Death in Mesopotamia*, ed. B. Alster (1980) 139-150
BM	Texts in the British Museum
Boyer *1958*	Boyer, Georges. ARM VIII: *Textes Juridiques*, 1958
Brecht *1962*	Brecht, Christoph Heinrich. *Zur Haftung der Schiffer im antiken Recht*, 1962
Burrows *1938*	Burrows, Millar. *The Basis of Israelite Marriage*, 1938
CAD	*The Assyrian Dictionary of the Oriental Institute of the University of Chicago*, 1956

A/i	1964
A/ii	1968
B	1965
D	1959
E	1958
G	1956
Ḫ	1956
I/J	1960
K	1971
L	1973
M/i	1977
M/ii	1977
N/i	1980
N/ii	1980
Q	1982
S	1984
Ṣ	1962
Z	1961

Cardascia *1958* Cardascia, Guillaume. "Le statut de l'étranger dans la Mésopotamie ancienne", *Recueils de la société Jean Bodin* 9 (1958) 105-117

Cardascia *1969* ——— *Les lois assyriennes*, 1969

Cardascia *1979* ——— "La place du talion dans l'histoire du droit pénal à la lumière des droits du Proche-Orient ancien", in *Mélanges offerts à Jean Dauvillier* (1979) 169-183

Cassin *1969* Cassin, Elena. "Pouvoirs de la femme et structures familiales", RA 63 (1969) 121-148

CH Code of Hammurabi

Christian *1933* Christian, Viktor. WZKM 40 (1933) 146-147 [Review of Lutz *1931*]

C.I. Codex Iustinianus

Civil *1965* Civil, Miguel. "New Sumerian Law Fragments", in *Studies in Honor of Benno Landsberger* (1965) 1-12

Clay *1915* Clay, Albert Tobias. *Miscellaneous Inscriptions in the Yale Babylonian Collection*, vol. I, 1915

CT Cuneiform Texts from Babylonian Tablets, in the British Museum

Daube *1944/1945* Daube, David. "Some Forms of Old Testament Legislation", *Abstract of Proceedings of the Oxford Society of Historical Theology* (1944/1945) 39-42

Daube *1947* ——— *Studies in Biblical Law*, 1947

Daube *1956* ——— *Forms of Roman Legislation*, 1956

Daube *1961* ——— "Direct and Indirect Causation in Biblical Law", VT 11 (1961) 249-269

David *1927* David, Martin. *Die Adoption im altbabylonischen Recht*, 1927

David *1934* —— *Vorm en wezen van de huwelijkssluiting naar de oud-oostersche rechtsopvatting*, 1934

David *1949* —— *Een nieuw-ontdekte babylonische wet uit de tijd vóór Hammurabi*, 1949

David, *1950* —— "The Codex Hammurabi and its Relation to the Provisions of Law in Exodus", *Oudtestamentische Studien* 7 (1950) 149-178

Diakonoff *1956* Diakonoff, Igor Mikhailovich. "*muškenum* i Povinostnoe Zemlevladenie na Tsarskoi Zemle pri Hammurabi", *Symbolae Raphaeli Taubenschlag Dedicatae* (= *Eos* 48/1 [1956] 37-62 [with English summary])

Diamond *1957* Diamond, Arthur Sigismund. "An Eye for an Eye", *Iraq* 19 (1957) 151-155

Donner-Röllig *1962* Donner, Herbert und Röllig, Wolfgang. *Kanaanäische und aramäische Inschriften*, 1962

Driver *1972* Driver, Godfrey Rolles. *Journal of the Royal Asiatic Society* (1972) 57-58 [Review of YLE]

Driver-Miles *1935* Driver, Godfrey Rolles and Miles, John. *The Assyrian Laws*, 1935

Driver-Miles *1952* —— *The Babylonian Laws* I:*Legal Commentary*, 1952

Driver-Miles *1955* —— *The Babylonian Laws* II: *Text, Translation, Philological Notes, Glossary*, 1955

Edzard *1957* Edzard, Dietz Otto. *Die "zweite Zwischenzeit" Babyloniens*, 1957

Edzard *1960* —— "Sumerer und Semiten in der frühen Geschichte Mesopotamiens", *Genava* 8 (1960) 241-258

Eger *1914* Eger, Otto. "Raptus", in RE, *Zweite Reihe, erster Halbband* (1914) col. 250-251

Eichler *1987* | Eichler, Barry L. "Literary Structure in the Laws of Eshnunna", in *Language, Literature and History: Philological and Historical Studies presented to Erica Reiner* (1987) 71-84 [Could not be utilized in this volume]

Eilers *1932* | Eilers, Wilhelm "Die Gesetzesstele Chamurabis", *Der alte Orient* 31, 3/4 (1932)

Eisser-Lewy | Eisser, Georg und Lewy, Julius. *Die altassyrischen Rechtsurkunden vom Kültepe*, 1930-1935

Ellis *1974* | Ellis, Maria de J. "The Division of Property at Tell Harmal", JCS 26 (1974) 133-153

Erdmann *1934* | Erdmann, Walter. *Die Ehe im alten Griechenland*, 1934

Evans *1963* | Evans, D. G. "The Incidence of Labour-Service in the Old Babylonian Period", JAOS 83 (1963) 20-26

Falkenstein *1956* | Falkenstein, Adam. *Die neusumerischen Gerichtsurkunden* II, 1956

Falkowitz *1978* | Falkowitz, Robert S. "Paragraph 59 of the 'Laws of Eshnunna'", RA 72 (1978) 79-80

Finet *1959* | Finet, André. "Une affaire de disette dans un district du royaume de Mari", RA 53 (1959) 57-69

Finet *1973* | ——— *Le Code de Hammurapi*, 1973

Finkelstein *1961* | Finkelstein, Jacob Joel. "Ammi-ṣaduqa's Edict and the Babylonian 'Law Codes'", JCS 15 (1961) 91-104

Finkelstein *1965* | ——— "Some New *misharum* Material and its Implications", in *Studies in Honor of Benno Landsberger* (1965) 233-246

Finkelstein *1966* | ——— "Sex Offenses in Sumerian Laws", JAOS 86 (1966) 355-372

Finkelstein *1967a* _____ "A Late Old Babylonian Copy of the Laws of Hammurapi", JCS 21 (1967) 39-48

Finkelstein *1967b* _____ *"ana bit emim šasu"*, RA 61 (1967) 127-136

Finkelstein *1968* _____ "Law in the Ancient Near East", *Encyclopaedia Biblica* V (1968) cols. 588-614 (Hebrew)

Finkelstein *1969a* _____ "The Laws of Ur-Nammu", JCS 22 (1969) 66-82

Finkelstein *1969b* _____ "The Laws of Ur-Nammu", in ANET *1969:* 523-525 [Translation not fully identical with that in Finkelstein *1969a*]

Finkelstein *1969c* _____ "The Edict of Ammi-ṣaduqa: a New Text", RA 63 (1969) 45-64

Finkelstein *1970* _____ "On Some Recent Studies in Cuneiform Law", JAOS 90 (1970) 243-256

Finkelstein *1981* _____ "The Ox that Gored", *Transactions of the American Philosophical Society* 71/2, 1981

Förtsch *1917* Förtsch, Wilhelm. *"šakanakku"*, ZA 31 (1917) 160-162

Friedrich *1959* Friedrich, Johannes. *Die hethitischen Gesetze*, 1959

Furlani *1935* Furlani, Giuseppe. *Rivista degli studi orientali* 15 (1935) 377-380 [Review of David *1934*]

Gadd *1963* Gadd, Cyril Jones. "Two Sketches from the Life at Ur", *Iraq* 25 (1963) 177-188

Gadd *1971* _____ "The Dynasty of Agade and the Gutian Invasion", in *Cambridge Ancient History*, 3rd ed., vol. I, part 2 (1971) 417-463

"Babylonia, c. 2120 — 1800 B.C.", *ibid.*, 595-643

GAG von Soden, Wolfram. *Grundriss der akkadischen Grammatik, Analecta Orientalia* 33 (1952)

Garelli *1963* Garelli, Paul. *Les Assyriens en Cappadoce*, 1963

Garelli *1964* —— "Tablettes cappadociennes de collections diverses", RA 58 (1964) 111-136

Gelb *1955* Gelb, Ignace Jay. *Old Akkadian Inscriptions in Chicago Natural History Museum*, 1955

Gevirtz *1961* Gevirtz, Stanley. "West-Semitic and the Problem of Origins of Hebrew Law", VT 11 (1961) 137-158

Goetze *1949* Goetze, Albrecht, "Mesopotamian Laws and the Historian", JAOS 69 (1949) 115-120

Goetze *1950b* —— "The Hittite Laws", in ANET, 1st ed. (1950) 188-197

Goetze *1957a* —— *Kulturgeschichte Kleinasiens,* 2. Aufl., 1957

Goetze *1957b* —— JCS 11 (1957) 79-82 [Review of CAD G, Ḫ]

Goetze *1958* —— "Fifty Old Babylonian Letters from Harmal", *Sumer* 14 (1958) 3-78

Greenberg *1968* Greenberg, Moshe. "Idealism and Practicality in Numbers 35: 4-5 and Ezekiel 48", JAOS 88 (1968) 59-66

Greengus *1966* Greengus, Samuel. "Old Babylonian Marriage Ceremonies and Rites", JCS 20 (1966) 55-72

Greengus *1969* —— "The Old Babylonian Marriage Contract", JAOS 89 (1969) 505-532

Greengus *1979* —— *Old Babylonian Tablets from Ishchali and the Vicinity*, 1979

Greengus *1986* —— *Studies in Ishchali Documents,* 1986

Gurney *1949* Gurney, Oliver Robert. "Texts from Durkurigalzu", *Iraq* 11 (1949) 131-149

Gurney *1983* —— *The Middle Babylonian Legal and Economic Texts from Ur*, 1983

Gurney *1987* —— WZKM 77 (1987) 195-198 [Review of Kraus *1984*]

Haase *1961* Haase, Richard. "Über die Berücksichtigung der Mitwirkung des Verletzten bei der Entstehung eines Schadens in keilschriftlichen Rechtssammlungen", *Iura* 12 (1961) 222-226

Haase *1963b* _____ "Körperliche Strafen in den altorientalischen Rechtssammlungen", RIDA 10 (1963) 55-75

Haase *1965* _____ "Keilschriftrechtliche Miszellen VI. Zum Recht von Ešnunna", ZverglRw 67 (1965) 143-148

Haase *1967* _____ "Die Behandlungen von Tierschäden in den Keilschriftrechten", RIDA 14 (1967) 11-65

Haase *1983* _____ WdO 14 (1983) 245-247 [Review of Innocenzo Cardellini, *Die biblischen "Sklaven"-Gesetze im Lichte des keilschriftlichen Sklavenrechts*, 1981]

Hallo *1964* Hallo, William Wolfgang. "The Slandered Bride", in *Studies Presented to A. Leo Oppenheim* (1964) 95-105

Harris *1955* Harris, Rivkah. 'The Archive of the Sin Temple in Khafajah" [Appendix: Copies by Thorkild Jacobsen] JCS 9 (1955) 31-120

Hartmann *1956* Hartmann, Louis Francis. *Catholic Biblical Quarterly* 18 (1956) 439-442 [Review of Goetze *1956*]

HG Kohler-Koschaker-Peiser-Ungnad, *Hammurabis Gesetz* I-VI, 1904-1923

Hirsch *1969* Hirsch, Hans. "Zur Frage der t-Formen in den keilschriftlichen Gesetzestexten", in *lišan mihurti — Festschrift Wolfram Freiherr von Soden ... gewidmet* (1969) 119-131

HL Hittite Laws

IM Texts in the Iraq Museum

Imparati *1964* Imparati, Fiorella. *Le leggi ittite*, 1964

ITT Inventaire des Tablettes de Tello, 1910-1921

Jackson *1973* Jackson, Bernard S. "The Problem of Exod. XXI 22-25", VT 23 (1973) 273-304

Jackson *1974* ____ "The Goring Ox Again", JJP 18 (1974) 55-93

Jackson *1982* ____ "Legal Drafting in the Ancient Near East in the Light of Modern Theories of Cognitive Development", in *Mélanges à la mémoire de Marcel-Henri Provost* (1982) 49-66

Jackson *1984* ____ "Distraint in the Laws of Eshnunna and Hammurabi", in *Studi in onore di Cesare Sanfilippo* V (1984) 409-419

JAOS *Journal of the American Oriental Society*

JCS *Journal of Cuneiform Studies*

Jean *1948* Jean, Charles François. "Lettres de Mari IV, transcrites et traduites", RA (1948) 53-78

JEOL *Jaarbericht Ex Oriente Lux*

JNES *Journal of Near Eastern Studies*

JSS *Journal of Semitic Studies*

Kaser *1971* Kaser, Max. *Das römische Privatrecht* I, 2. Aufl., 1971

Kaser *1975* ____ *Das römische Privatrecht* II, 2. Aufl., 1975

Kilian *1963* Kilian, Rudolf. "Apodiktisches und kasuistisches Recht im Licht ägyptischer Analogien", *Biblische Zeitschrift* 7 (1963) 185-202

Klíma *1948* Klíma, Josef. "Au sujet de nouveaux textes juridiques de l'époque préhammurapienne", Arch. Or. 16 (1948) 326-333

Klíma *1950a* ____ "Über neuere Studien auf dem Gebiete des Keilschriftrechts", Arch. Or. 18/4 (1950) 351-366

Klíma *1950b* —— "The *PATRIA POTESTAS* in the Light of Newly Discovered pre-Hammurabian Sources of Law", *Journal of Juristic Papyrology* 4 (1950) 275-288

Klíma *1952* —— "Über neuere Studien auf dem Gebiete des Keilschriftrechtes III", Arch. Or. 20 (1952) 539-571

Klíma *1953a* —— "Il diritto ereditario secondo le fonti giuridiche di Eshnunna", *Iura* 4 (1953) 192-197

Klíma *1953b* —— "La posizione degli schiavi secondo le nuove leggi pre-hammurapiche", in *Studi in onore di Vinczenzo Arangio Ruiz* IV (1953) 225-240

Klíma *1953c* —— "Zu den neuentdeckten Gesetzesfragmenten von Ur-Nammu", Arch. Or. 21 (1953) 442-447

Klíma *1956a* —— "Su un'analogia babilonese del sc. Macedoniano", in *Studi in onore di Ugo Enrico Paoli* (1956) 433-441

Klíma *1956b* —— "Intorno al principio del taglione nelle leggi pre-Hammurapiche", in *Studi in onore di Pietro De Francisci* III (1956) 2-13

Klíma *1957* —— Bi. Or. 14 (1957) 167-171 [Review of Goetze *1956*]

Klíma *1966* —— "[Gesetze] 5. Die Gesetze von Ešnunna", in RLA III, 4. Lief. (1966) 252-255

Klíma *1970* —— ZSS 87 (1970) 447-456 [Review of YLE]

Klíma *1976* —— "Im ewigen Banne der *MUŠKENUM*-Problematik?", *Acta Antiqua Academiae Scientiarum Hungaricae* 22 (1974, publ. 1976) 267-274

Kohler-Ungnad *1913* Kohler, Josef und Ungnad, Arthur. *Assyrische Rechtsurkunden*, 1913

Korošec *1938* Korošec, Viktor. "Ehe (in Ḫatti)", in RLA II (1938) 293-296

Korošec *1951* _____ "Über die Bedeutung der Gesetzbücher von Ešnunna und von Isin für die Rechtsentwicklung in Mesopotamien und Kleinasien" in *Proceedings of the 22nd Congress of Orientalists*, Istanbul 1951 (publ. 1957) 83-91

Korošec *1954* _____ "Das Gesetzbuch der Stadt Eshnunna und das Gesetzbuch von Lipit-Ishtar", *Iura* 5 (1954) 366-372

Korošec *1964* _____ "Keilschriftrecht", in *Handbuch der Orientalistik, Erste Abteilung, Ergänzungsband* III (1964) 49-219

Korošec *1968* _____ "Über die neuesten sumerischen Gesetzesfragmente aus Ur", Bi. Or. 25 (1968) 286-289

Koschaker *1917* Koschaker, Paul. *Rechtsvergleichende Studien zur Gesetzgebung Hammurapis, Königs von Babylon*, 1917

Koschaker *1932* _____ OLZ 35 (1932) col. 399-401 [Review of E. A. Speiser, "New Kirkuk Documents relating to Family Laws", AASOR 10, 1928/29]

Koschaker *1936* _____ "Randnotizen zu neueren keilschriftlichen Rechtsurkunden", ZA 43 (1936) 196-232

Koschaker *1950* _____ "Eheschliessung und Kauf nach antiken Rechten", Arch. Or. 18/3 (1950) 210-296

Koschaker *1951* _____ "Zur Interpretation des Art. 59 des Codex Bilalama", JCS 5 (1951) 104-122

Kramer *1963* Kramer, Samuel Noah. *The Sumerians*, 1963

Kraus *1947* Kraus, Fritz Rudolf. "Weitere Texte zur babylonischen Physiognomatik", *Orientalia* 16 (1947) 172-206

Kraus *1951* _____ *Nippur und Isin nach altbabylonischen Rechtsurkunden*, 1951

Kraus *1958* ____ *Ein Edikt des Königs Ammi-ṣaduqa von Babylon*, 1958

Kraus *1959/1962* ____ "Briefschreibübungen im altbabylonischen Schulunterricht", JEOL 16 (1959/1962) 16-39

Kraus *1960* ____ "Ein zentrales Problem des altmesopotamischen Rechtes: Was ist der Codex Hammu-rabi?", *Genava* 8 (1960) 283-296

Kraus *1965* ____ "Ein Edikt des Königs Samsu-Iluna von Babylon", in *Studies in Honor of Benno Landsberger* (1965) 225-231

Kraus *1969* ____ "Erbrechtliche Terminologie im alten Mesopotamien", in *Essays on Oriental Laws of Succession* (1969) 18-57

Kraus *1973* ____ *Vom mesopotamischen Menschen der altbabylonischen Zeit und seiner Welt*, 1973

Kraus *1974a* ____ "Das altbabylonische Königstum", in *Le Palais et la royauté*, ed. Paul Garelli (1974) 235-261

Kraus *1974b* ____ "Altbabylonische Heiratsprobleme", RA 68 (1974) 111-120

Kraus *1976* ____ "Akkadische Wörter und Ausdrücke X, *napṭarum/bit napṭarim"*, RA 70 (1976) 165-172

Kraus *1979* ____ "Akkadische Wörter und Ausdrücke XII, *ṣimdatum/ṣimdat šarrim"*, RA 73 (1979) 51-62

Kraus *1984* ____ *Königliche Verfügungen in altbabylonischer Zeit*, 1984

Krückmann *1932* Krückmann, Oluf. "Die Beamten zur Zeit der ersten Dynastie von Babylon", RLA I (1932) 444-451

Kutscher *1954* Kutscher, Eduard Yehezkel. "New Aramaic Texts", JAOS 74 (1954) 233-248

Kunkel *1956* Kunkel, Wolfgang. "Auctoratus", *Symbolae Raphaeli Taubenschlag Dedicatae (= Eos* 48/3 [1956]) 207-226

Landsberger *1915* Landsberger Benno. "Bemerkungen zur altbabylonischen Briefliteratur", ZDMG 69 (1915) 491-528

Landsberger *1925* ____ "Assyrische Handelskolonien in Kleinasien aus dem dritten Jahrtausend", *Der alte Orient* 24/4, 1925

Landsberger *1939* ____ "Die babylonischen Termini für Gesetz und Recht", in *Symbolae ad iura Orientis antiqui pertinentes Paulo Koschaker dedicatae* (1939) 219-234

Landsberger *1954* ____ "Assyrische Königsliste und 'dunkles Zeitalter'", JCS 8 (1954) 31-45, 47-73, 106-133

Landsberger *1964* ____ "Einige unerkannt gebliebene oder verkannte Nomina im Akkadischen", WdO 3 (1964/1966) 48-79

Landsberger *1967* ____ "Akkadisch-hebräische Wortgleichungen", in *Hebräische Wortforschung. Festschrift zum 80. Geburtstag von Walter Baumgartner* (1967) 176-204

Landsberger *1968* ____ "Jungfräulichkeit: ein Beitrag zum Thema 'Beilager und Eheschliessung' (mit einem Anhang: Neue Lesungen und Deutungen im Gesetzbuch von Ešnunna)", in *Symbolae iuridicae et historicae Martino David dedicatae* II (1968) 41-105

Larsen *1974* Larsen, M. T. "The City and its King", in *Le palais et la royauté*, ed. Paul Garelli (1974) 285-300

Lautner *1936* Lautner, Julius Georg. *Altbabylonische Personenmiete und Erntearbeiterverträge*, 1936

LE Laws of Eshnunna

Leemans *1950a* Leemans, W. F. *The Old Babylonian Merchant*, 1950

Leemans *1950b* —— "The Rate of Interest in Old Babylonian Times", RIDA 5 (1950) 7-34

Leemans *1981/1982* —— "The Interpretation of Sec. 38 of the Laws of Eshnunna", JEOL 27 (1981/1982) 60-64

Levy *1927* Levy, Ernst. "Verschollenheit und Ehe in antiken Rechten", in *Gedächtnisschrift für Emil Seckel* (1927) 145-193

Lewy *1949* Lewy, Hildegard. "Studies in Assyro-Babylonian Mathematics and Metrology", *Orientalia* 18 (1949) 40-67, 137-170

Lewy *1959* —— "The Synchronism Assyria — Ešnunna — Babylon", WdO 2 (1959) 438-453

Lewy *1959* Lewy, Julius. "On Some Akkadian Expressions for 'Afterwards' and Related Notions", WdO 2 (1959) 432-437

LI Laws of Lipit-Ištar

Loewenstamm *1957* Loewenstamm, Shmuel Efraim. *Israel Exploration Journal* 7 (1957) 192-198 [Review of Goetze *1956*]

Loewenstamm *1962* —— "Adultery and Murder in Biblical Law and in Mesopotamian Law", *Beth Miqra* 13 (1962) 55-59 (Hebrew)

LU Laws of Ur-Nammu [Sections of LU are quoted as LUY, referring to Yildiz *1981*, respectively as LUF, referring to Finkelstein *1969*. When the two editions overlap, LUY is preferred, with LUF added in brackets]

Lutz *1930* Lutz, Henry Frederick. "The Verdict of a Trial Judge in a Case of Assault and Battery", *University of California Publications in Semitic Philology* 9 (1930) 379-381

Lutz *1931* —— *Legal and Economic Documents from Ashjâli*, 1931

MAH — Texts in the collection of the Musée d'Art et d'Histoire, Geneva

Mahler *1927* — Mahler, Eduard. "Zum Par. 128 des Kodex Hammurabi", AfO 4 (1927) 147-152

MAL — Middle Assyrian Laws

Malamat *1966* — Malamat, Abraham. "Prophetic revelations: new documents from Mari and the Bible", *Supplement to Vetus Testamentum* 15 (1966) 207-227

Matouš *1959* — Matouš, Lubor. Bi. Or. 16 (1959) 94-96 [Review of Kraus *1958*]

MDP — Mémoires de la délégation en Perse

Meek *1946* — Meek, Theophile James. "The Asyndeton Clause in the Code of Hammurabi", JNES 5 (1946) 64-72

Meek *1950* — —— "The Code of Hammurabi", in ANET (1950) 163-180 [Identical in later editions of ANET]

Miles-Gurney *1949* — Miles, John and Gurney, Oliver Robert. "The Laws of Eshnunna", Arch. Or. 17/2 (1949) 174-188

Mitteis *1891* — Mitteis, Ludwig. *Reichsrecht und Volksrecht in den östlichen Provinzen des römischen Kaiserreichs*, 1891

Mommsen *1899* — Mommsen, Theodor. *Römisches Strafrecht*, 1899

Moran *1957* — Moran, William Lambert. *Biblica*, 38 (1957) 216-221 [Review of Goetze *1956*]

Müller *1903* — Müller, David Heinrich. *Die Gesetze Hammurabis und ihr Verhältnis zur mosaischen Gesetzgebung sowie zu den 12 Tafeln*, 1903

N — Texts (from Nippur) in the University Museum, Philadelphia

NBC — Texts in the Babylonian Collection, Yale University Library

Nörr *1958* — Nörr, Dietrich. "Zum Schuldgedanken im altbabylonischen Strafrecht", ZSS 75 (1958) 1-31

Nougayrol *1950* — Nougayrol, Jean. "Textes hépatoscopiques d'époque ancienne conservés au Musée du Louvre" (III) RA 44 (1950) 1-44

Nougayrol *1952* — ____ "Un fragment oublié du Code (en) sumérien", RA 46 (1952) 53-54

OLZ — *Orientalistische Literaturzeitung*

Oppenheim *1933* — Oppenheim, Adolf Leo. "Die Rolle der t-Formen im Codex Ḫammurapi", WZKM 40 (1933) 181-220

Oppenheim *1955* — ____ "'Siege Documents' from Nippur", *Iraq* 17 (1955) 69-89

P — Texts in the Collection Peiser

Paul *1970* — Paul, Shalom Morton. *Studies in the Book of the Covenant in the Light of Cuneiform and Biblical Law*, 1970

Petschow *1954* — Petschow, Herbert. "Der Surrogationsgedanke im neubabylonischen Recht", RIDA 1 (1954) 125-171

Petschow *1958* — ____ ZSS 75 (1958) 381-388 [Review of Falkenstein *1956*]

Petschow *1960* — ____ ZSS 77 (1960) 408-414 [Review of Kraus *1958*]

Petschow *1961* — ____ ZA 54 (1961) 264-273 [Review of Goetze *1956*]

Petschow *1965a* — ____ "Zu den Stilformen antiker Gesetze und Rechtssammlungen" ZSS 82 (1965) 24-38

Petschow *1965b* ——— "Zur Systematik und Gesetzestechnik im Codex Hammurabi", ZA 57 (1965) 146-172

Petschow *1968a* ——— "Zur 'Systematik' in den Gesetzen von Eschnunna", in *Symbolae iuridicae et historicae Martino David dedicatae* II (1968) 131-143

Petschow *1968b* ——— "Neufunde zu keilschriftlichen Rechtssammlungen", ZSS 85 (1968) 1-29

Petschow *1973a* ——— "Altorientalische Parallelen zur spätrömischen Calumnia", ZSS 90 (1973) 14-35

Petschow *1973b* ——— "Havarie", in RLA IV, 2./3. Lief. (1973) 233-237

Petschow *1975* ——— "Hehlerei", in RLA IV, 4./5. Lief. (1975) 247-251

Poebel *1915* Poebel, Arno. "Eine altbabylonische Abschrift der Gesetzessammlung Hammurabis aus Nippur", OLZ 18 (1915) 161-169, 193-200, 225-230, 257-265

van Praag *1945* van Praag, A. *Droit matrimonial assyro-babylonien,* 1945

van Praag *1950* ——— Bi. Or. 7 (1950) 80-81 [Review of David *1949*]

Preiser *1969* Preiser, Wolfgang. "Zur rechtlichen Natur der altorientalischen 'Gesetze'", in *Festschrift für Karl Engisch* (1969) 17-36

RA *Revue d'Assyriologie et d'Archéologie orientale*

Rabinowitz *1959* Rabinowitz, Jacob Johanan. "Sections 15-16 of the Laws of Eshnunna and section 7 of the Code of Hammurabi", Bi. Or. 16 (1959) 97

RE Paulys *Realencyclopädie der classischen Altertumswissenschaft*, neue Bearbeitung von G. Wissowa, W. Kroll, K. Mittelhaus, K. Ziegler

Rein *1844* Rein, Wilhelm. *Kriminalrecht der Römer*, 1844

Renger *1973* Renger, Johannes. "Who are all those People?", *Orientalia* 42 (1973) 259-273

Renger *1977* _____ "Wrongdoing and its Sanctions — On 'Criminal' and 'Civil' Law in the Old Babylonian Period", *Journal of the Economic and Social History of the Orient* 20 (1977) 65-75

Reschid *1965* Reschid, F. *Archiv des Nurušamaš und andere Darlehensurkunden aus der altbabylonischen Zeit*, 1965

RHD *Revue historique de droit français et étranger*

RIDA *Revue internationale des droits de l'antiquité*

RLA *Reallexikon der Assyriologie*, 1928 →

Römer *1982* Römer, Willem H. Ph. "Aus den Gesetzen des Königs Ur-Nammu von Ur", in TUAT I (1982) 17-23

Saarisalo *1934* Saarisalo, Aapeli. "New Kirkuk Documents relating to Slaves", *Studia Orientalia* 5/3, 1934

Sachau *1914* Sachau, Eduard. *Syrische Rechtsbücher* III, 1914

San Nicolò *1922* San Nicolò, Mariano. *Die Schlussklauseln der altbabylonischen Kauf- und Tauschverträge*, 1922

San Nicolò *1931* _____ *Beiträge zur Rechtsgeschichte im Bereiche der keilschriftlichen Rechtsquellen*, 1931

San Nicolò *1932* _____ "Parerga Babylonica V", Arch. Or. 4 (1932) 189-192

San Nicolò *1949* _____ "Rechtsgeschichtliches zum Gesetze des Bilalama von Ešnunna", *Orientalia* 18 (1949) 258-262

San Nicolò *1950a* _____ "Eshnunna", in "Rassegna di diritto cuneiforme", SDHI 16 (1950) 440-442

San Nicolò *1950b* ["Das Gesetzbuch Lipit-Ištars", I. A. Falkenstein, "Philologisches zum Gesetzbuch", *Orientalia* 19

(1950) 103-111;] II. M. San Nicolò, "Rechtsgeschichtliches zum Gesetzbuch", *ibid.*, 111-118

San Nicolò *1954* ——— "Raccolta di leggi di Ešnunna e codice di Lipit-Ištar", in "Rassegna di diritto cuneiforme II", SDHI 20 (1954) 502-504

Sauren *1986* Sauren, Herbert. "Le mariage selon le Code d'Eshnunna", RIDA 33 (1986) 45-86

Schorr *1913* Schorr, Moses. *Urkunden des altbabylonischen Zivil- und Prozessrechts*, 1913

SDHI *Studia et Documenta Historiae et Iuris*

Seif *1938* Seif, Miriam. *Über die altbabylonischen Rechts- und Wirtschaftsurkunden aus Iščâlí*, 1938

van Selms *1950a* van Selms, Adrianus. "The Goring Ox in Babylonian and Biblical Law", Arch. Or. 18/4 (1950) 321-330

van Selms *1950b* ——— "The Best Man and Bride — From Sumer to St. John, with a new Interpretation of Judges Chapters 14-15", JNES 9 (1950) 65-75

Sick *1984* Sick, Ulrich. *Die Tötung eines Menschen und ihre Ahndung in den keilschriftlichen Rechtssammlungen unter Berücksichtigung rechtsvergleichender Aspekte*, 1984

Simmons *1959* Simmons, Stephen D. "Early Old Babylonian Tablets from Ḫarmal and Elsewhere", JCS 13 (1959) 71-93, 105-119

1960 (continued) JCS 14 (1960) 23-32, 49-55, 75-87

[continued JCS 15 (1961) 49-58, 81-83]

von Soden *1933* von Soden, Wolfram. "Der hymnisch-epische Dialekt des Akkadischen. vii. Die Präfixe der 3. Person Singularis beim Verbum", ZA 41 (1933) 148-151 von Soden *1949* ____ "Kleine Beiträge zum Verständnis der Gesetze Hammurabis und Bilalamas" Arch. Or. 17/2 (1949) 359-373

von Soden *1956* ____ Bi. Or. 13 (1956) 32-34 [Review of Szlechter *1954*]

von Soden *1958* ____ "Neubearbeitungen der babylonischen Gesetzessammlungen", OLZ 53 (1958) 517-527

von Soden *1964* ____ "*muškenum* und die Mawālī des frühen Islam", ZA 56 (1964) 133-141

von Soden *1978* ____ Bi. Or. 32 (1978) 206-208 [Review of AbB vii]

von Soden *1985* ____ ZA 75 (1985) 133-135 [Review of Kraus *1984*]

Sollberger *1980* Sollberger, Edmond. "The so-called Treaty between Ebla and 'Ashur'", *Studi Eblaiti* III/9 (1980) 129-155

Speiser *1958* Speiser, Ephraim Avigdor. "The *muškenum*", *Orientalia* 27 (1958) 19-28

Szlechter *1949* Szlechter, Émile. "Essai d'explication des clauses: *muttatam gullubu, abbuttam šakanu* et *abbuttam gullubu*", Arch. Or. 17/2 (1949) 391-418

Szlechter *1952* ____ "Nouveaux textes législatifs babyloniens", *Iura* 3 (1952) 244-249

Szlechter *1956a* ____ "Revue critique des droits cunéiformes", SDHI 22 (1956) 478-499

Szlechter *1956b* ____ "La saisie illégale dans les lois d'Ešnunna et dans le Code de Hammurabi", in *Studi in onore di Pietro de Francisci* I (1956) 272-281

Szlechter *1958a* ____ *Tablettes juridiques de la 1re dynastie de Babylone*, 1958

Szlechter *1958b* ____ RA 52 (1958) 188-189 [Review of Goetze *1956*]

Szlechter *1959*	——— "Revue critique des droits cunéiformes IV", SDHI 25 (1959) 485-514
Szlechter *1962*	——— "La peine capitale en droit babylonien", in *Studi in onore di Emilio Betti* IV (1962) 146-178
Szlechter *1963a*	——— "Effets de la captivité en droit assyro-babylonien", RA 57 (1963) 181-192
Szlechter *1963b*	——— *Tablettes juridiques et administratives de la IIIe dynastie d'Ur et de la Ire dynastie de Babylone*, 1963
Szlechter *1965*	——— "Effets de l'absence (volontaire) en droit assyro-babylonien", *Orientalia* 34 (1965) 289-311
Szlechter *1967a*	——— "Des droits successoraux dérivés de l'adoption en droit babylonien", RIDA 14 (1967) 79-106
Szlechter *1967b*	——— "Nouveaux textes législatifs sumériens", RA 61 (1967) 105-126
Szlechter *1970*	——— "L'interprétation des lois babyloniennes", RIDA 17 (1970) 81-115
Taubenschlag *1929*	Taubenschlag, Rafael. "Die *materna potestas* im gräko-ägyptischen Recht", ZSS 49 (1929) 115-128
Taubenschlag *1955*	——— *The Law of Greco-Roman Egypt in the Light of the Papyri*, 2nd ed., 1955
Taubenschlag *1959*	——— *Opera Minora* I, 1959
TCL	Textes cunéiformes du Louvre
Thureau-Dangin *1907*	Thureau-Dangin, François. *Alt-sumerische und -akkadische Königsinschriften*, 1907
TRG	*Tijdschrift voor Rechtsgeschiedenis*
TUAT	*Texte aus der Umwelt des Alten Testaments*, 1982→
U	Texts from Ur, in the British Museum
UCBC	Texts in the University of California Babylonian Collection

UM — Texts in the Collections of the University Museum, Philadelphia

VAB — *Vorderasiatische Bibliothek*

VAT — Texts in the Collections of the Staatliche Museen, Berlin

VT — *Vetus Testamentum*

Walther *1917* — Walther, Arnold. *Das altbabylonische Gerichtswesen*, 1917

WdO — *Die Welt des Orients*

Westbrook *1985a* — Westbrook, Raymond. "Biblical and Cuneiform Law Codes", *Revue biblique* 92 (1985) 247-264

Westbrook *1985b* — ____ "The Price Factor in the Redemption of Land", RIDA 32 (1985) 97-127

Westbrook OBML — ____ *Old Babylonian Marriage Law* (forthcoming)

Westbrook-Wilcke *1977* — Westbrook, Raymond and Wilcke, Claus. "The Liability of an Innocent Purchaser of Stolen Goods in Early Mesopotamian Law", AfO 25 (1974-77) 111-121

Wilcke *1968* — Wilcke, Claus. "Einige Bemerkungen zum Par. 29 des Codex Lipitešṭar", WdO 4 (1968) 153-162

Williams *1964* — Williams, James G. "Concerning One of the Apodictic Formulas", VT 14 (1964) 484-489

Winckler *1903* — Winckler, Hugo. "Die Gesetze Hammurabis", *Der alte Orient* 4/IV, 1903

WZKM — *Wiener Zeitschrift für die Kunde des Morgenlandes*

Yaron *1959a* — Yaron, Reuven. "Jewish Law and Other Legal Systems of Antiquity", JSS 4 (1959) 308-331

Yaron *1959b* — ____ "Redemption of Persons in the Ancient Near East", RIDA 6 (1959) 155-176

Yaron *1960* _____ *Gifts in Contemplation of Death in Jewish and Roman Law*, 1960

Yaron *1961* _____ *Introduction* to the *Law of the Aramaic Papyri*, 1961

Yaron *1962a* _____ "Vitae necisque potestas", TRG (1962) 243-251

Yaron *1962b* _____ "Forms in the Laws of Eshnunna", RIDA 9 (1962) 137-153

Yaron *1963a* _____ "Matrimonial Mishaps at Eshnunna", JSS 8 (1963) 1-16

Yaron *1963b* _____ "A Royal Divorce at Ugarit", *Orientalia* 32 (1963) 21-31

Yaron *1963c* _____ "Duabus sororibus coniunctio", RIDA 10 (1963) 115-136

Yaron *1963d* _____ "On Section II 57 (= 72) of the Hittite Laws", RIDA 10 (1963) 137-146

Yaron *1963e* _____ "Divortium inter absentes", TRG 31 (1963) 54-68

Yaron *1964* _____ "De divortio varia", TRG 32 (1964) 533-557

Yaron *1965* _____ "The Rejected Bridegroom", *Orientalia* 34 (1965) 23-29

Yaron *1966a* _____ "SI ADORAT FURTO", TRG 34 (1966) 510-524

Yaron *1966b* _____ "The Goring Ox", *Israel Law Review* 1 (1966) 396-406

Yaron *1968* _____ "SI PATER FILIUM TER VENUM DUIT", TRG 36 (1968) 57-72

Yaron *1970* _____ "The Middle-Assyrian Laws and the Bible", *Biblica* 51 (1970) 549-557 [Review of Cardascia *1969*]

Yaron *1980* ____ "Biblical Law. Prolegomena", in *Jewish Law in Legal History and the Modern World*, ed. Bernard S. Jackson (1980) 27-44

Yaron *1985a* ____ "Quelques remarques sur les nouveaux fragments des lois d'Ur-Nammu", RHD 63 (1985) 131-142

Yaron *1985b* ____ "Akkadische Rechtssammlungen in deutscher Übersetzung", *Rechtshistorisches Journal* 4 (1985) 23-33

Yaron *1986* ____ "The Climactic Tricolon", *Journal of Jewish Studies* 37 (1986) 153-159

Yildiz *1981* Yildiz, Fatma. "A Tablet of Codex Ur-Nammu from Sippar", *Orientalia* 50 (1981) 87-97

YOS Yale Oriental Series, Babylonian Texts

ZA *Zeitschrift für Assyriologie und verwandte Gebiete*

ZDMG *Zeitschrift der Deutschen Morgenländischen Gesellschaft*

ZSS *Zeitschrift der Savigny-Stiftung für Rechtsgeschichte, Romanistische Abteilung*

ZverglRw *Zeitschrift für vergleichende Rechtswissenschaft*

INDEX OF SOURCES

A. Ancient Near Eastern Sources B. Biblical Sources
C. Talmudic Sources D. Greek Sources
E. Roman Sources F. Varia

C. Talmudic Sources

(a) Mishnah

(b) Tosefta

(c) Palestinian Talmud

(d) Babylonian Talmud

F. Varia

AKKADIAN WORDS AND PHRASES

abbuttum 162ff.
abbutum 158
(*abum*) *abiša u ummiša* 156ff.
aḫazum 173, 213, 219
aḫizanum 181f., 188ff.
alakum (*warki*) 214f., 218-221
(*alum*) *alšu u belšu* 115ff.
amtum 113, 161ff., 165ff., 276ff.
amat ekallim 168
ana 40, 120, 226
(*asakkum*) *asakkam akalum* 110
aššatum 25, 201ff., 283f.
(*awatum*) *awat napištim* 120
awilum 132-155 [*passim*]
awilum ša 106, 109f.
mar awilim 146ff., 155
mar awilim la zizu 158ff.
marat awilim 146ff., 155-158
warad awilim 147
awum 128

babtum 118f.
balaṭum: see *matum*
(*belum*) *alšu u belšu* 115ff.
bel tertim 118
biblum 174, 196
(*bitum*) *bit emim* 194f.
bit emutim 194f.

dababum 128
(*dinum*) *dinam šuḫuzum* 128f
din napištim 120, 259

egum 248, 251
ekallum 114f., 128, 168
ekallum u muškenum 26, 133, 143, 146
(*epešum*) *še'am ana kaspim* 244
(*erebum*) *ana bitišu irub* 173, 180

ibrum 58, 181, 198f
ina 40, 57
inuma 102f.
iwitum 67

kalbum šegum 300
kannum 163
kašum 58, 191, 197f.
kirrum 59, 173, 201f.
kunnum 130
kurullum 50, 273

-ma 39, 42
mad/ṭum 52f., 162
(*martum*) *marat awilim* 146f., 155-158
(*marum*)
mar awilim 146f., 160
mar awilim la zizu 158ff.
mar šiprim 164
maškanum 163
(*matum*) *imat ul iballuṭ* 259ff.
šumutum 267
meḫeṣ letim 120, 265, 285ff.
(*meḫrum*) *ana meḫrišu* 236
mudum 160, 235

GLOSSARY

The glossary is that of the text, as given in Chapter II, but the heading is omitted. The number of the section is printed in bold type; the first line reference (before the stroke) is to Tablet A, the second (after the stroke) to Tablet B. Thus, **38** 24/7 refers to a word occurring in sec. 38, in line 24 of Tablet A, line 7 of Tablet B. The letter H stands for Haddad 116. Where a word occurs only in one of the tablets, that tablet is indicated by the stroke, following the number or preceding it. Thus, **38** 24/ would refer to sec. 38, line 24 of Tablet A; **38** /7 to sec. 38, line 7 of Tablet B. For the sake of simplicity we have dispensed with the number of the column, trusting that this will cause no inconvenience in the use of the glossary.

abatum — "to flee": **30** 46/8
abbuttum — "slave mark" (?): **51** 8/12; **52** 12/16
abullum — "gate": written KÁ.GAL: **51** 9/13; **52** 11/15
abum — "father": **25** 28/; **26** 30/; **27**/ 32/, 33/; /**28** 35/
adi — "up to": **15** /11; **48** 42/1
agrum — "hired man": written LÚ.ḪUNGÁ: **9** 30/; **11** 36/
aḫazum — "to take, seize": /**18** /16; **27**/ 32/; /**28** 36/; **29** /6; **30** /9; **59** 30/; [*šuḫuzum* — "to cause to seize":] **48** 43/2
aḫizanum — "marrier": **18** /17
aḫum — "brother": **38** 24/8
alakum — "to go": **11** 37/; **17**/ 4/15; /**18** /17; **41** 31/15; **59** 32/
alpum — "ox": written GUD: **3** 21/; **40** 28/12; **50** 4/7; **53** 13[2]/17[2], 14[2]/18[2], 15/; **54** 15/, 16/, 17/
alum — "town": written URU.KI: **30** /8; written syllabically: **30** 45/
amarum — "to see": **33** 8/17
amtum — "slave woman": written GEMÉ: **15** /10; **22** 16[2]/, 18/; **23**/ 20/, 21[2]/; **31** /11, /12; **33** 6/16; **34**/ 9/19; /**35** 12/22; **40** 28/12; **49** /4, /5[2]; **50** /7; **51** 7/11; **52** 10/14

ana — "to, for": **1** 8ff. [10]/; **9** 30[2]/; **17**/ 2/13, 4/14, /15; /**18** /16, /17; **19** 8/21; **20** 10/, 11/; **21** 13/; **23**/ 21/; **25** 26/, 27/; **26** 29/; **27**/ 33/; /**28** 35/; **30** /10; **32** /13[2]; **33** 6/16; **34**/ 10[2]/20[2]; /**35** 13/23; **36**/ 14/24, 14/25; **38** /7; **39** 26/10; **48** 42/, /3; **50** /8; **52** 13/16 **54**/ 16/ **56**/ 20/; **58** 25/
appum — "nose": **42** 32/17
aptum — "window": **36**/ 16/26
arkum — "long" **29** 41/
aššatum — "wife": written DAM: /**24** 23/; **27**/ 34/; /**28** 36/; **29** 44/; **59** 29/; written syllabically: **29** /6, /7; **30** /9, /10
atḫu — "brothers, companions": **38** 23/7
awatum — "word, matter": **48** 44/
awilum — "man": written LÚ: **6** 27/; **9** 30/; **12** 37/; **13** 41/; **16** 1/12; **17**/ 2/13; **19** 8/; **20** 10/; **21** 13/; **22** 15[2]/, 16/; **23**/ 19[2]/, 20/; **25** 26/; **26** 29[2]/; **27**/ 31[2]/; /**28** 36/; **29** 38/3; **30** 45/8; **31** /11[2]; **32** /13; **33** 6/16; **36**/ 14/24; /**37** 18/1, /1; **39** 25/10; **40** 28/12; **42** 32[2]/17[2]; **43** 35/21, 35/; **44** 36/; **46** 39/ /H5[2]; **47** 40/ /H7, 41/ /H8; **47A** H9, 10; **49** /4; **54**/ 17/; **56**/ 22/; **58** 27/; **59** 29/; written syllabically: **43** /21; **44**/ 36/23; **46** 39/
awum — "to speak": **50** 7/10

babtum — "ward, quarter": **54**/ 16/; **56**/ 20/; **58** 25/
babum — "door": written KÁ: /**37** /3
balaṭum — "to live": **12** 40/3; **13** /7; /**28** 37/
balṭum — "live": **53** 14/18
balum — "without": **26** 30/; **27**/ 31/; **51** 9/13
bašum — "to be, exist": **40** 28/12; **50** /6; **59** 31/
belum — "owner, master, lord": **9A** 34/; **17**/ /15; **22** 16/; **23**/ 21/; **30** /8; **31** /12; **33** 8/17; /**37** 19/2, 20/3; **39** 27/11; **50** /6; **51** 9/13; **52** 13/16; **53** 15/; **54** 16/20, 17/; **56**/ 20/, 23/; **58** 25/
bitum — "house": written É: **13** /4, 41/4, /6; **17**/ 2/13; /**18** /16; **23**/ 20/; /**24** 24/; **25** 26/; **27**/ 33/; **36**/ 15/25; /**37** 18/1, 19/2, 20/3, 20/; **39** 26/10, 27/11; **50** 6/9; **59** 31/
bušum — "goods": **36**/ 14/24, 16/27, 17/28; /**37** /1, 21[2]/4[2]

dananum — "to grow strong": [*dunnunum* — "to strengthen":] **58** 26/
dinum — "(law) case, litigation": /**24** 24/; **26** 31/; **48** 43/

eburum — "harvest": **20** 12/
egum — "to be negligent": **5** 25/

ekallum — "palace": written É.GAL: **34**/ 9/19, 11/21; /**35** 12/22, 13/23; **50** /8, 6/10
eleppum — "boat": written GIŠ.MÁ: **4** 23/; **5** 25/; **6** 27/
eli — "upon, over": **22** 15/, 17/; **23**/ 19/; /**24** 22/; /**37** 23/6; **50** /9
ellum — "sesame oil": written Ì.GIŠ: **1** 10/; **2** 18/; **15** /11
emum — "father-in-law": **17**/ /13; **25** 26[2]/
enequm — "to suck": [*šunuqum* — "to suckle":] **32** /13
enešum — "grow weak, become impoverished": **39** 25/10
epešum — "to make, do": **20** 11/; /**37** 22/5
epšum — "wrought": **1** 17/
eqlum — "field": written A.ŠÀ: **12** 37/
erebum — "to enter": /**18** /16; **52** 11/15
ereqqum — "wagon": written GIŠ.MAR.GÍD.DA: **3** 21/
erum — "copper": written URUDU: **1** 16/, 17/
eṣedum — "to harvest": **9** 30/, 32[3]/
eṣidum — "harvester": written ŠE.KUD.KIN: **7** 28/
Ešnunna — **50** 5/8; **51** 7/11, 9/13; **52** 11/15
etequm — "to pass": [*šutuqum* — "to let pass":] **50** /10
ezebum — "to leave, divorce": **59** 30/

ḫabatum — "to abduct, carry off forcibly": **29** 40[2]/4[2]
ḫalaqum — "to lose": /**37** 19/2, 21/4; [*ḫulluqum* — "to cause to lose":] **50** /7
ḫalqum — "lost": **50** 3/7, 4[2]/7[2]; [fem. *ḫaliqtum*:] **50** /7
ḫalašum — "to scrape off": **36**/ 15/26
ḫarranum — "road, journey": written KASKAL: **29** 38/3
ḫašaḫum — "to want, desire": **38** 24/8
ḫa-x-x — a part of the body: **46** 39/
ḫepum — "to break": /**28** 34/
ḫulqum — "loss": /**37** 19/2

idum — "hire": written Á: **3** 22[2]/; **4** 23/, 24/; **7** 28/, 29/; **8** 29/; **9A** 33/; **10** 34/, 35/; **11** 36/; **14** /8[2], /9
idum — "to know": [*šudum* — "to make known":] **54**/ 16/; **56**/ 21/; **58** 26/
igarum — "wall": **58** 25[2]/, 26/, 27/
Ì.ÍD — "river oil" (Akkadian reading uncertain): **1** 12/; **2** 20/
ik/g-x-x — circumstance in which injury was inflicted: **44** 36/
ilum — "god": written DINGIR: **22** 16/; /**37** 20/3
imerum — "donkey": written ANŠE: **10** 34/; **50** 4/7

inu — "in, at, from, out of": **6** 27/; **12** 37/, 38[2]/, 39/; **13** 41[3]/**4**[3], 42/6, /6; **15** /10; **17**/ 3/14; **19** 9/; **20** 12/; **23**/ 20/; /**24** 24/; **27**/ 33/; /**28** 36/; **29** 38/3, /5; /**37** 20/3; **38** 23/7; **44** 36/; **47** 40/ /H7; **47A** H9; **49** /4; **50** 6/9; **59** 31/

inum — "eye": written IGI: **42** 33/19

inuma — "when, whenever": **29** /7; **30** /9; **33** 7/17

iprum — "food (allowance)": written ŠE.BA: **32** /14

išten (fem. *ištiat*) — "one": written 1. KAM: **11** 37/; **27**/ 33/; **50** /9; written syllabically: **17**/ /14; **38** 23/7

ištu — "from": **48** 42/

išum — "to have": **22** 16/, 17/; **23**/ 19/; /**24** 22/; /**37** 23/6

itti — "with, together with": /**37** 18/1, 21/4; **50** 7/10; **52** 10/14

iwitum — "evil, wrong": /**37** 21/5

ktl or *qtl* — meaning uncertain: **46** /H8

kalbum — "dog": written UR.ZÍR: **56**/ 20/, 21/, 23/

kallatum — "bride, young woman": /**18** /17

kalum — "to detain": **23**/ 20/; /**24** 24/; **50** 6/9

kalum — "all, whole": **3** 23/; **4** 24/; **10** 35/

kannum — "band, slave mark": **51** 8/11; **52** 12/15

kanum — "to last, endure": [*kunnum* — "to establish, prove":] **40** 29/13

kaspum — "silver": written KÙ.BABBAR: **1** 8ff. [10]/; **3** 22/; **6** 28/; **7** 29/; **9** 30/, 32/; **11** 36/; **12** 39/; **13** /5; **14** /8, /9; **15** /11; **17**/ /15; **20** 11/; **21** 13/, 14/; **22** 17/; **31** /12; **38** /7; **39** 26/10; **42** 33/18, 34/20; **43** 36/22; **44**/ 37/ /H2; /**45** 38/ /H4; **46** 40/ /H6; **47** 41/ /H8; **47A** H11; **54**/ 18/; /**55** 19/; **56**/ 23/; /**57** 24/

kašum — "to wrong, reject": **25** 27/

kilallan — "both": **17**/ 3/14; **53** 15/19

kirrum — "marriage feast": **27**/ 32/; /**28** 35/

kirrum — "collarbone": **46** /H6

kullum — "to hold": **9** 31/

kurrum — "kor" (measure of capacity): written GUR: **1** 8/, 14/, 15/; **4** 23/; **18A** 7/20; **20** 12/

kurullum — "sheaf, crop(?)": **12** 38/, 39/

kuṣirum(?) — "band": **9A** 33/

la — "not": **6** 27/; **9** 31/, 32/; **16** 1/12; **22** 16/, 17/; **23**/ 19/; /**24** 22/; **27**/ 33/; **32** /14; **36**/ 15/25, 15/26, 16/26; /**37** 22/5; **40** 29/13; **50** 5/9; **54**/ 16/; **56**/ 21/; **58** 26/

laqatum — "to collect, plunder": /**37** 18/1

lequm — "to take": /**18** 5/18; **20** 13/; **21** 15/; /**35** 12/22, 13/22
letum — "cheek": **42** 34/20
lu — "or, either ... (or)": /**18** /17[2](?); **29** 40/4; **34**/ 10/19, 11/21
lu — "verily" (particle of asseveration): /**37** /4
lubuštum — "clothing": written SÍG.BA: **32** /14
madum(?) — "much": **15** /11 (?)
maḫarum — "to receive": **15** /11; **25** 28/
maḫaṣum — "to hit": **46** 39/ /H5
maḫirum — "price, rate": **41** 31/15
mala — "as much as": **5** 26/; /**18** 4/18; **22** 18/; **40** 28/12; **50** /6; **59** 31/
malaḫum — "boatman": written MÁ.LAḪ: **4** 24/; **5** 25/
malum — "become full': [*mullum* — "to pay in full':] **5** 26/; **38** 25/9
manum — "mina" (unit of weight): written MA.NA: **1** 13/, 16/, 17/; **31** /12; **32** /14; **42** 33/18, 33[2]/19[2], 34/19; **43** 36/22; **44**/ 37/ /H2; /**45** 38/ /H4; **46** 40/ /H6; **47A** H11; **48** 42[2]/1[2]; **54**/ 18/; **56**/ 23/
maqatum — "to collapse": **58** 27/
martum — "daughter, girl": written DUMU.SAL: **25** 27/; **26** 29/; **27**/31/; **33** 6/16; **34**/ 10/19, 11/21; written syllabically: **25** 28/
marum — "son": written DUMU: **16** 1/12; **17**/ 2/13; /**24** 23/; **29** /6; **32** /13, 5/15, /15; **33** /16; **34**/ 9/19, 11/21; /**35** 12/22; **47A** H10; **52** 10/14; **58** 27/; **59** 29/
maṣṣartum — "deposit": **36**/ 14/25, 16/27; /**37** 18/1
maša'um — "to seize forcibly": **26** 30/
maškanum — "chain": **51** 8/11; **52** 12/15
maškanum — "threshing floor": **19** 9/22
matum — "land, country": **29** /5
matum — "to die": **12** 40/; **13** /7; /**24** 25/; **26** 31/; /**28** 36/; [*šumutum* — "to cause to die":] **23**/ 21/; /**24** 24/; **47A** H10; **53** 14/17; **54**/ 17; /**55** 19/; **56**/ 22/; /**57** 24/; **58** 27/
maṭum (?) — "little": **15** /11 (?)
meḫrum — "equivalent": **19** /21; /**35** 13/23
meḫṣum — "slap": **42** 34/20
mimma — "something, anything" (in LE only with negation: *la, ul):* **22** 15/, 17/; **23**/ 19/; /**24** 22/; **37** 22/6
mitum — "dead": **53** 14/18
mudum — "acquaintance (?), temporary visitor (?)": **41** 30/14
muṣlalum — "high noon, midday": **12** 38/; **13** 41/4

muškenum — written MAŠ.KAK.EN: **12** 37/; **13** 41/4; /**24** 23[2]; **34**/ 10/20; **50** /8

mušum — "night": **12** 39/; **13** 42/6

nadanum — "to give, sell, lend": **9** 31/; **19** 8/21; **20** 11/; **21** 14/; **25** 27/; **32** /13, /14; **33** 7/; **34**/ 11/20, 11/21; **36**/ 15/25, 17/27; /**37** 19/2; **38** 24/7; **39** 26/10, 27/11; **41** 30/14, 31/16 [*šuddunum* — "cause to give, collect, exact":] **19** 9/22

nadinanum — "seller": **40** 29/13

nadum(?) — "to throw, cast": **33** /16

naḫum — "lard": written Ì.ŠAḪ: **1** 11/; **2** 19/

nakapum — "to gore": **53** 13/17; **54**/ 17/; /**55** 18/; /**57** 24/

nakasum — "to cut off, sever": **42** 32/17; **43** 35/21

nakkapum — "gorer": written UL X UL: **54**/ 15/

napištum — "life": /**24** 24/; **26** 31/; **48** 44/3; **58** 28/

napṭarum — class designation: **36**/ 14/24; **41** 30/14

naqabum — "to deflower": **26** 30/; **31** /11

narum — "river, canal": written ÍD: **50** /6

nasaḫum — "to tear out": **36** 16/26; **59** 31/

naṣarum — "to guard, keep in custody": **52** 11/14, 13/16; **56**/ 21/

našakum — "to bite": **42** 32/17; **56**/ 22/

nepum — "to distrain": **22** 16/; **23**/ 20/; /**24** 23/, 25[2]/

niggallum (?) — "sickle": written URUDU.KIN.A: **9A** 33/

niputum — "distress" (i.e. person seized in distress): **23**/ 20/; /**24** 24/

nisḫatum — meaning uncertain: **2** 18/, 19/, 20/

nišum — "oath by": **22** 16/; /**37** 20/3

nullanum — meaning uncertain: **6** 27/

palašum — "to break into, force": **36**/ 15/25

panum — "initial, former" (?): **21** 13/

panum — measure of capacity: **3** 22/; **11** 36/

paṭarum — "to redeem": **39** 27/11

piššatum — "oil, ointment": written Ì.BA: **32** /14

qablitum — "average (price)" (?): **38** 24/9

qadum — "together with": **3** 21/

qab/pum — "threaten to fall down": **58** 25/

qapum — "to sell on credit, give credit": **16** /12

qatum — "hand": written ŠU: **44**/ 37/; written syllabically: **15** /10

qum — measure of capacity: **1** 9/, 10/, 11/; **2** 18/, 19[2]/, 20[2]/; **4** 23/, 24/; **9A** 33/

rabum — "to replace": **23**/ 21/; /**35** 13/23; **36**/ 17/28
rabum — "to grow up": **33** 7/17
ragamum — "to call, claim": **30** /**10**
ramum — "to love": **59** 32/ (?)
redum — "to drive": **3** 23/; **4** 24/; **10** 35/; **49** /5; **50** 5/9
redum — "driver": **3** 21/; **10** 35/
rešum — "head": **9** 31/
risbatum — "affray": **47A** H9
rikistum — "contract": **27**/ 32/; /**28** 34/1
ruštum — meaning uncertain: **1** 9/
sabitum — "ale wife": **15** /10; **41** 31/15
sakapum — "to throw to the floor": **44**/ 37/23
sakpum — "invasion": **29** 39/3
sararum — "to cheat": **33** 6/16
sartum — "fraud": /**37** 22/5
sippum — "threshold": **36**/ 15/26
sunum — "lap": /**28** 36/
sutum — unit of capacity: **1** 10/, 11/, 12/; **2** 18/, 19/; **3** 22/; **7** 28/; **8** 29/; **9A** 33/; **10** 34/, 35/; **18A** 7/20; **20** 12/
ṣabatum — "to seize, catch": **6** 28/; **12** 38/, 40/2; **13** /5, /6; /**28** 36/; **33** 8/18; **49** /5; **50** 5/8
ṣibtum — "interest": written MAŠ: **18A** 6/19, 7/20; **20** 12/; **21** 14/
ṣimdatum — "regulation, decree": **58** 28/
ša — "of, who, whom, which": **2** 18/, 19/, 20/; **12** 37/; **13** 41/4, 42/6; **19** 8/; /**24** 25/; **31** /12; **34**/ 11/21; /**35** 12/22; **36**/ 17/27; /**37** 19/2; **50** /8; **51** 7/11, 8/11; **52** 10/14; **59** 32/
šadištum — "one sixth": written IGI.6.GÁL: **18A** 6/19; **21** 14/
šaiamanum — "buyer": **39** 26/11
šakanum — "to place, put, fix, mark (with a slave mark)": **27**/ 33/; /**28** 35/2; **51** 8/12; **52** 12/16
šakkanakkum — a high-ranking official: written GÌR. NÍTA: **50** /6
šalalum (?) — "to carry off, capture": **29** 39/ (?)
šalašum — "three": written 3. KAM: **32** /14
šalum — "to ask": **26** 30/; **27**/ 31/
šaman ruštim — kind of oil: written Ì.SAG: **1** 9/
šamum — "to buy": **38** 24/8; **40** 29/13
šanum — "other": **26** 30/; **29** 42/6; **30** /9; **38** 25/9; [fem. *šanitum*:] **29** 41/5; **59** 30/
šapirum — "commissioner": **50** /6

šaqalum — "to weigh, weigh out, pay": written LÁ: **6** 28/; **9** 33/; **12** 39/; **13** /5; **22** 18/; **31** /12; **32** /15; **42** 33/18, 34/20, **43** 36/22; **44**/ 37/21 /H2; /**45** 38/25 /H4; **46** 40/; **47** 41/ /H8; **47A** H11; **54**/ 18/; /**55** 19/; **56**/ 23/; /**57** 24/

šaramum(?) — "cut down, cut off"(?): **54**/ 16 (?)

šarqum — "stolen": **49** /4; [fem. *šariqtum*:] **49** /4

šarraqum — "thief": **40** 29/13

šarrum — "king": written LUGAL: **48** /3; written syllabically: **58** 28/

šasum — "call, demand, claim": **25** 26/

šattum — "year": written MU: **27**/ 33/; **32** /14

šattum — "belonging to ...": **6** 27/

šeberum — "break": **44**/ 37/ /H2; /**45** 38/ /H3; **46** 39/ /H6

šegum — "vicious": **56**/ 20/

šeḫtum — "attack, raid": **29** 38/3

šelum(?) — "to injure(?): **47** 41/

šepum — "foot": written GÌR: /**45** 38/ /H3

še'um — "barley": written ŠE: **1** 8/; **2** 18/, 19/, 20/; **3** 22/; **7** 28/; **8** 29/; **10** 34/, 35/; **11** 36/; **18A** /20; written syllabically: **15** /11; **20** 11/, 12/

šigištum(?) — meaning uncertain: **46** /H7

šikarum — "beer": written KAŠ: **41** 30/14, 31/; written syllabically: **41** /16

šimtum — "fate": **17**/ 4/14; /**18** /17

šimum — "price, purchase": written ŠÁM: **22** 18/; written syllabically: **40** 28/12; **53** 14/18

šinnum — "tooth": written ZÚ: **42** 33/19

šipatum — "wool": written SÍG: **1** 13/; **15** /11

šiprum — "message, work": **52** 10/14

šiqlum — "shekel" (unit of weight): written GÍN: **1** 8ff. [10]/; **3** 22/; **6** 28/; **9** 30/, 32/; **11** 36/; **12** 39/; **13** /5; **14** /8[2], /9[2]; **18A** 6/19; **21** 14/; **42** 34/20; **47** 41/ /H8; /**55** 19/; /**57** 24/

širum — "flesh, carcass": written UZU: **53** 14/18

šu — "he": **40** 29/13

šumma — "if": **3** 22/; **5** 25/; **6** 27/; **7** 29/; **9** 31/; **17**/ 3/14; /**18** /16; **20** 10/; **21** 13/; **22** 15/; **23**/ 19/; /**24** 22/; **25** 26/; **26** 29/; **27**/ 31/; /**28** 34/; **29** 38/3; **30** /8; **31** /11; **32** /13; **33** 6/16; **34**/ 9/19; **36**/ 14/24; /**37** 18/1; **38** 23/7; **39** 25/10; **40** 28/12; **41** 30/14; **42** 32/17; **43** 35/21; **44**/ 36/ /H3; /**45** 38/; **46** 39/ /H5; **47** 40/ /H7; **47A** H9; **49** /4; **50** /6; **53** 13/17; **54**/ 15/; /**55** 18/; **56**/ 20/; /**57** 23/; **58** 25/; **59** 29/

šurqum — "theft": **50** 6/10
tabalum — "take back, away": **29** /7; **34**/ 12/21 (cf. *wabalum*)
tamkarum — "merchant": written DAM. GÀR: **15** /10
tarbitum — "upbringing": **32** /13, 5/15; **34**/ 10/20
târum — "return, revert": **9A** 34/; **17**/ /15; **29** /7; **30** /9; [*turrum* — "to hand back, return":] **25** 28/
tarûm — "take back": **32** 5/15; **33** 9/18
tašna — "twofold" (adv.): **25** 28/
terḫatum — "bride money": **17**/ /13; **25** 28/; **26** 29/
tertum — "order, authority" (in *bel tertim* — "official"): **50** 2/6
ᴰ*Tišpak* — Tishpak, the patron deity of Eshnunna: /**37** 20/3
ṭabtum — "salt": **1** 14/
ṭebum — "to sink": [*ṭubbum* — "cause to sink":] **5** 25/, 26/
u — "and, or": **3** 21/; **4** 24/; **9A** 33/; **10** 35/; **15** /10[2]; **16** /12; **18A** 6/19; **20** 12/; **21** 14[2]/; **26** 30/; **27**/ 32[3]/, 33/; /**28** 35, 35/2; **29** 39/3, 40/4, /6; **30** /8; **31** /12; /**35** 12/22; /**37** 22/5; **38** /8; **40** 28/12; **41** 30/14; **48** 42/; **50** /8; **52** 7/11, 8/12; **52** 10/14, 12/16; **53** 14/18; **59** 31/
ubanum — "finger": **43** 35/21
ubarum — class designation: written U.BAR: **41** 30/14
uḫulum — "potash": written NAGA: **1** 15/
ukullum — "provender": written ŠÀ.GAL: **11** 36/
ul — "not": **12** 40/3; **13** /7; **15** /11; **16** /12; /**18** 5/18; **27**/ 34/; /**28** 37/; **30** /10; /**37** 23/6; **51** 9/13
ummum — "mother": **26** 30/; /**27** 32/, 33/; /**28** 35/2
umum — "day": **3** 23/; **4** 24/; **10** 35/; **27**/ 33/; /**28** 36/; **29** 41/4; **39** 26/11; **50** /9
uṭṭetum — "grain": written ŠE: **7** 29/; **18A** 6/19
uznum — "ear": **42** 34/19
wabalum — "to bring, carry": **14** /8, /9; **17**/ /13; /**18** 4/18; **26** 29/
waladum — "to bear, give birth to": **29** 43/; [*wulludum* — "to beget":] **59** 29/
wardum — "slave": written SAG.ÌR: **15** /10; **16** /12; **40** 28/12; **49** /4, /5[2]; **50** 3/7; **51** 7/11; **52** 10/14; /**55** 18/; /**57** 23/
warḫum — "month": written ITU: **11** 37/; **50** /9
warki — "after": **59** 32/
waṣabum — "to bear (interest)": **18A** 6/19, 7/20
waṣum — "to go forth": **51** 9/13; [*šuṣum* — "to cause to go forth":] /**18** 5/18

wašabum — "to dwell": **27**/ 34/; **29** /5 (?)
watrum — "excess": /**18** 5/18
zakarum — "to swear, take an oath": **22** 16/; /**37** 20/3, 22/5
zarum — "winnower": **8** 29/
zazum — "to divide": **53** 15/19
zerum — "to hate": **30** /8
zittum — "share" **38** 23/7
zizum — "divided, separated" [*la zizum* — "not separated":] **16** 1/12